THE NEW PSYCHOLOGY OF LOVE

Second Edition

This is a much-needed development from the first edition that provides an update on the theory and research on love by world-renowned scientific experts. It explores love from a diverse range of standpoints: social-psychological, evolutionary, neuropsychological, clinical, cultural, and even political. It considers questions such as: How do men and women differ in their love? What makes us susceptible to jealousy and envy in relationships? How does love differ across cultures?

As the psychological basis of love is examined, this volume showcases what attracts people to one another, why love has developed the way it has over time and what evolutionary purpose it serves. It also analyses why and when love relationships both succeed and fail, which means readers will be rewarded with a better understanding of their own relationships and those of others, as well as what can be done to build a lasting, loving relationship.

ROBERT J. STERNBERG is Professor of Human Development at Cornell University, and is the author or editor of numerous books on love. He has also won the Grawemeyer Award in Psychology and the Cattell and James Awards of the Association for Psychological Science.

KARIN STERNBERG is a research associate and teaches in the Department of Human Development at Cornell University. She is the author of *Love 101* and co-author of *The Nature of Hate*.

THE NEW PSYCHOLOGY OF LOVE

Second Edition

EDITED BY

ROBERT J. STERNBERG

Cornell University

KARIN STERNBERG

Cornell University

CAMBRIDGE
UNIVERSITY PRESS

CAMBRIDGE
UNIVERSITY PRESS

University Printing House, Cambridge CB2 8BS, United Kingdom

One Liberty Plaza, 20th Floor, New York, NY 10006, USA

477 Williamstown Road, Port Melbourne, VIC 3207, Australia

314-321, 3rd Floor, Plot 3, Splendor Forum, Jasola District Centre, New Delhi - 110025, India

79 Anson Road, #06-04/06, Singapore 079906

Cambridge University Press is part of the University of Cambridge.

It furthers the University's mission by disseminating knowledge in the pursuit of education, learning and research at the highest international levels of excellence.

www.cambridge.org
Information on this title: www.cambridge.org/9781108468770
DOI: 10.1017/ 9781108658225

First edition © Yale University 2006
Second edition © Cambridge University Press 2019

First published 2006 by Yale University Press
This edition published 2019 by Cambridge University Press

A catalogue record for this publication is available from the British Library

Library of Congress Cataloging in Publication data
Names: Sternberg, Robert J., editor. | Sternberg, Karin, 1976– editor.
Title: The new psychology of love / edited by Robert J. Sternberg, Cornell
University, Karin Sternberg, Cornell University.
Description: Second edition. | Cambridge, United Kingdom;
New York, NY : Cambridge University Press, 2019. | Includes index.
Identifiers: LCCN 2018038854 | ISBN 9781108475686 (hardback) |
ISBN 9781108468770 (paperback)
Subjects: LCSH: Love – Psychological aspects.
Classification: LCC BF 575. L 8 N 48 2019 | DDC 152.4/1–dc23
LC record available at https://lccn.loc.gov/2018038854

ISBN 978-1-108-47568-6 Hardback
ISBN 978-1-108-46877-0 Paperback

This book is dedicated to Ellen Berscheid, whose pioneering work in collaboration with Elaine Hatfield created the scientific study of love.

Contents

Figure and Tables

Figure

Tables

Contributors

ARTHUR ARON
State University of New York,
Stony Brook

KRYSTYNA S. AUNE
University of Hawai'i at Mānoa

R. KELLY AUNE
University of Hawai'i at Mānoa

DAVID M. BUSS
University of Texas at Austin

STEPHANIE CACIOPPO
University of Chicago

MARGARET S. CLARK
Yale University

TERRI D. CONLEY
University of Michigan

LISA M. DIAMOND
University of Utah

BEVERLEY FEHR
University of Winnipeg

CYRILLE FEYBESSE
University of Porto, Portugal

HELEN E. FISHER
Indiana University and Rutgers
University

JUSTIN R. GARCIA
Indiana University

STACI GUSAKOVA
University of Michigan

ELAINE HATFIELD
University of Hawai'i
at Mānoa

CLYDE HENDRICK
Texas Tech University

SUSAN S. HENDRICK
Texas Tech University

JENNIFER L. HIRSCH
Yale University

WILLIAM JANKOWIAK
University of Nevada, Las Vegas

ROBERT NAVJOT KAUR
Cornell University

MARIO MIKULINCER
Interdisciplinary Center (IDC)
Herzliya, Israel

ELISABETH J. MISTUR
Cornell University

JOAN K. MONIN
Yale University

JENNIFER L. PIEMONTE
University of Michigan

PHILLIP R. SHAVER
University of California, Davis

KARIN STERNBERG
Cornell University

ROBERT J. STERNBERG
Cornell University

JENNIFER M. TOMLINSON
Colgate University

Preface

In 1975, Senator William Proxmire presented his Golden Fleece Award for waste in government spending to Ellen Berscheid (to whom this book is dedicated) and Elaine Hatfield (a contributor to this book). The target of his ire was work they were doing through a grant from the National Science Foundation on the scientific analysis of love.

Today, the scientific analysis of love is part and parcel of the field of psychological science. It has its own journals largely devoted to it, such as the *Journal of Social and Personal Relationships* and *Personal Relationships,* and has been the topic of numerous books, including a number by the contributors in this volume. One of the principal books in the field has been an earlier edition of this work, *The New Psychology of Love,* published in 2006.

It is more than a decade since the original edition of this book was published, and during that time theory and research in the field of love have exploded. The field as it was is barely recognizable. This is illustrated by the fact that more than half of the authors contributing to this book are new. Not only did they not contribute to the earlier volume, but at the time the earlier volume was published, some were still in secondary school, college, or graduate school! Some of the contributors in the earlier edition are no longer active researchers, either having passed on to other phases of their lives, or having passed away. The editors' recognition of how explosively much of the field has changed and expanded is what led to this new volume (with a new publisher, Cambridge University Press). We have asked the researchers we consider to be the most influential in the field to contribute, and we are delighted that they agreed to be part of this book.

There are many ways in which the field has changed as a whole since the early days of the study of love. First, it used to be fairly easy to characterize an essay on love as taking some kind of disciplinary approach: clinical, social, personality, biological, and so on. Today, that would be hard to do. Many investigators use a variety of approaches, so that the approaches blur together much more. Second, many of the early theories, whether they were psychoanalytical or not, directly showed the influence of Freud and his disciples. Today, one would struggle to find such influence. Third, contemporary research is much more rigorous scientifically than it was in the past. So the field you read about today will be very different from the field as it once was.

This book is intended to be readable for any educated person with an interest in love. Because almost everyone has some interest in love, if you are reading this Preface, then this book is written for you!

We hope you enjoy the book. We believe it represents some of the best scientific work currently being done in the field of love, and it will present to you many different perspectives, so you will be able to choose the perspective you prefer, or perhaps even combine perspectives to come up with your own.

CHAPTER I

Love as Expansion of the Self

Arthur Aron and Jennifer M. Tomlinson

What Is Love? And How Can the Self-expansion Model Help Us Understand It?

The self-expansion model of love was developed in the 1980s (Aron & Aron, 1986; for a recent review, see Aron, Lewandowski, Mashek, & Aron, 2013). It emerged from an integration of two diverse worlds of knowledge. The first world of knowledge was relevant social-psychological theories of basic human motivation, and the little research that existed at the time on attraction and relationships. The second world of knowledge was from classical concepts of love. From Western philosophy, for example, Plato's *Symposium* on love emphasizes the ultimate goal of growth from loving a specific person to universality. From Eastern philosophy, for example, the Upanishad discusses how close relationships lead to this kind of universality: "the love of the husband is not for the sake of the husband, but he is loved for the sake of the self which, in its true nature, is one with the Supreme Self" (and then continues the same for love of the wife, of children, and even of wealth).

Our focus then was mainly on romantic love, although since then the model has been applied much more widely, both to diverse types of love, and beyond love to fields such as intergroup relations and individual motivation. In this chapter, our focus is on romantic love, both intense passionate love and close relationships more generally.

We first describe key principles of the model, and then turn in more detail to its implications, focusing on initial attraction, the neural basis of being intensely in love, and the trajectories of romantic relationships over the lifespan. We then turn to implications for maintaining and enhancing relationships; then to understanding diverse problems that arise in relationships; and finally, briefly to other kinds of love. We conclude with examples of how the self-expansion model relates to some other major theories and discussion of future directions. We consider our model not as a competitor to other approaches, but rather as a partner, with the self-expansion model in some cases helping to deepen (or even "expand") other models, and in other cases, with other models helping to deepen and expand our model (and, of course, in some cases both).

The Self-expansion Model

What is the self-expansion model? The model has two key principles:

1. *Motivational principle:* People seek to expand their potential efficacy, to increase their ability to accomplish goals. That is, a fundamental human motive is what other scholars have described as exploration, effectance, self-improvement, curiosity, competence, or a broadening of one's perspective. (And experiencing rapid self-expansion should be particularly rewarding.) The motivational principle was influenced by White's (1959) work, arguing that the drive for efficacy or competence is similar to drives for basic needs such as hunger and thirst. Deci and Ryan's (1987) theory of intrinsic motivation, Bowlby's (1969) theory of secure base support for exploration, and Fredrickson's (2001) broaden-and-build model all touch on related motivational principles. See Aron, Aron, and Norman (2004) for a more detailed discussion.
2. *Inclusion-of-other-in-the-self principle:* One way people seek to expand the self is through close relationships, because in a close relationship the other's resources, perspectives, and identities are experienced, to some extent, as one's own.

And what does all of this mean for love? Based on this model, we define love as "the constellation of behaviors, cognitions, and emotions associated with a desire to enter or maintain a close relationship with a specific other person" (Aron & Aron, 1991, p. 26). That is, love is the desire to expand the self by including a desirable other in the self.

Example Research Support for the Motivational Principle

Aron, Paris, and Aron (1995) conducted a study with undergraduates in two large classes, in which every two weeks over a ten-week quarter, students completed standard self-concept measures along with a measure of whether they had fallen in love in the last two weeks. Those who fell in love in the previous two weeks showed significantly greater self-esteem, self-efficacy, and more traits listed in response to "Who are you today?" (a kind of literal self-expansion). And perhaps the most direct example for making clear what self-expansion motivation has to say about relationships is the consistent findings of greater relationship quality for those with higher scores on the widely used measure of relationship self-expansion, the Self-Expansion Questionnaire (SEQ; Lewandowski & Aron, 2002). Example items include "How much does your partner help to expand your sense of the kind of person you are?" "How much does your partner increase your ability to accomplish new things?" and "How much do you see your partner as a way to expand your own capabilities?"

Example Research Support for Inclusion-of-Other-in-the-Self

The inclusion principle has actually received the most scientific attention. The basic idea is that in a close relationship your mental construction of yourself (the way you spontaneously think of yourself) overlaps with your mental image of your close other. This has been shown in a particularly direct way by the "me-not-me response-time procedure": You rate yourself and a close other on various traits, and then later in another context, you are shown each trait on a computer screen and asked to press a "yes" or a "no" button for whether the trait is or is not true of yourself. The greater closeness between you and your close other, the slower you are in pressing the button for traits on which you and your close other differ. Other studies have shown, for example, that closeness predicts difficulty in distinguishing memories relevant to the self and the other, greater spontaneous sharing of resources with the others, and more overlapping neural areas when hearing the names of the self and the other. Indeed, a pictorial self-report measure of perceived overlap of the self and the other, the inclusion of the other in the Self Scale (Aron, Aron, & Smollan, 1992) has been used successfully in literally hundreds of studies to date (see Figure 1.1).

Implications for Different Types/Stages of Romantic Love

Attraction and Falling in Love

With whom are you likely to fall in love? Many studies on the predictors of initial interpersonal attraction have documented the importance of reciprocal liking (the other person liking you), desirable characteristics, and seeing the other as similar (see Zhou, Chelberg, & Aron, 2016, for a review). It feels good to be liked by others and it is also rewarding to be around others who validate our worldviews (Byrne, 1971). The findings on reciprocal liking and similarity taken together suggest that perceptions of

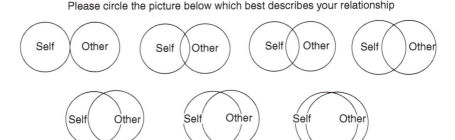

Figure 1.1 The inclusion of the other in the Self Scale.
(Originally printed in Aron et al., 1992.)

how others feel about the self are crucial in deciding with whom to engage in a relationship. The self-expansion model also sheds light on the processes of interpersonal attraction, suggesting that the standard situation works in part because reciprocal liking and similarity suggest a relationship (and thus expansion) is likely; and desirable characteristics are desirable at least in part because they are qualities that would expand the self if you had a relationship with this person. (Indeed, research going beyond attraction, examining people's experiences of falling in love, found that the most common situation was one in which a desirable other did something that indicated they liked the self; e.g. Riela, Rodriguez, Aron, Xu, & Acevedo, 2010.)

In addition, the model has pointed out some situations where, after reciprocal liking is established (and a relationship seems likely), opposites might attract. In one experiment, participants were given a measure of interests and a week later were shown the interest results of a supposed other person whom they were either told they were likely to get along with or about whom they were given no information. The first condition created an expectation for relationship certainty, establishing the idea that reciprocal liking was likely to occur. As predicted, based on the notion that different interests, if a relationship is possible, offer greater expansion of the self, participants in the relationship certainty condition reported liking dissimilar others more than similar others (Aron, Steele, Kashdan, & Perez, 2006).

Being Intensely in Love

So, you have now fallen in love. What does it mean to be passionately in love? One way researchers have explored this question is with brain imaging. We consider self-expansion (and especially the perceived opportunity for rapid expansion) through a relationship to be a powerful motivation. Passionate love specifically represents the intense desire for self-expansion through a relationship with the beloved (and thus, including him or her in oneself). Brain imaging can provide a clear picture of the degree of intense motivation experienced when one is in love.

Over the last dozen years, several functional magnetic resonance imaging (fMRI) studies have consistently demonstrated greater activation in the brain's key reward system when in-love individuals viewed a facial photo (or even when they were subconsciously presented with the name) of their romantic partner versus a facial photo of a familiar acquaintance. These findings have been replicated cross-culturally and across sexual orientation (for a review, see Acevedo, 2015). The key areas found again and again represent what is known as the dopamine reward system, the same brain areas that respond to cocaine. (Although the notion that romantic love is fundamentally a reward-based process is consistent in a general way with many models of love, it specifically supports the self-expansion model notion that passionate love should be considered more from a motivational than an emotional perspective, that it is associated more with expansion than survival, and that it is not primarily a more-specific brain system.)

This neural pattern has even been found in a study of long-term married individuals reporting high levels of passionate love (Acevedo, Aron, Fisher, & Brown, 2011). This study also explicitly measured key self-expansion model variables, and found that (a) activation of the dopamine system was correlated with greater inclusion of the other in the self (as measured by the IOS Scale) and that (b) participants also showed stronger dopamine system activation in association with greater relationship self-expansion (measured by the SEQ). Other fMRI studies provide further support for the centrality of this motivational system in passionate love. For example, when individuals experiencing intense romantic love are shown images of their partner (versus neutral acquaintances), it reduces brain responses to physical pain (Younger et al., 2010). And in a study of habitual smokers who are in love, viewing images of the beloved significantly reduced the brain's response to images of cigarettes (versus of pencils) (Xu, Wang, et al., 2012).

Ongoing Love and Relationship Closeness

Love as including each other in each other's self. In a love relationship, the identities of two partners become intricately intertwined. For example, partners know what the other is thinking, can finish each other's sentences, and have difficulty remembering what belongs to whom. As we noted earlier, describing the "me-not-me" procedure, this can happen so much so that reaction-time studies have shown that it takes longer to decide whether a trait belongs to yourself if it doesn't also belong to your partner; mental representations of the self include elements of close others. There are many studies showing this self-other overlap in a variety of ways. For example, Aron, Aron, Tudor, and Nelson (1991) asked participants to rate the extent to which they and a non-close other possessed pairs of traits (e.g. "carefree-serious"). Participants were given the option to report that only one trait, both traits, or neither trait applied to themselves and a non-close other. People reported both traits applied more when rating the self compared to a non-close other, because people are less likely to make dispositional attributions (seeing a person as all one-way) about the self compared to others (Sande, Goethals, & Radloff, 1988). Aron et al. (1991) showed that individuals also chose more "both apply" options when rating close others (similar to when rating the self). These results suggest that people treat close others in the same way that they treat themselves, spontaneously showing to some extent the same self–other dispositional bias for a close other as for the self. When in a close relationship, people demonstrate cognitive interdependence as well, which means they are more likely to use pronouns such as 'we' and 'us' compared to 'me' and 'my' (Agnew, Van Lange, Rusbult, & Langston, 1998). In addition, people are better at inferring intentions of close others compared to non-close others, owing to the activation of brain areas related to familiarity (Cacioppo, Juan, & Monteleone, 2017).

In such deeply interdependent relationships, perceived partner responsiveness, or the sense that the partner understands, validates (gets you), and cares for you, is central (Reis, Clark, & Holmes, 2004). One study suggests that perceptions of how much your partner includes you in their self are important in determining the extent to which you are willing to also include your partner in your own self (Tomlinson & Aron, 2013).

Love over time. Love and general relationship satisfaction consistently show typical declines over time (e.g. Karney & Bradbury, 1997; O'Leary, Acevedo, Aron, Huddy, & Mashek, 2012; Tucker & Aron, 1993). The self-expansion model argues that passion arises from the intensity of the rapid self-expansion that occurs in the formation of a relationship as one comes to include the other in the self; but once the other is largely included, the rate of expansion inevitably slows down. Indeed, in a large representative sample, how much passionate love one feels was associated with self-expansion in relationships over time (Sheets, 2014). The benefits of self-expansion are likely owing to increases in positive affect (Graham & Harf, 2015; Strong & Aron, 2006) and decreases in boredom (Tsapelas, Aron, & Orbuch, 2009). (As an aside, in a sense, passionate love is selfish in that it is focused on my feelings of self-expansion, but it is also unselfish in that because I include the other in the self, his or her self-expansion is also experienced as my own. So, we should be motivated to want the other to expand, and both partners should experience rapid self-expansion, but this has not been directly tested.)

Nevertheless, although passionate love (and satisfaction and love of all kinds) generally declines over time, the view that passionate love *inevitably* declines has not been demonstrated. It is clear that many long-term couples experience high levels of satisfaction. Indeed, in a four-year longitudinal study of newlyweds, Karney and Bradbury (1997) found that about 10% maintained or increased their level of satisfaction. Perhaps more surprising, in a representative US survey, 40% of individuals married for ten years or longer reported being "very intensely in love" with their partner (O'Leary et al., 2012). Further, interview data (Acevedo & Aron, 2005) suggests that at least some reports may correspond to how the relationship is actually being experienced and are not due merely to wanting to make a good impression or self-deception. These results were supported by fMRI data in partners reporting intense passionate love and married an average of 21.4 years, showing that brain activation is similar to that found in early stage passionate love (Acevedo et al., 2011). Further, brain activation in areas associated with passionate love and reward were positively correlated with satisfaction in long-term couples (Acevedo et al., 2011). There is also evidence that brain activation early on in a relationship predicts relationship stability and quality up to forty months later (Xu, Brown, et al., 2012).

Ways to Maintain/Enhance Love

How Can We Keep the Passion Alive?

Shared self-expansion activities. Once relationship partners can no longer gain substantial expansion from the initial development of the relationship, they can renew that sense to some extent by engaging in expanding activities together and thus associate the relationship and partner with the expansion from that shared expanding activity. Participation in shared self-expanding activities positively influences romantic relationship satisfaction

(Aron, Norman, Aron, McKenna, & Heyman, 2000). Reissman, Aron, and Bergen (1993) randomly assigned married couples to participate together each week in either an exciting or a pleasant but not exciting activity for ten weeks. The activities most often listed as exciting included things like attending musical concerts, plays, lectures, skiing, hiking, and dancing. Couples who participated in exciting activities had significantly greater increases in satisfaction after the ten weeks compared to those who participated in pleasant activities. Five other studies further established the impact of exciting activities above and beyond the effect of mundane activities on relationship satisfaction (Aron et al., 2000). For example, in three experiments, couples in the exciting condition participated in an obstacle course task together that included elements of novelty, challenge, and arousal. Further, a randomized clinical trial experiment asked couples to complete exciting activities for ninety minutes per week for four weeks (Coulter & Malouff, 2013). As in Reissman et al. (1993), couples chose the activities themselves after giving suggestions that were adventurous, passionate, sexual, exciting, interesting, playful, romantic, and spontaneous. Results showed that couples in the exciting group (compared to a waitlist control) had increased relationship excitement, positive affect, and satisfaction when tested four months later.

The self-expansion model suggests that exciting activities should be beneficial over more mundane or pleasant activities, but exactly what the exciting activities should look like has not been spelled out. The majority of the exciting activities that have been considered across studies contain elements of novelty, challenge, interest, and arousal (not necessarily sexual, but just general physical arousal). These initial studies did not identify which elements of excitement are most essential and if they vary by stage and type of relationship. Tomlinson, Hughes, Lewandowski, Aron, and Geyer (in press) sought to clarify this issue by comparing the effects of arousal and expansion in ongoing friendships and marriages. Across four studies, in both friend and married pairs, expansion was central to both individual and relationship outcomes, whereas arousal was not. These are only initial findings, but if future work continues to find this pattern, this suggests that elements of expansion, such as interest and fun, should be prioritized over physical arousal when selecting shared activities within ongoing relationships. That is, doing things together that are interesting and fun has more effect on love than just exercising together!

In addition to identifying the benefits of shared participation in exciting activities, research in this area also suggests that the mechanisms behind the benefits of exciting activities are owing to increases in positive affect (Coulter & Malouff, 2013; Graham & Harf, 2015; Strong & Aron, 2006) and decreases in boredom (Aron et al., 2000; Tsapelas et al., 2009). Daily diary research suggests that the increases in positive affect and decreases in boredom while participating in exciting activities may occur because of a sense of flow or optimal engagement in the activity (Graham, 2008). For optimal engagement to occur, it is important that the couple's skill levels are matched with the challenge level of the task. If a task is too challenging (in such a way that exceeds skill), couples did not experience benefits (Graham & Harf, 2015).

One type of shared activity many couples choose to seek out is a double date with another couple. Recent research experimentally tested the effects of engaging in a shared self-expansion task with another couple (Slatcher, 2010; Welker et al., 2014). In these studies, reciprocal and escalating levels of self-disclosure across couples provide the vehicle for self-expansion. Couples engaged in a forty-five-minute closeness building task. (This procedure, developed by Aron, Mellinat, Aron, and Vallone (1997) and usually done with pairs of strangers, is widely used in research and is known as "Fast Friends." It has become popular in the broader culture as "The 36 Questions for Closeness." There are a series of questions that are increasingly self-disclosing; each of the four answers each question, before proceeding to the next; and this continues for about forty-five minutes.) Those who did the closeness task, compared to pairs of couples who did a similarly long small talk task, felt closer to the couple that they got to know through the task, and more importantly, felt closer to one another (Slatcher, 2010). In addition, couples who engaged in the closeness task (compared to couples who made small talk) with another couple experienced increases in positive affect (Slatcher, 2010) and passionate love (Welker et al., 2014). These results suggest that simply sharing deep conversation with another couple might provide a way of enhancing and maintaining relationships over time.

Individual self-expansion activities. Although there is a clear benefit to engaging in shared activities with a partner, couples also spend a substantial portion of their time apart and engaging in hobbies, work, friendships, and other activities. There is a growing body of research that suggests that individual activities can provide an excellent vehicle for individual self-expansion (e.g. Mattingly & Lewandowski, 2013). Across a variety of experiments, individuals who engaged in novel, exciting, and interesting activities (compared to controls) experienced increased self-expansion and exerted greater effort (Mattingly & Lewandowski, 2013). Individual self-expansion activities lead to benefits because they increase the self-concept size and promote approach motivation (Mattingly & Lewandowski, 2014; Mattingly, McIntyre, & Lewandowski, 2012); a result that applies even in the work place (McIntyre, Mattingly, Lewandowski, & Simpson, 2014). By participating in individual self-expansion activities, whether they be leisure activities or a satisfying job, people can increase their own self-concepts and bring novel identities, perspectives, and resources back to the relationship and their partner.

Support for partner's self-expansion. Because participation in individual self-expansion activities has the potential to lead to relationship benefits, it would be advantageous for partners to encourage one another to seek out activities that might lead to expansion. Indeed, within long-term relationships, individuals whose partners actively encouraged them to seek out an opportunity for self-expansion (in comparison to those partners who only provided a passive acknowledgment) experienced increased relationship satisfaction (Fivecoat, Tomlinson, Aron, & Caprariello, 2015). In addition, people who perceive their partners to support their goal strivings experience increased feelings of capability of accomplishing the goal, which leads to self-growth, goal accomplishment, and self-esteem over time (Tomlinson, Feeney, & Van Vleet, 2016).

Self-expansion in retirement. Much of the research on self-expansion has been done with college students or relatively young married couples. However, there is evidence that older adults self-expand in a variety of life domains (Harris, Kemmelmeier, & Weiss, 2009). Retirement could be viewed as an opportunity to seek out activities that could lead to growth, which couples did not have time for while focusing on career goals. In a recent longitudinal study, we asked retirees to respond to the same question "Who are you today?" that we asked college students to answer in the Aron et al. (1995) study on falling in love. Interestingly, we found that during the transition to retirement, in general, people's self-concept size and diversity decreased, but partner support for self-expansion predicted an increase in self-concept size over a six-month period (Tomlinson, Yosaitis, Challener, Brown, & Feeney, 2015). In addition, partner support for self-expansion predicted relationship satisfaction, satisfaction with retirement, self-efficacy, goal accomplishment, and health over time (Tomlinson & Feeney, 2016).

Problems

Though there are many benefits and joys, especially to love relationships that are self-expanding rather than self-adulterating (Mattingly, Lewandowski, & McIntyre, 2014), there are also risks that are inherent to opening yourself up to closeness.

Over-idealization

When in love, partners tend to view one another with rose-colored lenses. Idealization is generally a good thing within relationships (Murray et al., 2011) and might even lead to self-expansion through which a partner helps you to reach your ideal self (Rusbult, Finkel, & Kumashiro, 2009). However, recent research suggests that perceived idealization has a kind of "U"-shaped relationship with satisfaction, such that too little or too much is detrimental (Tomlinson, Aron, Carmichael, Reis, & Holmes, 2014). Feeling over-idealized can be problematic because it sets up expectations that may be unwanted or unachievable, leading to a fear of discovery. In addition, the object of over-idealization may be less motivated to engage in pro-relationship behaviors, such as accommodation, if they feel that their partner thinks they walk on water. Over-idealization seems to be mainly an issue for more visible abilities within dating couples, but it is problematic for both traits and abilities for married couples.

Infidelity

Infidelity (or "cheating") is a major issue in romantic relationships (for a review, see Tsapelas, Fisher, & Aron, 2011). As we have seen, self-expansion has important implications for relationship quality; and dissatisfaction may cause people to seek extra-dyadic partners to fulfill these self-expansion needs. Indeed, several studies of dating college students (mostly in several-month-long exclusive relationships) have found that self-expansion in the current relationship predicts less interest in potential alternative partners. Lewandowski and Ackerman (2006) found that both inclusion of the other in the self and, especially, how much one sees their relationship as providing or potentially providing self-expansion, strongly predicted how much people reported the likelihood that they would engage in various infidelity behaviors. Similar results, using other methods were found in two studies conducted by VanderDrift, Lewandowski and Agnew (2011). In study 1, participants interacted by computer with what they were led to believe was an available attractive potential partner who provided standard answers that indicated high potential levels of self-expansion in a relationship with that person. Participants who had earlier reported low levels of self-expansion in their current relationship indicated that they liked the simulated partner and the overall interaction considerably more. In study 2, participants were told they could choose to be in a follow-up study involving a "get to know you" activity with a currently single opposite-sex student. They were then given a list of twelve very attractive potential interaction partners and asked to pick as many or few as they would like. Those with lower current-relationship self-expansion selected a greater number of the potential interaction partners. The two-dimensional model of relationship self-change finds that people who are in self-adulterating or self-contracting relationships (which add negative self-content or take away positive self-content) were more likely to demonstrate emotional and sexual infidelity (Mattingly et al., 2014).

Using a somewhat different focus, Tsapelas (2012) led participants to feel they did or did not have sufficient self-expansion in their lives. Participants were then shown pictures of several attractive others, each paired with self-expanding traits that their current partner either did or did not possess. After doing another task, participants who had been led to believe they had high self-expansion needs showed better memory for the alternatives that had self-expanding traits their partner did not have. Finally, in an fMRI study by Tsapelas and colleagues (in prep), participants showed less neural activity associated with perceiving attractive faces after viewing a video of their partner describing a self-expanding experience done together, versus after viewing a video of their partner describing a neutral activity done together (or even compared to a video of their partner describing an experience of showing their love for each other).

In sum, across multiple methods and studies, having self-expansion in a relationship (or even in one's life) seems to substantially help reduce the interest in cheating.

Unrequited Love

So, some problems with love involve feeling over-idealized or your partner being interested in someone else. But what if the person you love never loved you to begin with? Unrequited love is extremely common. In a large sample of college students, Baumeister and Wotman (1991) found that 93% reported having had at least one powerful or moderate experience of unrequited love in the last five years. Our own research with college students (described below) found it in 82%. Hatfield, Schmitz, Cornelius, and Rapson (1988) found it common even among children.

Unrequited love can be a major source of depression and even suicide. Yet, at the same time, even unrequited love can be desired by some. To quote the great poet Tennyson, "better to have loved and lost than never to have loved at all." So, what is going on? The study of unrequited love raises special motivational issues, as the usual sources of expansion from an actual relationship are lacking. Given the self-expansion model, desirability would probably be the major motivation for unrequited love, in the sense that if a relationship with this person is seen as being extremely self-expanding, then you might be attracted, even if the probability is low. (It is similar to betting on the lottery – small odds, but big potential winnings.) Probability may play the greater role in a second situation when you mistakenly felt a relationship was likely, developed an attraction, and later discovered the error. But in the context of unrequited love, the self-expansion model also suggests a third factor, which is a desire to be in love, in order to have the expansion associated with enacting the culturally scripted role of lover, to experience the close association of expansion with being in love that is culturally ingrained – but *not* necessarily really wanting an actual relationship. To examine this three-factor motivational approach, Aron, Aron, and Allen (1998) tested this in 733 undergraduates who had experienced unrequited love. Consistent with predictions, each of the three motivational factors significantly and independently predicted intensity. The strongest effect for most was for desirability, but probability and desire to be in love had the strongest effects for substantial numbers of individuals. (We will briefly discuss the individual differences that seem to determine this in a later section.)

Rejection

And what if you were already in a relationship, and then rejected? Fisher, Brown, Aron, Strong, and Mashek (2010) used the standard procedure from fMRI studies of individuals who were newly in love, but this time for a sample of participants who had been recently rejected but still were intensely in love with their partner. In interviews, these participants were quite upset, angry, depressed, and more (indeed, several participants when in the scanner looking at pictures of their partner were sobbing). The brain scans showed all of this – when looking at their rejecter (vs. neutral other) they showed activation in regions associated with anxiety, pain, and attempts at controlling anger; yet, they still showed the powerful activation in the dopamine reward areas found generally in studies of love. They were clearly upset, but also clearly still intensely seeking to be united with the partner – or as one way to understand this, the self-expansion opportunity was just too strong to let go. (The good news is that the longer it had been since the rejection, the less intense the findings. So, it seems time does typically help heal this wound.)

Breakup

The end of a self-expanding relationship, whether you were rejected, rejected the other, or something else happened, is challenging in many ways. Because the self grows through including the partner in the self, following a breakup, self-contraction can occur (Lewandowski, Aron, Bassis, & Kunak, 2006). The loss of a self-expanding relationship is especially detrimental to the self-concept post-dissolution. If you're feeling down after a breakup, one way to make yourself feel better could be to write about your feelings. Research shows that it is particularly helpful to write about the positive sides to a breakup, such as newfound time to hang out with friends or pursue a hobby (Lewandowski, 2009). However, if the relationship was low in self-expansion to begin with, results with undergraduate dating students suggest that people actually grow following a breakup due to rediscovery of the self, less loss due to the breakup, and increased positive emotions (Lewandowski & Bizzoco, 2007).

Beyond Romantic Love

Love is not just romantic love (although that is the main focus of this chapter). In this section, we briefly consider how the self-expansion model can help us understand the many kinds of love. What we love, whether a romantic partner or anyone or anything else, involves at least in part including or seeking to include these others in the self. Not surprisingly, parents include their children in the self and children include their parents (and the extent to which they do so predicts the quality of their relationship; e.g. Birditt, Fingerman, Lefkowitz, & Dush, 2008).

Furthermore, studies show that people even include nature in the self (e.g. Schultz, 2001). And beyond that, studies show that some people who include all people in the self have a general caring for all human beings (Leary, Tipsord, & Tate, 2008). And even further, being religious is associated with including God in the self (e.g. Hodges, Sharp, Gibson, & Tipsord, 2013). At the same time, the self-expansion model has been applied to love of products and brands (e.g. Riemann & Aron, 2009), with research showing that including a brand in the self predicts brand love, brand loyalty, and so forth.

Research in all of these areas has only begun recently, but has considerable promise. However, there are two areas that have received particular attention, namely compassionate love of other groups (especially involving undermining prejudice toward minorities) and love of friends.

Compassionate Love for Members of Other Groups

Compassionate love is love that "centers on the good of the other" (Underwood, 2009, p. 3). That is, it is about caring for and feeling concern and wanting to help the other when in need. And it follows from the self-expansion model, that if you are close to someone, and thus to some extent include this person in yourself, you will want the best for him or her, just as you would for yourself. Indeed, there is research showing that we spontaneously share resources more equally with those we include in the self (Aron et al., 1991, study 1). However, as spelled out in more detail in Brody, Wright, Aron, & McLaughlin-Volpe (2008), most of the application of self-expansion directly relevant to compassionate love has focused on processes that involve including groups in the self. It is well documented that you include your own groups (your college, your ethnicity, your gender, and so forth). But the situation in which this becomes especially interesting, in terms of compassionate love, is when you include an "out-group" in the self, especially a group that is discriminated against.

One major way in which this can happen is through having a friend in an out-group. Suppose you are a European American and you have a good friend, Jose, who is Mexican American. According to the self-expansion model, as your close friend, Jose is to some extent part of yourself. Thus, if someone insults Mexican Americans in general (or even disparages some individual Mexican American) you are likely to feel insulted. A meta-analysis of 135 studies testing this basic idea that a close friendship makes feelings toward out-groups more positive, has found strong evidence for this effect (Davies et al., 2011). What is especially interesting here from the point of view of compassionate love is that the effect is not just reducing prejudice or negative feelings, but actually increasing positive feelings, such as care, respect, and even admiration of the other group. And this effect is found not just in surveys, but in strong, random-assignment experiments. For example. various researchers have done experiments where participants are randomly assigned to get close (using the Fast Friends, or "36 questions" procedure) to a member of their own group or a member of another group and then are tested, for example, with hormonal response to expecting to meet a person from the out-group (Page-Gould, Mendoza-Denton, Alegre, & Siy, 2010). The findings are clear that getting close to a member of the other group substantially increases the effects on your feelings for the other group. Another example is a study that conducted a version of this experiment with the majority of an entering freshman class at a fairly racially diverse US university. During an early semester class session, freshmen were randomly paired to do Fast Friends together. The findings were clear – those that had been paired with a member of a different ethnic group showed much more positive feelings toward that other ethnic group than did those paired with a member of their own group (Davies, Aron, Wright, & McLaughlin-Volpe, 2007).

Finally, an especially interesting extension of the basic friendship effect based on the self-expansion model is called "extended contact." Just knowing about someone in your own group who has a friend in an out-group also causes more positive feelings toward the out-group! That is, suppose you are a Christian and you can see, sitting at the cafeteria table every day, that Mary (who you know is also a Christian because you see her at church) always sits with and clearly has a deep friendship with Fatima (who wears a headscarf and is known to be a Muslim). The findings from scores of studies (Zhou, Page-Gould, Aron, Moyer, & Hewstone, 2018) suggest that you will feel more positively about Muslims in general, and that one significant mechanism is via an indirect inclusion of other in the self (I include the in-group in the self and if I am aware of in-group members who include an out-group member in the self, it leads me to include that out-group).

Friendship Love

As expected, friendships (whether with someone of another group or of your own group) that are high in self-expansion are higher in satisfaction (Lewandowski and colleagues, unpublished data). Indeed, according to this study, people who are high in approach motivation seek out friendships that would expand the self. It can be intimidating to approach someone who is very different from us, but the opportunities for self-expansion are even greater when we get to know people who come from different backgrounds or groups. As discussed in the "Attraction and Falling in Love" section, Aron et al. (2006) found that if participants were told that they were likely to get along with another student, they were more interested in someone with dissimilar interests. These results have implications for forming friendships across difference and suggest that manipulating relationship certainty may help people to seek out a relationship that has the most opportunity for expansion. Indeed, intergroup friendships, in addition to what we have seen in terms of their potential for creating more positive intergroup attitudes (Davies et al., 2011), have important implications for individual self-expansion.

Relation to Other Approaches to Understanding Love

How does the self-expansion model relate to other approaches (such as the many covered in this book)? In this section, we give an example of this symbiotic relationship with each of a few of the many other important approaches.

Interdependence theory is one of the pioneering and ongoing most influential theories. A central, well-documented principle (Le & Agnew, 2003) is that commitment to a romantic relationship is largely predicted by a combination of high satisfaction, low quality of alternatives, and high investment in the relationship. The self-expansion model provides some clear predictors of part of what leads to each: more satisfaction (feeling self-expansion from the relationship); less interest in alternatives (the more self-expansion in the relationship the less appealing are alternatives, particularly those that do not offer any different expansion opportunities), and greater investment (inclusion of the other in the self would be lost without the relationship).

Attachment theory (Chapter 13, this volume), which is also enormously influential, includes a relationship-relevant individual difference, "attachment style." Largely owing to our early relationships with our parents, some of us are "secure" (and thus comfortable in close relationships); some avoidant (do not expect good outcomes from a close relationship); and some "anxious-ambivalent" (really want one, but do not expect the other will like us). As one example of the relation of attachment theory to our model, this classification helps explain the individual differences in the main motivations for unrequited love (as discussed earlier). Specifically, secures were most likely to have gotten into this situation by being misled into thinking the probability of a relationship was high, avoidants by desiring the experience of being in love (without having an actual relationship), and anxious ambivalents by desirability of the other (Aron et al., 1998).

Communal/exchange theory (Chapter 5, this volume) is a highly valuable model that suggests that in close relationships you do not keep score of who gets what and focus on just caring for each other's needs as they arise. We suggest that one source of communal caring is including each other in the self (e.g. Medvene, Teal, & Slavich, 2000).

Evolutionary theories (Chapters 3 and 10, this volume), as in all areas of human functioning, provide a very basic core understanding of why we do what we do. Romantic love clearly plays such an important role in shaping how we produce and raise offspring, and thus survive as a species! The main link with the self-expansion model is that we argue a key basic human motive beyond just survival, is expansion (often called exploration in the evolutionary literature), and that this motivation has been adapted to help create and maintain pair-bonds that will last at least through the raising of our large-brained babies.

Love as a story (e.g. Sternberg, Hojjat, & Barnes, 2001) suggests that there is a culturally validated script for falling in love (see Lamy, 2016). We suggest that these stories operate so strongly because they make explicit just how love can be a source of self-expansion.

The triangular theory of love (Sternberg, 1986) identifies three key aspects of love (also supported by Aron & Westbay, 1996). The self-expansion model suggests that each of these distinct qualities arises from the motivation to experience rapid expansion. Expansion occurs via including the other in the self (passion), ongoing expansion through shared experiences and deep inclusion of the other (intimacy), and the fear of losing self-expansion and IOS as described above regarding interdependence theory (commitment).

Conclusion

In this chapter, we have described the self-expansion model and how it describes and explains the nature of love. As you have seen, there is considerable research support for the basic principles as they apply to romantic love, from attraction to break up, and even beyond to other kinds of love. Love is so very important in the lives of almost all of us, which is why we have made understanding it the center of our research and thinking. As we have described in this chapter, the self-expansion model has proven very valuable in helping us understand love. But what has been done is only the beginning. More work is needed in all the different areas we have described, and many areas that have only minimally been studied that hold great promise for deepening and expanding what we know in important, useful ways. These include the following: the role of social class and culture in shaping our experiences of love; the way in which we move from attraction and falling in love to being in a relationship; how love operates in families; and how specific types of love operate in crucial contexts, such as compassionate love in long-term relationships and, not forgetting how it starts, passionate love in children. (Did you not fall in love with someone when you were a child? What was that about?)

What we can feel confident about at this point is that our understanding of love and relationships can be deepened by taking into account the basic motivation to expand the self, and that one way do so in a close relationship is by including the other in the self.

References

Acevedo, B. P. (2015). Neural correlates of human attachment: Evidence from fMRI studies of adult pair-bonding. In V. Zayas & C. Hazan (Eds.), *Bases of adult attachment: Linking brain, mind, and behavior* (pp. 185–194). New York: Springer.

Acevedo, B., & Aron, A. (2005, June). Intense romantic love in long-term relationships. Paper presented at the Positive Psychology Summer Institute, Philadelphia, PA.

Acevedo, B. P., Aron, A., Fisher, H. E., & Brown, L. L. (2011). Neural correlates of long-term intense romantic love. *Social Cognitive and Affective Neuroscience*, *7*, 145–159.

Agnew, C. R., Van Lange, P. A. M., Rusbult, C. E., & Langston, C. A. (1998). Cognitive interdependence: Commitment and the mental representation of close relationships. *Journal of Personality and Social Psychology*, *74*, 939–954.

Aron, A., & Aron, E. (1986). *Love and the expansion of self: Understanding attraction and satisfaction*. New York: Hemisphere.

(1991). *Love and sexuality*. In K. McKinney & S. Sprecher (Eds.), *Sexuality in close relationships* (pp. 25–48). Hillsdale, NJ: Lawrence Erlbaum.

Aron, A., Aron, E. N., & Allen, J. (1998). Motivations for unreciprocated love. *Personality and Social Psychology Bulletin*, *24*, 787–796.

Aron, A., Aron, E. N., & Norman, C. (2004). Self-expansion model of motivation and cognition in close relationships and beyond. In M. B. Brewer, M. Hewstone, M. B. Brewer, & M. Hewstone (Eds.), *Self and social identity* (pp. 99–123). Malden: Blackwell.

Aron, A., Aron, E. N., & Smollan, D. (1992). Inclusion of the other in the Self Scale and the structure of interpersonal closeness. *Journal of Personality and Social Psychology*, *63*, 596–612.

Aron, A., Aron, E. N., Tudor, M., & Nelson, G. (1991). Close relationships as including other in the self. *Journal of Personality and Social Psychology*, *60*, 241–253.

Aron, A., Lewandowski, G. W., Jr., Mashek, D., & Aron, E. N. (2013). The self-expansion model of motivation and cognition in close relationships. In J. A. Simpson & L. Campbell (Eds.), *The Oxford handbook of close relationships* (pp. 90–115). New York: Oxford University Press.

Aron, A., Melinat, E., Aron, E. N., & Vallone, R. (1997). The experimental generation of interpersonal closeness: A procedure and some preliminary findings. *Personality and Social Psychology Bulletin, 23*(4), 363–377.

Aron, A., Norman, C. C., Aron, E. N., McKenna, C., & Heyman, R. E. (2000). Couples' shared participation in novel and arousing activities and experienced relationship quality. *Journal of Personality and Social Psychology, 78*(2), 273–284.

Aron, A., Paris, M., & Aron, E. N. (1995). Falling in love: Prospective studies of self-concept change. *Journal of Personality and Social Psychology, 69,* 1102–1112.

Aron, A., Steele, J. L., Kashdan, T. B., & Perez, M. (2006). When similars do not attract: Tests of a prediction from the self-expansion model. *Personal Relationships, 13*(4), 387–396.

Aron, A., & Westbay, L. (1996). Dimensions of the prototype of love. *Journal of Personality and Social Psychology, 70,* 535–551.

Baumeister, R. F., & Wotman, S. R. (1991). *Breaking hearts: The two sides of unrequited love.* New York: Guilford Press.

Birditt, K. S., Fingerman, K. L., Lefkowitz, E. S., & Dush, C. M. K. (2008). Parents perceived as peers: Filial maturity in adulthood. *Journal of Adult Development, 15*(1), 1–12.

Bowlby, J. (1969). *Attachment and loss,* Vol. 1: *Attachment.* New York: Basic Books.

Brody, S., Wright, S. C., Aron, A., & McLaughlin-Volpe, T. (2008). Compassionate love for individuals in other social groups. In B. Fehr, S. Sprecher, L. G. Underwood, B. Fehr, S. Sprecher, & L. G. Underwood (Eds.), *The science of compassionate love: Theory, research, and applications* (pp. 283–308). Malden, MA: Wiley-Blackwell.

Byrne, D. (1971). *The attraction paradigm.* New York: Academic Press.

Cacioppo, S., Juan, E., & Monteleone, G. (2017). Predicting intentions of a familiar significant other beyond the mirror neuron system. *Frontiers in Behavioral Neuroscience, 11,* 1–12.

Coulter, K., & Malouff, J. M. (2013). Effects of an intervention designed to enhance romantic relationship excitement: A randomized-control trial. *Couple and Family Psychology: Research and Practice, 2,* 34–44.

Davies, K. M., Aron, A., Wright, S., McLaughlin-Volpe, T. (2007). The Stony Brook Fast Friends project: Some initial results. Poster presented at the Society for Personality and Social Psychology Annual Meeting, Memphis, TN.

Davies, K., Tropp, L. R., Aron, A., Pettigrew, T. F., & Wright, S. C. (2011). Cross-group friendships and intergroup attitudes: A meta-analytic review. *Personality and Social Psychology Review, 15*(4), 332–351.

Deci, E. L., & Ryan, R. (1987). The support of autonomy and the control of behavior. *Journal of Personality and Social Psychology, 53,* 1024–1037.

Fisher, H. E., Brown, L. L., Aron, A., Strong, G., & Mashek, D. (2010). Reward, addiction, and emotion regulation systems associated with rejection in love. *Journal of Neurophysiology, 104*, 51–60.

Fivecoat, H. C., Tomlinson, J. M., Aron, A., & Caprariello, P. A. (2015). Partner responsiveness to one's own self-expansion opportunities: Effects on relationship satisfaction. *Journal of Social and Personal Relationships, 32*(3), 368–385.

Fredrickson, B. L. (2001). The role of positive emotions in positive psychology: The broaden-and-build theory of positive emotions. *American Psychologist, 56*(3), 218–226.

Graham, J. M. (2008). Self-expansion and flow in couples' momentary experiences: An experience sampling study. *Journal of Personality and Social Psychology, 95*(3), 679–694.

Graham, J. M., & Harf, M. R. (2015). Self-expansion and flow: The roles of challenge, skill, affect, and activation. *Personal Relationships, 22*(1), 45–64.

Harris, S. G., Kemmelmeier, M., & Weiss, L. J. (2009). Do older adults (still) self-expand? Initial findings across six domains with adults aged 50+. Society of Personality and Social Psychology Annual Meeting, Tampa, FL.

Hatfield, E., Schmitz, E., Cornelius, J., & Rapson, R. L. (1988). Passionate love: How early does it begin? *Journal of Psychology & Human Sexuality,1*(1), 35–51.

Hodges, S. D., Sharp, C. A., Gibson, N. J., & Tipsord, J. M. (2013). Nearer my God to thee: Self–God overlap and believers' relationships with God. *Self and Identity, 12*(3), 337–356.

Karney, B. R., & Bradbury, T. N. (1997). Neuroticism, marital interaction, and the trajectory of marital satisfaction. *Journal of Personality and Social Psychology, 72*, 1075–1092.

Lamy, L. (2016). Beyond emotion: Love as an encounter of myth and drive. *Emotion Review, 8*(2), 97–107.

Le, B., & Agnew, C. R. (2003). Commitment and its theorized determinants: A meta-analysis of the investment model. *Personal Relationships, 10*(1), 37–57.

Leary, M. R., Tipsord, J. M., & Tate, E. B. (2008). All-inclusive identity: Incorporating the social and natural worlds into one's sense of self. In H. A. Wayment & J. J. Bauer (Eds.), *Transcending self-interest: Psychological explorations of the quiet ego* (pp. 137–147). Washington, DC: American Psychological Association.

Lewandowski, G. J. (2009). Promoting positive emotions following relationship dissolution through writing. *The Journal of Positive Psychology, 4*(1), 21–31.

Lewandowski, G. W., Jr., & Ackerman, R. A. (2006). Something's missing: Need fulfillment and self-expansion as predictors of susceptibility to infidelity. *The Journal of Social Psychology, 146*(4), 389–403.

Lewandowski, G. W., Jr., & Aron, A. (2002). Self-expansion scale: Construction and validation. Paper presented at the Society of Personality and Social Psychology Annual Meeting, Savannah, GA.

Lewandowski, G. W., Aron, A., Bassis, S., & Kunak, J. (2006). Losing a self-expanding relationship: Implications for the self-concept. *Personal Relationships, 13*, 317–331.

Lewandowski, G. J., & Bizzoco, N. M. (2007). Addition through subtraction: Growth following the dissolution of a low quality relationship. *The Journal of Positive Psychology*, *2*(1), 40–54.

Mattingly, B. A., & Lewandowski, G. W., Jr. (2013). The power of one: Benefits of individual self-expansion. *The Journal of Positive Psychology*, *8*, 12–22.

Mattingly, B. A., & Lewandowski, G. J. (2014). Expanding the self brick by brick: Nonrelational self-expansion and self-concept size. *Social Psychological and Personality Science*, *5*(4), 484–490.

Mattingly, B. A., Lewandowski, G. W., Jr., & McIntyre, K. P. (2014). "You make me a better/worse person": A two-dimensional model of relationship self-change. *Personal Relationships*, *21*, 176–190.

Mattingly, B. A., McIntyre, K. P., & Lewandowski, G. W., Jr. (2012). Approach motivation and the expansion of self in close relationships. *Personal Relationships*, *19*, 113–127.

McIntyre, K. P., Mattingly, B. A., Lewandowski, G. J., & Simpson, A. (2014). Workplace self-expansion: Implications for job satisfaction, commitment, self-concept clarity, and self-esteem among the employed and unemployed. *Basic and Applied Social Psychology*, *36*(1), 59–69.

Medvene, L. J., Teal, C. R., & Slavich, S. (2000). Including the other in self: Implications for judgments of equity and satisfaction in close relationships. *Journal of Social and Clinical Psychology*, *19*(3), 396–419.

Murray, S. L., Griffin, D. W., Derrick, J. L., Harris, B., Aloni, M., & Leder, S. (2011). Tempting fate or inviting happiness? Unrealistic idealization prevents the decline of marital satisfaction. *Psychological Science*, *22*(5), 619–626.

O'Leary, K. D., Acevedo, B. P., Aron, A., Huddy, L., & Mashek, D. (2012). Is long-term love more than a rare phenomenon? If so, what are its correlates? *Social Psychological and Personality Science*, *3*, 241–249.

Page-Gould, E., Mendoza-Denton, R., Alegre, J. M., & Siy, J. O. (2010). Understanding the impact of cross-group friendship on interactions with novel outgroup members. *Journal of Personality and Social Psychology*, *98*, 775–793.

Reimann, M., & Aron, A. (2009). Self-expansion motivation and inclusion of close brands in the self: Towards a theory of brand relationships. In J. Priester, D. MacInnis, & C. W. Park (Eds.), *Handbook of brand relationships* (pp. 65–81). Armonk, NY: M. E. Sharpe.

Reis, H. T., Clark, M. S., & Holmes, J. G. (2004). Perceived partner responsiveness as an organizing construct in the study of intimacy and closeness. In D. J. Mashek & A. Aron (Eds.), *Handbook of closeness and intimacy* (pp. 415–428). Mahwah, NJ: Lawrence Erlbaum.

Reissman, C., Aron, A., & Bergen, M. R. (1993). Shared activities and marital satisfaction: Causal direction and self-expansion versus boredom. *Journal of Social and Personal Relationships*, *10*(2), 243–254.

Riela, S., Rodriguez, G., Aron, A., Xu, X., & Acevedo, B. P. (2010). Experiences of falling in love: Investigating culture, ethnicity, gender, and speed. *Journal of Social and Personal Relationships*, *27*, 473–493.

Rusbult, C. E., Finkel, E. J., & Kumashiro, M. (2009). The Michelangelo phenomenon. *Current Directions in Psychological Science, 18*(6), 305–309.

Sande, G. N., Goethals, G. R., & Radloff, C. E. (1988). Perceiving one's own traits and others': The multifaceted self. *Journal of Personality and Social Psychology, 54*, 13–20.

Schultz, P. W. (2001). Assessing the structure of environmental concern: Concern for self, other people, and the biosphere. *Journal of Environmental Psychology, 21*, 1–13.

Sheets, V. L. (2014). Passion for life: Self-expansion and passionate love across the life span. *Journal of Social and Personal Relationships, 31*(7), 958–974.

Slatcher, R. B. (2010). When Harry and Sally met Dick and Jane: Experimentally creating closeness between couples. *Personal Relationships, 17*, 279–297.

Sternberg, R. J. (1986). A triangular theory of love. *Psychological Review, 93*, 119–135.

Sternberg, R. J., Hojjat, M., & Barnes, M. L. (2001). Empirical tests of aspects of a theory of love as a story. *European Journal of Personality, 15*, 199–218.

Strong, G., & Aron, A. (2006). The effect of shared participation in novel and challenging activities on experienced relationship quality: Is it mediated by high positive affect? In K. D. Vohs & E. J. Finkel (Eds.), *Self and relationships: Connecting intrapersonal and interpersonal processes* (pp. 342–359). New York: Guilford Press.

Tomlinson, J. M., & Aron, A. (2013). The path to closeness: A mediational model for overcoming the risks of increasing closeness. *Journal of Social and Personal Relationships, 30*, 805–812.

Tomlinson, J. M., Aron, A., Carmichael, C. L., Reis, H. T., & Holmes, J. G. (2014). The costs of being put on a pedestal: The effects of feeling over-idealized in married and dating relationships. *Journal of Social and Personal Relationships, 31*(3), 384–409.

Tomlinson, J. M., & Feeney, B. C. (2016). Helping each other grow: Benefits of partner support for self-expansion in retirement. Poster presented at The Society for Personality and Social Psychology Annual Meeting, San Diego, CA.

Tomlinson, J. M., Feeney, B. C., & Van Vleet, M. (2016). A longitudinal investigation of relational catalyst support of goal strivings. *The Journal of Positive Psychology, 11*(3), 246–257.

Tomlinson, J. M., Hughes, E. K., Lewandowski, G. W., Jr., Aron, A. & Geyer, R. (in press). Do shared self-expanding activities have to be physically arousing? *Journal of Social and Personal Relationships.*

Tomlinson, J. M., Yosaitis, A. J., Challener, S. A., Brown, R. R., & Feeney, B. C. (2015). Partners as a source of positive self-concept change during the transition to retirement. Paper presented at the International Association for Relationships Research Mini Conference, New Brunswick, NJ.

Tsapelas, I. (2012). Self-expansion as a predictor of attention to alternative romantic partners. *Dissertation Abstracts International, 72*, 7748.

Tsapelas I., Aron, A., & Orbuch, T. (2009). Marital boredom now predicts less satisfaction 9 years later. *Psychological Science, 20*, 543–545.

Tsapelas, I., Fisher, H. E., & Aron, A. (2011). Infidelity: When, where, why. In W. R. Cupach, B. H. Spitzberg, W. R. Cupach, & B. H. Spitzberg (Eds.), *The dark side of close relationships II* (pp. 175–195). New York: Routledge.

Tucker, P., & Aron, A. (1993). Passionate love and marital satisfaction at key transition points in the family life cycle. *Journal of Social and Clinical Psychology, 12*, 135–147.

Underwood, L. G. (2009). Compassionate love: A framework for research. In B. Fehr, S. Sprecher, & L. G. Underwood (Eds.), *The science of compassionate love: Theory, research, and applications* (pp. 3–25). Malden, MA: Wiley-Blackwell.

VanderDrift, L. E., Lewandowski, G. J., & Agnew, C. R. (2011). Reduced self-expansion in current romance and interest in relationship alternatives. *Journal of Social and Personal Relationships, 28*(3), 356–373.

Welker, K. M., Baker, L., Padilla, A., Holmes, H., Aron, A., & Slatcher, R. B. (2014). Effects of self-disclosure and responsiveness between couples on passionate love within couples. *Personal Relationships, 21*(4), 692–708.

White, R. W. (1959). Motivation reconsidered: The concept of confidence. *Psychological Review, 66*, 297–333.

Xu, X., Brown, L., Aron, A., Cao, G., Feng, T., Acevedo, B., & Weng, X. (2012). Regional brain activity during early-stage intense romantic love predicted relationship outcomes after 40 months: An fMRI assessment. *Neuroscience Letters, 526*, 33–38.

Xu, X., Wang, J., Lei, W., Aron, A., Westmaas, L., & Weng, X. (2012). Intense passionate love attenuates cigarette cue-reactivity in nicotine-deprived smokers: An fMRI study. *PLoS ONE, 7*(7), e42235.

Younger, J., Aron, A., Parke, S., Chatterjee, N., & Mackey, S., (2010). Viewing pictures of a romantic partner reduces experimental pain: Involvement of neural reward systems. *PLoS ONE, 5*(10), 1–7.

Zhou, S., Chelberg, M. B., & Aron, A. (2015). Interpersonal attraction, psychology of. In J. D. Wright (editor-in-chief), *International encyclopedia of the social and behavioral sciences* (2nd ed., Vol 12. pp. 626–630). Oxford: Elsevier.

Zhou, S., Page-Gould, E., Aron, A., Moyer, A., & Hewstone, M. (2018). The extended contact hypothesis: A meta-analysis on 20 years of research. *Personality and Social Psychology Review*. doi: 10.1177/1088868318762647.

Entraining, Becoming, and Loving

Krystyna S. Aune and R. Kelly Aune

A perusal of any number of internet sites that purport to help us with our relationships will reiterate the common wisdom "Don't expect him/her to change after marriage." This is an aphorism that is drilled into young people's minds to the point that it has become a truism. But is it true? Is there evidence (besides the insistent and hard-won anecdotes of a few friends) that what we see in the beginnings of our pair-bond relationships is what we will get, and continue to get long down the road?

In this chapter, we are going to argue that the old chestnut "don't expect them to change" could not be farther from the truth. While we are not suggesting that one can or should try to affect a partner's core personality or value system over the course of a relationship, we underscore the premise that relating is a verb, not a noun. Likewise, "personing" is a verb, not a noun. We, too, are not static, unchanging individuals over the course of our lives. Accordingly, we will argue that an important characteristic of the most successful pair-bond relationships is not simply accepting our partner for who they are, and expecting the same in return. Successful relationships develop because we *do* change over time. We change in large part because interacting with our partners changes us, and our relationships thrive because we embrace, value, and even celebrate the changes in ourselves.

We will show that simply communicating with our partner changes us at the most fundamental levels. We will argue that the extent to which we acknowledge these changes, and welcome these changes, is experienced as a facet of what we have come to know as love. Ultimately, what we experience as love for another is, in the most general sense, a reflection of our satisfaction, even our happiness, with who we have become and continue to become in our relationship. Our view is that love is a reflection of the happiness that we find in who we are and who we are becoming with our partner.

Personal Background

Our own love story began when we met in graduate school thirty years ago. Krystyna was an incoming first-year doctoral student, and Kelly was a fourth-year doctoral student working on his dissertation. Falling for each other was not at all convenient; it wasn't what either of us sought out or expected to happen. But it happened nonetheless, through a powerful attraction and growing bond that we could not ignore. After only a few months together as a couple, Kelly began his career as an assistant professor at the University of Hawai'i at Mānoa and Krystyna continued with the doctoral program at the University of Arizona. We endured a long-distance relationship, staying linked as well as late 1980s technology and academic conference trips would allow. After a long three years apart, we transitioned to the next phase of our relationship as spouses and colleagues. Today, almost twenty-seven years later, we are still personally and professionally entwined. Our differing areas of research in human communication are complementary and inform the approach to love that we describe in this chapter. Krystyna studies emotions and relationships; Kelly focuses on message processing. Our understanding of love is a reflection of Krystyna's interests in relational communication and relational dynamics fused with Kelly's interests in the cooperative and collaborative efficiencies of communication in developed relationships. In the following pages, we will discuss our perspective of love as arising from communicative processes that facilitate cognitive and neurological states of entrainment. We bridge the literatures of communication, social psychology, and neuroscience to offer a different view of this most fundamental construct of love.

Foundational Theories

Theorists have offered various perspectives of love over the last few decades, as is evidenced by the numerous chapters in this book. Perhaps somewhat distinctively, our approach to the understanding of love and relationships traverses several different scientific domains, ranging from the most distal – evolutionary psychology – to a more proximal level of explanation in the domain of social psychology, and finally to the most proximal level of neuroscience (Fletcher, Simpson, Campbell, & Overall, 2013). The theoretical foundations that most directly frame our perspective come from the sociobiological/evolutionary approaches and social-psychological approaches to love.

Jankowiak and Fischer's (1992) approach to love is broad, highlighting the near universality of romantic love, and offering support for an evolutionary perspective of love. Buss's (1988) evolutionary approach maintains that love is a natural category of actions that have evolved to perpetuate the species. Love is not just an affective state but is a sequence of love *acts* that fulfill primal *goals*: to attract and retain a mate; to reproduce; and to invest in offspring. Likewise, Fisher and her colleagues (Fisher, Aron, & Brown, 2006; Fisher, Aron, Mashek, Li, & Brown, 2002) describe lust, attraction, and attachment as the human emotion-motivation systems that have evolved to initiate mating, prefer specific mating partners, and cooperate in order to accomplish parenting duties.

Social-psychological perspectives frame our own thinking about love most directly. Given our relational history, it may be no surprise that these perspectives include the self-expansion model (Aron & Aron, 1996; Aron, Aron, Tudor, Nelson, & Miller, 1991; Aron, Paris, & Aron, 1995; Graham & Harf, 2014) and interdependence theory (Kelley & Thibaut, 1978; Rusbult & Van Lange, 2003). These approaches both champion the idea that relationships change us as individuals. Aron and Aron, along with their colleagues, argue that people are fundamentally motivated to expand the self, and broaden their experiences and identity. One important way to do so is to become close to someone who will facilitate this. Falling in love provides an ideal opportunity to facilitate self-expansion by engaging in new and interesting experiences with another person (Aron, Norman, Aron, McKenna, & Heyman, 2000). As partners become close, they incorporate the other within the self and merge identities reciprocally. But even before extensive communication and shared experiences occur, Slotter and Gardner (2009) found evidence of *anticipatory* self–other integration among individuals motivated to enhance romantic closeness with another. This may reflect how primal the need to expand ourselves is.

Mattingly, Lewandowski, and McIntyre (2014) elaborated on how being in a relationship can change us by developing a two-dimensional model of relationship self-change. These dimensions include direction (increase versus decrease in content) and valence (positivity and negativity of content). Their results showed that self-expansion and self-pruning (decreasing negative content) were associated with romantic love. So partners in a romantic relationship develop a sense of cognitive interdependence, where they think of themselves as a unit rather than individuals. Romantic partners may begin to have trouble seeing where one of them stops and the other begins. Mattingly et al. argue that – in the context of our relationship – we may expand or contract our sense of self, in positive and negative ways. We learn new skills and develop new interests as a function of interacting with our partner. Our worlds expand. Conversely, activities that we might have engaged in before the current relationship, interests we had that are less relevant in the current relationship, might atrophy, and ultimately disappear from our lives.

The second, and related, foundational social-psychology theory that frames our perspective on love is interdependence theory. The fundamental premise of interdependence theory, traced to Kelley and Thibaut (1978; Thibaut & Kelley, 1959), is that interpersonal interaction is the core of a close relationship. Interdependence necessarily entails mutual influence. Internal processes triggered by interaction ultimately lead to transformation of the self, the other, and the relationship as a whole. Interdependence manifests in cognitive, affective, and behavioral outcomes, idiosyncratic to the partner and relationship (Agnew & Etcheverry, 2006). In other words, how we think, feel, and act is impacted by the interdependence we have with a close partner. This process of increasing cognitive, affective, and behavioral interdependence involves the inclusion of the partner in the self and vice versa.

There is an interesting information-processing aspect to this relational interdependence. Wegner and his colleagues invoke a construct of transactive memory, which they describe as the process by which relationship partners develop a collective and interdependent system for storing memories and information. Our relational partners serve, in essence, as external hard drives for our own memories. This arrangement allows people in relationships access to a higher breadth and depth of information than they would as individuals (Wegner, Erber, & Raymond, 1991). These interdependent memory systems accompanying relationship commitment involve self–partner attributions and *cognitive restructuring* (Agnew, Van Lange, Rusbult, & Langston, 1998).

Agnew et al. (1998) point out that self-expansion and Interdependence Theory share similarities. Specifically, both theories focus on partners' evolution toward increasing interdependence, the rewards of everyday interaction, and the fulfillment of human needs that comes from interaction with a close other. Whereas self-expansion theory zeroes in on the expansion need gratified by relationships, Interdependence Theory suggests that many different needs are met in romantic relationships. Invoking a theme that rings true to our perspective on love, Agnew et al. claim that commitment brings about cognitive restructuring that includes incorporating one's close relationship partner into the self. We will expand on this perspective in the following sections.

Primacy of Close Relationship Partners

Although other dyadic relationships can certainly impact the self, romantic partners have a "privileged status" to influence us (Agnew & Etcheverry, 2006, p. 275). Influencing a close other is not just a side effect of being a relational partner; in some respects it is a partner's responsibility. Rusbult, Kumashiro, Kubacka, and Finkel (2009) note that we are shaped by those we love. The Michelangelo phenomenon refers to the sculpting of close partners to achieve, or at least get closer to, the ideal self (Drigotas, Rusbult, Wieselquist, & Whitton, 1999; Rusbult, Finkel, & Kumashiro, 2009). Fundamental to this idea of interpersonal sculpting is the idea of behavioral confirmation – a process by which a partner's expectations about the self bring about such behaviors that confirm those expectations. Importantly, they argue that as partners adapt to each other in specific interactions, these adaptations accumulate over time through a process of perceptual and behavioral affirmation, moving toward the ideal self, and ultimately personal and relational well-being.

Why do we morph to a new and better version of ourselves? Kumashiro, Rusbult, Wolf, and Estrada (2006) note that striving for self-growth is a *fundamental* human goal, referencing Freud's motive of ego idea and Maslow's concept of self-actualization, among others. They theorize that the Michelangelo phenomenon promotes relational well-being for a number of reasons. Specifically, perceptual affirmation reflects empathic understanding and that this understanding "should enhance feelings of love" (p. 322). Relatedly, they argue that behavioral affirmation leads to more coordination, synchrony which leads to greater adjustment, sense of security, and attachment, as well as partner and relationship value. In short, over time, close partners adapt to each other in what initially begins as interaction-specific moments, and ultimately transcends into gestalt patterns and affect (Kumashiro et al., 2006). An interesting hypothesis noted by Rusbult, Kumashiro, Kubacka, and Finkel (2009) is that over extended interaction with affirmation, positivity, and movement toward the ideal selves, partners actually come to resemble one another. On a concretely physical level, Zajonc, Adelmann, Murphy, and Niedenthal (1987) showed that perceived resemblance was higher for couples married for twenty-five years compared with when they were first married. Zajonc et al. theorize that the explanatory mechanism is vascular emotional efference; that empathic facial muscular mimicry actually creates greater convergence of facial features of close partners over time.

Thus far we have outlined a view of love stemming from an evolutionary perspective that points to fundamental drives as the basis of pair-bonding. We incorporated social-psychology theories of self-expansion and interdependence theories to discuss how being part of a pair-bond can affect us and shape us as individuals. Next, we will turn our attention to communication in dyads, drawing particular attention to neurological approaches to communication, in order to bring home the argument that our relationships influence us and shape us in the most fundamental ways possible.

Talk as the Foundation of the Relationship

The fundamental core of any relationship is behavioral, and particularly communicative, interaction. Relational behavior is, at its most fundamental, communicative behavior. Self-expansion and interdependence theories both acknowledge that the key component of relationships is interaction. Early scholarly work on communicative events and interaction often focused on highly deliberate, mindful acts – for example, the public speech, the persuasive appeal, and the conflict resolution. It took a significant change of theorists' attention to recognize the relational importance of the most ordinary behaviors. The dialogic work of Steve Duck (1990a, 1990b, 1995; Duck, Rutt, Hurst, & Strejc, 1991) and colleagues argues that everyday talk not only has instrumental functions (such as actually increasing closeness) and indexical functions (*revealing* how close people are to one another), but ordinary talk "actually *embodies* the relationship and defines it" (p. 21). Duck (1995) points out that the interpretation of the behavioral chains, the *meaning* derived from modes of expression, are paramount. It is important to understand that we are not referring to highly intentional discussions between partners *about* their relationship. We are referring to *ordinary* talk, routine conversations; the stuff of scores of interactions every day. Duck and his colleagues argue that everyday, mundane talk and the constructive interpretation of that talk *comprise* the dynamic process of relating.

Embracing Duck's view that relationships are constituted in talk, Goldsmith and Baxter (1996) identified a taxonomy of twenty-nine speech events, organized into six overarching clusters. Consistent with Duck's premise that the mundane, everyday talk is the foundation of a relationship, Goldsmith and Baxter found that in-depth speech events were not very common in their diary data. Six kinds of talk events were prominent across relationship types: gossip, making plans, joking around, catching up, small talk, and recapping the day's events. Among romantic partners, informal talk was predominant (including the subcategories of recapping, morning talk, joking around, gossip, bedtime chat), followed by involving positive talk and less formal goal-directed talk. These data affirm that even in romantic relationships, the building blocks are not predominantly composed of in-depth interactions and conversations, but ordinary fleeting moments that take on meaning in the dynamic process of relating.

It seems clear that these ordinary conversations have relational impacts, that they provide the continuity and the glue for the relationship. But might these communicative acts serve other functions in the relationship? To answer this question we will turn our attention to the most proximal domain of the study of relationships and human communication (Fletcher et al., 2013).

Neurobiology and Love

We are seeing more data arising from neurological studies that tell us about the brain in love. Neuroimaging studies have produced data that are consistent with the self-expansion model of love. De Boer, Van Buel, and Ter Horst (2012) reviewed existing data on the neurobiological mechanisms of love and attachment. Overall, there is support for the presence of neural circuits in the brain to promote attraction to partners and to develop and maintain long-term pair-bonds. There is also evidence that areas of the brain associated with mentalizing and Theory of Mind (needed to assess others' motivational states, feelings, and intentions) are activated. The latter would certainly be a precursor to any valid sense of merging with another.

Using functional magnetic resonance imaging (fMRI) to examine neural correlates of long-term romantic love, Acevedo, Aron, Fisher, and Brown (2012) found that regions of the brain associated with reward are activated when respondents think of their partners. Further, reward activity was correlated with scores on the Inclusion of Other in Self scales, providing neurological data consistent with self-expansion hypotheses.

Ortigue and colleagues (Origue & Bianchi-Demicheli, 2008; Ortigue, Bianchi-Demicheli, Hamilton, & Grafton, 2007) explored the neural basis of love. Ortigue et al. (2007) found that subliminal presentations of a beloved's name (as compared to a friend's name) activated parts of the brain that had been associated with love in prior studies. Ortigue and

Bianchi-Demicheli (2008) articulate a mirror neuron system hypothesis of love supporting a self-expansion framework. The authors claim that people in love not only showed more activation of self-related brain networks, but performed better on a cognitive decision-making task – recognizing personally meaningful versus meaningless stimuli – than did people not in love. Invoking self-expansion, Ortigue and Bianchi-Demicheli (2008) suggest that being exposed to a loved one's name activates the self-related brain network, which accelerates the subject's ability to recognize personally meaningful stimuli. They also report that couples in love were faster at comprehending and anticipating the intentions of their partner relative to a neutral other person, consistent with their hypothesis about the role of the mirror neuron system in love.

Neurobiology and Communication

One limitation to the neurological studies described above is the fact that they were exploring neurological data related to being in romantic relationships, but the data were collected from individuals. The data are certainly revealing and informative but limited in their ability to show us something about the dyadic process of relating.

Similarly, researchers in communication have often examined communicative processes by looking at the individuals involved in those processes, and examining how communicators create and comprehend messages. More current theorizing – at both cognitive and neurological levels – is focusing on the dyad as the fundamental unit of analysis for understanding communicative processes. An important motivation for this evolution in methodology is offered by Pickering and Garrod (2004). They argue that the former approach to design and data analysis is more *monologic* in nature. In monologic approaches, we study message sources to understand message production processes, and message receivers to understand message comprehension processes.

A *dialogic* perspective, on the other hand, allows us to focus on the more cooperative and collaborative nature of the communicative process. By focusing on the dyad and the dialogic process, we can see how two persons, using sounds and kinesic behavior, are able to achieve *states of understanding*. In this perspective, understanding is not synonymous with comprehension. Comprehension can be understood as an outcome of a *single* mind processing a message. Understanding, however, is conceptualized as a transient state into which *two* minds enter, and a form of cognitive and neurological *entrainment*, resulting from their successful communicative interaction (Gasiorek & Aune, 2017; Hasson, Ghazanfar, Galantucci, Garrod, & Keysers, 2012). Gasiorek and Aune describe this entrainment as "a dynamic operational alignment of two brains and a convergence of two cognitions" (2017, p. 2). In our classes, we refer to understanding as an *isomorphic meme state*. Stolk, Verhagen, and Toni (2016) describe it as conceptual alignment, and – when both parties are aware they have achieved this state – mutual understanding. Perez, Carreiras, and Duñabeitia (2017) refer more specifically to brain-to-brain entrainment as a process of interbrain coupling or synchronization that is indicative of understanding rather than simply arising from common signal (speech) processing.

Hasson and colleagues (Hasson et al., 2012; Silbert, Honey, Simony, Poeppel, & Hasson, 2014; Stephens, Silbert, & Hasson, 2010) had similar concerns about the state of message processing in cognitive neuroscience. They point out that the dominant approach to studying neurological behavior included separating people from their environment and looking at individual neurological responses to stimuli. Hasson et al. suggested that a focus on individuals limits our ability to see how brains act on each other in dyadic situations. Focusing on individuals ignores the extent to which our cognitive faculties are products of rich, interpersonal environments.

In an attempt to remedy this situation, Stephens et al. (2010) asked speakers subjected to fMRI to engage in fifteen-minute-long unrehearsed narratives that were recorded and played back to listeners also in fMRI scanners. In general, listeners' brain activity mirrored the brain activity of the speakers. Further, the extent of the neural coupling was positively related to the degree to which understanding was achieved between speaker and listener. It is important to point out that the neural coupling was not fixed in time. The manner in which Stephens et al. (2010) assessed neural coupling allowed them to see how coupling was often slightly delayed between the speaker and the listener; that is, the listener's brain reflected the speaker's brain as comprehension was achieved. However, there were also instances where the listener's brain showed *anticipatory* coupling. The listener's brain reflected the speaker's brain *ahead* of the speaker. Further, the listener's anticipatory neural coupling was positively correlated with understanding as well. Silbert, Honey, Simony, Poeppel, and Hasson (2014) have demonstrated that the neural coupling that accompanies the achievement of understanding between speakers and listeners is widespread and bilateral, encompassing production- and comprehension-related processing functions across both linguistic and nonlinguistic areas of the brain.

From the communicative and relational perspectives, the upshot of Hasson's and colleagues' work cannot be overstated. They demonstrate, in real time, the form and range of neurological entrainment that arises from successful communication. Understanding – whether we think of it as an isomorphic meme state or conceptual alignment – is provided an empirical instantiation in the results of these studies. As we will discuss in the next section, what this implies about pair-bond relationships is particularly fascinating.

Implications of Neurological Research for Pair-bond Relationships

Relationship partners who engage in long-term, frequent communicative activity, likely spend a significant amount of time in neurologically coupled states. The very act of engaging in communication with somebody with whom we frequently achieve understanding is likely to be intrinsically pleasurable. Morelli, Torre, and Eisenberger (2014) have demonstrated that when we feel understood we experience greater activity in those portions of the brain related to reward, social connection, and mentalizing. They also report that feeling understood is associated with increased reports of interpersonal closeness from the participants toward their responders. Conversely, not feeling understood is associated with greater activation in areas related to negative affect, social pain, and reports of feeling socially distant from others.

Having a history of achieving neurological entrainment also increases the likelihood that a couple experiences greater conceptual fluency when communicating (Fazendeiro, Chenier, & Winkielman, 2007). Greater conceptual fluency, in turn, leads to increasing communicative efficiencies, allowing the relational partners to achieve understanding with less cognitive expenditure. This, too, should add to the positive relational outcomes that could be expected to develop with frequent successful communicative interactions.

Finally, we know from learning research (e.g. Takeuchi et al., 2010; Zatorre, Fields, & Johansen-Berg, 2012) as well as gaming and internet research (e.g. Kuss & Griffiths, 2012) that the brain is plastic, and capable of structural change over time with repeated exposure to stimuli. Consequently, it is reasonable to expect that long-term partners, who spend a significant amount of time influencing each other's neurological patterns of activation in achieving understanding, probably are concomitantly engaging in mutual neurological structuration as well. That is, *couples who*

engage in frequent, successful communication may actually be creating struc-
tural and operational commonalities with each other at the neurological level.
The interdependence experienced by relationship partners may be, in part,
hardwired by the couple themselves.

Summary and Conclusion

The argument we have advanced here is that at its most general level,
love can be thought of as an enduring satisfaction – happiness, even –
with the person we have become and are becoming through our ongoing
interactions with our pair-bond partner. A variety of arguments and theories from distal to proximal perspectives weave a coherent tapestry consistent with this perspective of love. Evolution tells us that we are driven
to enter into pair-bond relationships. Social psychology shows us that
our successful romantic relationships are maintained through symbiotic
growth, spurred by our mutual desire to become a better person and help
our romantic partner become a better person. Communication describes
how this symbiotic dance is made up of the innumerable and routine
activities and conversations in which we engage with our partner every
day. Finally, neurobiology shows us that when these communicative activities are successful, that is, when understanding is achieved, our brains
become coupled, structurally and operationally entrained. It is likely that
the more we engage in such interactions with our partners, the more easily
we can achieve these states, as we can expect repeated entrainment to be
reflected in more durable, long-term changes to our brains. Further, it is
highly likely that we find these states rewarding, pleasurable even, and will
endeavor to achieve them more completely and more frequently. This, we
argue is what is experienced as love.

It is not lost on us that the dynamics we describe in this paper are not
limited to the pair-bond relationship. We may have significant numbers of
interactions with friends every day. We talk with people at work on a daily
basis. There is no reason to believe that these conversations, should they
result in successfully achieving understanding, would not produce neural
coupling as well. We would simply argue that the pair-bond relationship
is the greatest forum for these dynamics. The pair-bond relationship is
typically the most salient to individuals, characterized by more frequent
communicative interactions, covering the widest bandwidth from trivial
to significant matters of any of our dyadic relationships. Thus, the pair-
bond relationship, certainly the romantic relationship, is the focus of most
discussions of love.

But we do not see the fact that these dynamics are not limited to the pair-bond relationship as a limitation in our depiction of love. Rather we see this as a feature, not a bug in our conceptualization. These same processes can help explain the love we feel for our family, our friendship network, our co-workers, and our community. In our conceptualization, love is not exclusive to the pair-bond relationship; rather it is epitomized and maximized in the pair-bond relationship. In all of these other social contexts, we endeavor on a mutual basis to help each other achieve our goals and satisfy our needs, we entrain with them, and we enjoy and embrace the personal outcomes of these interactions and entrainments; or we do not. To the extent that our response is the former, we can say some aspect of love characterizes our relationship with these people and the communities we share with them.

If our response to successive interactions and entrainments with another is not rewarding, if we do not like the person we are becoming in the relationship, we may find ourselves drifting away from our relationship. For most with a social network and a professional life, there will be no shortage of others with whom we can interact. It is likely that somebody (or multiple others) across those interactions could provide the self-expanding entrainment that we are not getting in our primary relationship. This need not lead directly to a new romantic relationship and the dissolution of our pair-bond relationship, though that is certainly a possibility. It could just as easily lead to spending increasing amounts of time with friends or work relationships that make us feel good about ourselves and who we are becoming, thus indirectly leading to relational decline or even dissolution. The point is that if our regular communication in our pair-bond relationship is not providing the entrainment and subsequent positive growth rewards that we expect or hope for, then we will likely gravitate toward where these rewards can be found.

There are two overriding takeaways from our conceptualization of love. The first is that love, as we describe it here, is not something reserved for the pair-bond relationship. It may have its ultimate manifestation in the pair-bond relationship, achieving something the couple experiences as transcendent, but the magic itself can be found in the fleeting interaction with a stranger. Essentially, every interaction with another is an opportunity to – quite literally – merge and harmonize with another, at the most fundamental level.

The second, related takeaway associated with our conceptualization of love is that, in a very material way, we become someone different as a result of our relationship with another. The self-expansion discussed above largely refers to cognitive changes and growth – changes that certainly can lead to behavioral changes. But more recent neurological studies suggest that our communicative interactions with others can produce neurological changes as well. When we experience such changes in the context of our relationship with another, we will find this process rewarding, *or not*, and we will continue or discontinue that relationship accordingly. This sense of reward and pursuit of that reward via continuing the relationship is maximized in the pair-bond relationship. It is safe to say that the experience of this process in the pair-bond relationship – particularly in the early stages – is so intense as to warrant its own phenomenological label. That intense state is what "love" refers to in common vernacular. But we are suggesting that the process is the same: communicate – entrain – reshape – and continue, or end.

We opened this chapter by arguing that partners in a romantic couple should not only expect to experience change but they should hope to find it rewarding as well, if the relationship is to thrive. We also referenced our own relationship as an example. We have worked together as spouses for almost twenty-seven years and throughout our time together we have frequently speculated on how are lives might have been different had we not met in graduate school. Certainly the logistics of our lives would have been different – universities, departments, career trajectories, geographies, and of course families. On the other hand, long before we pieced the research together that led to this chapter, we had had discussions about how we personally and specifically changed through relating with each other. From more superficial areas such as musical tastes, through temperament and emotional responses, all the way to fundamental values, nothing about us as individuals has been immune to change. As we have argued above, we believe our relationship has thrived because we value these changes and value the persons we have become through our relationship with each other. We are also well aware that these changes occurred as a direct result of how we were shaped by each other. However, we would think of these changes and the processes that produced them as "cognitive," and had not given much thought to how these changes might manifest neurologically. But now, after almost three decades of personal and professional lives together – raising children, doing research, writing papers, and discussing our careers – we have to wonder what an fMRI would show us about our brains, particularly as we communicate. Do they easily move into synchronization, showing structural and operational commonalities? We are betting "yes!"

References

Acevedo, B., Aron, A., Fisher, H. E., & Brown, L. L. (2012). Neural correlates of long-term intense love. *SCAN*, *7*, 145–159. doi: 10.1093/scan/nsq092.

Agnew, C. R., & Etcheverry, P. E. (2006). Cognitive interdependence: Considering self-in-relationship. In E. Finkel & K. Vohs (Eds.), *Self and relationships: Connecting intrapersonal and interpersonal processes* (pp. 274–293). New York: Guilford Press.

Agnew, C. R., Van Lange, P. A. M., Rusbult, C. E., & Langston, C. A. (1998). Cognitive interdependence: Commitment and the mental representation of close relationships. *Journal of Personality and Social Psychology*, *74*, 939–954. doi: 10.1037/0022-3514.74.4.939.

Aron, E. N., & Aron, A. (1996). Love and expansion of the self: The state of the model. *Personal Relationships*, *3*, 45–58. doi: 10.1111/j.1475-6811.1996.tb00103.x.

Aron, A, Aron, E. N., Tudor, M., Nelson, G., & Miller, N. (1991). Close relationships as including other in the self. *Journal of Personality and Social Psychology, 60*(2), 241–253. doi: 10.1037/0022-3514.60.2.241.

Aron, A., Norman, C. C., Aron, E. N., McKenna, C., & Heyman, R. E. (2000). Couples' shared participation in novel and arousing activities and experienced relationship quality. *Journal of Personality and Social Psychology, 78*(2), 273–284. doi: 10.1037/0022-3514.78.2.273.

Aron, A., Paris, M., & Aron, E. N. (1995). Falling in love: Prospective studies of self-concept change. *Journal of Personality and Social Psychology*, *69*, 1102–1112. doi: 10.1037/0022-3514.69.6.1102.

Buss, D. M. (1988). Love acts: The evolutionary biology of love. In R. J. Sternberg & M. L. Barnes (Eds.), *The psychology of love* (pp. 100–118). New Haven, CT: Yale University Press.

De Boer, A., Van Buel, E. M., & Ter Horst, G. J. (2012). Love is more than just a kiss: Neurobiological perspective on love and affection. *Neuroscience, 201*, 114–124. doi: 10.1016/j.neuroscience.2011.11.017.

Drigotas, S. M., Rusbult, C. E., Wieselquist, J., & Whitton, S. W. (1999). Close partner as sculptor of the ideal self: Behavioral affirmation and the Michelangelo phenomenon. *Journal of Personality and Social Psychology, 77*(2), 293–323. doi: 10.1037/0022-3514.77.2.293.

Duck, S. (1990a). Where do all the kisses go? Rapport, positivity, and relational-level analyses of interpersonal enmeshment. *Psychological Inquiry, 1*, 308–309. doi: 10.1207/s15327965pli0104_7.

(1990b). Relationships as unfinished business: Out of the frying pan and into the 1990s. *Journal of Social and Personal Relationships*, *7*, 5–28. doi: 10.1177/0265407590071001.

(1995). Talking relationships into being. *Journal of Social and Personal Relationships*, *12*, 535–552. doi: 10.1177/0265407595124006.

Duck, S., Rutt, D. J., Hurst, M. H., & Strejc, H. (1991). Some evident truths about conversations in everyday relationships: All communications are not created equal. *Human Communication Research, 18*, 228–267. doi: 10.1111/ j.1468–2958.1991.tb00545.x.

Fazendeiro, T., Chenier, T., & Winkielman, P. (2007). How dynamics of thinking create affective and cognitive feelings: Psychology of neuroscience of the connection between fluency, liking, and memory. In E. Harmon-Jones & P. Winkielman (Eds.), *Social neuroscience: Integrating biological and psychological explanations of social behavior* (pp. 271–289). New York: Guilford Press.

Fisher, H. E., Aron, A., & Brown, L. L. (2006). Romantic love: A mammalian brain system for Mate choice. *Philosophical Transactions of the Royal B Society, 361*, 2173–2186. doi: 10.1098/rstb.2006.1938.

Fisher, H. E., Aron, A., Mashek, D., Li, H., & Brown, L. L. (2002). Defining the brain systems of lust, romantic attraction, and attachment. *Archives of Sexual Behavior, 31*, 413–419. doi: 10.1023/A:1019888024255.

Fletcher, G., Simpson, J. A., Campbell, L., & Overall, N. C. (2013). *The science of intimate relationships*. Chichester, UK: Wiley-Blackwell.

Gasiorek, J., & Aune, R. K. (2017). Text features related to message comprehension. In *Oxford research encyclopedia of communication*. Retrieved from http://communication.oxfordre.com/view/10.1093/acrefore/9780190228613.001.0001/ acrefore-9780190228613-e-303.

Goldsmith, D. J., & Baxter, L. A. (1996). Constituting relationships in talk: A taxonomy of speech events in social and personal relationships. *Human Communication Research, 23*, 87–114. doi: 10.1111/j.1468–2958.1996.tb00388.x.

Graham, J. M., & Harf, M. R. (2014). Self-expansion and flow: The roles of challenge, skill, affect, and activation. *Personal Relationships, 22*, 45–64. doi: 10.1111/pere.12062.

Hasson, U., Ghazanfar, A. A., Galantucci, B., Garrod, S., & Keysers, C. (2012). Brain-to-brain coupling: A mechanism for creating and sharing a social world. *Trends in Cognitive Science, 16*(2), 114–121. doi: 10.1016/j.tics.2011.12.007.

Jankowiak, W. R., & Fischer, E. F. (1992). A cross-cultural perspective on romantic love. *Ethnology, 31*, 149. doi: 10.2307/3773618.

Kelley, H. H., & Thibaut, J. W. (1978). *Interpersonal relations*. New York: Wiley.

Kumashiro, M., Rusbult, C. E., Wolf, S. T., & Estrada, M. J. (2006). The Michelangelo phenomenon: Partner affirmation and self-movement toward one's ideal. In E. Finkel & K. Vohs (Eds.), *Self and relationships: Connecting intrapersonal and interpersonal processes* (pp. 317–341). New York: Guilford Press.

Kuss, D. J., & Griffiths, M. D. (2012). Internet and gaming addiction: A systematic literature review of neuroimaging studies. *Brain Sciences, 2*, 347–374. doi: 10.3390/brainsci2030347.

Mattingly, B. A., Lewandowski, G. W., & McIntyre, K. P. (2014). "You make me a better/worse person": A two-dimensional model of relationship self-change. *Personal Relationships, 21*, 176–190. doi: 10.1111/pere.12025.

Morelli, S. A., Torre, J. B., & Eisenberger, N. I. (2014). The neural bases of feeling understood and not understood. *Social Cognitive and Affective Neuroscience, 9*, 1890–1896. doi: 10.1093/scan/nst191.

Ortigue, S., & Bianchi-Demicheli, F. (2008). Why is your spouse so predictable? Connecting mirror neuron system and self-expansion model of love. *Medical Hypotheses, 71,* 941–944. doi: 10.1016/j.mehy.2008.07.016.

Ortigue, S., Bianchi-Demicheli, F., Hamilton, A. F. de C., & Grafton, S. T. (2007). The neural basis of love as a subliminal prime: An event-related functional magnetic resonance imaging study. *Journal of Cognitive Neuroscience, 19,* 1218–1230. doi: 10.1162/jocn.2007.19.7.1218.

Perez, A., Carreiras, M., & Duñabeitia, J. A. (2017). Brain-to-brain entrainment: EEG interbrain synchronization while speaking and listening. *Scientific Reports, 7,* 1–11. doi: 10.1038/s41598-017-04464-4.

Pickering, M., & Garrod, S. (2004). Toward a mechanistic psychology of dialogue. *Behavioral and Brain Sciences, 27*(2), 169–190. doi: 10.1017/S0140525X04000056.

Rusbult, C. E., Finkel, E. J., & Kumashiro, M. (2009). The Michelangelo phenomenon. *Current Directions in Psychological Science, 18,* 305–309. doi: 10.1111/j.1467-8721.2009.01657.x.

Rusbult, C. E., Kumashiro, M., Kubacka, K. E., & Finkel, E. J. (2009). "The part of me that you bring out": Ideal similarity and the Michelangelo phenomenon. *Journal of Personality and Social Psychology, 96,* 61–82. doi: 10.1037/a0014016.

Rusbult, C. E., & Van Lange, P. A. M. (2003). Interdependence, interaction, and relationships. *Annual Review of Psychology, 54,* 351–375. doi: 10.1146/annurev.psych.54.101601.145059.

Silbert, L. J., Honey, C. J., Simony, E., Poeppel, D., & Hasson, U. (2014). Coupled neural systems underlie the production and comprehension of naturalistic narrative speech. *Proceedings of the National Academy of Sciences, 111,* E4687–E4696. doi: 10.1073/pnas.1323812111.

Slotter, E. B., & Gardner, W. L. (2009). Where do you end and I begin? Evidence for anticipatory, motivated self-other integration between relationship partners. *Journal of Personality and Social Psychology, 96,* 1137–1151. doi: 10.1037/a0013882.

Stephens, G. J., Silbert, L. J., & Hasson, U. (2010). Speaker-listener neural coupling underlies successful communication. *PNAS, 107,* 14425–14430. doi: 10.1073/pnas.1008662107.

Stolk, A., Verhagen, L., & Toni, I. (2016). Conceptual alignment: How brains achieve mutual understanding. *Trends in Cognitive Sciences, 20,* 180–191. doi: 10.1016/j.tics.2015.11.007.

Takeuchi, H., Sekiguchi, A., Taki, Y., Yokoyama, S., Yomogida, Y., Komuro, N., Yamanouchi, T., Suzuki, S., & Kawashima, R. (2010). Training of working memory impacts structural connectivity. *The Journal of Neuroscience, 30,* 3297–3303. doi: 10.1523/jneurosci.4611-09.2010.

Thibaut, J. W., & Kelley, H. H. (1959). *The social psychology of groups.* New York: Wiley.

Wegner, D., Erber, R., & Raymond, P. (1991). Transactive memory in close relationships. *Journal of Personality and Social Psychology, 61,* 923–929. doi: 10.1037/0022-3514.61.6.923.

Zajonc, R., Adelmann, B., Murphy, P., & Niedenthal, K. (1987). Convergence in the physical appearance of spouses. *Motivation and Emotion, 11*(4), 335–346. doi: 10.1007/BF00992848.

Zatorre, R. J., Fields, R. D., & Johansen-Berg, H. (2012). Plasticity in gray and white: Neuroimaging changes in brain structure during learning. *Nature Neuroscience, 15,* 528–536. doi: 10.1038/nn.3045.

CHAPTER 3

The Evolution of Love in Humans

David M. Buss

"Love is blind," according to a common saying. "Love is a recent invention, a mere few hundred years old," some social scientists have argued. "Love is limited to Western cultures," according to others. This chapter explains why all these beliefs are radically wrong. From an evolutionary perspective, love is an adaptation, or more accurately a complex suite of adaptations, designed to solve specific problems of survival and reproduction. It is an exquisitely honed set of psychological devices that for humans served critical utilitarian functions in highly specific contexts. These functions are sufficiently numerous to give credence to another aphorism that gets closer to the truth: "Love is a many splendored thing."

The Adaptive Functions of Love

Solitary creatures such as giant pandas and porcupines have little need for love. They live alone and survive alone, coming together only briefly to mate before parting ways. Humans, in contrast, are "the social animal" (Aronson, 2003). Group living is what we do. Other humans are the "vehicles" on which our survival and genetic legacy critically depend. Some of those vehicles are so critical that we bestow them with our psychological, emotional, and material investments. Some are so critical to our reproduction that we willingly sacrifice our lives so that they can thrive.

Natural selection, the driving engine of the evolutionary process, favors the creation of adaptations. Adaptations are anatomical, physiological, or psychological solutions to recurrent problems of survival and reproduction, defined in its modern inclusive fitness formulation (Hamilton, 1964). A strict requirement for the evolution of adaptations is the cross-time statistical recurrence of an environmental structure. Statistical regularities can be of many sorts – a link between abrasive surfaces and damage to the skin; a correlation between a discrepancy in mate value and the odds of infidelity; a correlation between prolonged eye gaze and sexual interest; a correlation between symmetrical features and absence of environmental insults.

When these statistical regularities recur generation after generation, and when they afford information that is tributary to reproductive success, selection can exploit these statistical regularities to create adaptations designed to detect and act upon them. Thus, a callus-producing adaptation can solve the problem of damage due to repeated exposure to abrasive surfaces. A jealousy adaptation can alert an individual about an increased risk of a partner's infidelity (Buss, 2000). Courtship initiation adaptations can be designed to respond to signals of sexual interest (Greer & Buss, 2004). And standards of attractiveness can form around cues recurrently associated with physical health (Symons, 1979; Sugiyama, 2005).

These hypothesized adaptations are solutions to recurrent problems of survival or reproduction. Callus-producing mechanisms are solutions to a problem of survival, protecting the body against damage from the physical environment. Courtship initiation subroutines, jealousy, and standards of beauty solve specialized problems of mating, and hence historically contributed to reproductive success.

Could the complex psychological state we call "love," which includes emotional states, information-processing devices, and manifest acts of love be an adaptation that evolved to solve problems of reproduction (Buss, 1988a)? This chapter explores several hypotheses about the adaptive functions of love. According to an earlier evolutionary analysis, love evolved to serve several functions (Buss, 1988a, 2006):

- displaying reproductively relevant resources;
- providing sexual access;
- signaling sexual fidelity;
- providing psychological and emotional resources;
- promoting relationship exclusivity through mate guarding;
- displaying commitment – love as a commitment device;
- promoting actions that lead to successful reproductive outcomes; and
- providing signals of parental investment.

This chapter expands this evolutionary theory by postulating, and providing empirical evidence for, additional adaptive functions of love. Although conclusive proof does not yet exist to support any one of these hypotheses, enough empirical evidence exists to support the notion that a complete understanding of the psychology of love cannot be attained without understanding its possible functions – the adaptive problems it was designed to solve (see also Fletcher et al., 2015). Theoretically, the major addition to this evolutionary conception of love center on the notion of *fitness interdependence*.

Fitness Interdependence and the Evolution of Love

Theoretical progress in understanding the evolution of cooperative relationships centers on the concept of fitness interdependence: "The degree to which two or more organisms positively or negatively influence each others' success in replicating their genes" (Aktipis et al., in press). Genetic relatives provide the most obvious example of fitness interdependence. An individual's fitness is heavily dependent on the reproductive success of close genetic relatives – an insight that led to the inclusive fitness revolution in evolutionary biology (Hamilton, 1964). The concept of fitness interdependence applies more generally to cooperation among non-kin, including dyadic friendships and coalitional groups. And love relationships often reach a pinnacle of fitness interdependence.

Three conditions of romantic love promote maximal fitness interdependence: (1) *mutually produced offspring*, in which each parent has an equal genetic stake in promoting the welfare of children; (2) *monogamy*, with little or no chance of infidelity in or defection from the relationship; and (3) *lack of genetic kin in close proximity* (Alexander, 1987). Conversely, conditions that deviate from these conditions reduce or even undermine fitness interdependence. For example, each additional child a couple has decreases the likelihood of divorce, suggesting higher levels of commitment, whereas childless couples have the highest probability of divorce (see Buss, 2016). Infidelity and a couple's infertility, to take two other examples, are leading causes of divorce worldwide (Betzig, 1989), suggesting a rupture in commitment, love, and fitness interdependence. To my knowledge, the impact of kin from either partner in close proximity, which would create the potential conflict of one partner channeling pooled resources preferentially to their genetic relatives, has not been examined empirically.

In short, fitness interdependence and the conditions that promote or undermine it, should be key predictors of love, and especially the commitment component of love. People, of course, do not directly track fitness interdependence any more than they track fitness. Rather, the conditions that promote or impede fitness interdependence have acted as forces of selection that created, in part, the psychological adaptations involved in promoting love as well as the shattering of love.

Importantly, this hypothesis does not imply that the psychological adaptations created by selection pressures of fitness interdependence are currently adaptive or currently track fitness. For example, men's adaptations for sexual jealousy upon discovery of a love partner's sexual infidelity get fully activated, even if his partner is taking birth control and her infidelity has no chance of compromising his paternity (and hence the level of fitness interdependence he has with his partner). I anticipate that the conditions that promote and impede fitness interdependence will continue to illuminate the evolution of love.

We now turn to additional empirical evidence for an evolutionary theory of love, starting with whether love shows universality across cultures.

The Universality of Love

One straightforward prediction from the evolutionary theory proposed here is that the psychological circuits dedicated to love should be universal, not limited to Western cultures. Universality of psychological adaptation, of course, does not mean universality of manifest experience. Just as a person could go through life without ever having their jealousy circuit activated – if a partner never displayed cues to infidelity or defection, for example – a person could go through life never experiencing love. Nonetheless, most humans should possess the psychological circuitry, and hence love should be experienced by some people in every single culture around the world – a testable prediction not generated by non-evolutionary theories of love.

One testament to the universality of love and its obstinate refusal to be extinguished can be found in societies that have attempted to banish it (Jankowiak, 1995). In the nineteenth century, the Oneida society articulated the view that romantic love was merely disguised sexual lust, and saw no reason to encourage such deceit. The Shakers, to take another example, declared romantic love undignified and threatening to the goals of the larger community, and so sought to banish it. The Mormons in the nineteenth century also viewed romantic love as disruptive, and sought to discourage it. In all three societies, however, romantic love persisted among individuals, sometimes underground, refusing banishment, hidden from the harsh eyes of the group's elders. Within cultures, as the story of Romeo and Juliet declares with universal resonance, love can be fueled by the efforts of others to suppress it. Lovers have no choice; they can quell their feelings temporarily or muffle their expression, but they cannot exorcise them entirely.

Cultures that impose arranged marriage and permit polygyny provide a test case, for what system could be better designed to undermine love? Does love have any place within a mating system where a man's first wife is chosen for him? Even when his elders choose a man's first wife for him, such as in polygynous Arabic cultures, men often marry a second wife for love. Taita women, in fact, state that they prefer to be the second or third wife, not the first. They feel that they will be more likely to be married for love, and hence anticipate that they will receive more favorable treatment from their husband and experience more emotional closeness (Jankowiak, 1995, p. 11).

Another testament to the universality of love comes from studies that simply ask men and women whether or not they are currently in love. Susan Sprecher and her colleagues interviewed 1,667 women and men from three different cultures (Sprecher, Aron, Hatfield, Cortese, Potapova, & Levitskaya, 1994). Seventy-three% of the Russian women and 61% of the Russian men confessed to being currently in love. The comparable figures from Japan were 63% for women and 41% for men. Americans reported roughly the same levels, with 63% of the women and 53% of the men admitting that they were currently in love. Another study of ethnographies across cultures revealed that the overwhelming majority contained explicit references to the experience of love – observed declarations of love, love songs, expressions of pain upon unrequited love, and many others (Jankowiak & Fisher, 1992).

Finally, in the most massive study ever conducted of mate preferences – in thirty-seven cultures located on six continents and five islands, consisting of 10,047 participants – "mutual attraction and love" proved to be at or near the top in every single culture (Buss, 1989; Buss et al., 1990). If the experience and expression of love were limited to only some cultures, the evolutionary theory of love would be a non-starter. Available evidence suggests that love indeed is a universal experience; no cultures have been shown to lack the experience of love. Universality of love, however, does not imply that the psychological design of love adaptations is identical in women and men.

Sex Differences in the Psychological Design of Love

Among the half dozen or so more replicable findings in the human mating literature is that men place a greater premium than women on physical appearance in their selection of a long-term mate (Buss, 1989, 2016). This is not because men are superficial or brainlessly judge a book by its cover. Physical appearance provides a wealth of information about a woman's health and youth, and hence her fecundity (probability that an act of sexual intercourse would lead to successful conception, barring use of modern birth control) and reproductive value (future reproductive potential). The features of physical appearance that embody standards of female attractiveness all support the attractiveness-fertility link – clear skin, smooth skin, lustrous hair, long hair, symmetrical features, absence of open sores, pustules, or lesions, relatively small waist, relatively large breasts, and a low waist-to-hip ratio (see Sugiyama, 2005, for comprehensive summaries of the empirical evidence).

Many of the qualities critical to women's selection of a long-term mate are not readily assessed through physical appearance. These include a man's ambition, industriousness, drive, and status trajectory – qualities linked with resource acquisition (Buss, 1989, 2016; Buss & Schmitt, 1993). These contrast with what women want in a short-term mate, including signals of good genes, which can be evaluated partly through physical appearance (Gangestad & Thornhill, 1997; Sugiyama, 2005). Love, however, is not an emotion typically linked with casual sex. It emerges mainly in the context of long-term mating.

Because love is an emotion tethered to long-term mating; because reproductive value is so critical to men in selecting a long-term mate; and because physical appearance provides an abundance of cues to a woman's reproductive value, we can predict that men will experience "love at first sight" more often than women. The empirical evidence supports this prediction. Men, more than women, report falling in love at first sight (Brantley, Knox, & Zusman, 2002; Kanin, Davidson, & Scheck, 1970). This evidence supports one hypothesized sex difference in the design of the psychological circuitry of love. Other evidence centers on commitment.

Short-term mating, on average, tends to be most costly and less beneficial for women than for men (Buss & Schmitt, 1993). By engaging in short-term mating, women historically risked conceiving by a less-than-ideal man – perhaps one with inferior genes or one who will not stick around to invest in her and her children. Although women can benefit from short-term mating in some circumstances (Buss, Goetz, Duntley, Asao, & Conroy-Beam, 2017; Greiling & Buss, 2000), casual sex historically did not translate into direct linear increments in reproductive success, as it did for men. Because men can reproduce with as little investment as a single act of sex, whereas women require an obligatory nine-month pregnancy to reproduce, selection has favored in men a more powerful motivation to desire and seek casual sex.

Would you agree or disagree with the statement "Sex without love is OK"? If you are a man, the chances are that you would agree with this statement. Women, on average, disagree. Indeed, attitudes toward casual sex without love remain one of the largest sex differences in the sexual domain, as revealed by meta-analyses (Olivia & Hyde, 1993) and the cross-cultural evidence (Buss, 2016; Schmitt, 2005).

These findings support a critical hypothesis about sex differences in the psychological design of love. For women, love and sex are closely linked. Men find it easier to have sex without love. This brings us to another hypothesis anchored in an evolutionary theory of love – the emotional experience of love as a means to increase the odds of commitment.

Love as a Commitment Device

If love is a universal human emotion, why did evolution install it in the human brain to begin with? Keys to the mystery come from three unique departures of the human animal from their most recent primate ancestors: the evolution of long-term mating; the concealment of female ovulation; and the heavy investment by men in their children. Chimpanzees, our closest primate relatives, mate primarily when the female enters estrus. Her bright red genital swellings and olfactory scents send males into a sexual frenzy. Outside of estrus, males are largely indifferent to females. Among humans, ovulation is concealed or cryptic, at least for the most part. Although there might be subtle physical changes in women – a slight glowing of the skin or an almost imperceptible increase in her sexual desire – there is no solid evidence that men can actually detect when women ovulate.

The concealment of ovulation coincided with several other critical changes. Men and women started having sex throughout the menstrual cycle, not just around ovulation. Men and women engaged in long-term pair-bonded mating over the expanse of years or decades. And men, unlike their chimpanzee cousins, began investing heavily in offspring. Meat from the hunt went to provision the children, not just the wife and kin.

It requires taking a step back to realize how extraordinary these changes are. Some females began allocating their entire reproductive careers to a single male, rather than to whoever happened to be the reigning alpha male when they happened to be ovulating. Males began to guard their partners against rival males who might be tempted to lure their mates. Surplus resources that in many species go to the female as a specific inducement to copulation now get channeled to the wife and children. Indeed, males now had added incentive to acquire surplus resources, mostly in the form of hunted meat. Long-term mating, in short, involved the allocation of reproductively relevant resources to a single mate over a virtually unprecedented span of time.

Elementary economics tells us that those who hold valuable resources do not give them away indiscriminately. Indeed, evolution would ruthlessly select against those who frittered away reproductively valuable resources in long-term mateships that had no payoff. The evolution of long-term mating required installing in the human psychological architecture a set of circuits designed to ensure a reasonable reproductive payoff to allocating all of one's resources to a single partner. It required some means for determining that one particular mate, above all other potential mates, would be there through thick and thin, through sickness and health. It required a solution to the problem of commitment.

My own initial outline of an evolutionary theory of love (Buss, 1988a) accords with that of evolutionary economist Robert Frank – that the emotion we call love is, in part, an evolved solution to the problem of commitment (Frank, 1988). If a partner chooses you for rational reasons, he or she might leave you for the same rational reasons: finding someone slightly more desirable on all of the "rational" criteria. This creates a commitment problem: How can you be sure that a person will stick with you? If your partner is blinded by an uncontrollable love that cannot be helped and cannot be chosen, a love for only you and no other, then commitment will not waver when you are in sickness rather than in health, when you are poorer rather than richer. Love overrides rationality. It is the emotion that ensures that you won't leave when someone more desirable comes along. Love, in short, may be a solution to the commitment problem, providing a signal to the partner of strength of long-term intent and resolve.

The causal arrow almost certainly also runs in reverse. Love may be the psychological reward we experience when the problem of commitment is successfully being solved. It is a mind/body opium that signals that the adaptive problems of mate selection, sexual congress, devotion, and loyalty have met with triumph (Fisher, 2004). The scientific explanation is that evolution has installed in the human brain reward mechanisms that keep us performing activities that lead to successful reproduction. The disadvantage is that the drug sometimes wears off (Fisher, 2004).

Love is both a solution to the commitment problem and an intoxicating reward for successfully solving it. The astonishingly intricate entwinement of love was first revealed in my own study (Buss, 1988a). I started by asking several hundred women and to describe the behaviors that signal that a person is in love. A separate sample then diagnosed each of the 115 love acts on how much it indicated being in the thrall of love.

Signals of commitment emerged as most diagnostic, but commitment can take many forms. A partner can commit resources such as food, shelter, and physical protection to a lover over the long term. A lover can commit sexual resources by remaining sexually faithful and by making love with wild abandon. Lovers commit reproductive resources to their beloved, as in successful conception, pregnancy, and childbirth. And it follows that lovers commit parental resources to their mutual children, the natural result of the love union.

Many of these acts conveyed self-sacrifice: putting one's own interests aside for the greater needs of the loved one, making a sacrifice of great importance for the partner, and giving up large amounts of free time to be with the partners. Other signals involved a sexual openness and trust that may be lacking in lesser relationships: trying out different sexual positions, swallowing during oral sex, acting out the lover's deepest sexual fantasies.

Emotional commitment emerged throughout the acts of love, including listening to problems with real attention and interest, giving up fun activities to be with the lover when he or she really needed it, and showing great concern for a partner's problems. Several people described how a partner had gone out of his or her way emotionally when they were in the most desperate psychological state. Several lovers described how their partner provided hope during their darkest hours of need, reaching down to pull them out of a pit of depression when the walls of life seemed steep and unscalable.

These findings support another critical set of design features hypothesized to be linked to love – specialized forms of commitment. Evidence for love as a commitment device, first posited independently by Buss (1988a) and Frank (1988), has accrued increasing empirical support (e.g. Fletcher et al., 2015).

Snakes in the Garden of Love

Unfortunately, that is not the happy end to the evolutionary story. There are snakes in the garden, troubles in emotional paradise. One sort of trouble comes from the dual strategies in the human menu of mating. Once the desire for love exists, it can be exploited and manipulated. Men deceive women about the depth of their loving feelings, for example, just to gain short-term sexual access (Haselton, Buss, Oubaid, & Angleitner,

2005). As Ovid noted hundreds of years ago, "love is … a sexual behavior sport in which duplicity is used in order that a man might win his way into a woman's heart and subsequently into her boudoir." Women, in turn, have coevolved defenses against being sexually exploited by imposing a longer courtship process before to consenting to sex, attempting to detect deception, and evolving superior ability to decode nonverbal signals (Buss, 2016). The coevolutionary arms race of deception and detection of deception continues with no end in sight.

Jealousy as a Functional but Dangerous Emotion Guarding Love

Jealousy poses a paradox. Consider these findings: 46% of a community sample stated that jealousy was an *inevitable* consequence of true love (Mullen & Martin, 1994). St. Augustine noted this link when he declared that "He that is not jealous, is not in love" (quoted in Claypool & Sheets, 1996). Shakespeare's tormented Othello "dotes, yet doubts, suspects, yet strongly loves." Women and men typically interpret a partner's jealousy as a sign of the depth of his or her love; a partner's absence of jealousy as a lack of love.

Mathes asked a sample of unmarried, but romantically involved, men and women to complete a jealousy test (Mathes, 1986). Seven years later, he contacted the participants again and asked them about the current status of their relationship. Roughly 25% of the participants had married, whereas 75% had broken up. The jealousy scores from seven years earlier for those who married averaged 168, whereas the scores for those who broke up registered significantly lower at 142. These results must be interpreted cautiously; it is one study with a small sample. Nonetheless, it points to the possibility that jealousy might be inexorably linked with long-term love.

Contrast this with another finding: In a sample of 651 university students who were actively dating, more than 33% reported that jealousy posed a significant problem in their current relationship (Riggs, 1993). The problems ranged from the loss of self-esteem to verbal abuse, from rage-ridden arguments to the terror of being stalked.

Jealousy, paradoxically, flows from deep and abiding love, but can shatter the most harmonious relationships. The paradox was reflected in O. J. Simpson's statement: "Let's say I committed this crime [the killing of his ex-wife, Nicole Brown Simpson]. Even if I did do this, it would have to have been because I loved her very much, right?" (*Newsweek*, December 28, 1998, p. 116). The emotion of jealousy, designed to shelter a relationship from intruders, "turns homes that might be sanctuaries of love into hells of discord and hate" (E. Gillard; quoted in Ellis, 1950, Vol. 2, ch. 11).

Jealousy is one of the most commonly found correlates of being in love (Mathes, 1991). It evolved to protect love not merely from the threat of loss but more profoundly from the threat of loss to a rival. Consider which of the following scenarios would make you more jealous:

> *Loss due to fate:* Your [partner], with whom you are deeply in love, is killed in an automobile accident.
>
> *Loss due to partner's destiny:* Your [partner], with whom you are deeply in love, obtains a promotion and moves to a far away city. You know that you will never see him (her) again.
>
> *Loss due to rejection:* Your [partner], with whom you are deeply in love, explains that he (she) does not love you anymore and ends the relationship. You know that you will never see him (her) again.
>
> *Loss due to a rival:* Your [partner], which whom you are deeply in love, falls in love with another and ends his (her) relationship with you. You know that you will never see him (her) again. (Mathes, 1991, pp. 93–94)

In an experiment, Mathes asked men and women "If this happened to you, would you feel jealous?" Out of a possible range of four to twenty-eight, loss of a love due to fate scored only seven on the jealousy scale. Loss due to destiny scored nearly double at thirteen. Loss due to rejection came out at sixteen. But loss to a rival provoked the greatest jealousy scores at twenty-two. Evolution designed jealousy not just to protect the loss of love. Because evolution is an inherently competitive process, jealousy evolved to prevent the "double-whammy" of the loss of love and a rival's gain of that love.

In my studies, I discovered that signs of jealousy are accurately interpreted as acts of love (Buss, 1988b). When a man drops by unexpectedly to see what his partner is doing, this mode of jealous vigilance functions to preserve exclusivity while simultaneously communicating love. When a woman loses sleep thinking about her partner and wondering whether he is with someone else, it indicates simultaneously the depth of her love and the intensity of her jealousy. When a man tells his friends that he is madly in love with a woman, it serves the dual purposes of conveying love and communicating to potential rivals to keep their hands off.

The failure of most "open marriages" that became popular in the late 1960s and early 1970s is a stark testament to the failure of experiments to expunge jealousy from the lives of lovers. Few marriages can endure third-party intruders. One of the positive benefits of jealousy is to preserve that inner sanctum, protecting it from interlopers who have their own hidden agendas. According to the Ayala Pines, protecting love is the primary function of jealousy: "jealousy aims to protect romantic relationships. It is not a useless flight of irrationality, but a useful signal people can learn to interpret correctly … Jealousy makes people examine their relationship … It teaches couples not to take each other for granted … ensures that they continue to value each other and … indicates that people value the love relationship it protects" (Pines, 1998, pp. 205–206).

The recent surge of interest in *polyamory* or *consensual non-monogamy* where individuals engage in open consensual love and sex with multiple partners, may pose a challenge to these views (e.g. Moors, 2017), but the field awaits good empirical evidence of their viability. There is evidence that polyamorous relationships are often, although not always, initiated by men who seek sexual variety, and sometimes women go along as a mate-retention tactic (Buss, 2016). Moreover, jealousy is a pervasive problem in consensually non-monogamous relationships.

Safe havens, however, are rarely possible in the modern world. As journalist Judith Viorst noted, "Unfortunately there is an endless supply of women out there in the big world – secretaries and dental assistants and waitresses and women executives … And wives with traveling husbands have an even wider selection of potential temptations to get aggravated over – TWA stewardesses, San Francisco topless dancers, old flames in Minneapolis, new models in Detroit" (Viorst, 1998, p. 24).

The maintenance of love, ironically, may hinge on the ever-present threat of rivals and the jealousy they evoke. "On those days when I happen to be feeling mature and secure," Viorst observes, "I'm also going to admit that a man who wasn't attractive to other women, a man who wasn't alive enough to enjoy other women, a man who was incapable of making me jealous, would never be the kind of man I'd love" (Viorst, 1998, p. 24).

When Love Kills

Another problem is that what comes up often comes down. People fall out of love as crashingly as they fall in love. We can not predict with certainty who will fall out of love, but recent studies provide some critical clues. Just as the fulfillment of desire looms large when falling in love, violations of desire portend conflict and dissolution. A man who was chosen in part for his kindness and drive may get dumped when he turns cruel or lazy. A woman chosen in part for her youth and beauty may lose out when a newer model beckons her partner. An initially considerate partner may turn condescending. And a couple's infertility after repeated episodes of sex prompts each to seek a more fruitful union elsewhere (Betzig, 1989).

The most crushing blow to long-term love comes from the harsh metric of the mating market. A mated couple initially equivalent on overall desirability may experience a widening gap over time. Consider an entry-level professional couple. If the woman's career skyrockets and the man gets fired, it puts a strain on both because their market values now differ. When actress Meg Ryan's career surpassed that of her husband Dennis Quaid, she promptly had an affair with rising star Russell Crowe. Sudden increases in status open up new mating opportunities. A "9" who was previously out of reach now becomes available. In the evolutionary jungle of mating, we may admire a woman who stands by her loser husband. But few of those who did are our ancestors. Modern humans descended from those who traded up when the increment was sufficient to outweigh the manifold costs that people experience as a consequence of breaking up (Buss, 2000).

Falling out of love has many dark sides. "Love's pleasure lasts but a moment; love's sorrow lasts all through life" (Celestine, a French writer of fables). The crash can be physically dangerous for women and psychologically traumatic for both sexes. Hearts broken from love lost rate among the most stressful life events a person can experience, exceeded in psychological pain only by horrific events such as a child dying. Men who get rejected by the woman with whom they are in love abuse them often emotionally and sometimes physically. Some men start stalking their exes with repeated phone calls, unexpected visits, and threats of violence. Victims of stalking experience psychological terror, disruption of work, and interference with new mateships. In our recent studies, we found that an alarming number of men who are unceremoniously dumped begin to have homicidal fantasies (Buss, 2005). Unfortunately, these fantasies sometimes turn into reality.

The mere loss of love is enough to make a man homicidal. The following case, from a systematic compilation of all homicides that occurred within one year in the city of Houston, Texas, illustrates the centrality of power of love and its loss.

> Case No. 191 begins as a domestic quarrel. A 37-year-old White woman and her 42-year-old husband were drinking and quarreling. The woman first ran next door to her sister's apartment but only found her 11-year-old nephew awake. She left her sister's house to seek assistance from a neighbor. Her husband intercepted her as she crossed their driveway, a further argument ensued, and the woman shouted for help as she walked away from her husband. The neighbors found the woman lying bleeding on the sidewalk and

called an ambulance. The husband told police that the whole thing started because his wife did not love him anymore … [this] led him to pull out a pocketknife and stab his wife in the chest. (Lundsgaarde, 1977)

Losing love, in short, remains traumatic, both for the dumper and the dumpee. Just as evolution has installed serotonin reward mechanisms that flood our brains with pleasure when we successfully mate, it has also equipped us with brain circuits that deliver searing psychological pain when we experience mating failure. The many failures of love can bring catastrophic costs, creating adaptive problems of great moment.

In the United States between 1976 and 1984, 4,507 women were murdered annually on average (Campbell, 1992). Race was no barrier. Just over a third of the victims were African-American women; two-thirds were American women of European descent. The majority were killed by men who loved them deeply. One study of women murder victims in Dayton, Ohio, reveals proportions similar to those of most studies: 19% were murdered by their husbands, 8% by a current boyfriend, 17% by an estranged husband, and 8% by a prior sex partner. These total to an astonishing 52% of women killed in Dayton by their lovers or former lovers. In sharp contrast, in a typical year, only 3% of male murder victims die at the hands of a female lover.

Dayton is not unique. In a massive study of homicides committed within the United States between 1976 and 1998, more than a third of the women were killed by an intimate partner, whereas only 4% of the men were killed by a wife or lover (Greenfield et al., 1998). Similar statistics show up worldwide, from the Australian aborigines to murder among the Munda of India (Easteal, 1993; Saran, 1974).

It may seem strange to have the warm fuzzy emotion of love lead to vicious and bloody death. After all, love is what leads to romance. Love leads to passion. Love leads to the birth of new life. Killing seems the opposite – destruction, demolition, and final demise. How can these apparent opposites be fused in the human mind, in a jarring tangle of paradoxical emotions? Consider the following case.

Then she said that since she came back in April she had fucked this other man about ten times. I told her how can you talk about love and marriage and you been fucking this other man. I was really mad. I went to the kitchen and got the knife. I went back to our room and asked: Were you serious when you told me that? She said yes. We fought on the bed, I was stabbing her. Her grandfather came up and tried to take the knife out of my hand. I told him to go and call the cops for me. I don't know why I killed the woman, I loved her. (Confession of a thirty-one-year-old man to police

after he stabbed his twenty-year-old wife to death, following their reunion
after a six-month separation)

The killing of a mate, however, poses a more serious puzzle. How could
this bizarre form of behavior possibly have evolved? Killing a mate destroys
a key reproductive resource. Evolution by selection should favor pre-
serving, not destroying, vital reproductive resources. Mate killing seems
outrageously counter to self-interested reproductive survival.

The solution to this mystery requires delving into the underlying
particulars of mating market logic (Buss, 2005). First, in most cases, killing
a mate who has been unfaithful usually *would* have been detrimental to the
killer. An unfaithful woman might still be a valuable reproductive resource
to her husband. If she *continues* to be his sexual resource, then killing her
would be damaging his own fitness, an instance of futile vengeful spite. As
Margo Wilson and Martin Daly correctly observe, "murdered women are
costly to replace" (Wilson & Daly, 1998). If the woman has borne him children, then killing her dramatically hurts his children's chances to survive
and thrive. Finally, by killing her, the cuckolded man risks retribution. The
woman's brother or father might be motivated to extract vengeance. For all
these reasons, killing a mate is usually a remarkably ineffective solution to
the problem of cuckoldry.

But sometimes the elements in the cost–benefit equation become
rearranged. An infidelity might signal the man's *permanent* loss of sexual
access to his mate, not just a temporary or fractional loss. She might *not*
have children by him, and hence killing her would not impair his existing
children's survival. She might lack a father or brothers in the vicinity, something quite common in traditional societies where marriage is usually exog-
amous where women migrate away from their own kin group and move
in with her husband's kin group when they marry. Furthermore, a man's
social reputation might be so severely damaged by his wife's infidelity that
his social status would plummet unless he engaged in dramatic action to
staunch the slide. Status loss cascades into a decline in mate value, undermining the man's ability to attract another mate. Finally, the man's sexual
loss might become a rival's sexual gain, a valuable reproductive resource
flowing to an arch enemy.

Consider for a moment the logic of the argument outside the context of mating. If you have just killed a game animal to feed yourself and
your hungry family, and a scavenging animal comes along and steals it
before you can eat it, you suffer a loss. But if your rival steals the meat, the
loss becomes compounded in the currency of evolutionary fitness, since

selection operates on the principle of *relative* reproductive success. Your loss becomes a gain for your immediate rival, whose children survive and thrive whereas yours go hungry or perish.

The same logic applies to mating. If your mating loss bestows a sexual gain on your immediate rival, then the fitness costs of being cuckolded become compounded. This theory leads to a counterintuitive prediction: The younger, healthier, and more attractive the woman, the greater the loss to the cuckolded man and the greater the gain for the rival who now sleeps in her bed. This leads to a disturbing prediction of the theory – that the more appealing, healthy, and fertile the woman, the more motivated the man will be to kill her upon discovering a sexual infidelity.

What is extraordinary is that roughly half of the 3,400 women who are murdered in America every year are killed by the ones who presumably love them – their husbands, boyfriends, ex-husbands, or ex-boyfriends – in circumstances that are remarkably similar. The permanent loss of love sometimes activates evolved homicidal circuits in men.

What an Evolutionary Perspective on Love Adds to Existing Theories of Love

Psychological theories of love and the empirical research they have generated have led to important insights and discoveries. These include Berscheid and Hatfield's (1978) distinction between passionate and companionate love; Sternberg's triangular theory of love, with the key components of passion, intimacy, and commitment (Sternberg, 1986); Fehr's (1988, 2015) prototype analysis of love, which identifies caring and intimacy as the most central and passion as important but less central; and Aron and Aron's (1986) self-expansion model of love. Important progress has also been made in identifying the neurobiological substrates of love (e.g. Aron et al., 2005; Cacioppo, Bianchi-Demicheli, Frum, Pfaus, & Lewis, 2012).

An evolutionary perspective does not contradict any of these theories and discoveries, but rather importantly complements them. Most centrally, it poses the question: *Has there been selection pressure over evolutionary time for adaptations for love, and if so, what are the functions of these adaptations?* Just as it is important for a medical researcher to discover *how* the heart, liver, and lungs work, it is equally important to discover the *adaptive functions* of these organs (e.g. to pump blood to the brain and muscles; to break down toxins; etc.). Analogously, if there exist psychological adaptations for love, as I have argued, it is critical to identify their adaptive functions – the specific ways in which these adaptations have contributed to fitness or reproductive success over evolutionary time.

Evolution-based theories of love have emphasized passion and sex drive, which function to promote *sex and hence successful conception* (e.g. Buss, 1988a; Fisher, 1998); attachment, which is critical for the function of *investing in offspring* (Shaver, Hazan, & Bradshaw, 1988); commitment, which is critical for the function of *investing in those offspring over the long term* needed in our highly altricial species; and love as a commitment device, which functions to *channel reproductively relevant resources preferentially to a partner* (e.g. Buss, 1988a; Frank, 1988; for a recent treatment, see Fletcher, Simpson, Campbell, & Overall, 2015).

Buss's theory of love extends these core ideas by specifying in detail precisely what those reproductively relevant resources are (e.g. not just sex, but exclusive sexual access, signals of sexual fidelity, curtailing contact with potential alternative mates), as well as the *mate-retention adaptations* crucial for protecting love relationships from infidelity and mate poachers. The current evolutionary perspective adds the important concept of fitness interdependence, together with the conditions that promote it, with romantic love being one pinnacle of maximal fitness interdependence (another pinnacle is parental love for their children, another example of high fitness interdependence). The notion of fitness interdependence dovetails nicely with Aron and Aron's (1986) notion of love as self-expansion, giving that theory an evolutionary functional foundation. In these ways, an evolutionary perspective provides an important complement to existing psychological theories of love by bringing in the selective pressures likely to have created the psychological components of love and plausible hypotheses about the adaptive functions of those psychological components.

Conclusions

The evolutionary theory of love proposed here contains a key feature lacking in non-evolutionary theories of love – hypotheses about its functionality in solving specific adaptive problems that have recurrently faced humans over deep time in the quest for mating success. It also contains testable, hence potentially falsifiable, predictions about the psychological design of love, including critical sex differences in design features. Although the full theory requires more extensive empirical tests, the available evidence supports several key predictions from the evolutionary theory of love.

First, evidence suggests that the experience of love is universal in the sense that some individuals in all cultures for which we have relevant data experience love. Second, the evidence supports the hypothesis that love emerges primarily in the context of long-term mating. Third, evidence points to the functions of love as a commitment device (Buss, 1988a; Frank, 1988). Specifically, Buss (1988a) found that love signals the commitment of the following: (1) displaying reproductively relevant resources; (2) providing sexual access; (3) signaling sexual fidelity; (4) promoting relationship exclusivity through mate guarding; (5) promoting actions that historically led to successful reproductive outcomes; and (6) providing signals of high parental investment in resulting children.

Although the emotion of love contains these universal psychological circuits and adaptive functions, men and women differ in a few psychological design features of love. Men experience "love at first sight" more than women – a design feature that supports the notion that physical appearance and physical attractiveness is more central to men's than to women's activation of love circuits. Women more than men *disagree* with the attitude statement "sex without love is OK," supporting the hypothesis that love and sex are more closely linked in the minds of women than men. Because of men's short-term mating strategy, they are more able to dissociate sex and love and find it easier to have sex with strangers with whom they are not in love. Although some women are like some men in this respect, women on average find it more difficult to have sex without the accompanying emotion of love.

Jealousy shows links to love in ways precisely predicted by the current evolutionary theory. Women more than men experience more intense jealousy when a partner falls in love with someone else, whereas men more than women experience more intense jealousy at signals of sexual infidelity (despite some claims to the contrary, the sex differences in the design of jealousy are extremely robust across methods – see Buss, 2018a; Edlund & Sagarin, 2017; Sagarin et al., 2012; Pietrzak, Laird, Stevens, & Thompson, 2002).

Finally, loss of love, particularly when a woman permanently leaves a man who loves her, places women in peril of violence, stalking, and murder – findings that support the hypothesis that men's psychology of love contains design features that motivate them to keep a woman they love and take desperate measures to prevent male rivals from possessing her. Infidelity and defection from the relationship lead to a rival's access to a lover's reproductively valuable resources, which in turn compromises fitness interdependence – a key criterion for the evolution of love.

Acknowledgment

The author thanks Athena Aktipis for constructive comments on an earlier version of this chapter.

References

Aktipis, A. et al. (in press). How should we study fitness interdependence? Opportunities and challenges of investigating cooperation and conflict across systems. *Nature: Human Behavior*.

Alexander, R. D. (1987). *The biology of moral systems*. Hawthorne, NY: Aldine DeGruyter.

Aron, A., & Aron, E. N. (1986). *Love and the expansion of self: Understanding attraction and satisfaction*. New York: Hemisphere.

Aron, A., Fisher, H., Mashek, D., Strong, G., Li, H., & Brown, L. (2005). Neural systems in intense romantic attraction: An fMRI study. *Journal of Neurophysiology*, *94*, 327–337.

Aronson, E. (2003). *The social animal* (9th ed.). New York: Worth.

Berscheid, E., & Hatfield [Walster], E. H. (1978). *Interpersonal attraction* (2nd ed.). Reading, MA: Addison-Wesley.

Betzig, L. (1989). Causes of conjugal dissolution. *Current Anthropology*, *30*, 654–676.

Brantley, A., Knox, D., & Zusman, M. E. (2002). When and why gender differences in saying "I Love You" among college students. *College Student Journal*, *36*, 614–615.

Buss, D. M. (1988a). *Love acts: The evolutionary biology of love*. In R. Sternberg & M. Barnes (Eds.), *The psychology of love* (pp. 100–118). New Haven, CT: Yale University Press.

(1988b). From vigilance to violence: Tactics of mate retention. *Ethology and Sociobiology*, *9*, 291–317.

(1989). Sex differences in human mate preferences: Evolutionary hypotheses testing in 37 cultures. *Behavioral and Brain Sciences*, *12*, 1–49.

(2000). *The dangerous passion: Why jealousy is as necessary as love and sex*. New York: Free Press.

(2005). *The murderer next door: Why the mind is designed to kill*. New York: The Penguin Press.

(2006). The evolution of love. In R. J. Sternberg & K. Weis (Eds.), *The new psychology of love* (pp. 65–86). New Haven, CT: Yale University Press.

(2016). *The evolution of desire: Strategies of human mating* (rev. and updated ed.). New York: Basic Books.

(2018). Sexual and emotional infidelity: Evolved gender differences in jealousy prove robust and replicable. *Perspectives in Psychological Science*, *13*, 155–160.

Buss, D. M., Abbott, M., Angleitner, A., Asherian, A., Biaggio, A., et al. (1990). International preferences in selecting mates: A study of 37 cultures. *Journal of Cross-Cultural Psychology*, *21*, 5–47.

Buss, D. M., Goetz, C., Duntley, J. D., Asao, K., & Conroy-Beam, D. (2017). The mate switching hypothesis. *Personality and Individual Differences, 104,* 143–149.

Buss, D. M., & Schmitt, D. P. (1993). Sexual strategies theory: An evolutionary perspective on human mating. *Psychological Review, 100,* 204–232.

Cacioppo, S., Bianchi-Demicheli, F., Frum, C., Pfaus, J., & Lewis, J. W. (2012). The common neural bases between sexual desire and love: A multilevel kernel density fMRI analysis. *Journal of Sexual Medicine, 9,* 1048–1054.

Campbell, J. C. (1992). "If I can't have you, no one can": Power and control in homicide of female partners. In J. Radford & D. E. H. Russell (Eds.), *Femicide: The politics of woman killing* (pp. 99–113). New York: Twayne.

Claypool, H., & Sheets, V. (1996). Jealousy: Adaptive or destructive? Paper presented to the Human Behavior and Evolution Society, Evanston, IL, June, 1996.

Easteal, P. W. (1993). *Killing the beloved: Homicide between adult sexual intimates.* Canberra, ACT: Australian Institute of Criminology.

Edlund, J. E., & Sagarin, B. J. (2017). Chapter Five – Sex differences in jealousy: A 25-year retrospective. *Advances in Experimental Social Psychology, 55,* 259–302.

Ellis, H. (1950). *Studies in the psychology of sex*, Vol. 2, ch. 11. London: Heinemann.

Fehr, B. (1988). Prototype analysis of the concepts of love and commitment. *Journal of Personality and Social Psychology, 55,* 557–579.

(2015). Love: Conceptualization and experience. In M. Mikulincer, P. R. Shaver, J. A. Simpson, & J. F. Dovidio (Eds.), *APA handbook of personality and social psychology*, Vol. 3: *Interpersonal relations* (pp. 495–522). Washington, DC: American Psychological Association. Retrieved from http://dx.doi.org/10.1037/14344-018.

Fisher, H. E. (1998). Lust, attraction, and attachment in mammalian reproduction. *Human Nature, 9*(1), 23–52.

Fisher, H. (2004). *Why we love: The nature and chemistry of romantic love.* New York: Henry Holt.

Fletcher, G. J., Simpson, J. A., Campbell, L., & Overall, N. C. (2015). Pair-bonding, romantic love, and evolution: The curious case of homo sapiens. *Perspectives on Psychological Science, 10*(1), 20–36.

Frank, R. (1988). *Passions within reason.* New York: Norton.

Gangestad, S. W., & Thornhill, R. (1997). The evolutionary psychology of extrapair sex: The role of fluctuating asymmetry. *Evolution and Human Behavior, 18,* 69–88.

Greenfeld, L. A., Rand, M. R., Craven, D., Klaus, P. A., Perkins, C. A., Ringel, C., Warchol, G., Maston, C., & Fox, J. A. (1998). *Violence by intimates.* Washington, DC: US Department of Justice, NCJ-167237.

Greer, A., & Buss, D. M. (1994). Tactics for promoting sexual encounters. *The Journal of Sex Research, 5,* 185–201.

Greiling, H., & Buss, D. M. (2000). Women's sexual strategies: The hidden dimension of extra-pair mating. *Personality and Individual Differences, 28,* 929–963.

Hamilton, W. D. (1964). The genetical evolution of social behavior. I and II. *Journal of Theoretical Biology, 7*, 1–52.

Haselton, M., Buss, D. M., Oubaid, V., & Angleitner, A. (2005). Sex, lies, and strategic interference: The psychology of deception between the sexes. *Personality and Social Psychology Bulletin, 31*, 3–23.

Jankowiak, W., & Fisher, E. (1992). Romantic love: A cross-cultural perspective. *Ethnology, 31*(2), 149–155.

Jankowwiak, W. (Ed.) (1995). *Romantic passion: A universal experience?* New York: Columbia University Press.

Kanin, E. J., Davidson, K. D., & Scheck, S. R. (1970). A research note on male-female differentials in the experience of heterosexual love. *The Journal of Sex Research, 6*, 64–72.

Lundsgaarde, H. P. (1977). *Murder in space city: A cultural analysis of Houston homicide patterns* (pp. 60–61). New York: Oxford University Press.

Madigan, N. (2003, February 13). Trial in killing of orthodontist goes to jury. *New York Times*, p. A25.

Mathes, E. W. (1986). Jealousy and romantic love: A longitudinal study. *Psychological Reports, 58*, 885–886.

(1991). *Jealousy: The psychological data.* New York: University Press of America.

Moors, A. C. (2017). Has the American public's interest in information related to relationships beyond "the couple" increased over time? *The Journal of Sex Research, 54*(6), 677–684.

Mullen, P. E., & Martin, J. (1994). Jealousy: A community study. *British Journal of Psychiatry, 164*, 35–43.

Muller, W. (1917). *Yap, band 2, halbband 1* (HRAF Trans.). Hamburg: Friederischesen.

Oliver, M. B., & Hyde, J. S. (1993). Gender differences in sexuality: A meta-analysis. *Psychological Bulletin, 114*(1), 29–51.

Pietrzak, R., Laird, J. D., Stevens, D. A., & Thompson, N. S. (2002). Sex differences in human jealousy: A coordinate study of forced-choice, continuous rating-scale, and physiological responses on the same subjects. *Evolution and Human Behavior, 23*, 83–94.

Pines, A. M. (1998). *Romantic jealousy: Causes, symptoms, cures.* New York: Routledge.

Riggs, D. S. (1993). Relationship problems and dating aggression: A potential treatment target. *Journal of Interpersonal Violence, 8*, 18–35.

Sagarin, B. J., Martin, A. L., Coutinho, S. A., Edlund, J. E., Patel, L., Skowronski, J. J., & Zengel, B. (2012). Sex differences in jealousy: A meta-analytic examination. *Evolution and Human Behavior, 33*(6), 595–614.

Saran, A. B. (1974). *Murder and suicide among the Munda and the Oraon.* Delhi: National Publishing House.

Schmitt, D. P. (2005). Sociosexuality from Argentina to Zimbabwe: A 48-nation study of sex, culture, and strategies of human mating. *Behavioral and Brain Sciences.*

Shaver, P. R., Hazan, C., & Bradshaw, D. (1988). The integration of three behavioral systems. In R. Sternberg & M. Barnes (Eds.), *The psychology of love* (pp. 68–99). New Haven, CT: Yale University Press.

Sprecher, S., Aron, A., Hatfield, E., Cortese, A., Potapova, E., & Levitskaya, A. (1994). Love: American style, Russian style, and Japanese style. *Personal Relationships*, *1*, 349–369.

Sternberg, R. J. (1986). A triangular theory of love. *Psychological Review*, *93*(2), 119–135.

Sugiyama, L. (2005). Physical attractiveness in adaptationist perspective. In D. M. Buss (Ed.), *The handbook of evolutionary psychology* (pp. 1–68). New York: Wiley.

Symons, D. (1979). *The evolution of human sexuality*. New York: Oxford University Press.

Viorst, J. (1998). Confessions of a jealous wife. In G. Clanton & L. G. Smith (Eds.), *Jealousy* (3rd ed., pp. 17–24). New York: University Press of America.

Wilson, M., & Daly, M. (1992). Till death do us part. In J. Radford & D. E. H. Russell (Eds.), *Femicide: The politics of woman killing* (pp. 83–98). New York: Twayne.

(1998). Lethal and nonlethal violence against wives and the evolutionary psychology of male sexual proprietariness. In R. E. Dobash & R. P. Dobash (Eds.), *Violence against women: International and cross-disciplinary perspectives* (pp. 199–230). Thousand Oaks, CA: Sage.

CHAPTER 4

Neuroimaging of Love in the Twenty-first Century

Stephanie Cacioppo

If you have ever driven under the influence of love but were not charged with DUI (driving under the influence), this could change soon. Neuroimaging research in rodents suggests that love has a similar brain signature to drugs like alcohol or cocaine – subjecting the afflicted to compulsive tendencies that interfere with ordinary responsibilities. If true, would anyone arrested for "love driving" also need to complete some sort of addiction treatment before they can drive again, including detoxification, medication, rehabilitation, and long-term follow-up to prevent relapse? Or is it possible that the true nature of human love is not fully captured by the rodent brain model of love? If human love is really just an addiction with no redeeming feature, why do people keep looking for lasting love rather than temporary connections? Why do people want to change their partner when they experience self-doubts? What does one's sense of self have to do with social connections? These are some of the questions that led me to start a quest to understand the love network in the human brain more than a decade ago.

The investigation of the neural bases of love in the human brain is not new. In a case report from 250 BCE, Greek physician and anatomist Erasistratos accurately diagnosed Antiochus' ailment as lovesickness, marking the beginning of the first objective neurological case report of love. In the mid-nineteenth century, phrenologists such as Franz Joseph Gall, who first developed his theory on the relationship between shape of the scalp and function of the brain within that scalp, identified a couple of brain areas associated with love and its subtypes, such as "conjugal love," parental love, and friendship.

Since the nineteenth century, further advances have been made in the development of methods allowing investigators to gain a better understanding of the brain signature of love and identify an entire brain network (rather than one brain area) as the neurobiological substrates of love. In the past two decades, neuroimaging of love has been fueled by significant neuroimaging developments and refinement, such as, for instance, significant improvement in terms of neuroimaging power (e.g. from 1T to 3T or 7T for fMRI; from 32 electrodes to 64 and then to 128 electrodes or 256 electrodes for surface EEG; S. Cacioppo & Cacioppo, 2017), computational capacities and analytic tools, and statistical approaches (multi-kernel density analyses, multi-voxel pattern analyses, network modeling of brain connectivity; graph theoretical analyses; Bullmore & Sporns, 2009; S. Cacioppo, Frum, et al., 2013; Wager et al., 2013; Wager, Lindquist, Nichols, Kober, & Van Snellenberg, 2009). In addition to traditional physiological measures (e.g. facial electromyography, impedance cardiography and electrocardiography, eye-tracking, electrodermal activity(J. T. Cacioppo, Tassinary, & Berntson, 2017), contemporary neuroimaging techniques (such as positron emission tomography, PET; fMRI; electro-encephalogram (EEG) and event-related potentials (ERPs), magneto-encephalography (MEG), or transcranial magnetic stimulations, TMS) offer an unprecedented opportunity to grasp better the complexity of brain functions that manifest at very different levels of organization, ranging from networks of computations and information-processing operations to behavior in a social context. The integrative, interdisciplinary field of neuroimaging of love has not only emerged as these methods and technology were burgeoning, but also as lesion studies, comparative research, and animal models began to focus more on the biological basis of social structures and processes.

Also of importance in the neuroimaging of love in the twenty-first century are the advances made in genetics and molecular biology. For instance, a growing body of research demonstrates that the social environment can modulate gene expression, thereby influencing neural and neuroendocrine functioning. In line with the fact that most of our human social behavior arises from neurobiological and psychological mechanisms shared with other social species, methods and models are also being developed in social neuroscience to bridge the gap between animal and human research to understand the neural, hormonal, chemical, and genetic bases of social behavior (e.g. J. T. Cacioppo, Cacioppo, & Cole, 2013). Such interdisciplinary investigations across social species (and across cultures within social species) are becoming more common in the field. Because of space limitations, however, I limit the focus here on the neuroimaging technique most used by social neuroscientists investigating the human brain network of love – fMRI.

Together these methods offer unprecedented access to the human brain network of love during normal waking states. A key challenge in the study of the neuroimaging of love resides, however, in determining how psychological states and processes map onto patterns of brain activity and also how this activity is modulated by social compositions and social behaviors. With more than 85 billion brain cells working together in malleable networks to produce our mind, consciousness, and behavior, the scientific investigation of the human brain network of love represents one of the most complex and exciting scientific frontiers in the twenty-first century.

Measuring Love in a Scanner

Functional magnetic resonance imaging (fMRI) measures changes in blood flow oxygenation (hemodynamic response) that are produced in the brain in response to the presentation of a broad variety of stimuli. In fMRI studies of love changes in response to partner-related stimuli are measured. These stimuli can theoretically be visual, auditory, tactile, or olfactory. To date, however, mostly visual stimuli (i.e. faces, names, pictures, and video clips) of a loved one (such as a romantic partner, friends, children, and pets) have been used in neuroimaging of love. Together these studies in healthy volunteers point to a specific set of brain regions as activated when love is evoked but not when other biological drives are evoked, including sexual desire (S. Cacioppo, Bianchi-Demicheli, Hatfield, & Rapson, 2012; S. Cacioppo, 2017; S. Cacioppo, Bianchi-Demicheli, Frum, Pfaus, & Lewis, 2012; S. Cacioppo & Hatfield, 2013).

Functional MRI of love provides a wealth of data on *what* neural networks may be selectively activated or co-activated in response to the presentation of stimuli related to the subject's significant other. Because fMRI is non-invasive, it has an important role to play in the development, testing, and refinement of the component processes underlying social behaviors. The brain does not operate exclusively at the spatial level of molecules, cells, nuclei, regions, circuits, or systems, however. Thus, before designing or interpreting fMRI research, it is important to understand that fMRI is a correlative measure. Additional experimental studies including lesion, transcranial magnetic stimulation, and pharmacological interventions (e.g. ligands, drugs) in human and nonhuman animals are essential to elucidate further the causal role of any given neural structure, circuit, or process in a given task. Any single neuroimaging methodology provides only a partial view of brain activity within a very limited range of spatial and temporal levels. Each of these angles has limitations, but the confluence of the three can provide a more complete picture of the neuroimaging of love and facilitate advances in our understanding of the neural mechanisms underlying the component processes of social behaviors (S. Cacioppo & Cacioppo, 2017).

The Love Brain Network (LBN)

The first neuroscientists to use the fMRI approach to attempt to identify the brain regions associated with passionate love were Andreas Bartels and Semir Zeki (2000). They also recruited participants via the Internet. Seventy young men and women from eleven countries and several ethnic groups responded. Respondents were asked to write about their feelings of love and to complete the Passionate Love Scale (PLS; (E. Hatfield & Rapson, 1996; E. Hatfield & Sprecher, 1986)). Seventeen men and women (six men and eleven women), ranging in age from twenty-one to thirty-seven, were selected for the study. Participants were then placed in an fMRI scanner (Bartels & Zeki, 2000). Bartels and Zeki (2000) gave each participant a color photograph of their beloved at which to gaze, alternating the beloved's picture with pictures of a trio of casual friends. They then digitally compared the scans taken while the participants viewed their beloved's picture with those taken while they viewed a friend's picture, creating images that represented the brain regions that became more (or less) active in both conditions. These images, the researchers argued, revealed for the first time the brain regions involved when a person experiences passionate love. Not surprisingly, the Bartels and Zeki (2000, 2004) research sparked a cascade of fMRI research. Since 2000, a growing body of fMRI studies of passionate love has been performed in social neuroscience.

Because individual neuroimaging studies with small sample size tend to have low statistical power, reduce the likelihood of detecting a true effect, and increase the likelihood of detecting false effect, we used a meta-analytic approach to investigate the brain network of love. This approach allowed us to identify brain areas that are statistically activated beyond chance level, in response to love. Our results reinforced and expanded prior empirical findings and qualitative reviews. Overall, our results showed that love, independently of its type (e.g. romantic/passionate love, maternal love), activates a specific brain network within and beyond the emotional brain network.It is interesting to note that these LBN brain areas involve an interaction of both excitatory and inhibitory neural pathways and their associated neurotransmitters (e.g. dopamine; serotonin) and hormone receptors (e.g. oxytocin; vasopressin). For instance, excitation involves cues activating the emotional limbic system, the oxytocin system (which in turn stimulates pair-bonding, trust, and attachment), and the dopaminergic system (which stimulates attention, motivation, and pleasure). On the other hand, inhibition involves the recruitment of serotonin that occurs in several brain regions, such as the prefrontal cortex.

The LBN can be decomposed into four functional systems: autonomous/appetitive, motivational/reward, emotional, and cognitive. Based on the function of these four systems, it is assumed that the loving brain first begins by evaluating all the images that come to it from the retina, through sensory pathways. Later (or in parallel), the brain evaluates/interprets the stimuli as being potentially love-relevant. Finally (or in parallel), the cognitive system includes an appraisal process that categorizes stimuli as lovable, and increases attention for these stimuli. The motivational system is underpinned by specific areas, such as the insula and striatum. This motivational system is fundamental to sustaining and maintaining the sexual response. The emotional system, on the other hand, involves specific structures such as the insula and the somatosensory cortex (i.e. brain regions involved in the specific hedonic quality of a love experience). Finally, the autonomic system includes the anterior cingulate gyrus – the brain area related to autonomic responses (e.g. cardiovascular and respiratory).

The activation of subcortical dopaminergic-rich areas and the limbic system during experiences of love is in line with psychological studies defining love as a rewarding, positive, and motivating experience. Most of these regions were those that are active when people are under the influence of euphoria-inducing drugs, such as opiates or cocaine. Activity was also noted in other parts of the brain, notably in brain areas mediating emotion, somato-sensorial integration, and reward processes (e.g. the insula and anterior cingulate cortex).

To our surprise, these twelve areas were not located only in the limbic system and/or emotional regions of the brain, but also in associative (more cognitive) brain regions (e.g. angular gyrus/temporo-parietal junction) that mediate more complex and associative cognitive functions, such as self-expansion, body image, self-representation, metaphors, attention, memory, and abstract representations (Ortigue, Bianchi-Demicheli, Hamilton, & Grafton, 2007). The fact that love recruits brain areas that are involved both in basic instincts, dopaminergic-like rewarding experiences, and craving *and* in higher-order cognitive functions suggests that love is not only a [putatively addicting] emotion, it is also a cognition (Bianchi-Demicheli, Grafton, & Ortigue, 2006; Ortigue, Bianchi-Demicheli, Patel, Frum, & Lewis, 2010). The activation of brain regions mediating self-representation is in line with the cognitive and social-psychological model of the self-expansion of love (Aron & Aron, 1996), which suggests that people fall in love with another individual when they detect (consciously and/or automatically) a cognitive opportunity to expand their own self (Aron & Aron, 1996; Aron, Paris, & Aron, 1995), and include their significant other in their cognitive sphere to represent themselves as possessing their significant other's characteristics/ qualities (Aron & Aron, 1996; Aron, Aron, Tudor, & Nelson, 1991). In 1996, Aron and Aron specified this concept by suggesting that individuals, who are in love, seek to enhance their potential self-efficacy by "increasing the physical and social and cognitive resources, perspectives, and identities that facilitate achievement of any goal that might arise" (Aron & Aron, 1996; Aron et al., 1991). This self-expansion model of love is also in line with a universal and key evolutionary purpose of love, which manifests itself in the maintenance and upholding of a species by ensuring the formation of firm bonds between individuals (Beauregard, Courtemanche, Paquette, & St-Pierre, 2009; Fisher, Aron, & Brown, 2005). By highlighting the spatial dimension of love in the human brain, the brain-imaging techniques used in social neuroscience allow a better understanding of the brain mechanisms that mediate this complex phenomenon as a motivation to attain the resources to be able to achieve such a self-expansion goal (Aron & Aron, 1996; Aron et al., 1991).

It is interesting to note that no studies have revealed a correlation between the activation of brain areas underlying this self-expansion mechanism (e.g. angular gyrus) and the length of time during which the participants were in love. This absence of a correlation underlines the assumption that the role of the angular gyrus in love is not directly "time dependent." This is coherent with a previous study that assessed this question and showed changes in several regions as the relationship changes, but not in the angular gyrus (Aron et al., 2005; Acevedo, Aron, Fisher, & Brown, 2012). In 2005, for instance, Aron and colleagues instead showed a right-insula, right-cingulate cortex, and a right-posterior cingulated/retrospenial cortex activity related to the length of the relationship.

Neural Bases of Love versus Different Types of Biological Drives

Compared to other types of love, such as companionate love (feelings of calm, social comfort, emotional union, and the security felt in the presence of a long-term mate; Hatfiled & Rapson, 1996), unconditional love, or parental (maternal and/or paternal) love, passionate love activates very similar associative cortical areas (see S. Cacioppo et al., 2012 for reviews). The main difference is noted at the subcortical level (e.g. stronger activation of the PAG in maternal love than passionate love) rather than at the cortical level. This result suggests a more basic difference among the different types of love than a cognitive difference.

Compared to sexual desire, fMRI studies on passionate love show that both sexual desire and passionate love spark increased activity in the subcortical brain areas that are associated with euphoria, reward, and motivation, as well as in the cortical brain areas that are involved in self-representation and social cognition (S. Cacioppo et al., 2012; Cacioppo, 2017). The co-activation of subcortical emotion-related areas and higher-order cortical areas that mediate more complex cognitive functions (e.g. body image, mental associations, and self-representation) reinforces the top-down neurofunctional model of interpersonal relationships and the potential role of past experiences on future emotional feelings and behaviors.

It is interesting to note that neural differences also exist between love and desire. These differences mostly occur at the insula and subcortical parts of the brain.

Compared to sexual desire, passionate love shows a diminished activity in the ventral striatum, hypothalamus, amygdala, somatosensory cortex, and inferior parietal lobule. Those reductions are in keeping with sexual desire as a motivational state with a very specific, embodied goal, whereas passionate love could be thought of as a more abstract, flexible, and behaviorally complex goal that is less dependent on the physical presence of another person. On the other hand, love is associated with a more intense activation of the ventral tegmental area, and a specific recruitment of activity in the more dorsal regions of the right striatum, which are two dopamine-rich regions involved generally in motivation, reward expectancy, and habit formation. Those findings reinforce the importance of specific goal-directed incentives if one's mind is to fall "head over heels in love." The activation of these subcortical dopaminergic-rich areas during experiences of passionate love is in line with psychological studies defining love as a rewarding, positive, and motivating experience.

Further neural differences exist between desire and love with a posterior-to-anterior insula pattern, from desire to love, suggesting that love is a more abstract representation of the pleasant sensorimotor experiences than desire. The anterior part of the insula is activated significantly by feelings of love, whereas the posterior part of the insula is activated significantly by feelings of sexual desire. This posterior-to-anterior insular distinction between sexual desire and love again reinforces the neurofunctional characteristic of a posterior-to-anterior progression of integrative representations of affective bodily feelings to an ultimate representation of all feelings. This is in line with the view that love is an abstract construct, which is partly based on the mental representation of repeated past emotional moments with another. In other words, this specific pattern of activation suggests that love builds upon a neural circuit for emotions and pleasure, adding regions associated with reward expectancy, habit formation, and feature detection. In particular, the shared activation within the insula, with a posterior-to-anterior pattern, from desire to love, suggests that love grows out of and is a more abstract representation of the pleasant sensorimotor experiences that characterize desire.

From these results, one may consider sexual desire and love on a spectrum that evolves from integrative representations of affective visceral sensations to an ultimate representation of feelings incorporating mechanisms of reward expectancy and habit learning. Although love is not a prerequisite for sexual desire, our recent neuroimaging meta-analyses suggest that desire might be a prerequisite for love based on the researchers' interpretation of their results that desire is grounded in a relatively concrete representation of sensorimotor experiences, whereas love is a more abstract representation of those experiences in the context of a person's current and prior experiences. If this interpretation is correct, then a lesion in the anterior (or posterior) insula should be associated with a diminished capacity to ignite normal responses to love (or desire) in particular.

In 2013, we had the rare opportunity to test a patient (a forty-eight-year-old heterosexual man from Argentina) who suffered from a circumscribed ischemic lesion in the LBN-related anterior insula. Although the patient did not report any changes in feelings of love or desire, behavioral testing revealed a selective deficit for love (but not desire). Specifically, the patient performed a neuropsychological computer task in which he viewed a series of photographs. Half of the photographs depicted attractive females in short, revealing dresses, and half depicted equally attractive women in long dresses. Following each presentation, the patient pressed a button to indicate whether the stimulus was related to love (yes/no) on half of the trials and to indicate if the stimulus was related to desire (yes/no) on half of the trials. Stimuli were presented in a counterbalanced randomized repeated design (ABBA).

Statistical analyses revealed that the patient took significantly longer than a control group that was gender, ethnicity, and age-matched ($N = 7$) to respond when asked about the relevance for love than when asked about the relevance for desire. These findings provide the first clinical (and causal, rather than correlational) evidence that the anterior insula contributes to love but not desire. The specific interference of the anterior insula damage on the speed of judgments of love (but not desire) further suggests that the anterior insula may play a role not only in concrete feelings but also in more abstract forms of human emotions. These data also support the notion of a posterior-to-anterior insular gradient, from sensorimotor to abstract representations, in the evaluation of anticipatory rewards in interpersonal relationships (S. Cacioppo, Frum, et al., 2013).

The Speed of Love in the Human Brain

A key theoretical objective in the neuroimaging of love is not only to specify what brain areas are recruited during the presentation of the photograph of your beloved partner or friend, but also to specify when and in what specific combinations they are activated (e.g. S. Cacioppo, Weiss, Runesha, & Cacioppo, 2014; S. Cacioppo, Grafton, & Bianchi-Demicheli, 2012). By providing detailed information about the relationship between neuronal activity (i.e. post-synaptic dendritic potentials of a considerable number of neurons that are activated in a pattern that yields a dipolar field) and the temporal resolution (millisecond by millisecond) of each component in the information-processing operation required for behavioral performance, high-density electroencephalographic (EEG) recordings and averaged EEG (event-related potentials, ERPs) have provided a useful additional tool in investigations of brain function. Whereas fMRI analyses are performed in source space, EEG/ERP analyses are performed in sensor space, with high-density sensor recordings producing more detailed information about changes in brain activity measured across time and sensor space. To date, however, only a few neuroscientists have investigated the spatiotemporal dynamics of love (Cacioppo et al., 2012).

The first modern-day neuroscientists to study passionate love were Niels Birbaumer and his Tübingen colleagues (1993). They performed a series of electrophysiological surface recordings from fifteen different locations on the scalp of healthy participants. Participants' brain electrical activity was recorded during love-related imaging tasks (imagining a time in their past in which they had been joyously in love [without sexual imagery] and imagining the same scene [with sexual imagery]) compared to sensory tasks (such as determining which of two pieces of sandpaper was the smoothest) (Birbaumer, Elbert, Flor, & Rockstroh, 1993). Based on their assessment of the participants' EEGs, the authors suggested the frontal and posterior groupings showed similar dimensions on the romantic imagery tasks, whereas smaller dimensions were found in the frontal as compared to the posterior electrode sites on the four sensory tasks. The authors then concluded that passionate imagery involves a significantly higher brain complexity than does sensory stimulation at all brain sites, but particularly at frontal regions (Birbaumer et al., 1993). Although these electrophysiological findings shed light on the temporal mechanisms of love, they don't provide enough high spatiotemporal resolution because of the limited method and number of electrodes available at that time.

Since the first EEG study by Birbaumer, significant developments and refinement have been made in terms of neuroimaging power (e.g. from 15 electrodes to 64 and then to 128 electrodes or 256 electrodes for surface EEG; S. Cacioppo & Cacioppo, 2016), numerous techniques have been developed for investigating the brain state dynamics of EEG, including standard wave-form analyses, Fourier analysis, independent component analysis (ICA), principal component analysis (PCA), *k*-means cluster analyses, and high-performance electrical neuroimaging (S. Cacioppo, Bangee, et al., 2015; S. Cacioppo, Weiss, et al., 2014).

In 2008, Başar et al. investigated the oscillatory brain dynamics of love using facial stimuli of a "loved person" in twenty women (Başar, Schmiedt-Fehr, Oniz, & Başar-Eroğlu, 2008). Their main results showed that a specific frequency band (i.e. the delta band here) and a high amplitude generated by the brain may be evoked by the photo of a "loved person" compared with an "unknown person," and with the picture of the "appreciated person" (Başar et al., 2008). In 2010, Vico and colleagues also investigated central and peripheral electrophysiological indices associated with the perception of loved faces. In another experiment, Vico et al. (2010) tested thirty female undergraduate students (ranging in age between twenty and twenty-seven years) while they were viewing black-and-white photographs of faces that belonged to one of five categories: loved ones, famous people (preselected by the participants), unknown people, babies from the International Affective Picture System, and neutral faces from the Ekman and Friesen system. Subcategories of loved faces included romantic partner, parents, siblings, second-degree relatives, and friends. Participants were informed that the purpose of the study was to examine physiological responses to familiar faces (Vico, Guerra, Robles, Vila, & Anllo-Vento, 2010). One of the selection criteria was that participants were required to have a current romantic relationship and to reside in close proximity to five loved ones, including the partner, so as to be able to take their photograph.

Heart rate, skin conductance, electromyography of the zygomatic muscle, and ERPs were obtained while participants passively viewed the pictures of their love ones and control faces. Both central and peripheral electrophysiological measures differentiated faces of loved ones from all other categories by eliciting higher heart rate, skin conductance, and zygomatic activity, as well as larger amplitudes of the late ERP components P3 and LPP (Vico et al., 2010). These waveform analyses about the latency of some components remain, however, limited in their interpretation. Over the years, some have argued that measuring peaks and troughs was sufficient to the temporal processing of the brain, while others (e.g. Donchin & Heffley, 1978) argued, quite persuasively, that another approach, such as a statistical decomposition of the evoked brain states, was necessary. Using a microstate decomposition of the ERP, we analyzed surface high-density brain activity recorded from twenty healthy participants while they were performing a cognitive priming paradigm known to activate LBN (S. Cacioppo, Bianchi-Demicheli, Frum, et al., 2012; S. Cacioppo, Bianchi-Demicheli, Hatfield, et al., 2012). Our results showed that when a person is feeling high passionate love, the subliminal presentation of their beloved's name evokes specific brain states that are mediated by generators located in the pleasure, reward and cognitive brain pathways very quickly after the stimulus onset (i.e. between 80 ms and 220 ms after stimulus onset and between 120 and 220 ms). Inverse solutions applied on this data set revealed that visual areas were activated first, followed by activation of higher-order associative brain areas, such as those involved in self-related processes (e.g. the angular gyrus/temporo-parietal junction). Finally, a flow of backward activation occurred from these associative brain areas to the primary visual and emotional brain areas. These results reinforce the neurofunctional top-down model of interpersonal relationships, suggesting that associative brain areas may prime more basic brain areas at a pre-conscious stage (i.e. starting at 80 ms post-stimulus onset) of information processing. This raises the question of the various states of consciousness in people feeling in passionate love. Further studies with a larger sample size need to be done to address this question.

Implications

The fact that the LBN is recruited very quickly (below the level of awareness) in response to a loved stimulus indicates that you are probably unaware that your brain is implicitly activated when you see someone you love or even when you are on the lookout for potential mates. We tested this hypothesis recently using eye-tracking measurements while neurologically healthy college students were looking at visual stimuli. We asked them to look at photographs of potentially desirable or lovable individuals. In one block, the participants were asked to look at each photograph and decide as rapidly and as precisely as possible whether they perceived the photograph as eliciting feelings of lust (sexual desire). In the other block, the participants were asked to look at each photograph and decide as rapidly and as precisely as possible whether they perceived the photograph as eliciting feelings of romantic love. The same photographs of attractive individuals were presented in each block. Responses were made by pressing one of two response keys ("K" for "yes," and "L" for "no") on a keyboard with fingers of the right hand (response "yes" with the index and response "no" with the middle finger). The order of these experimental instructions was counterbalanced across participants (see Bolmont et al., 2014 for details).

Overall results showed that when participants were asked to indicate whether the photographs could elicit feelings of romantic love (a sentimental and tender state of longing for union with another, that is not necessarily associated with sexual feelings) or lust (the presence of feelings of sexual interest, and of sexual thoughts or fantasies related to the image depicted in the photograph), their decision making about lust (rather than that for romantic love) was associated with specific eye gaze to the torso and face (Bolmont, Cacioppo, & Cacioppo, 2014). Participants' decision making for romantic love was more focused on the face per se (Bolmont et al., 2014). These eye movements were performed extremely quickly (in less than one second). For instance, time to the first fixation toward the torso (*Mean* = 0.19 s, 95% Confidence Interval = [0.111, 0.275]) was shorter than time to the first fixation toward the face (*Mean* = 0.42 s, 95% Confidence Interval = [0.27, 0.575]; $F(1, 8) = 7.13$, $p = .03$, $\eta^2 = 0.37$).

These findings reinforce our neuroimaging of love as well as prior behavioral studies showing that love and lust are distinctive emotions with unique behavioral scripts (Cacioppo & Hatfield, 2013; Diamond, 2004; Hatfield & Rapson, 2009). Such identification of categorical thinking and other information about what a person captures about their environment during a social interaction might have theoretical and clinical importance in couples therapy when patients' self-reports fail to disentangle romantic love and lust (S. Cacioppo, Couto, et al., 2013; S. Cacioppo, Bolmont, & Monteleone, 2017).

The Quest to Understand Further the Human Love Brain Network Matters

Pair-bond satisfaction matters. People who are in a salutary and fulfilling reciprocal relationship live longer and are happier. Analysis of data from the General Social Surveys of 1972–96, for instance, shows that the likelihood that married individuals report being happy with life is higher than in those who have never been married or have been previously married (other factors held constant, Waite, 2000). However, marital status is not the main factor associated with better health. Rather, marriage quality and how one partner feels connected or disconnected from the other partner plays the crucial role (J. Cacioppo & Patrick, 2008). In other words, the person's subjective position along the continuum of social connections (how they feel in their relationship, i.e. connected or disconnected; S. Cacioppo & Cacioppo, 2012) is a key factor.

As demonstrated by Cacioppo and colleagues over the past twenty years, feeling socially isolated (lonely) from one's significant other is strongly predictive of decrements in health and well-being (e.g. J. Cacioppo & Cacioppo, 2018). For instance, a recent meta-analysis of seventy prospective studies involving more than 3 million participants who were followed for an average of seven years found that individuals who feel lonely have a 26% increased risk of premature mortality, even after controlling for objective social isolation and potential confounding variables (Holt-Lunstad, Smith, Baker, Harris, & Stephenson, 2015). Moreover, evidence from experimental studies (J. Cacioppo et al., 2006), latent growth modeling (J. Cacioppo et al., 2006), and case-based matching designs (VanderWeele, Hawkley, Thisted, & Cacioppo, 2011) indicates that loneliness increases depressive symptomatology, and parallel decrements have been found for subjective/psychological well-being and physical health (J. Cacioppo, Cacioppo, Capitanio, et al., 2015; Steptoe, Owen, Kunz-Ebrecht, & Brydon, 2004; VanderWeele et al., 2011).

From a psychological viewpoint, loneliness contributes to aggressive behaviors, social anxiety, and impulsivity (J. Cacioppo & Cacioppo, 2018; J. Cacioppo, Cacioppo, Capitanio, et al., 2015; J. Cacioppo, Cacioppo, Cole, et al., 2015; S. Cacioppo, Capitanio, & Cacioppo, 2014). It also increases an automatic (nonconscious) hypervigilance for social threats (J. Cacioppo & Hawkley, 2009; S. Cacioppo, Balogh, & Cacioppo, 2015; S. Cacioppo, Bangee et al., 2015; S. Cacioppo et al., 2014). In addition, in the physical sphere loneliness is a risk factor for obesity (Lauder, Mummery, Jones, & Caperchione, 2006), decreased sleep salubrity (J. Cacioppo, Hawley, Crawford, et al., 2002), diminished immunity (Pressman et al., 2005) in part due to affecting the composition of white blood cells (Cole, 2008), elevated blood pressure (J. Cacioppo et al., 2002), recurrent stroke (S. Cacioppo et al., 2014), and premature mortality (Luo, Hawkley, Waite, & Cacioppo, 2012).

One mechanism of loneliness-related health risks takes place via alterations in hypothalamic–pituitary–adrenal (HPA) axis regulation of inflammatory biology in leukocytes and antiviral immunity and alterations in genome-wide transcription of glucocorticoid target genes and NF-kappaB target genes (Cole, Hawkley, Arevalo, & Cacioppo, 2011). These loneliness-related alterations in leukocyte biology may stem from a functional desensitization of the glucocorticoid receptor in lonely individuals, which in turn, is reciprocally related to NF-kappaB expression, a key factor in regulation of cellular responses to infection, cancer, and inflammation (Cole et al., 2011). Impaired transcription of glucocorticoid response genes and increased activity of pro-inflammatory transcription control pathways provide a functional genomic explanation for elevated risk of inflammatory disease in individuals who experience chronically high levels of loneliness (J. Cacioppo, Cacioppo, Capitanio, et al., 2015).

Because the prefrontal cortex (a part of your brain that is involved in abstract thinking, executive function, decision making, and self-insights) modulates the HPA activity and its relationship with the limbic system (a part of your brain involved in love, emotion regulation, emotional and social processes, habit formation, and conditioning) based on environmental appraisals, including appraisals of the quality of your relationship with someone, a cascade of signals travels between these regions when you feel isolated or rejected from a significant other. Within the limbic system, specific brain areas that are associated with anger-related emotional processing (Siegel & Brutus, 1990) or fear and anxiety conditioning (Davis, 1998) will, in turn, differentially regulate HPA activation (Choi et al., 2007; Ulrich-Lay & Herman, 2009). For instance, the amygdala (an almond-shape brain area in your limbic system) is especially important for rapid-onset, short-duration behaviors that occur in response to specific threats, whereas another brain area called the bed nucleus of the stria terminalis (BNST, a brain area that plays the role of communication integration center in the limbic system and monitors valence processing) mediates slower-onset, longer-lasting emotional responses that frequently accompany sustained threats (or the surveillance for threats) and that may persist even after threat termination (J. Cacioppo, Cacioppo, Capitanio, et al., 2015; Walker, Toufexis, & Davis, 2003).

The systematic study of these communication exchanges within (and beyond) the HPA-limbic system circuitry is critical to better understand our emotions while in a close relationship. In turns, this systematic study of the influences between the biological levels of organization and social connections along and beyond the HPA axis will allow for a better specification of the neural, hormonal, cellular, and genetic mechanisms underlying social behavior – a core concept of social neuroscience (J. Cacioppo & Berntson, 2001).

Future Perspectives and Applications

Neuroimaging of love is a growing field of research, which only recently has become the topic of intensive and rigorous scientific investigations. Given the small sample size in most of the early functional neuroimaging studies, small but theoretically important effects have likely been undetected (owing to low statistical power), thereby providing at best an incomplete and at worst a misleading depiction of underlying neural mechanisms. The recent use of statistical (rather than narrative) fMRI meta-analyses with large sample sizes has elevated this field to a more rigorous understanding of the neural mechanisms underlying the component processes of close relationships. Future researchers should keep performing highly powered studies, treating social neuroscience as a cumulative rather than an all-or-none process, and addressing the question of the neurobiology of love from an interdisciplinary and integrating viewpoint beyond correlation studies.

Further, researchers need to combine methods that facilitate a dynamic (rather than static) investigation of love. Functional MRI is not the most suited technique to investigate or monitor dynamic aspects of a dyadic relationship, although some exceptions can be found (e.g. Montague et al., 2002). Rather, interbrain relationships, dynamic cooperation/exclusion, or synchronization may be better assessed using hyperscanning techniques, such as dual EEG (Babiloni et al., 2006; Koike, Tanabe, & Sadato, 2015), or functional near-infrared spectroscopy (fNIRS; Balconi & Vanutelli, 2016; Funane et al., 2011). Although hyperscanning has limitations and hyperscanning results still need to be interpreted with caution (Babiloni et al., 2006; Burgess, 2013), this method for studying two individuals simultaneously may offer a new avenue toward the understanding of dynamic covariations and individual differences when the human brain interacts with or relates to the brain of a significant other during social interactions.

Finally, social neuroscientists interested in the study of close relationships and shared representations in the social brain should also dedicate more time and effort to identifying the role of top-down influences and self-other overlap or cognitive interdependence on emotional sharing within (and beyond) the couple (Wegner, Giuliano, & Hertel, 1985; Wegner, Erber, & Raymond, 1991). The systematic study of individual brain differences and brain differences across-gender and within-gender might help clinicians better comprehend the pathological behaviors in a passionate love relationship. The integration of neuroimaging findings of love with standard approaches in couple therapy, such as emotionally focused couple therapy (Johnson, 2004; Moser et al., 2016), might allow the development of new psychobiological models of the human sexual response and neurofeedback training. Combining knowledge from various disciplines that investigate the hard problem of salutary close relationship maintenance has the potential to answer age-old questions as to the nature and function of love. The better our understanding is of lasting salutary close relationships, the greater our respect is for the significance and potency of its role in mental and physical health.

References

Acevedo, B. P., Aron, A., Fisher, H. E., & Brown, L. L. (2012). Neural correlates of long-term intense romantic love. *Social Cognitive and Affective Neuroscience*, 7(2), 145–159. doi: 10.1093/scan/nsq092. Epub 2011 Jan 5. PubMed PMID: 21208991; PubMed Central PMCID: PMC3277362.

Aron, A., & Aron, E. N. (1996). Love and expansion of the self: The state of the model. *Personal Relationships*, 3, 45–58.

Aron, A., Aron, E. N., Tudor, M., & Nelson, G. (1991). Close relationships as including other in the self. *Journal of Personality and Social Psychology*, 60, 241–253.

Aron, A., Paris, M., & Aron, E. N. (1995). Falling in love: Prospective studies of self-concept change. *Journal of Personality and Social Psychology*, 69(6), 1102–1112.

Aron, A., Fisher, H., Mashek, D. J., Strong, G., Li, H., & Brown, L. L. (2005). Reward, motivation, andemotion systems associated with early-stage intense romantic love. *Journal of Neurophysiology*, 94(1), 327–337. Epub 2005 May 31. PubMed PMID: 15928068.

Babiloni, F., Cincotti, F., Mattia, D., Mattiocco, M., De Vico Fallani, F., Tocci, A., Bianchi, L., Marciani, M. G., & Astolfi, L. (2006). Hypermethods for EEG hyperscanning. *Conf Proc IEEE Engineering in Medicine and Biology Society*, 1: 3666–3669. PubMed PMID: 17945788.

Balconi, M., & Vanutelli, M. E. (2017). Interbrains cooperation: Hyperscanning and self-perception in joint actions. *Journal of Clinical and Experimental Neuropsychology*, Aug; 39(6), 607–620. doi: 10.1080/13803395.2016.1253666. Epub 2016 Nov 13. PubMed PMID: 27841088.

Bartels, A., & Zeki, S. (2000). The neural basis of romantic love. *Neuroreport*, 11(17), 3829–3834. Retrieved from www.ncbi.nlm.nih.gov/pubmed/11117499 (2004). The neural correlates of maternal and romantic love. *Neuroimage*, 21(3), 1155–1166. PubMed PMID: 15006682.

Başar, E., Schmiedt-Fehr, C., Oniz, A., & Başar-Eroğlu, C. (2008). Brain oscillations evoked by the face of a loved person. *Brain Research, 1214*, 105–115. Retrieved from https://doi.org/10.1016/j.brainres.2008.03.042.

Beauregard, M., Courtemanche, J., Paquette, V., & St-Pierre, E. L. (2009). The neural basis of unconditional love. *Psychiatry Research, 172*(2), 93–98. Retrieved from https://doi.org/S0925-4927(08)00188-1[pii]10.1016/j.pscychresns.2008.11.003.

Bianchi-Demicheli, F., Grafton, S. G. T. S., & Ortigue, S. (2006). The power of love on the human brain. *Social Neuroscience, 1*(2), 90–103. Retrieved from https://doi.org/10.1080/17470910600976547.

Birbaumer, N., Lutzenberger, W., Elbert, T., Flor, H., & Rockstroh, B. (1993). Imagery and brain processes. In N. Birbaumer & A. Öhmann (Eds.), *The structure of emotion* (pp. 298–321). Toronto: Hogrefe and Huber.

Bolmont, M., Cacioppo, J. T., & Cacioppo, S. (2014). Love is in the gaze: An eye-tracking study of love and sexual desire. *Psychological Science, 25*(9), 1748–1756. Retrieved from https://doi.org/10.1177/0956797614539706.

Brown, K. S., Ortigue, S., Grafton, S. T., & Carlson, J. M. (2010). Improving human brain mapping via joint inversion of brain electrodynamics and the BOLD signal. *NeuroImage, 49*(3), 2401–2415. Retrieved from https://doi.org/10.1016/j.neuroimage.2009.10.011.

Bullmore, E., & Sporns, O. (2009). Complex brain networks: Graph theoretical analysis of structural and functional systems. *Nature Reviews. Neuroscience, 10*(3), 186–198. Retrieved from https://doi.org/10.1038/nrn2575.

Burgess, A. P. (2013). On the interpretation of synchronization in EEG hyper-scanning studies: A cautionary note. *Frontiers in Human Neuroscience, 7*, 881.

Cacioppo, J. T., & Berntson, G. G. (2001). Social neuroscience. In N. J. Smelser & P. B. Baltes (Eds), *International encyclopedia of the social and behavioral sciences* (pp. 14388–14391). Oxford: Pergamon Press.

Cacioppo, J. T., & Cacioppo, S. (2018). The growing problem of loneliness. *Lancet. 391*(10119), 426. doi: 10.1016/S0140-6736(18)30142-9. PubMed PMID: 29407030.

Cacioppo, J. T., Cacioppo, S., Capitanio, J. P., & Cole, S. W. (2015). The neuroendocrinology of social isolation. *Annual Review of Psychology, 66* (9.1–9.35). doi: 10.1146/annurev-psych-010814-015240.

Cacioppo, J. T., Cacioppo, S., & Cole, S. W. (2013). Social neuroscience and social genomics: The emergence of multi-level integrative analyses. *International Journal of Psychological Research, 6*, 1–6. Retrieved from http://mvint.usbmed.edu.co:8002/ojs/index.php/web/article/view/647.

Cacioppo, J. T., Cacioppo, S., Cole, S. W., Capitanio, J. P., Goossens, & Boomsma, D. I. (2015). Loneliness across phylogeny and a call for comparative studies and animal models. *Perspectives on Psychological Science, 10*, 202–212. doi: 10.1177/1745691614564876.

Cacioppo, J. T., & Patrick, B. (2008). *Loneliness: Human nature and the need for social connection.* New York: W. W. Norton.

Cacioppo, J. T., Tassinary, L. G., & Berntson, G. G. (2017). *Handbook of psychophysiology* (4th ed.). New York: Cambridge University Press.

Cacioppo, S. (2017). Neuroimaging of female sexual desire and hypoactive sexual desire disorder. *Sexual Medicine Reviews, 5*(4). Retrieved from https://doi.org/10.1016/j.sxmr.2017.07.006.

Cacioppo, S., Balogh, S., & Cacioppo, J. T. (2015a). Implicit attention to negative social, in contrast to nonsocial, words in the Stroop task differs between individuals high and low in loneliness: Evidence from event-related brain microstates. *Cortex, 70,* 213–233.

Cacioppo, S., Bangee, M., Balogh, S., Cardenas-Iniguez, C., Qualter, P., & Cacioppo, J. T. (2015b). Loneliness and implicit attention to social threat: A high performance electrical neuroimaging study. *Cognitive Neuroscience.* doi: 10.1080/17588928.2015.1070136.

Cacioppo, S., Bianchi-Demicheli, F., Frum, C., Pfaus, J. G., & Lewis, J. W. (2012). The common neural bases between sexual desire and love: A multi-level kernel density fMRI analysis. *The Journal of Sexual Medicine, 9*(4), 1048–1054. Retrieved from https://doi.org/10.1111/j.1743-6109.2012.02651.x.

Cacioppo, S., Bianchi-Demicheli, F., Hatfield, E., & Rapson, R. L. (2012). Social neuroscience of love. *Clinical Neuropsychiatry, 9*(1), 3–13.

Cacioppo, S., Bolmont, M., & Monteleone, G. (2017). Spatio-temporal dynamics of the mirror neuron system during social intentions. *Social Neuroscience.* Retrieved from https://doi.org/10.1080/17470919.2017.1394911.

Cacioppo, S., & Cacioppo, J. T. (2012). Decoding the invisible forces of social connections. *Frontiers in Integrative Neuroscience, 6,* Article 51, 1–7. doi: 10.3389/fnint.2012.00051.

(2013). Lust for life. *Scientific American Mind,* (November 2013), 56–60. Retrieved from https://doi.org/10.1038/scientificamericanmind1113-56.

(2016). Research in social neuroscience: How perceived social isolation, ostracism, and romantic rejection affect your brain. In P. Riva & J. Eck (Eds). *Social exclusion* (pp. 73–88). Switzerland: Springer. doi: 10.1007/978-3-319-33033-4_4.

(2017). Cognizance of the neuroimaging methods for studying the social brain. *Shared Representations,* (May), 86–106. Retrieved from https://doi.org/10.1017/CBO 9781107279353.006.

Cacioppo, S., Couto, B., Bolmont, M., Sedeno, L., Frum, C., Lewis, J. W., et al. (2013). Selective decision-making deficit in love following damage to the anterior insula. *Current Trends in Neurology, 7,* 15–19.

Cacioppo, S., Frum, C., Asp, E., Weiss, R. M., Lewis, J. W., & Cacioppo, J. T. (2013). A quantitative meta-analysis of rejection, 10–12. Retrieved from https://doi.org/10.1038/srep02027.

Cacioppo, S., Grafton, S. T., & Bianchi-Demicheli, F. (2012). The speed of passionate love, as a subliminal prime: A high-density electrical neuroimaging study. *Neuroquantology, 10*(4), 715–724. Retrieved from www.neuroquantology.com/index.php/journal/article/view/509.

Cacioppo, S., & Hatfield, E. (2013). From desire to love: New advances from social neuroscience. In L. Bormans (Ed.), *The world book of love* (pp. 1–2). Tielt, Belgium: Lannoo.

Cacioppo, S., Weiss, R. M., Runesha, H. B., & Cacioppo, J. T. (2014). Dynamic spatiotemporal brain analyses using high performance electrical neuroimaging: Theoretical framework and validation. *Journal of Neuroscience Methods, 238,* 11–34. Retrieved from https://doi.org/10.1016/j.jneumeth. 2014.09.009.

Choi, D. C., Furay, A. R., Evanson, N. K., Ostrander, M. M., Ulrich-Lai, Y. M., & Herman, J. P. (2007). Bed nucleus of the stria terminalis subregions differentially regulate hypothalamic-pituitary-adrenal axis activity: Implications for the integration of limbic inputs. *The Journal of Neuroscience, 27,* 2025–2034.

Cole, S. W, Hawkley, L. C., Arevalo, J. M., & Cacioppo, J. T. (2011). Transcript origin analysisidentifies antigen-presenting cells as primary targets of socially regulated geneexpression in leukocytes. *Proceedings of the National Academy of Sciences of the United States of America, 108*(7), 3080–3085. doi: 10.1073/pnas.1014218108. Epub 2011 February 7. PubMed PMID: 21300872; PubMed Central PMCID: PMC3041107.

Cole, S. W., Hawkley, L. C., Arevalo, J. M., Sung, C. Y., Rose, R. M., & Cacioppo, J. T. (2007). Social regulation of gene expression in human leukocytes. *Genome Biology, 8*(9), R189. PubMed PMID: 17854483; PubMed Central PMCID: PMC2375027.

Davis, M. (1998). Are different parts of the extended amygdala involved in fear versus anxiety? *Biological Psychiatry, 44,* 1239–1247.

Diamond, L. M. (2004). Emerging perspectives on distinctions between romantic love and sexual desire. *Current Directions in Psychological Science, 13*(3), 116–119.

Fisher, H., Aron, A., & Brown, L. L. (2005). Romantic love: An fMRI study of a neural mechanism for mate choice. *The Journal of Comparative Neurology, 493*(1), 58–62.

Hatfield, E., & Rapson, R. L. (2009). The neuropsychology of passionate love. In E. Cuyler & M. Ackhart (Eds.), *Psychology of relationships* (pp. 1–26). Nova Science.

(1996). *Love and sex: Cross-cultural perspectives.* Boston, MA: Allyn and Bacon.

Hatfield, E., & Sprecher, S. (1986). Measuring passionate love in intimate relations. *Journal of Adolescence, 9,* 383–410.

Montague, P. R., Berns, G. S., Cohen, J. D., McClure, S. M., Pagnoni, G., Dhamala, M., et al. (2002). Hyperscanning: simultaneous fMRI during linked social interactions. *Neuroimage, 16,* 1159–1164. doi: 10.1006/nimg.2002.1150.

Moser, M., Johnshon, S. M., Dalgleish, T. L., Lafontaine, M. F., Wievbe, S. A., & Tasca, G. A. (2016). Changes in relationship-specific attachment in emotionally focused couple therapy. *Journal of Marital and Family Therapy, 42,* 231–245.

Ortigue, S., Bianchi-Demicheli, F., Hamilton, A. F. D. C., & Grafton, S. T. (2007). The neural basis of love as a subliminal prime: An event-related functional magnetic resonance imaging study. *Journal of Cognitive Neuroscience, 19*(7), 1218–1230. Retrieved from https://doi.org/10.1162/jocn.2007.19.7.1218.

Ortigue, S., Bianchi-Demicheli, F., Patel, N., Frum, C., & Lewis, J. (2010). Neuroimaging of love: fMRI meta-analysis evidence towards new perspectives in sexual medicine. *Journal of Sexual Medicine, 7*(11), 3541–3552.

Siegel, A., & Brutus, M. (1990). Neural substrate of aggression and rage in the cat. *Progress in Psychobiology and Physiological Psychology*, *14*, 135–233.

Ulrich-Lai, Y. M., & Herman, J. P. (2009). Neural regulation of endocrine and autonomic stress responses. *Nature Reviews Neuroscience*, *10*, 397–409.

VanderWeele, T. J., Hawkley, L. C., Thisted, R. A., & Cacioppo, J. T. (2011). A marginal structural model analysis for loneliness: Implications for intervention trials and clinical practice. *Journal of Clinical and Consulting Psychology*, *79*, 225–235. doi: 10.1037/a0022610.

Vico, C., Guerra, P., Robles, H., Vila, J., & Anllo-Vento, L. (2010). Affective processing of loved faces: Contributions from peripheral and central electrophysiology. *Neuropsychologia*, *48*(10), 2894–2902. Retrieved from https://doi.org/10.1016/j.neuropsychologia.2010.05.031.

Wager, T. D., Atlas, L. Y., Lindquist, M. A., Roy, M., Woo, C.-W., & Kross, E. (2013). An fMRI-based neurologic signature of physical pain. *The New England Journal of Medicine*, *368*(15), 1388–1397. Retrieved from https://doi.org/10.1056/NEJMoa1204471.

Wager, T. D., Lindquist, M. A., Nichols, T. E., Kober, H., & Van Snellenberg, J. X. (2009). Evaluating the consistency and specificity of neuroimaging data using meta-analysis. *NeuroImage*, *45*(1 Suppl.), S210–S221. Retrieved from https://doi.org/10.1016/j.neuroimage.2008.10.061. www.nytimes.com/2017/11/08/style/modern-love-neuroscience.html. Credit: Stephanie Cacioppo.

Waite, L. J. (2000). Trends in men's and women's well-being in marriage. In L. J. Waite, C. Bachrach, M. Hindin, E. Thomson, & A. Thornton (Eds.), *The ties that bind: Perspectives on marriage and cohabitation* (pp. 368–392). New York: Aldine de Gruyter.

Walker, D. L., Toufexis, D. J., & Davis , M. (2003). Role of the bed nucleus of the stria terminalis versus the amygdala in fear, stress, and anxiety. *European Journal of Pharmacology*, *463*, 199–216.

Wegner, D. M., Erber, R., & Raymond, P. (1991). Transactive memory in close relationships. *Journal of Personality and Social Psychology*, *61*(6), 923.

Wegner, D. M., Giuliano, T., & Hertel, P. T. (1985). Cognitive interdependence in close relationships. In Ickes, W. J. (Ed.), *Compatible and incompatible relationships* (pp. 253–276). New York: Springer.

CHAPTER 5

Love Conceptualized as Mutual Communal Responsiveness

Margaret S. Clark, Jennifer L. Hirsch, and Joan K. Monin

The term *love* is used in many ways. It has been used to refer to sexual feelings for another person, motivation to be with a person, and selfless devotion to another (just to name a few). Many times it refers to a combination of these things. Very often the term is used without definition. No one usage is the right one. Each has value. Yet in conducting research and in writing about love for academic purposes, it is important to make one's own conceptual definition clear.

Love conceptualized as (usually) mutual, communal, responsiveness. Here we define love as having a strong communal relationship with another person (see Clark & Mills, 2012). This refers to partners assuming special responsibility for one another's welfare (over and above the responsibility most humans assume for most strangers). Each relationship member manifests love defined in this way by striving to understand, accept, and care for the other *and* by expecting and seeking the same from the other in accord with the special level of responsibility that has been assumed. Such responsiveness should be present to the best of each person's ability and should occur in a noncontingent way; that is, acts of responsiveness should not be conditional on receiving a repayment nor should the motivation to be responsive be to make a repayment (Clark & Mills, 2012; Reis & Clark, 2014).

Love, defined in this way, captures love that characterizes close friendships, family relationships, and romantic relationships alike. The term "love," used in this way, represents a sense of each person "being there" for the other in good times and bad, that is, of each being both a safe haven for the other and each also being a supportive secure base (as adult attachment theorists' use those terms; Mikulincer & Shaver, 2013). It includes feeling protective of one's partner as well as feeling dependent upon one's partner.

This type of love, occasionally, is one sided. For instance, when an infant is born, almost all parents immediately assume responsibility for that infant's welfare – indeed, they do so even before the infant is born. They strive to understand, accept, and care for the infant whereas the infant has no ability to reciprocate. When parents behave communally toward their infants, they feel authentic and experience enhanced emotional well-being themselves (Le & Impett, 2015) – feelings that are intimately tied up with feelings of love and, indeed, constitute much of those feelings. This fits our definition of love. The infant experiences love as well as a function of being the target of her parents' efforts to understand, accept, and care for her and those experiences too fit our definition. However, the love we discuss most often is characterized by *mutual* responsiveness of each member of a pair of friends, family relationship or romantic couple. Interestingly, there is evidence that *being* responsive may be even more important for one's own feelings of love than receiving responsiveness (Reis, Maniaci, & Rogge, 2017). However, it is important to point out that when both members of a relationship have the ability to be responsive, both enacting responsiveness *and* seeking/accepting it (in accord with those abilities) must occur for optimal feelings of bonding and love to emerge (see Le, Impett, Lemay, Muise, & Tskhay, 2018). One-sided caring or seeking of care when both members have the capacity to enact love can be just plain odd and disconcerting, undermining overall feelings of love in the relationship.

Levels of love. It is important to note that loving, responsive, relationships vary in communal strength (Mills et al., 2004). Communal strength refers to the extent to which people assume responsibility for a partner's welfare and expect the same from that partner. Most people have multiple communal relationships – with romantic partners, with family members, and with friends. The degree of responsibility the members assume for their partners (and vice versa) varies within that set of relationships. Such variation is reflected in the amount of time, effort, and money each member expends to enact responsiveness for one another. For instance, many people have both spouses and friends, and among those who have both types of relationship, many assume more responsibility for a spouse and expect more responsibility from a spouse than they do for their friends. Of course, not everybody orders the communal strength of relationships with spouses, friends, children, and parents in the same way. Such ordering varies both between people and between cultures (Monin, Clark, & Lemay, 2008; Pataki, Fathelbab, Clark, & Malinowski, 2013).

Agreeing on levels of love. Members of a given relationship generally implicitly agree on the communal strength of their relationships and will, as a result, use these levels as guides for giving and seeking responsiveness in their relationship. They also typically understand much about the strength of other communal relationships. This means people will understand if, say, a friend is not responsive to them by, say, attending their birthday party because that friend has a higher level of communal strength in another relationship in which a similar need exists at the same time, because, say, the person is attending his own child's birthday party.

The fact that implicitly agreed-upon levels of communal strength vary means that it is entirely possible to be *too* responsive to a partner, making that partner uncomfortable and interfering with processes that would normally lead to feeling loved. Imagine, for example, the unlikely scenario of having your friend buy you a fancy car and giving it to you "no strings attached." You would likely feel very uncomfortable and feel as if the gesture was "too much." As a result, feelings of love might actually drop. The bottom line is that feelings of love are most likely to flourish when members of relationships assume and enact a certain level of responsibility for one another and also act in accord to a mutually and generally implicitly agreed upon level of communal strength. People simply cannot have very strong communal relationships with too many others at one time because they have limited ability to enact high levels of responsiveness. Instead, most people have relationships of different levels of communal strength, with just a very few very strong ones. Consequently, although they feel love as defined here in many relationships, they also feel different levels of love.

In this chapter we discuss interpersonal processes that comprise and facilitate communal responsiveness and, consequently, felt love. We also discuss processes that detract from communal responsiveness and, hence, from felt love. In talking about communal responsiveness, we build upon a long-standing program of research on communal relationships (see Clark & Mills, 1979, 1993, 2012; Mills & Clark, 1982) as well as upon discussions of the nature of responsiveness (Reis & Clark, 2014; Reis, Clark, & Holmes, 2004).

What Is Communal Responsiveness?

We have said communal responsiveness entails understanding, accepting, and caring for another person but we have yet to provide concrete examples of its enactment. Consider each of the following examples.

A young child bursts into tears. A classmate has teased him about his haircut. His mother hugs him, and then listens carefully to what he is saying. She provides assurances and says she thinks his hair looks just fine, but also takes care not to dismiss his concerns – she truly wants to understand and to validate his experience. She asks what *he* thinks and he says he does not like his haircut. She assures him she believes him and accepts his view. "If *you* want a new haircut, let's go get you one." Her focus is squarely on understanding, accepting, and caring for her child's needs. She comforts and cheers him up in the moment. She further suggests that, perhaps if the teaser felt good about himself, he would not be so mean – thus also preparing her child for future resilience as well as compassion toward others. The result? Her son feels loved; she feels loving.

Now picture a young woman talking with her older brother. She trusts her brother and feels comfortable being vulnerable with him. She says she is both losing interest in and is stressed by her current high-pressure sales job. She wants to return to school, to get her master's degree in biology, and to teach high school biology. Her brother is surprised. *He,* personally, would love to have her current high-paying, powerful, and prestigious position. Yet he maintains a focus on *her.* He asks her questions about her current unhappiness as well as about her ambitions. He strives to understand her current concerns and to communicate that he not only understands but also accepts those concerns, saying, "I get it. I didn't realize how much pressure you were under – wanting to switch paths makes sense now." He points out other perspectives, but ultimately supports his sister in moving toward and growing in the direction *she* desires, helping her become whom she wishes to become (see Rusbult, Finkel, & Kumashiro, 2009).

Next, consider a woman who, in the midst of a meeting, realizes that she has missed a lunch date with a friend. She feels awful, leaves the meeting, and calls to apologize and to express her guilt and embarrassment. Her friend feels hurt because she expected this woman to care about her needs, but her friend does not feel anger or a desire to retaliate both because she cares about this woman and because she values their relationship (Lemay, Overall, & Clark, 2012). The woman expresses guilt and embarrassment and doing so mitigates the friend's hurt feelings (see Feinberg, Willer, & Keltner, 2012; Semin & Manstead, 1982). This shifts the friend's focus from her hurt feelings toward this woman's own negative feelings and needs (see Clark, Graham, Williams, & Lemay, 2008). The friend reassures the woman that she understands how busy and stressed the woman has been, adding that she, herself, has made such mistakes in the past, intentionally providing a comforting social comparison. The transgressor feels gratitude for her friend's understanding and expresses it. Her friend appreciates the gratitude (see Algoe,

Haidt, & Gable, 2008). Both members of the relationship end their interaction feeling understood, accepted, and supported.

Finally, consider two good friends who have gone out to dinner together at a shared, favorite restaurant. Neither has pressing needs nor worries. Both truly are comfortable and relaxed with one another. Neither closely monitors what is said nor worries about acceptance by the other. They can focus outward on their shared experience of the new dishes they try (see Clark et al., 2008). They share a number of these dishes with one another and are able to savor each and to enjoy the fact that the other shares their pleasure. Each person's experience is enhanced because it is shared (see Boothby, Clark, & Bargh, 2014; Boothby, Smith, Clark, & Bargh, 2017; Reis, O'Keefe, & Lane, 2017).

Each of these relationships involves communal responsiveness and the positive fallout of that responsiveness. What these situations have in common is that each person feels a special responsibility for the other. Each feels comfortable, understood, accepted, and cared for by the other. They can let down their guards, be vulnerable, give and accept support as needed and desired. They easily focus outward on joint activities when neither requires support. They can do so without protecting themselves – without worrying about whether they are saying the right thing or acting the right way. Their comfort allows them to savor the activities themselves and they also gain pleasure from the fact that their partner is enjoying the activity as well (Boothby & Clark, 2017).

Responsiveness takes different forms in each of these examples. It shows up as seeking to remediate a partner's distress (in the case of the child who was teased), supporting progress toward a partner's desired goals (in the case of the brother and sister), as accommodation and avoiding self-focused, angry reactions (in the case of the friend who was left waiting at lunch), and as involving the partner in enjoyable activities (in the case of the friends at dinner). In all cases, partners trust each other and their actions reinforce that trust. Importantly, the partners do *not* exploit one another's vulnerabilities to their own advantage. Moreover, partners are noncontingently responsive – that is, they are not supporting one another because they feel a debt or want to create a debt of the other to them.

All of this this is not the result of communal relationships being completely unselfish (Clark, 2011; Clark & Mills, 1993) and we do not equate love with unselfish altruism (which is another definition of love – but not ours.) People retain concern about the self and expect the other to care. They seek and expect support from the other if and when they need it and when the other has the ability to respond.

They can, and do, however, shift their focus of attention from themselves to their partner when the partner has needs and they do not. Importantly, in our examples, the mother did *not* worry that having an unpopular child would reflect poorly on her. The brother did *not* calculate his own costs in helping his sister explore educational opportunities. The friend did *not* stop talking to the woman who missed their planned lunch date nor did she demand an apology. The responsive partners in all our scenarios likely felt good about themselves for having been responsive and for living up to the norms of a communal relationship (see Williamson & Clark, 1989).

Because partners focus on one another's needs and welfare and are confident that their partner will do the same both members feel safer, more secure, and more loved within mutual, communally responsive relationships. Such responsiveness includes providing benefits to one's partner, both tangible and intangible, that fulfill the partner's needs (e.g. taking a partner to get a new haircut), enhancing the partner's enjoyment of life (e.g. savoring meals and activities together), and supporting a partner's growth toward goals (e.g. researching a partner's career options). Although we have not included an example to illustrate this, communal responsiveness also can be largely symbolic, as when one person writes another a supportive note, sends a card or flowers, or simply expresses affection. When people state that they love another, we think they often mean they are, and intend to be, communally responsive toward the other, and that they have experienced and anticipate continuing to experience the same from the other.

Stating that a loving relationship involves individuals' communal responsiveness places the emphasis on the person who is responsive, and might be taken to imply that all that is needed for a loving relationship is for two people to be willing and able to be responsive to one another. As our opening comments should make clear, though, we place *at least equal* emphasis on the attitudes and self-generated actions of the person who is to be the recipient of responsiveness. Potential recipients of responsiveness must trust that the other will care and act accordingly. In other words, they must be open about their needs, what they enjoy, what their goals are, and even what their transgressions have been (and how they feel about those transgressions). They must be willing to be vulnerable and dependent. This is also illustrated in the scenarios above. The child revealed that he was upset about being teased. The sister revealed her worries and goals. The friend acknowledged her transgression and her feelings of distress and guilt. This opens the door for people *to* understand, validate, and respond communally to their partners – three processes that we already have emphasized in this chapter and three qualities that Reis and his colleagues (Reis & Clark, 2014; Reis & Patrick, 1996; Reis & Shaver, 1988) have identified as central to establishing intimacy. It is not just about being responsive *for* a partner; one must also be willing to seek and accept gestures of responsiveness *from* a partner. For instance, in one study by Graham and colleagues (Graham, Huang, Clark. & Helgeson, 2008, Study 2), college students were given the task of watching a peer give a speech and were allowed to, if they wished, help that peer by looking up material on the Internet relevant to the topic of the speech and providing it to the peer. If the peer both showed nonverbal evidence of being nervous and openly acknowledged it verbally – actually stating he or she was nervous – the speech giver peer received significantly more help than he did if he showed no emotion or only nonverbal signs of fear. In another study from the same paper, students who self-reported being willing to express their negative emotions to others before going to college subsequently developed more friendships and more intimate friends during their first semester of college. Expressing vulnerability openly and intentionally invites and encourages partners to be responsive. In the case of this work, just needing the support was not enough. Another example of the importance of willingness to express needs within close communal relationships is provided by the work of Monin and colleagues (Monin, Matire, Schulz & Clark, 2009). In this study of older adults with osteoarthritis and their spousal caregivers, when care recipients were more willing to express vulnerabilities to their spousal caregivers, the caregivers reported feeling less caregiving stress and also having provided more sensitive care to their partners.

How Can One Tell If Love, as Exemplified by Communal Responsiveness, Characterizes a Relationship?

Defining a loving relationship as one characterized by mutual communal responsiveness (to the best of each person's ability) straightforwardly suggests that the best way to measure the presence (or absence) of love is to look for the presence (or absence) of behaviors that index or promote communal responsiveness. That is, if one wishes to understand feelings of love as defined in this chapter then measuring the giving, seeking and acceptance of communally responsive acts is superior to using (especially exclusively using) other, very common methods of assessing relationship quality. These include having a person rate how satisfied they are with a relationship (see Weidmann, Schonbrodt, Ledermann, & Grob, 2017), counting the number of conflicts in a relationship or examining whether a relationship remains stable or not (e.g. Kirkpatrick & Davis, 1994).

Using those other indices of "love" – as is very commonly done, especially by people new to relationship research – is not ideal, in our opinion. Considering satisfaction first, interdependence theorists' construct of comparison levels is relevant. People have expectations for close relationships based on past relationships experienced or observed. If a current relationship exceeds comparison levels, even if those levels are very low, a person may be satisfied. So too can one person in a relationship report high satisfaction and the other low satisfaction, perhaps because only one person's needs are being met (Rusbult & Buunk, 1993).

Second, consider, the presence of conflict as an index of (poor) relational quality. From our perspective, conflict is not necessarily bad. When conflict consists of constructive complaints about neglected needs and is responded to with attention, possibly guilt or embarrassment, and efforts by each partner to understand, accept, and care in response, conflict can promote communal responsiveness. Indeed, constructive conflict paired with resolution has been shown to be important for problem solving in relationships. Clinical relationship psychologists and developmental psychologists see this as an important part of parenting as well. Children learn to be communally responsive and to solve problems from observing parents do this (McCoy, Cummings, & Davies, 2009) and constructive conflict even seems to have health benefits (El-Sheikh, Kelly, Koss, & Bauer, 2015)

Finally, why is stability not a great index of relationship quality? Relationships may be stable simply because people have poor alternative options (Rhatigan & Axsom, 2006; Rusbult & Martz, 1995) or because members feel they must remain in a relationship because of personal or social prescriptives, such as a personal belief or a strong cultural norm that divorce is unacceptable (Cox, Wexler, Rusbult, & Gaines, 1997; Lehmiller & Agnew, 2006), or because of how much they have already invested in the relationship (including children conceived and raised jointly and or years invested in a relationship) (Rhatigan & Axsom, 2006). If we want to understand feelings of love that arise from, co-occur with, and encourage noncontingent responsiveness, then we must look to that noncontingent responsiveness and factors that encourage or interfere with it.

What Relationship Processes Characterize High-quality, Loving Relationships?

Most straightforwardly, repeated, noncontingent acts of being communally responsive to one's partner, and one's partner being communally responsive to oneself index high-quality, loving relationships. So too can the repeated occurrence of mutual efforts to engage in activities that benefit both parties index and contribute to a sense of love, be it within a friendship, a romantic relationship, or a family relationship. The longer the time period over which such responsiveness occurs, the more it is welcomed and successfully enhances partner happiness (see Monin, Poulin, Brown, & Langa, 2017), the longer it is expected to continue (see Lemay, 2016 for a discussion of the importance of expectancies in relationships), and the fewer lapses there are in such behavior, the greater should be members' senses of love.

Of course, as already suggested, there are different types of responsiveness. One type occurs when a person has lost something or has experienced some harm, and aid could be used, as well as when a person provides something desirable to a person (who lacks it, whereas most others in that person's situation have it). This is commonly called helping, and has received considerable research attention (Clark, Ouellette, Powell, & Milberg, 1987; Monin, Poulin, Brown, & Langa, 2017). Another type involves supporting a partner as that partner works toward a goal, short-term or long-term, shared or individual. This type of partner support helps facilitate goal progress and well-being for the goal striver (Feeney, 2004; Jakubiak & Feeney, 2016a). This has come to be referred to in the relationships literature as the Michelangelo phenomenon, wherein a person helps to sculpt a partner into that partner's ideal self (Drigotas, Rusbult, Wieselquist, & Whitton, 1999; Rusbult, Finkel, & Kumanshiro, 2009). For instance, a partner may want to make the Olympic trials in the marathon, lose ten pounds, or go on a dream vacation. Supporting a partner's goals, such as these, may take the form of listening to the person articulate a dream, indicating understanding and acceptance, offering encouragement, stifling an urge to label the goal as crazy or unrealistic, or offering concrete help. Importantly, it may also take the form of cheering for the person as successful steps are made toward the goal and celebrating the person's attainment of the goal, helping them to capitalize on their success (Gable, Reis, Impett, & Asher, 2004).

A third type of responsiveness involves combining forces with another person to create something enjoyable and beneficial to one or both – an enjoyable conversation, a puzzle, tennis game, creating music together, a collaborative project, or a dance (see Reis, O'Keefe, & Lane, 2017). It can also consist of merely engaging in a pleasant activity side by side with a close person, something that has recently been shown to enhance the positivity of pleasant activities (Boothby, Clark, & Bargh, 2014; Boothby, Smith, Clark, & Bargh, 2016, 2017).

A fourth category of positive responsiveness includes caring behaviors in response to a transgression by one's partner. If one's natural reaction in such a situation is to retaliate or express anger, merely restraining one-self from doing so must be counted as responsiveness (Rusbult, Verette, Whitney, Solvik, & Lipkus, 1991) and it is a process that may become automatic in some relationships (Perunovic & Holmes, 2008). Forgiveness (Van Tongeren, Green, Hook, Davis, Davis, & Ramos, 2015), reassurance of continuing care, and indications of understanding are responsive in this sense (as in the earlier example of a friend forgiving her partner's having missed a lunch appointment.)[1]

A final, important type of responsiveness to another person is symbolic responsiveness. It may occur in the absence of any clear need for support or of any joint participation in an activity. It consists of conveying that one really does care about the partner and will be there if needed. This can be done through words (e.g. saying "I love you"), physical actions like a hug or a touch (Jakubiak & Feeney, 2016b), sending cards or flowers, expressions of appreciation and gratitude (Monin, Poulin, Brown, & Langa, 2017), and even, when trust is high, in the form of affectionate teasing. It can be conveyed by merely "being there" for a partner; attending a partner's graduation ceremony, musical performance, or athletic competition, or listening to a partner who is practicing a speech (Jakubiak & Feeney, 2016a). The mere presence of and/or touch from a partner can reduce felt threat (Coan, Beckes, & Allen, 2013; Conner, Siegle, McFarland et al., 2012; Eden, Larkin & Abel, 1992; Kamarch, Manuck & Jennings, 1990; Lougheed, Koval & Hollenstein, 2016; Schnall, Harber, Stefannucci & Proffitt, 2008).[2] The mere presence of communal partners can also enhance pleasures (Aron, Norman, Aron & Lewandowski, 2003; Boothby et al., 2014; Reis et al., 2017).

Why Responsiveness Is So Important

Most obviously, responsiveness provides partners with support, goods, information, appraisals, and money that they can use. Less visibly, but

---

[1] An important caveat: Forgiveness in the face of especially harmful behaviors on a partner's part – particularly behaviors that are not likely to end – can mean that forgiveness, albeit responsive toward one's partner, is unwise (McNulty, 2010a; McNulty & Russell, 2016). Indeed, many seemingly positive, responsive behaviors can be unwise and lead to exploitation if a communal relationship is not truly mutual (McNulty, 2010b).

[2] So too should it be noted that responsibility for a communal partner, especially a child, can increase felt threat (e.g. Eibach, Libby & Gilovich, 2003; Fessler, Holbrook, Pollack & Hahn-Holbrook, 2014). These relationships do have their burdens as well.

probably even more importantly for most people, it provides partners with an ongoing sense of security – a sense of security that allows them to relax, enjoy life, explore, and achieve, knowing that another person is looking out for one's welfare. Knowing that another person is watching out for one's welfare provides respite from protecting the self, permitting a person to focus attention elsewhere, including on a relationship partner and on an enjoyable activity (Boothby et al., 2017; Clark, Graham, Williams, & Lemay, 2008; Mikulincer, Shaver, Gillath, and Nitzberg, 2005). It allows a person to feel comfortable opening up, revealing emotions, stating needs, seeking and accepting help, sharing goals, revealing creations, and engaging the other in joint activities. These are all things that, in turn, elicit further responsiveness. In the absence of evidence that the partner cares, disclosure of goals and attempts to be creative are often closely guarded because a partner who does not care can use this information to exploit or harm a person. Likewise, people are less willing to express emotions in the absence of perceived care (Von Culin, Hirsch, & Clark, 2017). In the presence of a caring, responsive person, one feels confident of social approval, one can be more authentic, and one feels warmer and less shy (Venagalia & Lemay, 2017).

Unsurprisingly, perceiving that partners care comes, in large part, from partners truly being caring (Lemay & Clark, 2008; Lemay, Clark & Feeney, 2007; Von Culin, Hirsch, & Clark, 2017). However, people also vary in the degree to which they are prone to trust others generally, presumably as a result of their own past experiences in relationships. Adult attachment theorists have long emphasized this (see Mikulincer & Shaver, 2013 for a review of such literature). More recently, Lemay and others have shown with multiple studies that people project their own feelings of trust on relationship partners and that this too is an important source of perceived communal responsiveness (Lemay & Clark, 2008; Lemay Clark, & Feeney, 2007; Von Culin, Hirsch, & Clark, 2017).

The Importance of Responsiveness Being Noncontingent

For responsiveness to promote a sense of security, as noted above, it is essential that it be noncontingent. In this regard, consider a target's reaction to noncontingent responsiveness. Say, for instance, that a husband states that he will be happy to have his wife's relatives visit, with no further comment, versus agreeing to the same thing *if* she promises to do all the house cleaning for a month. To what will she attribute his willingness to have her family visit? In the first case, she is likely to attribute it to her spouse's concern for her; in the second case, the thought that it is due to his concern for her will be discounted to the extent that she believes what he really wants is for her to clean the house. Now, consider the same scenario from the husband's perspective. To what will he attribute his *own* actions in each case? Self-perception suggests that he will see himself as caring in the former case, but, perhaps as manipulative or selfish in the second case. The upshot of the former (but *not* the latter) offer should be a wife who feels loved and a husband who feels loving.

Promoting attributions of care and nurturance both on the part of both care recipients and caregivers constitutes one category of reasons why *noncontingent* responsiveness is so important, but there is another, very important, reason as well. It is that the initial impetus for noncontingent responsiveness is, naturally, the recipient's needs and desires. In sharp contrast, the impetus for contingent responsiveness will be the *giver's* desire to receive something in return or the giver's desire to eliminate a perceived debt. As a result, not only may it be the case a partner's needs will be neglected when the donor needs nothing from that person or is not indebted to that person, it may also be the case that a partner will receive undesired or harmful "benefits," simply because a person wishes to eliminate a debt or to create one.

The Importance of Acceptance of Responsiveness Being Noncontingent

Noncontingent acceptance of support also is an important quality of communal relationships. This refers, simply, to being willing to accept a partner's acts of responsiveness without repaying and without indicating that one feels the necessity to repay (or even wishes they could repay). Gracious acceptance with no protest sends the message that one feels comfortable with the gesture, welcomes it, and desires the relationship. Insisting on repayment or displaying discomfort upon receiving benefits suggests that one might prefer that the communal relationship not exist (or that it be less strong). Noncontingent acceptance of a benefit, however, combined with feeling and expressing gratitude or thanks is acceptable and, in our view, often important. Indeed, research suggests that the mere act of expressing gratitude to a partner increases the expresser's sense of the communal strength of a relationship (Lambert, Clark, Durtschi, Fincham, & Graham, 2010) and receiving an expression of gratitude from one's partner appears to increase the recipient's desire for a stronger communal relationship (Williams & Bartlett, 2015). The latter may occur because a person who has been responsive may be somewhat uncertain of whether the responsiveness was appropriate or desired; the recipient's expression of gratitude eliminates that uncomfortable uncertainty by signaling that, yes, the gesture *was* welcome. Indeed, expressions of gratitude that specifically praise the caregiver (e.g. "*You* were so nice to have done that! I appreciate *you*.") as opposed to just mentioning the help itself (e.g. "That helped me finish the task") seem especially effective in this regard (Algoe, Kurtz, & Hilaire, 2016). Such expressions of gratitude likely not only make the responsive person happy but also encourage further responsiveness on that person's part toward the expresser (Algoe, Frederickson & Gable, 2013).

The Importance of Signaling Needs and Desires and Seeking Responsiveness

Responsiveness is key to establishing a sense of love in a relationship, and, as already noted, gracious acceptance of responsiveness is also a sign of a well-functioning communal relationship and the presence of love. Yet for a partner to be responsive, that partner must know what to do to enhance the other's welfare. At times it is obvious because the situation is a strong cue. If you're walking down a sidewalk with your friend, he drops a sheaf of papers, the wind is blowing, and he is frantically attempting to gather them, it is pretty clear some help is in order and probably would be welcome. Yet, frequently, partner needs, desires, goals, and fears are not obvious. Thus, for high levels of communal responsiveness to characterize a relationship (and to be felt by its inhabitants), its members must be willing to express their vulnerabilities, needs, goals, desires, and fears freely. This can be accomplished through self-disclosure in the form of verbal statements of needs or, often, through nonverbal expressions of emotion with happiness inviting capitalization efforts, sadness inviting comforting efforts, and so forth. Thus, willingness to self-disclose and to express emotion are signs of love as are active requests for support. Indeed, being as willing to reveal one's authentic self and to seek responsiveness when it is needed as one is to give responsiveness is likely a sign that people are committed to a mutually caring and loving relationship (Beck & Clark, 2010; Clark, Beck & Aragon, 2018).

Do More Responsiveness and More Bids for Dependency Always Signal More Love in a Relationship?

It is important to keep in mind that more responsiveness and more dependency on a person's part is not always better for communal relationships nor does it always enhance feelings of love. Recall the discussion above regarding people assuming differing levels of responsibility for the welfare of different partners and of partners implicitly agreeing on this. One-sided violations of the implicit agreement by being too responsive (as in giving a friend a new car) or by seeking too much dependence will likely decrease feelings of love in many relationships. Thus, an important part of loving relationships is adhering to the implicitly agreed upon strength of the relationship and mutually desired trajectory of the relationship – be it as one stable in strength or as one growing in strength across time.

Other Considerations

Returning to the question of what constitutes a loving relationship, it is our sense that the terms *love* and *loving* are used to refer to a communal relationship when that relationship surpasses some implicit threshold of communal strength. We also believe that loving relationships are those in which people share assumptions about the strength of the relationship and consistently enact the expected (or, if relationship growth is desired, surpass expectations of) responsiveness in that relationship. However, other factors may influence a person's sense that a communal relationship is characterized by love, such as the length of time a particular relationship has been characterized by a high level of communal responsiveness and the length of time a high level of communal responsiveness is expected to continue.

In thinking about what contributes to a sense of love, it is interesting to return to our point that communal relationships need not be symmetrical in strength. As stated earlier, parents typically feel more responsibility for the welfare of their young children than those children feel for the welfare of their parents. However, does this mean that the parents love the children more than the children love the parents? Not necessarily. The reason is straightforward. *Both* feeling a strong communal responsibility for another person *and* perceiving that another person feels a strong communal responsibility for the self contribute to a sense of love (whether the relationship is symmetrical or not). Hence, even when a relationship is characterized by asymmetrical communal strength, it need not be characterized by asymmetry in the amount of love the participants feel for one another (although it may be).

What those thresholds of communal strength must be for the term *love* to be used undoubtedly differs between people and cultures. Just how it differs and what factors weigh in (e.g. how long a history of communal responsiveness one must endure, how long it is expected to continue, and where a relationship sits in a person's hierarchy of communal relationships) is a matter for future research.

The Importance of Certainty

Communal relationships differ not only in strength and in placement within a person's hierarchy of other communal relationships, but also in felt certainty about the communal nature of the relationship (Mills & Clark, 1982). We can be absolutely sure about the level of communal strength of a given relationship, somewhat uncertain, or very uncertain. Many factors drive certainty. An obvious one is the length of time a communal relationship has existed. All else being equal, the longer a communal relationship has existed, the more certainty should exist. Indeed, uncertainty about the nature of relationships is part and parcel of the initiation phase of close relationships (Clark, Beck & Aragon, 2018). A person's history in other communal relationships may well influence their certainty about the strength of a present one. A history of failed communal expectations may well carry over and influence one's certainty about a current relationship. Variability over time in a partner's responsiveness is also a factor, with greater variability creating more uncertainty. Finally, the extent to which a partner has sacrificed their own self-interest to be responsive ought to increase certainty (Holmes and Rempel, 1989). Uncertainty of the communal strength of relationships likely undermines the sense that the relationship is characterized by love.[3]

Placement of the Self in One's Communal Hierarchy

People feel responsible not just for communal partners' needs; they also feel responsible for their own needs. They place themselves in their own hierarchy of communal relationships, mostly at or near the top. Placement of the self in the hierarchy has implications for the sense of love that the self feels for a partner as well as for the sense of love that the partner feels for the self. In particular, if the self is placed far above the partner, then even the strongest communal partner's needs will not take precedence over the needs of the self. Sacrifices will not be made for the partner. Forgiving a partner for transgressions against the self will be rare. The very fact that the self's welfare always takes precedence over that of the partner should serve as an indicator to both parties that the love is not exceptionally strong.

---

[3] It is interesting to note that others have defined love as involving arousal plus a label (e.g. Dutton and Aron, 1974; Berscheid and Walster, 1974). Uncertainty and variability may be associated with greater anxiety and arousal that may contribute to a sense of love defined in that manner, but probably not to a sense of love as discussed in this chapter.

If the self is placed either at the same level as the partner (as many long-term romantic partners may do) or at a level lower than the partner (as parents may often do with their child), the story is very different. In such cases, sacrifices *will* be made, the needs of the partner *will* sometimes (given equal strength) or even often (if the self is placed below the partner) take precedence over the needs of the self, forgiveness will take place regularly, and so on. The few relationships a person has that fit this category are often considered the *most* loving relationships. The placement of self, relative to a partner, is, we believe, a potent determinant of this.[4] This is why sacrificing self-interest to be responsive to a partner promotes certainty about the communal nature of the relationship (Holmes and Rempel, 1989).

Numbers of Communal Relationships at Various Levels

Reis et al. (2004; see also Clark & Mills, 2012) suggested that communal relationships are typically arranged in terms of a hierarchy of communal strength and also that, when arranged in such hierarchies, they tend to form triangles with many very low strength communal relationships at the base, fewer in the middle, and a few, very high strength relationships at the top. If one is uniquely high in another person's hierarchy of relationships, one may feel especially loved.

What Is Ideal Relative to What Is Real

The amount of communal responsibility a person wishes or professes to assume for another person and the amount enacted toward that person can differ. Moreover, the amount of communal responsibility a person ideally expects from another person and the amount actually received can differ. In assessing what produces a sense of love, the perception of actual responsiveness received relative to what is expected or desired will be important. So too will the amount of responsiveness given relative to the giver's sense of what should, ideally, be given be important. Actual responsiveness coming closer to relationship members' ideals for responsiveness should enhance feelings of love.

---

[4] An important caveat is that some people are high in a trait known as unmitigated communion (Helgeson & Fritz, 1998). They place the needs of a partner above their own needs, neglect their own needs, and fail to alert a partner to their own needs. This trait may arise from a person having low self-esteem, feeling unworthy of care, and/or having a great desire to win others over and to please them. This is *not* a trait we believe contributes to optimal communal responsiveness nor to mutual feelings of love and it is a trait that has been linked to low psychological well-being (Aube, 2008).

The Importance of Individual Differences in Expectancies that Others Will Be Communally Responsive

Thus far we have discussed a loving relationship as being one that is objectively characterized by communal responsiveness. Of course, there is variability between individuals in their general, chronic tendencies to be communally responsive (and to behave in such a way as to elicit communal responsiveness). There is also variability between individuals in their tendencies to *perceive* that others are communally responsive to them (given the same objective circumstances).

Many (conceptually overlapping) traits are relevant in this regard (Reis et al., 2004). They include communal orientation (Clark et al., 1987), self-esteem (Leary & Baumeister, 2000; Leary, Haupt, Strausser, & Chokel, 1998; Murray et al., 1998; Murray, Bellavia, Rose, & Griffin, 2003), rejection sensitivity (Downey & Feldman, 1996), and attachment styles (Ainsworth, Blehar, Waters, & Wall, 1978; Bowlby, 1982; Hazan & Shaver, 1987; Shaver, Hazan, & Bradshaw, 1988). People who are high in communal orientation, high in self-esteem, low in rejection sensitivity, and securely attached undoubtedly are more likely, on average, to be communally responsive to their partners in any given relationship (Simpson, Rholes, & Nelligan, 1992; Clark et al., 1987), to reveal vulnerabilities, to ask for help from partners (Simpson et al., 1992), and to perceive their partners as communally responsive, especially in ambiguous situations (Collins & Feeney, 2004; Downey & Feldman, 1996). They also are less likely to be threatened by negative information about their partner, and less likely to withdraw from dependency on their partner in the face of any sign of rejection (Murray et al., 2003). Indeed, people who are generally confident in their partners' positive regard even find positives in their partners' faults (Murray & Holmes, 1993, 1999).

What Promotes Communal Responsiveness?

What encourages communally responsive acts? We believe most people have *knowledge* of basic communal norms. That is, if explicitly asked, most people readily would agree that helping, providing support toward goals, including partners in enjoyable activities, willingness to forgive partners (except for extremely negative behaviors), and conveying care through words and symbolic actions promote the formation, maintenance and repair of close relationships. Indeed, most people are quite adept at immediately behaving communally when they desire a new friendship or romantic relationship (Berg & Clark, 1986; Clark & Mills, 1979; Clark

& Waddell, 1985; Clark, Ouellette, Powell, & Milberg, 1987; Clark et al., 1986; Clark et al., 1989; Williamson & Clark, 1989; and see Clark et al., 2018 for a discussion of the role of strategically presenting oneself as a communally oriented person during relationship initiation). Yet knowledge of the desirability of communal responsiveness is not sufficient to generate communal relationships.

Trust Is Central

What matters far more to being *able* to form, deepen, and, especially, to maintain communal relationship in the face of challenges, are (a) *trusting* that a particular partner truly cares about one's welfare and, simultaneously, will not exploit or hurt one, as well as (b) *trusting* that a partner desires to be a recipient of one's care and will accept such care, along with a mutual communal relationship. The former type of trust affords one the courage to reveal needs and seek support; the latter type of trust affords one the courage to offer support.

Trust in a particular partner within a specific relationship is what is crucial to a loving relationship. Such trust is primarily built up by having a partner who is truly responsive to one's welfare even in the face of their conflicting self-interests (Holmes & Rempel, 1989; Holmes, 2002). Of course, the propensity to trust is the central part of the individual differences that were just discussed as relevant to communal responsiveness. Yet, the trust that inheres in a particular partner within a particular relationship remains important to achieving a sense of love. No matter how generally secure and trusting a person is, that person likely does not experience love until the trust is manifested within a particular relationship.

Trust in a particular partner's felt communal strength toward oneself need not be entirely based in reality for it to promote relationships. There are now numerous studies that have shown that people tend to project their own felt communal strength (or lack thereof) onto partners, seeing those partners as feeling about as much communal strength toward them as they feel toward that partner (Lemay et al., 2007; Lemay & Clark, 2008; Von Culin, Hirsch, & Clark, 2017). This encourages them to behave communally toward their partner, which, in turn, can become a self-fulfilling prophecy if the partner welcomes the behavior and responds in kind (Lemay & Clark, 2008). Recipients' of responsiveness can have and often do have biased perceptions of the support they actually receive based upon their own desires to come across as more or less responsive (Lemay & Neal, 2014). This, too, almost certainly influences how loved they feel.

To What Relationship- and Love-enhancing Processes
Does Trust Give Rise?

It is our sense that trust that a particular partner truly cares for one gives rise to a host of processes, which promote the formation, maintenance, and strengthening of communal relationships. It is, perhaps, easiest to understand how trust in a partner's care facilitates behaviors that elicit support, such as revealing one's own vulnerabilities; self-disclosing needs, goals and desires; willingness to express emotions (Clark et al., 2004; Clark & Finkel, 2005; Von Culin, Hirsch, & Clark, 2017); and issuing straight-forward requests for help. Trust is necessary to engaging in these behaviors because the other can turn one down (thereby hurting one's feelings and/or embarrassing one) or even exploit one's revealed vulnerabilities. Trust is also crucial to noncontingently accepting benefits from partners, since one is signaling a willingness to be dependent on the other by doing so.

Trust is also integral to the process of noncontingently providing support. People like partners more when those partners do not repay them for benefits received and do not ask for repayment of benefits given (Clark & Mills, 1979). Yet, especially early in relationships when one does care noncontingently, one is doing so with no guarantee that the person will welcome the support and no guarantee that the other will be similarly responsive to the self. Trust, we believe, provides the courage to believe that noncontingent responsiveness will be welcome, and the reassurance that the other will be responsive to the self *if and when* such responsiveness is needed.

It is interesting to note that high trust also appears to give rise to a host of positive cognitive biases that support mutual noncontingently caring relationships and, hence, ought to increase feelings of love in relationships (see Murray & Holmes, 2017 and Lemay & Clark, 2015 for discussions that go beyond what can be covered here). This point has been made clearly by Murray, Holmes, and their colleagues in talking about dependency regulation (Murray, Holmes, & Griffin, 2000). They suggest that having faith that one's partner regards one positively (and, we would say, more specifically, having trust that the partner is likely to care about one's wel-fare) allows one to "take a leap of faith" and to hold positive illusions about that partner. The illusions they study consist largely in viewing part-ners as having traits, such as kindness, which should allow people both to risk revealing vulnerabilities and to believe that their own communal gestures will be accepted. Other processes to which trust may give rise, and that may also foster maintaining or increasing dependence on one's partner, include making benign attributions for a partner's less than perfect behavior (Fincham, 2001), being accommodating (Rusbult, Verette, Whitney, Slovik, & Lipkus, 1991; Wieselquist, Rusbult, Foster, & Agnew, 1999), and seeing one's partner as being superior to alternative partners (Rusbult, Van Lange, Wildschut, Yovetich, & Verette, 2000). Lemay and colleagues also have provided extensive evidence that people who are highly motivated to form or maintain communal relationships with partners positively bias their perceptions of partners and situations in ways that support those goals (Lemay et al., 2007; Lemay & Clark, 2008; Von Culin, Hirsch, & Clark, 2017, Study 2), meaning people who are especially motivated to communally care for partners project those feelings onto partners, seeing them as equally as communally motivated as they are themselves. This is the case even when controlling for those partners' self-reports of their own communal motivation and, in some cases, controlling for objective observers' sense of the partner's motivation to behave communally. Experiments too support the notion that a person's own communal motivations can bias perceptions of partner communal motivations. Specifically, participants exposed to manipulations designed to alter their felt care for a partner in the moment, change perceptions of partner responsiveness in a congruent way (Lemay et al., 2007; Lemay & Clark, 2008).

People highly motivated to have communal relationships also selectively attend to information that is consistent with that goal and "remember" information from the past in ways biased to reflect positively on the relationship. Lemay & Neal (2013), in a daily diary study, for instance, found that perceivers who are chronically motivated to bond with partners have more positive memories of their partner's responsiveness across days. Also, their daily fluctuations in motivation to bond are positively associated with daily fluctuations in memories of partner responsiveness (while simultaneously controlling for those partners' own reports of their own responsiveness on the relevant days and even controlling for perceivers' initial perceptions of partners' responsiveness of the relevant day). Additional work by Lemay & Melville (2014) found evidence that when a partner has not been particularly responsive, communally motivated people underestimate the extent to which they self-disclosed their needs and desires to that partner thereby providing an excuse for the partner's low responsiveness and, presumably, allowing them to maintain their own communal motivation.

In sum, it seems that people who are highly motivated to form, maintain or strengthen communal relationships create a world in which perceptions of their partners' desires and behaviors match their own motivation.

Happily, it appears that their motivations and biased perceptions often become self-fulfilling prophecies (Lemay & Clark, 2008; Lemay & Neal, 2013; Lemay et al., 2007). Such biases give people the courage to be responsive to partners and then partners respond in kind. We are, in ways we both realize and may not realize, creators of our own loving relationships.

How Might a Lack of Trust Detract from Communal Responsiveness?

We view low trust in others' care as the primary factor that interferes with the development of ongoing communal responsiveness and love in a relationship. Mistrust heightens a person's focus on self-protection, which, in turn, typically (a) moves the self above the partner, sometimes far above the partner, in a person's hierarchy of communal relationships; (b) makes a person very reticent to reveal vulnerabilities; and (c) heightens a person's reluctance to be noncontingently responsive to the other, lest the other reject communal overtures (which would hurt) or not respond to the person's own needs (in mutual communal relationships) when needs arise. The ultimate fallout is independence from others at best, and conflict, suspicion, tendencies to interpret partner behaviors in negative, defensive ways (Collins, 1996; Collins & Allard, 2001), and outright negative interactions at worst.

We have studied two processes that, we believe, arise from a relative lack of trust in others' care and a resultant felt need to protect the self: One is following contingent norms within close relationships – what Clark & Mills (1979, 2012) have called exchange rules. Another is having a tendency to functionally segregate positive and negative information about partners in memory (Graham & Clark, 2006, 2007).

Consider following contingent norms for giving and accepting benefits first. Doing so is certainly "fair" and, indeed, has been advocated as a positive technique for maintaining the quality of relationships (Walster, Walster, & Berscheid, 1978). Yet, as we have already noted, following contingent norms undermines both the giver's sense of being nurturing and the recipient's sense of being the object of care. It also results in responsiveness being dictated as much or more by the provider's needs than by the potential recipient's needs, desires, or goals.

People do prefer noncontingent to contingent rules for giving benefits in close relationships; people who have been led to desire a communal relationship like their partners less when those partners appeared to follow exchange norms by repaying them for benefits received or asking for repayments for benefits given (Clark & Mills, 1979; Clark & Waddell, 1985), as well as avoid keeping track of benefits when a communal relationship was desired (Clark, 1984; Clark, Mills, & Corcoran, 1989). Other evidence comes from studies of ongoing marriages, which show that although almost all couples start out with the view that communal norms are ideal for their relationships (Clark et al., 2010; Grote & Clark, 1998) and make efforts to be communally responsive, stressful times can cause members to begin calculating fairness, which, in turn, increases conflict (see Clark, Lemay, Graham, Pataki, & Finkel, 2010; Grote & Clark, 2001 for avoidant persons) and appears to be associated with both low trust and decreased marital satisfaction (Clark et al., 2010).

Yet another process to which low faith in others appears to give rise is thinking of partners as "all positive" or "all negative" at a single point in time (Graham & Clark, 2006, 2007). Graham and Clark reasoned that whereas all people feel a need to belong (Baumeister & Leary, 1995), those low in trust that others will care for them (as indexed by low self-esteem or anxious attachment) find approaching a less than seemingly perfect other very difficult. Hence, in times of low threat, they tend to defensively see others as perfect, which allows them both to approach and interact with such people and to feel that partners will reflect positively upon them. However, once they detect a fault in others, they quickly conjure up all other faults, which provide an excuse to avoid depending upon the person and to avoid being embarrassed by them. The result, Graham and Clark claim, and for which they provide evidence, is a tendency to think of partners as "all good" or "all bad" at a given point in time – a tendency that does not characterize people high in self-esteem (and trust of others), who appear to view partners in more realistic and stable ways. Our sense is that a tendency to segregate a partner's positive and negative attributes instead of integrating them will detract from communal responsiveness in a number of ways. First, a balanced sense of a partner's strength and weaknesses ought to support both being optimally communally responsive to that person *and* optimal seeking of support from that partner. For instance, if one knows that one's partner has great mathematical skills and also is forgetful, one can both recommend that he or she apply for a desirable job requiring those skills and remind them of the deadline for applications; and if one needs some tutoring in mathematics for a course one is taking, one can both ask for that help and call to remind them of when the help is needed. Beyond this, having a balanced view ought to allow for a steadiness in views of and communal responsiveness toward the partner across time and events (Graham & Clark, 2006; Wortman, 2005) that should, in turn, as noted above, increase trust and felt love. All-positive and all-negative views of partners, in contrast, ought to lead, respectively, to expecting too much from partners and believing they need little support (when views are positive) and avoiding supporting or relying on partners (when views are negative).

Moreover, just as high trust leads to cognitive biases that support communal relationship functioning, low trust often does just the opposite. The work by Lemay and colleagues reviewed additionally demonstrates people do project their own low felt communal strength toward partners onto those partners putting the brakes on their own communal behavior (Lemay et al., 2007; Lemay & Clark, 2008). Moreover, people low in trust of others (e.g. low self-esteem or insecure attachment) show biases to see their partners in a negative light. For instance, Beck & Clark (2010) have found that avoidant people and people who are experimentally induced to feel avoidant in the moment, tend to perceive benefits that they have been given as having been non-voluntarily given (dictated by the situations) rather than given voluntarily as a result of partner's truly caring for them. This likely prevents them from responding communally in return and from feeling loved as a result of having received the benefit.

Finally, some recent work has shown that having a *partner* who is low in trust can even undermine a person's *own* communal behavior. For example, MacGregor and colleagues (MacGregor, Fitzsimons, & Holmes, 2013; MacGregor & Holmes, 2011) find evidence that people who merely know their partner is low (rather than high) in self-esteem (and therefore likely to be low in trust that others care about them) caused those people to withhold disclosures of their own accomplishments. This in turn prevented their partners' possible responsiveness in the form of capitalization (e.g. celebrating their successes). Further, Lemay and Dudley (2009) have found that people who perceive partners to be insecure begin to express inauthentic positive affect toward them. Whereas this seems to be effective in making their partner feel more valued, their own relationship satisfaction dropped. These studies together suggest that low trust not only undermines a person's own ability to freely self-disclose (a trait that promotes mutual communal responsiveness) but also, when detected by partners, inhibits their partner's authenticity and willingness to disclose.

Summary and Conclusions

To summarize, we believe that repeated and consistent giving and receipt of communal responsiveness results in experiencing relationships as loving ones. In mutual communal relationships, such responsiveness is dependent upon each member trusting that the other cares and will accept care. Beyond this, sensing where one is in a partner's hierarchy of other communal relationships and where one places one's partner in one's own hierarchy can have an impact on felt love with higher placements, enhancing felt love. Trust gives rise to a wide variety of interpersonal processes, including actual acts of communal responsiveness (indicating understanding, validation, and noncontingent helping; including the other in joint activities; supporting; signaling felt care) and acts that often directly elicit receipt of care (expressing emotion, self-disclosure, asking for support). Less obviously, high trust encourages processes – such as viewing one's partner in a very positive light and more positively than alternatives, making benign attributions for partner misdeeds, accommodation, and forgiveness – that permit a person to remain comfortably within the relationship and to continue acting in communally responsive ways.

Low trust, in contrast, discourages communal responsiveness and revealing information about the self that may elicit communal responsiveness from others. Instead, it gives rise to behaviors, some of which, on the surface, may seem acceptable (and even admirable) but which, simultaneously, undermine communal responsiveness. Such behaviors include relying on the self even when receipt of support might be very useful, suppressing emotions, giving and accepting benefits only on a contingent basis, and behaving in a wide variety of defensive ways that may lead to harmful chronic ways of thinking about partners, such as segregating positive and negative thoughts about partners. Behaviors that are chronically associated with high rather than low communal responsiveness will come to elicit high rather than low feelings of love. Low trust also may be detected by partners and lead them to inhibit their own comfortable disclosures of their own feelings and successes thereby inhibiting optimal responsiveness to them.

We do not claim that communal responsiveness and the interpersonal processes with which it is associated are the only ways in which love can be productively defined. However, we do think that the term is often used to refer to a relationship characterized by chronic communal responsiveness and comfort, and the security and warm feelings that accompany it and that this applies to friendships, romantic relationships, and family relationships alike. Communal responsiveness is also, we firmly believe, the most important factor contributing to the now well-documented fact that having close, loving, relationships is tremendously beneficial to one's mental and physical health (Holt-Lunstad, Smith, & Layton, 2010).

Acknowledgments

This chapter is a revision and update of a chapter on the same topic published in an earlier edition of this book. It retains some of the structure and much material from the earlier version. Preparation of the earlier version was supported by National Science Foundation grant BNS 9983417. The ideas and opinions expressed in the chapter are those of the authors, and do not necessarily reflect those of the National Science Foundation. We thank Tatum A. Jolink for her clerical support in preparing this manuscript.

References

Ainsworth, M. D. S., Blehar, M. C., Waters, E., & Wall, S. (1978). *Patterns of attachment: A psychological study of the strange situation*. Hillsdale, NJ: Lawrence Erlbaum.

Algoe, S. B., Fredrickson, B. L., & Gable, S. L. (2013). The social functions of the emotion of gratitude via expression. *Emotion, 13*(4), 605.

Algoe, S. B., Haidt, J., & Gable, S. L. (2008). Beyond reciprocity: Gratitude and relationships in everyday life. *Emotion, 8*(3), 425–429.

Algoe, S. B., Kurtz, L. E., & Hilaire, N. M. (2016). Putting the "you" in "thank you": Examining other-praising behavior as the active relational ingredient in expressed gratitude. *Social and Personality Science, 7*, 658–666.

Aron, A., Norman, C. C., Aron, E. N., & Lewandowski, G. (2003). Shared participation in self-expanding activities: Positive effects on experienced marital quality. In P. Noller & J. Feeney (Eds.), *Understanding marriage: Developments in the study of couple interaction* (pp. 177–194). New York: Cambridge University Press.

Aube, J. (2008). Balancing concern for other with concern for self: Links between unmitigated communion, communion, and psychological well-being. *Journal of Personality, 76*, 101–134.

Baumeister, R. F., & Leary, M. R. (1995). The need to belong: Desire for interpersonal attachments as a fundamental human motivation. *Psychological Bulletin, 117*, 497–529.

Beck, L. A., & Clark, M. S. (2010). Looking a gift horse in the mouth as a defense against increasing intimacy. *Journal of Experimental Social Psychology, 46*, 676–679.

Berg, J., & Clark, M. S. (1986). Differences in social exchange between intimate and other relationships: Gradually evolving or quickly apparent? In V. Derlega & B. Winstead (Eds.), *Friendship and social interaction* (pp. 101–128). New York: Spring-Verlag.

Berscheid, E., & Walster, E. (1974). A little bit of love. In T. L. Huston (Ed.), *Foundations of interpersonal attraction* (pp. 36–379). New York: Academic Press.

Boothby, E. J., & Clark, M. S. (2017). Side by side: Two ways merely being with a close or familiar other enhances well-being. In D. Dunn (Ed.), *Positive psychology: Psychological frontiers of social psychology.* New York: Taylor Francis/Routledge.

Boothby, E. J., Clark, M. S., & Bargh, J. A. (2014). Shared experiences are amplified. *Psychological Science, 25,* 2209–2216.

Boothby, E., Smith, L., Clark, M. S., & Bargh, J. (2016). Psychological distance moderates the amplification of shared experience. *Personality and Social Psychology Bulletin, 42,* 1431–1444.

(2017). The world looks better together: How close others enhance our visual experiences. *Personal Relationships,*24(3), 694–714.

Bowlby, J. (1982). *Attachment and Loss,* Vol. 1: *Attachment* (2nd ed.). New York: Basic Books.

Clark, M. S. (1984). Record keeping in two types of relationships. *Journal of Personality and Social Psychology, 47,* 549–557.

(2011). Communal relationships can be selfish and give rise to exploitation. In R. M. Arkin (Ed.), *Most underappreciated: 50 prominent social psychologists describe their most unloved work* (pp. 77–81). New York: Oxford University Press.

Clark, M. S., Beck, L. A., & Aragon, O. R. (2018). Relationship initiation: How do we bridge the gap between initial attraction and well-functioning communal relationships? In B. Friese (Ed.), *American Psychological Association handbook for contemporary family psychology.* Washington, DC: American Psychological Association Press.

Clark, M. S., & Finkel, E. J. (2004). Does expressing emotion promote well-being? It depends on relationship context. In L. Z. Tiedens & C. Leach (Eds.), *The social life of emotions* (pp. 105–126). New York: Cambridge University Press.

(2005). Willingness to express emotion: The impact of relationship type, communal orientation and their interaction. *Personal Relationships, 12,* 169–180.

Clark, M. S., Fitness, J., & Brissette, I. (2004). Understanding people's perceptions of relationships is crucial to understanding their emotional lives. In M. B. Brewer & M. Hewstone (Eds.), *Emotion and motivation* (pp. 21–46). Malden, MA: Blackwell.

Clark, M. S., Graham, S. M., Williams, E., & Lemay, E. P. (2008). Understanding relational focus of attention may help us understand relational phenomena. In J. Forgas & J. Fitness (Eds), *Social relationships: Cognitive, affective and motivational processes* (pp. 131–146). New York, NY: Psychology Press.

Clark, M. S., Lemay, E., Graham, S. M., Pataki, S. P., & Finkel, E. (2010). Ways of giving benefits in marriage: Norm use, relationship satisfaction, and attachment-related variability. *Psychological Science, 21,* 944–951.

Clark, M. S., & Mills, J. (1979). Interpersonal attraction in exchange and communal relationships. *Journal of Personality and Social Psychology, 37,* 12–24.

(1993). The difference between communal and exchange relationships: What it is and is not. *Personality and Social Psychology Bulletin, 6,* 684–691.

(2012). A theory of communal (and exchange) relationships. In P. A. M. Van Lange, A. W. Kruglanski, & E. T. Higgins (Eds.), *Handbook of theories of social psychology,* Vol. 2 (pp. 232–250). Thousand Oaks, CA: SAGE Publications.

Clark, M. S., Mills, J., & Corcoran, D. M. (1989). Keeping track of needs and inputs of friends and strangers. *Personality and Social Psychology Bulletin, 15,* 533–542.

Clark, M. S., Mills, J., & Powell, M. C. (1986). Keeping track of needs in communal and exchange relationships. *Journal of Personality and Social Psychology, 51,* 333–338.

Clark, M. S., Ouellette, R., Powell, M., & Milberg, S. (1987). Recipient's mood, relationship type, and helping. *Journal of Personality and Social Psychology, 52,* 94–103.

Clark, M. S., & Waddell, B. (1985). Perceptions of exploitation in communal and exchange relationships. *Journal of Personal and Social Relationships, 2,* 403–418.

Coan, J. A., Beckes, L., & Allen, J. P. (2013). Childhood maternal support and social capital moderate the regulatory impact of social relationships in adulthood. *International Journal of Psychophysiology, 88,* 224–231.

Collins, N. (1996). Working models of attachment: Implications for explanation, emotion, and behavior. *Journal of Personality and Social Psychology, 71,* 810–832.

Collins, N. L., & Allard, L. M. (2001). Cognitive representations of attachment: The content and function of working models. In G. J. O. Fletcher & M. S. Clark (Eds.), *Blackwell handbook of social psychology: Interpersonal processes* (pp. 60–85). Oxford: Blackwell.

Collins, N. L., & Feeney, B. C. (2004). Working models of attachment shape perceptions of social support: Evidence from experimental and observational studies. *Journal of Personality and Social Psychology, 87*(3), 363–383.

Conner, O. L., Siegle, G. J., McFarland, A. M., Silk, J. S., Ladouceur, C. D., Dahl, R. E., et al. (2012). *Mom – It helps when you're right here! Attenuation of neural stress markers in anxious youths whose caregivers are present during fMRI. PloS ONE, 7*(12), e50680. doi: 10.1371/journal.pone.0050680.

Cox, C. L., Wexler, M. O., Rusbult, C. E., & Gaines, S. O. (1997). Prescriptive support and commitment processes in close relationships. *Social Psychology Quarterly, 60,* 79–90.

Downey, G., & Feldman, S. I. (1996). Implications of rejection sensitivity for intimate relationships. *Journal of Personality and Social Psychology, 70,* 1327–1341.

Drigotas, S. M., Rusbult, C. E., Wieselquist, J., & Whitton, S. W. (1999). Close partner as sculptor of the ideal self: Behavioral affirmation and the Michelangelo phenomenon. *Journal of Personality and Social Psychology, 77*(2), 293–323.

Dutton, D. G., & Aron, A. P. (1974). Some evidence for heightened sexual attraction under conditions of high anxiety. *Journal of Personality and Social Psychology, 30,* 510–517.

Eden, J. L., Larkin, K. T., & Abel, J. L. (1992). The effect of social support and physical touch on cardiovascular reactions to mental stress. *Journal of Psychosomatic Research, 36*, 371–382.

Eibach, R. P., Libby, L. K., & Gilovich, T. D. (2003). When change in the self is mistaken for change in the world. *Journal of Personality and Social Psychology, 84*, 917–931.

El-Sheikh, M., Kelly, R. J., Koss, K. J., & Rauer, A. J. (2015). Longitudinal relations between constructive and destructive conflict and couples' sleep. *Journal of Family Psychology, 29*, 349–359.

Feeney, B. (2004). A secure base: Responsive support of goal strivings and exploration in adult intimate relationship. *Journal of Personality and Social Psychology, 87*, 631–648.

Feinberg, M., Willer, R., & Keltner, D. (2012). Flustered and faithful: Embarrassment as a signal of prosociality. *Journal of Personality and Social Psychology, 102*(1), 81–97.

Fessler, D. M. T., Holbrook, C., Pollack, J. S., & Hahn-Holbrook, J. (2014). Stranger danger: Parenthood increases the envisioned bodily formidability of menacing men. *Evolution and Human Behavior, 35*, 109–117.

Fincham, F. D. (2001). Attributions in close relationships: From Balkanization to integration. In G. J. O. Fletcher & M. S. Clark (Eds.), *Blackwell handbook of social psychology: Interpersonal processes* (pp. 3–31). Oxford: Blackwell.

Gable, S. L., Reis, H. T., Impett, E. A., & Asher, E. R. (2004). What do you do when things go right? The intrapersonal and interpersonal benefits to sharing positive events. *Journal of Personality and Social Psychology, 87*, 228–245.

Graham, S. M., & Clark, M. S. (2006). The Jekyll-and-Hyde-ing of relationship partners. *Journal of Personality and Social Psychology, 90*, 652–665.

(2007). Segregating positive and negative thoughts about partners: Implications for context dependence and stability of partner views. *Current Research in Social Psychology, 12*, 124–133.

Graham, S. M., Huang, J. Y., Clark, M. S., & Helgeson, V. H. (2008). The positives of negative emotions: Willingness to express negative emotions promotes relationships. *Personality and Social Psychology Bulletin, 34*, 394–406.

Grote, N. K., & Clark, M. S. (1998). Distributive justice norms and family work: What is perceived as ideal, what is applied and what predicts perceived fairness? *Social Justice Research, 11*, 243–269.

(2001). Perceiving unfairness in the family: Cause or consequence of marital distress? *Journal of Personality and Social Psychology, 80*, 281–293.

Hazan, C., & Shaver, P. (1987). Romantic love conceptualized as an attachment process. *Journal of Personality and Social Psychology, 52*, 511–524.

Helgeson, V. S., & Fritz, H. L. (1998). A theory of unmitigated communion. *Personality and Social Psychology Review, 2*, 173–183.

Holmes, J. G. (2002). Interpersonal expectations as the building blocks of social cognition: An interdependence theory perspective. *Personal Relationships, 9*, 1–26.

Holmes, J. G., & Rempel, J. K. (1989). Trust in close relationships. In C. Hendrick (Ed.), *Close relationships: A sourcebook* (pp. 187–220). Thousand Oaks, CA: Sage.

Holt-Lunstad, J., Smith, T. B., & Layton, J. B. (2010). Social relationships and mortality risk: A meta-analytic review. *PLoS: Medicine*, *7*(7), e1000316.

Jakubiak, B. K., & Feeney, B. C. (2016a). Daily goal progress is facilitated by spousal support and promotes psychological, physical, and relational well-being throughout adulthood. *Journal of Personality and Social Psychology*, *111*(3), 317–340.

(2016b). Keep in touch: The effects of imagined touch support on stress and exploration. *Journal of Experimental Social Psychology*, *65*, 59–67.

Kamarck, T. W., Manuck, S. B., & Jennings, J. R. (1990). Social support reduces cardiovascular reactivity to psychological challenge: A laboratory model. *Psychosomatic Medicine*, *52*, 42–58.

Kirkpatrick, L. A., & Davis, K. E. (1994). Attachment style, gender, and relationship stability. *Journal of Personality and Social Psychology*, *66*, 502–512.

Lambert, N. M., Clark, M. S., Durtschi, J., Fincham, F. D., & Graham, S. M. (2010). Benefits of expressing gratitude: Expressing gratitude to a partner changes one's view of the relationship. *Psychological Science*, *21*(4), 574–580.

Le, B. M., & Impett, E. A. (2015). The rewards of caregiving for communally motivated parents. *Social Psychological and Personality Science*, *6*, 458–765.

Le, B. M., Impett, E. A., Lemay, E. P., Muise, A., & Tskhay, K. O. (2018). Communal motivation and well-being in interpersonal relationships: An integrative review and meta-analysis. *Psychological Bulletin*, *144*, 1–25.

Leary, M. R., & Baumeister, R. F. (2000). The nature and function of self-esteem: Sociometer theory. In M. P. Zanna (Ed.), *Advances in experimental social psychology*, Vol. 32 (pp. 1–62). San Diego, CA: Academic Press.

Leary, M. R., Haupt, A. L., Strausser, K., & Chokel, J. T. (1998). Calibrating the sociometer: The relationship between interpersonal appraisals and the state of self-esteem. *Journal of Personality and Social Psychology*, *74*, 1290–1299.

Lehmiller, J. J., & Agnew, C. R. (2006). Marginalized relationships: The impact of social disapproval on romantic relationship commitment. *Personality and Social Psychology Bulletin*, *32*, 40–51.

Lemay, E. P. (2016). The forecast model of relationship commitment. *Journal of Personality and Social Psychology*, *111*, 34–52.

Lemay, E. P., & Clark, M. S. (2015). Motivated cognition in relationships. *Current Opinion in Psychology*, *1*, 72–75.

Lemay, E. P., & Dudley, K. L. (2009). Implications of reflected appraisals of interpersonal insecurity for suspicion and power. *Personality and Social Psychology Bulletin*, *35*, 1672–1686.

Lemay, E. P., & Melville, M. C. (2014). Diminishing self-disclosure to maintain security in partners' care. *Journal of Personality and Social Psychology*, *106*, 37–57.

Lemay, E. P., & Neal, A. M. (2014). Accurate and biased perceptions of responsive support predict well-being. *Motivation and Emotion*, *38*, 270–286.

(2013). The wishful memory of interpersonal responsivenss. *Journal of Personality and Social Psychology*, *104*, 653–672.

Lemay, E. P., & Clark, M. S. (2008). How the head liberates the heart: Projection of communal responsiveness guides relationship promotion. *Journal of Personality and Social Psychology, 94*, 647–671.

Lemay, E. P., Clark, M. S., & Feeney, B. C. (2007). Projection of responsiveness to needs and the construction of satisfying communal relationships. *Journal of Personality and Social Psychology, 92*, 834–853.

Lemay, E. P., Overall, N. C., & Clark, M. S. (2012). Experiences and interpersonal consequences of hurt feelings and anger. *Journal of Personality and Social Psychology, 103*, 982–1006.

Lougheed, J. P., Koval, P., & Hollenstein, T. (2016). Sharing the burden: The interpersonal regulation of emotional arousal in mother-daughter dyads. *Emotion, 16*, 83–93.

MacGregor, J. C., Fitzsimons, G. M., & Holmes, J. G. (2013). Perceiving low self-esteem in close others impedes capitalization and undermines the relationship. *Personal Relationships, 20*(4), 690–705.

MacGregor, J. C. D., & Holmes, J. G. (2011). Rain on my parade: Perceiving low self-esteem in close others hinders positive self-disclosure. *Social and Personality Science, 2*, 523–530.

McCoy, K., Cummings, E. M., & Davies, P. T. (2009). Constructive and destructive marital conflict, emotional security and children's prosocial behavior. *Journal of Child Psychology and Psychiatry, 50*(3), 270–279.

McNulty, J. K. (2010a). When positive processes hurt relationships. *Current Directions in Psychological Science, 19*, 167–171.

(2010b). Forgiveness increases the likelihood of subsequent partner transgressions in marriage. *Journal of Family Psychology, 24*, 787–790.

McNulty, J. K., & Russell, V. M. (2016). Forgive and forget, or forgive and regret? Whether forgiveness leads to less or more offending depends on offender agreeableness. *Personality and Social Psychology Bulletin, 42*, 616–631.

Mikulincer, M., & Shaver, P. R. (2013). The role of attachment security in adolescent and adult close. In J. A. Simpson & L. Campbell (Eds.), *The Oxford handbook of close relationships* (pp. 66–89). New York: Oxford University Press.

Mikulincer, M., Shaver, P. R., Gillath, O., & Nitzberg, R. A. (2005). Attachment, caregiving, and altruism: Boosting attachment security increases compassion and helping. *Journal of Personality and Social Psychology, 89*, 817–839.

Mills, J., & Clark, M. S. (1982). Communal and exchange relationships. In L. Wheeler (Ed.), *Review of personality and social psychology*, Vol. 3 (pp. 121–144). Beverly Hills, CA: Sage.

Mills, J., Clark, M. S., Ford, T. E., & Johnson, M. (2004). Measurement of communal strength. *Personal Relationships, 11*, 213–230.

Monin, J., Clark, M. S., & Lemay, E. P. (2008). Expecting more responsiveness from and feeling more responsiveness toward female than to male family members. *Sex Roles, 59*, 176–188.

Monin, J. K., Matire, L. M., Schulz, R., & Clark, M. S. (2009). Willingness to express emotions to caregiving spouses. *Emotion, 9*(1), 101–106.

Monin, J. K., Poulin, M. J., Brown, S. L., & Langa, K. M. (2017). Spouses' daily feelings of appreciation and self-reported well-being. *Health Psychology*, *36*(12), 1135.

Murray, S. L., Bellavia, G. M., Rose, P., & Griffin, D. W. (2003). Once hurt, twice hurtful: how perceived regard regulates daily marital interactions. *Journal of Personality and Social Psychology*, *84*(1), 126–147.

Murray, S. L. & Holmes, J. G. (2017). *Motivated cognition in relationships: The pursuit of belonging*. New York: Routledge/Taylor & Francis Group.

    (1993). Seeing virtues in faults: Negativity and the transformation of interpersonal narratives in close relationships. *Journal of Personality and Social Psychology*, *65*, 707–722.

    (1999). The (mental) ties that bind: Cognitive structures that predict relationship resilience. *Journal of Personality and Social Psychology*, *65*, 707–722.

Murray, S. L., Holmes, J. G., & Griffin, D. W. (2000). Self-esteem and the quest for felt-security: How perceived regard regulates attachment processes. *Journal of Personality and Social Psychology*, *78*, 478–498.

Murray, S. L., Holmes, J. G., MacDonald, G., & Ellsworth, P. (1998). Through the looking glass darkly? When self-doubts turn into relationship insecurities. *Journal of Personality and Social Psychology*, *75*, 1459–1480.

Pataki, S. P., Fathelbab, S., Clark, M. S., & Malinowski, C. H. (2013). Communal strength norms in the United States and Egypt. *Interpersona: An International Journal on Personal Relationships*, *7*, 77–87.

Perunovic, M., & Holmes, J. G. (2008). Automatic accommodation: The role of personality. *Personal Relationships*, *15*, 57–70.

Reis, H. T., & Clark, M. S. (2014). Responsiveness. In J. Simpson & L. Campbell (Eds.), *Handbook of close relationships* (pp. 400–423). Oxford, UK: Oxford University Press.

Reis, H. T., Clark, M. S., & Holmes, J. G. (2004). Perceived partner responsiveness as an organizing construct in the study of intimacy and closeness. In D. J. Mashek & P. Aron (Eds.), *Handbook of closeness and intimacy* (pp. 201–225). Mahwah, NJ: Lawrence Erlbaum.

Reis, H. T., Maniaci, M. R., & Rogge, R. D. (2017). Compassionate acts and everyday emotional well-being in newly-weds. *Emotion*, *17*, 751–763.

Reis, H. T., O'Keefe, S. D., & Lane, R. D. (2017). Fun is more fun when others are involved. *The Journal of Positive Psychology*, *12*(6), 547–557.

Reis, H. T., & Patrick, B. C. (1996). Attachment and intimacy: Component processes. In E. T. Higgins & A. W. Kruglanski (Eds.), *Social psychology: Handbook of basic principles* (pp. 523–563). New York: Guilford Press.

Reis, H. T., & Shaver, P. (1988). Intimacy as an interpersonal process. In S. Duck (Ed.), *Handbook of personal relationships: Theory, relationships, and interventions* (pp. 367–389). Chichester, UK: Wiley.

Rhatigan, D. L., & Axsom, K. K. (2006). Using the investment model to understand battered women's commitment to abusive relationships. *Journal of Family Violence*, *21*, 153–162.

Rusbult, C. E., & Buunk, B. P. (1993). Commitment processes in close relationships: An interdependence analysis. *Journal of Social and Personal Relationships, 10*(2), 175–204.

Rusbult, C. E., Finkel, E. J., & Kumashiro, M. (2009). The Michelangelo phenomenon. *Current Directions in Psychological Science, 18*, 305–309.

Rusbult, C. E., & Martz, J. M. (1995). Remaining in an abusive relationship: An investment model analysis of nonvoluntary commitment. *Personality and Social Psychology Bulletin, 21*, 558–571.

Rusbult, C. E., Van Lange, P. A. M., Wildschut, T., Yovetich, N. A., & Verette, J. (2000). Perceived superiority in close relationships: Why it exists and persists. *Journal of Personality and Social Psychology, 79*, 521–545.

Rusbult, C. E., Verette, J., Whitney, G. A., Slovik, L. R., & Lipkus, I. (1991). Accommodation processes in close relationships: Theory and preliminary empirical evidence. *Journal of Personality and Social Psychology, 60*, 53–78.

Schnall, S., Harber, K. D., Stefanucci, J. K., & Proffitt, D. R. (2008). Social support and the perception of geographical slant. *Journal of Experimental Social Psychology, 44*(5), 1246–1255.

Semin, G. R., & Manstead, A. S. (1982). The social implications of embarrassment displays and restitution behaviour. *European Journal of Social Psychology, 12*(4), 367–377.

Shaver, P., Hazan, C., & Bradshaw, D. (1988). Love as attachment. In R. J. Sternberg & M. L. Barnes (Eds.), *The psychology of love* (pp. 68–99). New Haven, CT.: Yale University Press.

Simpson, J. A., Rholes, W. S., & Nelligan, J. S. (1992). Support seeking and support giving within couples in an anxiety-provoking situation: The role of attachment styles. *Journal of Personality and Social Psychology, 62*, 434–446.

Van Tongeren, D. R., Green, J. D., Hook, J. N., Davis, D. E., Davis, J. L., & Ramos, M. (2015). Forgiveness increases meaning in life. *Social Psychological and Personality Science, 6*(1), 47–55.

Venaglia, R. B., & Lemay, E. P. (2017). Hedonic benefits of close and distant interaction partners: The mediating roles of social approval and authenticity. *Personality and Social Psychology Bulletin, 43*(9), 1255–1267.

Von Culin, K., Hirsch, J., & Clark, M. S. (2017). Willingness to express emotion depends upon perceiving partner care. *Cognition and Emotion, 32(3)*, 641–650.

Walster, E., Walster, G. W., & Berscheid, E. (1978). *Equity: Theory and research.* Boston: Allyn and Bacon.

Weidmann, R., Schonbrodt, F. D., Ledermann, T., & Grob, A. (2017). Concurrent and longitudinal dyadic polynomial regression analyses of Big Five traits and relationship satisfaction: Does similarity matter? *Journal of Research in Personality, 70*, 6–15.

Wieselquist, J., Rusbult, C. E., Foster, C. A., & Agnew, C. R. (1999). Commitment, pro-relationship behavior, and trust in close relationships. *Journal of Personality and Social Psychology, 77*, 942–966.

Williams, L. A., & Bartlett, M. Y. (2015). Warm thanks: Gratitude expression facilitates social affiliation in new relationships via perceived warmth. *Emotion, 15*, 1–5.

Williamson, G., & Clark, M. S. (1989). Providing help and desired relationship type as determinants of changes in moods and self-evaluations. *Journal of Personality and Social Psychology, 56*, 722–734.

Wortman, J. (2005). Mood and perceptions of siblings among those high and low in self-esteem. Senior honors thesis, Carnegie Mellon University, Pittsburgh, PA.

CHAPTER 6

Love Is Political: How Power and Bias Influence Our Intimate Lives

Terri D. Conley, Staci Gusakova, and Jennifer L. Piemonte

Love[1] is political. Not political in the sense of governments or elections – though we would argue that such institutions do regulate love – but in a broader sense. In her book, *Sexual Politics*, Kate Millett (1970) used the term "politics" to refer to the ways in which people jockey for power within groups. We borrow this approach as we address the issue of love. Love politics, we argue, refers to the ways in which love can be used to manipulate power dynamics in relationships, the ways in which love processes may reflect societal inequalities, and how loving relationships are often embedded in larger social structures. By deeming love political, we mean to suggest that love is a power-laden dynamic and the social structures that we inhabit influence how power unfolds in loving contexts. Some groups have (presently and historically) more power in society than others. When members of groups with different social statuses interact in loving relationships, power differences manifest themselves, making the process of loving others more complex and challenging. We suggest that being aware of this power dynamic could lead to smoother sailing as we navigate our relationships. In this chapter, we will consider how a variety of social positions (i.e. one's status as a member of a particular gender or racial/ethnic group, sexual orientation, body-type category, relationship status, etc.) can shape the experience of love, sex and relationships.

Most people assume (sensibly) that when they tumble into a loving relationship, they are there of their own volition – they alone are making decisions about their dyad. We take a different approach. We suggest that people are in the company of countless thousands of others who have

---

[1] In this chapter, we will use the term "love" broadly to refer to sexual/romantic relationships and the institutions that support them, inter alia dating, marriage, commitment, and so on, although we acknowledge that certain incarnations of love may not occur in each of these relationships. We also will focus on romantic love, although we believe that love politics infuses friendships and family relationships as well.

shaped their expectations of their partners and their beliefs about how to love and what love is supposed to be. In this way, love, far from the private endeavor most of us think of it as, has a distinctly communal and civic flavor.

In this chapter, we examine five politicized aspects of love, sex, and relationships. First, we address the politics of falling in love – are our attractions to others based on innate motivations or are they swayed by the larger social context in which we live? Second, we address the politics of finding true love – what are the contexts in which we determine our beliefs about whether "the one" is out there? Third, we address the politics of keeping love alive, and more specifically, the notion that love *should* be kept alive. Fourth, we address the politics of making love. How do our social contexts determine how we interact with partners sexually? And finally, we address politics in researching love – how our deeply entrenched beliefs about love affect scientists' approach to the topic.

Politics of Falling in Love

Within social psychology, *attraction* – one of the major determinants of whom we fall in love with – is understood as the proportion of positive feelings in the total array of positive and negative feelings aroused within someone by an individual (Byrne, 1971). Despite the subjective nature of attraction, it is common for people to consider their experiences of feeling attraction as quite immutable and inherent. The belief that people have a "type" of physical appearance to which they are primarily or solely attracted is a comforting notion: It can be a component of our self-schemas (Fiore & Donath, 2005), and it corroborates psychological research that emphasizes the utility of heuristics (e.g. categories and labels) in judgment and decision making (Campbell, 2015).

Much of the psychological research on interpersonal attraction focuses on individual factors, such as personality traits, and dyadic dynamics, such as complementarity. However, such an approach precludes discussion of how macro factors, such as societal structures and institutionalized hierarchies, influence attraction and romantic love. We wish to consider the ways that sociopolitical systems also impact desire, dating, and ultimately the phenomenon we know as love.

Psychologists have studied myriad factors that lead to interpersonal attraction, all rooted in social reinforcement, or the notion that an individual's positive and negative interactions with others constitute the individual's propensity to pursue or avoid further interactions. Essentially, people are drawn to those with whom they have good experiences and to relationships that are rewarding. Social reinforcement principles include the mere exposure effect (the more we are exposed to someone, the more we like them; Zajonc, 1968), the matching hypothesis (we partner with those with whom we are equally matched in social attributes, such as wealth; Walster, Aronson, & Abrahams, 1966), and the similarity-attraction effect (perceived familiarity is comforting and comfort is alluring; Bryne, 1961). These concepts are a psychologist's way of describing the common patterns of romantic relationship development: People experience attraction toward, interest in, and love for those to whom they are regularly exposed, and with whom they regularly interact.

But what determines how frequently we are exposed to various people? How does societal organization (e.g. segregation) influence our ability to regularly interact with a variety of others? How much of what goes into a person's attractiveness is determined by sociocultural factors beyond the interpersonal dynamic? In fact, the sociopolitical institutions that structure a given culture or community also structure the loving relationships between inhabitants.

Politics of Attraction

Imagine swiping through the profiles in a mobile-dating application, and coming across the following soundbites: "Must love dogs," "Looking for Mr. Right," and "No Asians, no blacks." One of these should stand out as markedly different. When the criteria for our romantic and/or sexual partners includes absolute prohibitions of groups of people based on physical characteristics or racial/ethnicity group, are those merely preferences, or a symbol of something larger and systemic?

In an exemplary manifestation of "the personal is political," something as individual and personal as one's intimate desires and attractions are indeed connected to a broader political system that ranks people according to various physical dimensions such as skin color, body size, or ability. And these physical dimensions are not arbitrary; rather, they are part and parcel of systems of oppression and power that maintain a system whereby dominant group characteristics are favored and valued over groups with less power or status. Therefore, people's "types" (i.e. those for whom they lust and love) are not organically spawned in a sociopolitical vacuum, but rather are produced by social hierarchies of race, gender, sexuality, and other identities (e.g. disability, body type; Koski, Xie, & Olson, 2015).

Popular theories about love and attraction that go beyond the individual or dyadic level tend to jump all the way to universality, claiming that there are objective standards of beauty and attractiveness (e.g. facial symmetry, waste-to-hip ratio) that are anchored in the evolutionary drive to reproduce (Paris, 2017). However, empirical evidence suggests that cultural or learned factors are stronger influences on preferences than facial symmetry or waist-to-hip ratio (Germine et al., 2015). For example, different ethnicities within the same society report different preferences for female body types (Flynn & Fitzgibbon, 1998). Thus, what is desirable in a given sociocultural context becomes distilled by evolutionary psychologists into mate preferences held by individual members of that society. Even more specifically, what is acceptable, tolerated, or prohibited by an individual's immediate environment (e.g. family, religious community) regulates that individual's preferences regarding the identity of their mate.

Once we are willing to acknowledge the ways our attractions are environmentally shaped, the evidence becomes ubiquitous and omnipresent. For example, gender roles (e.g. masculinity, femininity), pathologized bodies (e.g. fat, disabled), and even stereotypes about hair color (e.g. "dumb blonde") are all aspects of culture that inform understandings of people based on the bodies they inhabit. The transmission of common beliefs across a community or culture is what makes those ideologies a social system, rife with politics about who has access to resources, social capital, and status.

Social norms dictate which bodies and appearances are, and are not, considered attractive, advantageous to a partner's status, and worthy of love. Those that fall into the "not" category are marginalized, fetishized, and expected to be grateful for any attention they receive. Racism in particular is blatantly codified in standards of beauty and desirability (Zota & Shamasunder, 2017). The pressure for women of color to engage in skin bleaching and chemical hair straightening potently demonstrates cultural preferences for European white features, which are consequently privileged by individuals in their personal attractions, as well.

Strong resistance is the common knee-jerk reaction to the idea that our desires are not, in fact, innate and static drives rooted deep within our loins. Many people feel that such a unique and personal phenomenon as our intimate attractions should be protected from critique (Callander, Newman, & Holt, 2015). This apprehension is understandable; it is difficult and uncomfortable to acknowledge the ways in which we have been unwittingly shaped by external influences, even against our conscious sensibilities. In other words, a White woman who prides herself on her progressive, antiracist values may be upset by and resistant to the idea that her desire for a White relationship partner is not, in fact, a predetermined trait, but something she absorbed from her personal and cultural surroundings. To acknowledge this risks acknowledging the ways in which our relationships have been culturally determined, as well as the potential for change in our desires.

Yet research consistently demonstrates that individual-level cognitive and physiological phenomena, such as attitudes, beliefs, or arousal, are all malleable processes and subject to shaping by environmental factors (e.g. the mere exposure effect or sexual imprinting; Irwin & Price, 1999; Moreland & Zajonc, 1982). Furthermore, it does not take extensive reflection to realize the strength of the impact of cultural messaging about beauty, sexuality, and human value on the intimate sphere. Our collective unwillingness to interrogate sources of influence on our intimate preferences demonstrates the strength of the narrative that personal tastes are not up for debate and must be respected as an individual's prerogative (Callander, Holt, & Newman, 2015). We encourage reflection on the sources and implications of even such intimate touchstones as our sexual desires or, as we will discuss in the next section, our romantic relationships.

Politics of True Love

According to one poll, two-thirds of Americans believe in soul mates (Monmouth University Poll, 2017). But does "the one" exist? With plenty of fish in the sea, can we ever be certain that we have truly found "the one" when we are constantly faced with hundreds of choices and an ever-increasing list of personal demands? With countless books, pop-press articles, and psychological research, the cultural and scientific preoccupation with finding and sustaining "true love" is not going to diminish any time soon. In this section, we argue that people's obsession with true love rests in our society's orientation toward monogamy as the ideal relationship configuration.

In the United States, there is a deeply entrenched idea that monogamy *should* be the norm. The idea of true love likely takes hold in childhood: The fairy tales our parents read to us and the Disney movies we watched (e.g. *Cinderella*; *Snow White and the Seven Dwarves*) often told stories about a princess waiting for her Prince Charming, suggesting that "the one" is out there. In our adulthood, many of us watch romantic comedies and read romance novels that have us dreaming about finding our ideal relationship. As we peruse the Internet, we find articles telling us what qualities we should look for in a potential partner to make sure we find the perfect match. Computer algorithms have even been invented via dating websites that promise to help users meet "the one," despite evidence that these algorithms do not work (Finkel, Eastwick, Karney, Reis, & Sprecher, 2012).

Clearly, we are oversaturated with messages regarding true love. This obsession with true love seems like a clear-cut application of social learning theory – people imitate what they observe in real life and in the media, which is searching and finding our soul mate. Unfortunately, finding your one true love is not always as easy as logging into your online dating account and waiting for a computer algorithm to match you up with your soul mate; Instead, there are obstacles people must navigate depending on the social identities which they hold.

First Comes Love, Then Comes Marriage

In the prototypical loving relationship, most people follow a relationship script in which the ultimate goal is to get married to signal your love for one another. However, marriage has been, and continues to be, a heavily regulated institution, which only recognizes certain forms of love. Interracial marriage was outlawed in the United States until 1967. Until 2015, same-sex marriage was illegal in most of the United States, suggesting that true love should only recognized between heterosexual couples. The Supreme Court decision remains contentious to this day, leaving the state of same-sex love in a precarious position and the people in same-sex marriages stigmatized. Moreover, the United States continues to outlaw marriage between more than two people, suggesting that true romantic love cannot and should not exist between people who are consensually non-monogamous (i.e. people mutually agree to have other romantic or sexual relationships; Conley, Moors, Matsick, Ziegler, & Valentine, 2011). In these ways, it seems obvious that monogamy is politically mandated, such that only some people are qualified to be beneficiaries of societal and governmental sanctions and others who fail to love a certain way are victims of structural inequality and stigma.

At this point, you may be wondering: So what? What harm comes from wishful thinking about finding your soul mate and why does it matter if the government only recognizes and promotes love between certain people? To illustrate the repercussions of idealizing true love, we turn to research that illustrates how viewing monogamy as the ideal can have negative consequences for both monogamous and consensually non-monogamous (CNM) people.

In monogamous relationships, viewing your partner as a "soul mate" can have negative effects on relationship satisfaction when conflicts are salient. In one experiment, people were primed to think of their relationship as a perfect match (a love-as-unity-framework) or to think of their relationship as something that must be worked on (a love-as-journey framework) (Lee & Schwarz, 2014). When participants thought about relational conflicts, they reported lower relationship satisfaction in the unity, compared to the journey, prime. In other words, people are willing to compromise potentially rewarding relationships just because they believe in soul mates. Although thinking that someone is your perfect match is romantic, it might not be the ideal relationship approach once conflict (inevitably) emerges. This is especially problematic when people live in a society that is obsessed with soul mates and considers monogamy to be the ideal. If someone in search of a soul mate consistently breaks up with their partner, how many potentially rewarding relationships are they leaving behind? Moreover, people's beliefs about love may not always be autonomous; instead, people's "own" ideals about a partner are governed by societal standards of what they should look for in a romantic partnership. This could result in people internalizing society's beliefs that love is supposed to be perfect or that we can only find true love with specific types of people, as we addressed in the "Politics of Falling in Love" section. Partners who do not meet society's standards are, thus, not viewed as soul-mate material.

Another reason why wishful thinking about soul mates is potentially problematic is that research on marriage trends in the United States suggests that people are increasingly looking to their partners for not only economic needs, but for companionate and self-expressive needs as well (Finkel, Cheung, Emery, Carswell, & Larson, 2015; Finkel, Hui, Carswell, & Larsen, 2014). Specifically, married people, and we would argue relationships in general, are looking to their partners to meet their self-esteem, self-expressive, and personal growth needs. Finkel and colleagues suggest that as the United States moves toward a self-expressive era, people are struggling to meet their partners' increasing needs. Overall, greater reliance on a single person to meet all your needs seems to have become the norm. This can be difficult when one person stops fulfilling all of your needs and conflict in the relationship arises, but your only option is to stay with the person unhappily or dissolve the relationship entirely because society tells you that you should be monogamous.

For people in CNM relationships, the political standpoint that monogamy is the ideal and that there is only *one* true love out there can be detrimental to CNM relationships. The general perception of CNM relationships is that they are of lower quality than monogamous relationships, with the perception that CNM people experience greater jealousy, lower trust in their partners, lower relationship satisfaction, and low sexual satisfaction – this is despite research pointing to evidence to the contrary (Conley, Matsick, Moors, & Ziegler, 2017; Conley, Piemonte, Gusakova, & Rubin, 2018). The research by Conley and colleagues suggests that the general public's perception of CNM people and of CNM relationships are unwarranted, instead providing evidence that people can flourish in different types of relationships. In addition, viewing monogamy as ideal has consequences for research conducted on CNM individuals, which we discuss in the "Politics in Researching Love" section.

In sum, we encourage skepticism regarding the idea of soul mates. People's belief that true love can only be found in a soul mate is likely a fabricated ideal that we internalize as a result of being socialized in a political world. In the next section, we investigate the challenges of keeping love alive.

Politics of Keeping Love Alive

Regardless of whether people believe in soul mates, the verdict remains clear: People want long-lasting relationships. One poll demonstrated that 86% of people believe that once they find the person who they will marry, they will stay together until the day they die (Clark University Poll, 2012). Lifetime partners are assumed to provide many benefits to relationships, including relationship stability, economic stability, personal growth, and freedom from STDs (Ley, 2009). In this section, we argue that the pressure for keeping love alive is a result of political and societal forces, which create an undue burden on relationships.

It seems that almost everywhere we look we are continually bombarded with information on how to keep love alive. As discussed in the previous section, because many people are relying on their marriages to fulfill most, if not all, of their needs, most of the marriages and relationships today are under constant strain to perform up to societal expectations of a happy couple (Finkel et al., 2014; Finkel et al., 2015). Rather than acknowledging that it is okay for bad relationships to end, both the relationship science literature and societal relationship scripts urge couples to work things out.

Working at (Not Falling Out of) Love

Although we agree it is important to put work into love and relationships, one question remains: Why do people feel compelled to persist at relationships when they fall out of love? One answer may lie in people's commitment to the Protestant work ethic (PWE). The PWE (Weber, [1904–05] 1958) suggests that people who hold a strong work ethic will be the ones who are rewarded. Typically, the PWE has been examined in work and unemployment research; however, the PWE can be examined in related areas, including love and relationship research. People are told that the key to a successful loving relationship is to keep on working at it even if they fall out of love with one another. If, and only if, people continually work at their relationships will they see a payoff. Unfortunately, living in a culture that endorses the PWE can make falling out of love especially difficult. Admitting you are not in love with your partner anymore may be interpreted as giving up and not being willing to work at your relationship. After putting in so much effort to sustain a relationship, people may feel helpless to end it – to do so would be giving up on years, if not decades, of labor (Rusbult, 1980).

A hard-work ethic pins the success of love and relationships directly on individuals themselves and fails to consider how societal forces determine whether relationships prosper or fail. It is a person's responsibility to work harder and harder at their relationships. However, research indicates that many factors outside a person's control predict if a relationship prospers, including stigma, education, and financial strain. Racial and ethnic discrimination has been shown to be a relationship stressor (Trail, Goff, Bradbury, & Karney, 2012). Women and men who are well educated typically have longer-lasting first marriages compared to their less-educated counterparts (Copen, Daniels, Vespa, & Mosher, 2012). Financial strain has also been linked to relationship dissatisfaction (Vinokur, Price, & Caplan, 1996). In these ways, it seems clear that the world is often working against people and their love toward one another – and yet, the pressure on people themselves to maintain their love is high.

The pressure to keep love alive can lead to the stigmatization of failed relationships, such as divorces (Konstam, Karwin, Curran, Lyons, & Celen-Demirtas, 2016; Thornton & Young-Demarco, 2001). In a series of interviews with divorced women in their twenties and thirties, several themes regarding stigma were prevalent throughout (Konstam et al., 2016). Women reported experiencing stigma from others because they were divorced. Women also felt as though they were failures because they could not make their relationship work. Some women never even disclosed that they were divorced due to feeling that they would be stigmatized. In essence, society's obsession with keeping love alive is not innocuous; rather, it has real-world repercussions, such that people who "give up" on their relationships are stigmatized. In society's eyes, divorced people have failed to live up to the expectations of the PWE.

Reconsidering Ideals: Falling Out of Love Can Be Good

In considering the broader context within which love and relationships are embedded, we must understand how scripts and norms in our cultures are prevalent. Maybe it is worth reconsidering the dominant discourse that relationship stability and longevity is good and ideal – that staying together is good and that breaking up is bad, that lifelong love is good and falling out of love is bad. Rather than lamenting a relationship gone awry, perhaps we should be celebrating a transition and recognizing that people who fall out of love and break up can go on to lead happy and fulfilling lives?

Love is not something that can be controlled, even if we toil endlessly. People can reevaluate their expectations of love from their partner and understand that if we ask too much of our partner and demand unconditional love, that they will often fall short of those expectations. Moreover, the expectation of one true love for eternity may not be realistic. Instead, we can fall in and out of love with many people, sometimes at the same time. Overall, we encourage people to develop good communication and problem-solving skills while acknowledging that the politics of love will continue to influence who and how we love.

Politics in Making Love

Most of us assume (sensibly) that when we jump into bed with a partner, the two of us are there alone. Unlike the dating process, which is often enacted in the public eye, or even deep committed relationships, which are typically embedded in relationships with other people (our parents, our children, our friends), our sexual relationships are generally just between two people, and those experiences are rarely communicated to others. However, we argue that even in these most intimate moments, we are affected by our society's rules about how people should behave and that power dynamics regulate these intimate experiences. McClelland (2010) has proposed an intimate-justice framework to understand how our larger sociopolitical environment may determine intimate details of our lives.

According to McClelland, "intimate injustice focuses our attention on how social and political inequities impact intimate experiences, affecting how individuals imagine, behave, and evaluate their intimate lives" (p. 672). McClelland considered intimate justice in the context measurement of sexual satisfaction. Here we use this framework to consider related dimensions of sexuality.

We can start by discussing bodies. Women have more negative thoughts about their bodies than men do (Sanchez & Kiefer, 2007). These thoughts did not idiosyncratically emerge in individual women's heads. Indeed, it would be difficult to overestimate the volume of messages – many direct and countless more indirect – that people (especially women) receive about their bodies throughout their lives – from the media, from parents, from peers and from potential relationship partners, as well. Women are led to believe that their bodies in their normal (e.g. not airbrushed) states are not good enough and hence would not be appealing to a partner. Think about body types that are represented in the media – we see far many more images of women than of men and the women represented tend to be of a very specific type (Grabe, Ward, & Hyde, 2008). Women have many more products marketed to them for the purpose of improving their appearance than men do. Women also receive much more feedback from people they know about their appearance than men do (Bailey & Ricciardelli, 2010). In sum, women live in a world in which their physical appearance is made a preoccupation, a matter of open debate, with unending advice about how it can be improved (see, e.g., Grabe, Ward, & Hyde, 2008, for a review; Fredrickson & Roberts, 1997; Rudd & Lennon, 2000).

This is an avenue through which love politics infiltrates our sexual encounters. Via the social control of appearance, politics can also influence how enthusiastic we are about making love and how much we enjoy making love. We now consider a few examples.

Politics and Desire

Let us first consider the politics of desire for sex. In general, people who feel negatively about their bodies report less sexual desire. (Hoyt & Kogan, 2001; Koch Mansfield, Thurau, & Carey, 2005). Given that women feel more poorly about their bodies than men do, this may translate into women having less sexual desire than men do. One group of researchers (Seal, Bradford & Meston, 2009) asked women about their body self-esteem (how positively they felt about their bodies) and their sexual desire. They found that women with more positive views of their bodies reported greater desire. Women in this study also watched erotica in the lab and reported their responses to these images. Women with more negative body esteem reported less physical response to erotica than women who had more positive perceptions of their bodies. Therefore, the messages that society sends us can end up influencing what we may think of as instinctual or hard wired – our sex drive. In other words, love politics affects our desire to make love.

Politics and Sexual Enjoyment

In a related vein, we can consider what actually happens in a given sexual encounter; we suggest that societal messages about attractiveness guide the ways people behave sexually – how people experience love making. Imagine two people involved in an encounter, one of whom is able to immerse fully in pleasurable sexual sensations, another who is preoccupied with the appearance of his or her body to the outside world. Researchers refer to this as spectatoring – thinking about how an outsider views you rather than attending to your sexual pleasure (Trapnell, Meston & Gorzalka, 1997). Who would you expect to have more sexual pleasure?

You likely predicted what researchers typically find. Spectatoring can really kill the buzz of a sexual encounter. Those who are thinking more about their bodies experience less sexual pleasure (Sanchez & Kiefer, 2007)

Not surprisingly, distracting thoughts about their bodies strike women more frequently than they do men (Meana & Nunnink, 2006). As a result, when women are involved in sexual encounters, they often are thinking not about the pleasurable sensations that they are experiencing. Instead, they are thinking about how they appear to their partner, wondering, for example, if their thighs spread out when they are lying flat in a way that is unappealing to their partners. In sum, sex is not something humans undertake as free agents. Social and cultural dynamics envelop our sexual selves.

Politics in How We Make Love

The anonymous people inhabiting our sexual encounters from the recesses of our mind also determine how we respond to our partners, that is, the choices we make about what to do in bed. In her book *Performing Sex*, Fahs (2011) documents how most women find themselves in a bind sexually. They are led to believe that society takes a liberated view of women's sexuality, but the only types of liberation that are deemed appropriate for women seem to be those that are known to be appealing to men. Thus, women receive the message that they are "liberated" if they dress in sexy clothing or make out with other women for an audience of men. Meanwhile, menstruating women, women with body hair and heavy women are considered disgusting (Basow & Braman, 1998; Hebl & Heatherton, 1998; Roberts, Goldenberg, Power, & Pyszczynski, 2002). Therefore, women's sexual liberation is highly constrained – women are given messages about who can be liberated and how they can express this liberation (Fahs, 2011).

Because allowable liberation is that which pleases men, the lines between performing sexually for others and enjoying sexuality for one's self become blurred for women. For example, *Girls Gone Wild* was a franchise that created videos of college-aged women stripping, kissing other women, and otherwise behaving in visually sexual ways (Levy, 2005; Rupp & Taylor, 2010). Whereas this series has been provided as evidence for the sexual empowerment of women (i.e. women are not being prudish and anti-sex in these videos), and the celebration of expressive sexuality, Fahs (2011) and others demonstrate that the types of activities the *Girls Gone Wild* series portrays are performances for audiences, specifically audiences of men. The message is confusing for women. Is it empowering to engage in a brand of sexuality that is geared toward the pleasure of other people?

Thus, a woman may technically be in bed with just her partner, but her choices of how to behave in that context are effectively micromanaged by society's representations of female sexuality. A woman may be asking herself – what activities make me most appealing to my partner? Women may try to enjoy sexuality for themselves, but find their own pleasure difficult to identify or navigate because so much of women's sexual expression is connected to pleasing a male audience. Thus, once again, our society is in bed with us as we make love. An intimate justice approach would entail locating sexual experiences in these larger political structures.

These thoughts about making love are not intended to put a damper on anyone's sex life. We suggest that it is worth pausing to think about how the social environment in which we are immersed could affect how we interface with sexuality. Perhaps by doing so we could expand whom we are able to love and the ways in which that love is enacted.

Politics in Researching Love

We have discussed many ways in which love itself is political, but we would like to end with a way in which love politics affects all of the authors in this book – as well as consumers of research about love. That is, researching love is also political. This circumstance is of relevance to consumers of research on love, because it might well affect the type of questions that people ask about love or the information that we receive.

Our experiences in researching love center around the topic of consensual non-monogamy. We find that consensually non-monogamous relationships are at least as happy and well-adjusted as monogamous relationships (e.g. Conley et al., 2017). These findings sometimes raise eyebrows, even among our peers in our field who are trained to be unbiased. In our early experiences of publishing these results, our peers who reviewed our work seemed unable to believe that people who love non-monogamously could be just as happy as those who love monogamously. We were told that our very writing was biased in favor of CNM. We often thought that our review experiences reflected a greater level of hostility than was typical in the review process. Sheff (2013), who studied children of polyamorous families, reported similar experiences: "The specific tone of the reviews and the recurrent nature of the negative feedback signal a deeper, institutionalized issue of sex negativity." Sheff continues by expressing that, although all researchers receive critiques about their research, "not every critique is so defensive and vitriolic in tone" (p. 127). Sheff's experiences resonated with us. When reporting that monogamy has drawbacks, researchers reviewing our paper seemed to have a personal investment in the results. However, is it possible that, instead, researchers who address CNM are just being overly sensitive? And that research demonstrating favorable outcomes for CNM really is written in a biased manner?

We conducted a little study to try to answer this question (Conley et al., 2017). We presented participants with one of two descriptions of fictional research – in one, the fictitious researchers found that monogamous relationships were higher quality than polyamorous relationships; in the other, the fictitious researchers found that polyamorous relationships are higher in quality than monogamous relationships. The only aspect of the two descriptions that differed was whether the researchers found that *monogamous* or, alternately, *polyamorous* people had more rewarding romantic relationships – all the other words were exactly the same across the two descriptions. Take a moment and consider what you think happened. Would researchers who report better outcomes for monogamy be perceived differently than those who report better outcomes for polyamory?

We suspect you intuited the results. The participants who received the passage in which polyamorous relationships were reported to be better thought that the researchers who conducted the study were more biased and generally worse scientists than the researchers associated with the study demonstrating monogamy's superiority.

This type of bias is probably prevalent in many research domains, but when we are discussing our closest relationships – the relationships with people we love – these biases are imbued with more meaning. If monogamy was something that you found challenging, but you sacrificed relationships with others because you really loved someone, you might prefer to be rewarded for your efforts by learning that this type of love really is worth it, despite the hardships you endured. Hearing that maybe all your loving efforts at maintaining monogamy were unnecessary – that you could have been happy *without* monogamy – may be jarring to some people.

We have had experiences with one type of love research – consensual non-monogamy. But there was a time when researchers were suspicious of the possibility that love between two women or two men could be as fulfilling as that between a woman and a man – to the extent that lesbians and gay men were considered mentally ill. Hooker (1957) conducted groundbreaking work demonstrating that clinicians could not distinguish between gay and heterosexual men based on results from a battery of psychological tests. Her work contradicted the prevailing view that lesbians and gay men were maladjusted; thus, although she took pains to be objective, the research had rather political outcomes.

Many of us have been inculcated with the idea that science is a fully objective endeavor and scientists have been lauded for their unbiased approach. But of late, the pendulum seems to have swung in the other direction. Our current political environment has drawn upon the sense that everyone with whom you disagree is inherently biased – if this is indeed true, one can feel free to ignore any scientific findings with which they disagree. To concede the point that scientists are biased and thus give up trying to understand the world would entail succumbing to nescience – which we don't believe is useful (and certainly isn't pragmatic). It is crucial to always seek objectivity and to do our very best to approximate it in every circumstance.

Yet those of us who are scientists recognize that, although we are, through our training, substantially more capable of recognizing our biases and avoiding them than the average person, we can never be entirely free from some partiality. But even though we won't necessarily be perfectly objective, we can try, and we do a pretty good job. What about the biases that seep in? Standpoint theory (Hartsock, 1983) addresses how scientists can never really be completely objective and that scientists emerging from distinct social and political contexts will have diverse viewpoints. For example, the way a student perceives a classroom environment will be different from the way that a faculty member construes the same context. Drawing on standpoint theory, Harding (1992) argues instead for strong objectivity – having multiple perspectives involved in our research inquiries, particularly from those who are in lower positions of power.

What does this mean about how you learn about love? It means that researchers may ask questions based on their own particular view of love, that when scientists study love they may be inclined to interpret findings in ways that are consistent with their world-views. It means that they may question a particular finding a little bit more – be a little more careful or cautious in reporting it – if it contradicts these beliefs. People who question any dominant love paradigm may be perceived more negatively than those who operate within that paradigm – and therefore researchers may have difficulty in telling a different story that departs from the dominant narrative, at least at first. These are all correctable problems, and indeed we believe they are usually corrected through the normal progression of science. As a specific antidote, drawing from Standpoint Theory, we advocate for the inclusion of people who love differently as researchers in love – and for people who love in different ways to involve themselves in research on these topics.

Conclusion

How can knowing that love is political inform your choices about love? You may want to know what good this information is to you as you navigate your own love life. We offer a few tentative suggestions.

First, it is crucial to be aware of how you fit into the larger social and political world that surrounds you. Each member of a relationship may want to consider how the larger social context in which they operate regulates their individual decisions about love. Think about your relationship choices. Why are you attracted to members of some ethnic groups but not others? Could prejudice play a role in forming your attractions? If so, how can you address this issue? Why do you want to be monogamous? Do you believe that you are a failure if a relationship dissolves? What are the social contexts that would promote this concern?

We can also think about power more explicitly. Do you belong to a group that has historically oppressed other groups? If so, then people may view you with a bit of trepidation. Rather than feel offended by their misgivings, you may want to attribute them to complicated social structures that we all have to slowly unlearn, and be a part of that unlearning process. People who belong to groups that have been hurt in the past may be wary, but this is about their position in society – not you as an individual. If you are dating someone who is a member of a group that has historically been in a higher power position, you may want to examine how that affects your behaviors in the relationship. Are your reservations about your partner's group membership severe enough that you have qualms about being in a relationship with him or her? You may also want to understand that being on guard may put your partner at ill-ease. Are there strategies that the two of you can employ to counter these external forces?

We are most obviously referencing gender here – men typically have had more power in contemporary societies than women have, but people who love across lines of race, class, nationality or other group differences will likely encounter similar problems. Try to take your partner's perspective and honestly share your own. Learn about how people in higher and lower positions of power operate and use that information to help interpret your own and your partner's behaviors.

Within our culture of late, we seem to be witnessing a dearth of understanding of one another. Partisanship and hatefulness have intensi-fied over the past few years (Bartlett, Reffin, Rumball, & Williamson, 2014; Druckman, Peterson, & Sluthuus, 2013). Perhaps one of the best ways to counter such incivility is to promote understanding in the relationships of those that we love.

References

Bailey, S. D., & Ricciardelli, L. A. (2010). Social comparisons, appearance related comments, contingent self-esteem and their relationships with body dis-satisfaction and eating disturbance among women. *Eating Behaviors, 11*(2), 107–112.

Bartlett, J., Reffin, J., Rumball, N., & Williamson, S. (2014). Anti social-media. Retrieved from www.demos.co.uk/files/DEMOS_Anti-social_Media.pdf.

Basow, S. A., & Braman, A. C. (1998). Women and body hair: Social perceptions and attitudes. *Psychology of Women Quarterly, 22*(4), 637–645.

Bryne, D. (1961). Interpersonal attraction and attitude similarity. *Journal of Abnormal and Social Psychology, 62*, 713–715.

  (1971). *The attraction paradigm.* New York: Academic Press.

Callander, D., Newman, C. E., & Holt, M. (2015). Is sexual racism really racism? Distinguishing attitudes toward sexual racism and generic racism among gay and bisexual men. *Archives of Sexual Behavior, 44*(7), 1991–2000.

Campbell, L. (2015, April 24). *Do your preferences for a romantic partner influence your actual choice of romantic partner?* Retrieved from www.scienceofrelationships.com/home/2015/4/24/do-your-preferences-for-a-romantic-partner-influence-your-ac.html.

Clark University Poll. (2012). Clark University Poll of emerging adults. Retrieved from www.clarku.edu/article/new-clark-poll-18-29-year-olds-are-traditional-about-roles-sex-marriage-and-raising-children

Conley, T. D., Matsick, J. L., Moors, A. C., & Ziegler, A. (2017). Investigation of consensually nonmonogamous relationships: Theories, methods, and new directions. *Perspectives on Psychological Science, 12*(2), 205–232.

Conley, T. D., Moors, A. C., Matsick, J. L., & Ziegler, A. (2013). The fewer the merrier? Assessing stigma surrounding consensually non-monogamous romantic relationships. *Analyses of Social Issues and Public Policy, 13*(1), 1–30.

Conley, T. D., Moors, A. C., Matsick, J. L., Ziegler, A., & Valentine, B. A. (2011). Women, men, and the bedroom: Methodological and conceptual insights that narrow, reframe, and eliminate gender differences in sexuality. *Current Directions in Psychological Science, 20*(5), 296–300.

Conley, T. D., Piemonte, J. L., Gusakova, S., & Rubin, J. D. (2018). Sexual satisfaction among individuals in monogamous and consensually non-monogamous relationships. *Journal of Social and Personal Relationships, 35*(4), 509–531.

Copen, C. E., Daniels, K., Vespa, J., & Mosher, W. D. (2012). First marriages in the United States: Data from the 2006–2010 national survey of family growth. *National Health Statistics Reports, 49*, 1–22.

Druckman, J. N., Peterson, E., & Slothuus, R. (2013). How elite partisan polarization affects public opinion formation. *American Political Science Review, 107*(1), 57–79.

Fahs, B. (2011). *Performing sex: The making and unmaking of women's erotic lives.* Albany, NY: State University of New York Press.

Faith, M. S., & Schare, M. L. (1993). The role of body image in sexually avoidant behavior. *Archives of Sexual Behavior, 22*(4), 345–356.

Fiore, A. T., & Donath, J. S., MIT Media Library. (2005). *Homophily in online dating: When do you like someone like yourself?* Portland: ACM Publications.

Finkel, E. J., Cheung, E. O., Emery, L. F., Carswell, K. L., & Larson, G. M. (2015). The suffocation model: Why marriage in America is becoming an all-or-nothing institution. *Current Directions in Psychological Science, 24*(3), 238–244.

Finkel, E. J., Eastwick, P. W., Karney, B. R., Reis, H. T., & Sprecher, S. (2012). Online dating: A critical analysis from the perspective of psychological science. *Psychological Science in the Public Interest, 13*(1), 3–66.

Finkel, E. J., Hui, C. M., Carswell, K. L., & Larson, G. M. (2014). The suffocation of marriage: Climbing Mount Maslow without enough oxygen. *Psychological Inquiry, 25*(1), 1–41.

Flynn, K. J., & Fitzgibbon, M. (1998). Body images and obesity risk among black females: A review of the literature. *Annals of Behavioral Medicine, 20*(1), 13–24.

Fredrickson, B. L., & Roberts, T. (1997). Objectification theory: Toward understanding women's lived experiences and mental health risks. *Psychology of Women Quarterly, 21*(2), 173–206.

Germine, L., Russell, R., Bronstad, P. M., Blokland, G. A. M., Smoller, J. W., Kwok, H., Anthony, S. E., Nakayama, K., Rhodes, G., & Wilmer, J. B. (2015). Individual aesthetic preferences for faces are mostly shaped by environments, not genes. *Current Biology, 25*(20), 2684–2689.

Grabe, S., Ward, L. M., & Hyde, J. S. (2008). The role of the media in body image concerns among women: A meta-analysis of experimental and correlational studies. *Psychological Bulletin, 134*(3), 460–476.

Harding, S. (1992). After the neutrality ideal: Science, politics, and "strong objectivity." *Social Research, 59*(3), 567–587.

Hartsock, N. (1983). The feminist standpoint: Developing the ground for a specifically feminist historical materialism. In S. Harding & M. Hintikka (Eds.), *Discovering reality: Feminist perspectives on epistemology, metaphysics, methodology, and philosophy of science* (pp. 283–310). Boston, MA: D. Reidel.

Hawkins, A. J., Amato, P. R., & Kinghorn, A. (2013). Are government-supported healthy marriage initiatives affecting family demographics? A state-level analysis. *Family Relations, 62*(3), 501–513.

Hebl, M. R., & Heatherton, T. F. (1998). The stigma of obesity in women: The difference is black and white. *Personality and Social Psychology Bulletin, 24*(4), 417–426.

Hooker, E. (1957). The adjustment of the male overt homosexual. *Journal of Projective Techniques, 21*(1), 18–31.

Hoyt, W. D., & Kogan, L. R. (2001). Satisfaction with body image and peer relationships for males and females in a college environment. *Sex Roles, 45*(3), 199–215.

Irwin, D. E., & Price, T. (1999). Sexual imprinting, learning, and speciation. *Heredity, 82*, 374–354.

Koch, P. B., Mansfield, P. K., Thurau, D., & Carey, M. (2005). "Feeling frumpy": The relationships between body image and sexual response changes in midlife women. *Journal of Sex Research, 42*(3), 215–223.

Konstam, V., Karwin, S., Curran, T., Lyons, M., & Celen-Demirtas, S. (2016). Stigma and divorce: A relevant lens for emerging and young adult women? *Journal of Divorce and Remarriage, 57*(3), 173–194.

Koski, J., Xie, H., & Olson, I. R. (2015). Understanding social hierarchies: The neural and psychological foundations of status perception. *Social Neuroscience, 10*(5), 527–550.

Lee, S. W., & Schwarz, N. (2014). Framing love: When it hurts to think we were made for each other. *Journal of Experimental Social Psychology, 54*, 61–67.

Levy, A. (2005) *Female chauvinist pigs: Women and the rise of raunch culture.* New York: Free Press.

Ley, D. L. (2009) *Insatiable wives: Women who stray and the men who love them.* Landham, MD: Rowman & Littlefield.

McClelland, S. I. (2010). Intimate justice: A critical analysis of sexual satisfaction. *Social and Personality Psychology Compass*, *4*(9), 663–680.

Meana, M., & Nunnink, S. E. (2006). Gender differences in the content of cognitive distraction during sex. *Journal of Sex Research*, *43*(1), 59–67.

Millett, K. (1970). *Sexual politics*. Garden City, NY: Doubleday.

Monmouth University Polling Institute. (2017). Monmouth University Poll. Retrieved from www.monmouth.edu/polling-institute/reports/Monmouth Poll_US_020917/.

Moreland, R. L., & Zajonc, R. B. (1982). Exposure effects in person perception: Familiarity, similarity, and attraction. *Journal of Experimental Social Psychology*, *18*, 395–415.

Paris, W. (2017). Why you want who you want. Retrieved from www.psychologytoday.com/articles/201707/why-you-want-who-you-want.

Roberts, T. A., Goldenberg, J. L., Power, C., & Pyszczynski, T. (2002). "Feminine protection": The effects of menstruation on attitudes towards women. *Psychology of Women Quarterly*, *26*(2), 131–139.

Rudd, N. A., & Lennon, S. J. (2000). Body image and appearance-management behaviors in college women. *Clothing and Textiles Research Journal*, *18*(3), 152–162.

Rupp, L. J., & Taylor, V. (2010). Straight girls kissing. *Contexts*, *9*(3), 28–32.

Rusbult, C. E. (1980). Commitment and satisfaction in romantic associations: A test of the investment model. *Journal of Experimental Social Psychology*, *16*(2), 172–186.

Sanchez, D. T., & Kiefer, A. K. (2007). Body concerns in and out of the bedroom: Implications for sexual pleasure and problems. *Archives of Sexual Behavior*, *36*(6), 808–820.

Seal, B. N., Bradford, A., & Meston, C. M. (2009). The association between body esteem and sexual desire among college women. *Archives of Sexual Behavior*, *38*(5), 866–872.

Sheff, E. (2013). *The polyamorists next door: Inside multiple-partner relationships and families*. Lanham, MD: Rowman & Littlefield.

Thornton, A., & Young-DeMarco, L. (2001). Four decades of trends in attitudes toward family issues in the United States: The 1960s through the 1990s. *Journal of Marriage and the Family*, *63*, 1009–1038.

Trail, T. E., Goff, P. A., Bradbury, T. N., & Karney, B. R. (2012). The costs of racism for marriage: How racial discrimination hurts, and ethnic identity protects, newlywed marriages among Latinos. *Personality and Social Psychology Bulletin*, *38*(4), 454–465.

Trapnell, P. D., Meston, C. M., & Gorzalka, B. B. (1997). Spectatoring and the relationship between body image and sexual experience: Self-focus or self-valence? *Journal of Sex Research*, *34*(3), 267–278.

Vinokur, A. D., Price, R. H., Caplan, R. D. (1996). Hard times and hurtful partners: How financial strain affects depression and relationship satisfaction of unemployed persons and their spouses *Journal of Personality and Social Psychology*, *71*(1), 166–179.

Walster, E., Aronson, V., & Abrahams, D. (1966). Importance of physical attractiveness in dating behavior. *Journal of Personality and Social Psychology, 4*, 508–516.

Weber, M. (1958) *The Protestant ethic and the spirit of capitalism* (T. Parsons, Trans). New York: Charles Scribner's Sons. (Original work published 1904–05.)

Zajonc, R. B. (1968). Attitudinal effects of mere exposure. *Journal of Personality and Social Psychology Monograph Supplement, 9*(2, part 2), 1–27.

Zota, A. R., & Shamasunder, B. (2017). The environmental injustice of beauty: Framing chemical exposures from beauty products as a health disparities concern. *American Journal of Obstetrics and Gynecology, 217*(4), 418.e1–418.e6.

CHAPTER 7

Love, Desire, and Sexual Fluidity

Lisa M. Diamond

I considered myself a sexuality researcher long before I considered myself a relationship researcher, and so when I first started studying the phenomenon of romantic love, it was in the context of studying sexual desire. My particular focus was on *same-sex* desire, a phenomenon that remains highly stigmatized in our culture and around the globe. My first research project as a new graduate student at Cornell University in the early 1990s involved interviewing young sexual-minority women. *Sexual-minority* is a catch-all term used to denote individuals with same-sex attractions. (Unlike the acronym "LGBT" or the terms "lesbian/gay/bisexual," the term *sexual-minority* makes no assumptions about whether someone with same-sex attractions chooses to openly identify as "lesbian," "gay," "bisexual," "queer," etc.). I was interested in understanding the process by which young women first began to question their sexuality and first begin experiencing and expressing same-sex desire. The women that I recruited for my study were all between sixteen and twenty-three years of age, and I interviewed each of them for roughly ninety minutes about their history of sexual feelings, their intimate relationships with women and men, and about how they thought about their identity.

Right away, I noticed a powerful theme in the data. For many women, their *very first* experience of same-sex attraction occurred in the context of a powerful emotional attachment to a female friend. For example, one woman recounted that she had had an extremely close relationship with her very best friend for over five years. They were roommates and spent their evenings cuddling together on the couch and watching movies, talking all hours of the night. They used affectionate nicknames for one another, held hands, and spent practically all their free time together. "It was totally like a romantic relationship, except without the sex," she told me. Their other friends frequently remarked that they seemed to be closer than most lovers, but they never worried about it. "But then something changed," she told me. According to her story, one night they were lying in bed, cuddling and talking, their faces close together, and she was struck by a sudden desire to *kiss* her friend. Their eyes were locked and she sensed that her friend felt the same way. She took the risk and soon they were kissing passionately, rolling on the bed, stroking one another, and stripping off their clothes. That night was the beginning of a passionate love affair that lasted for two years. My interviewee remarked that, initially, they were both confused by the fact that they did not seem to have sexual attractions for any other women, only each other. "It was almost like the sexual feelings just spilled over from our emotional feelings," she said. I found the story compelling and startling, but I had no way to make sense of it. As the interview ended, she said to me "I'm still not sure if we're lesbians or not. What do you think? Am I a lesbian if I only feel this way about her?" I told her, with some embarrassment, that I honestly had no way to answer that question!

Soon I found that this woman's story was not uncommon. Although some of my interviewees had been aware of their attractions to women from a very early age, others reported that their attractions suddenly "spilled over" from powerful emotional attachments to female friends. These female friendships seemed remarkable to me for their passionate intensity – these were more than just typical "best friendships," but contained all of the infatuation, preoccupation, and separation distress that most of us only experience in romantic relationships. "What is going on in these intense friendships?," I asked myself. How could an emotional attachment be so intense that it could give rise to utterly novel sexual feelings? These questions became even more pressing when I talked to self-identified lesbians who reported nearly the same type of experience, but with *male* friends. One twenty-year-old woman told me that she had known she was a lesbian from a very early age, and she had enjoyed many satisfying relationships with women over the years. "But last summer," she recounted, "I got sexually involved with my closest male friend – I don't really know how it happened." She said that she had never experienced sexual attractions for men before, but this particular relationship with her closest male friend was extremely emotionally intimate and physically affectionate. One night they were hanging out, horsing around and cuddling on the bed, and all of a sudden, she wanted to kiss him. She was shocked by her feelings, and so was he, but they both realized that they wanted a physical relationship. "I don't get it," she said "I don't feel this way for any other men, and I know I'm still a lesbian because I'm still totally attracted to women, but it's like he's an exception, because I love him so much."

What Was This Thing Called Love?

I was struck by these reports, and the fact that they centered on love. Something about these powerful romantic feelings was strong enough to utterly reshape these women's erotic vocabularies, turning their lives upside down and sometimes completely upending their sexual identities. Some of the women that I interviewed went on to develop additional same-sex attractions for other women, and ended up identifying as lesbian or bisexual. But for others, their sudden and unexpected attractions were completely limited to one singular and transformative relationship. I knew that if I wanted to understand these remarkable experiences, and to understand their relationship to sexual desire and orientation, I needed to know more about *love*. What was it, after all? I had never actually asked myself that question before (since I considered myself a sexuality researcher, not a love researcher), but now it seemed to be central to understanding women's sexuality.

Fortunately, one of the world's experts on romantic love was just down the hall from me in my graduate program at Cornell University: Dr. Cindy Hazan, a world-renowned researcher who studied adult *romantic attachment* (basically, the scientific term for *romantic love*). I was vaguely aware of her research on "adult attachment," but I didn't know much about it. I tentatively made an appointment to meet with her, and in preparation, I read her most prominent and influential articles (Hazan & Shaver, 1987; Shaver & Hazan, 1988, 1993; Shaver, Hazan, & Bradshaw, 1988). Soon I discovered why she was so famous – she and her mentor, Phil Shaver, had been the first to argue that adult romantic love is basically analogous to the powerful emotional attachments that infants develop to their caregivers.

Attachment is the word that scientists use to describe this powerful bond between infants and their caregivers. As elegantly and powerfully described by John Bowlby in his many writings on the topic (Bowlby, 1973a, 1973b, 1980, 1982), attachment is a fundamental human drive – it evolved to keep vulnerable human infants in close proximity to their caregivers, and it is typically characterized by intense desires for proximity (just imagine an infant reflexively reaching up for the mother), the seeking of comfort and safety from the caregiver (running to mom's side when distressed), separation distress (crying and wailing if suddenly separated from the caregiver), and the seeking of security from the caregiver (feeling safe and sound just from the sight of her). Bowlby described attachment as a "cradle to grave" phenomenon: No matter how old we become, we continue to need a basic feeling of safety and security in order to function well.

Cindy Hazan's contribution was to argue that as we mature from children to adults, we gradually "transfer" these basic attachment needs *to our romantic partners* (Hazan, Hutt, Sturgeon, & Bricker, 1991). As adults, we continue to need a singular figure in our lives who makes us feel safe, to whom we turn when distressed, and with whom we would rather be than anyone else. But as adults, it is no longer our mother or father that we typically put in this lofty position: *It is a romantic partner*. Hazan and Shaver's research showed that romantic relationships have all the classic hallmarks of attachment bonds: the intense desires for proximity, the seeking of comfort and support, the profound distress that comes from physical separation, the emotional security (Hazan & Shaver, 1987). Romantic relationships are also characterized by many unique behaviors that are only otherwise observed between infants and their caregivers: extended chest-to-chest holding and cuddling; extended mutual gazing; long strokes of the entire body; and the use of private affectionate language (Hazan & Zeifman, 1994). In Hazan's view, these were all indicators of the *emotional primacy* of attachment bonds, and adults typically develop these types of bonds only with sexual partners.

"But wait a second," I thought, reading Hazan and Shaver's powerful articles. "It seems as if my interview subjects *are* developing these types of bonds – full-blown adult romantic attachments – except with *platonic friends* instead of lovers." This could explain why these friendships seemed so unusually intense and passionate, and why other friends and family members would often tell the girls that they were "too close" or that they seemed to be "more than friends." Hazan and Shaver's research implied that adult romantic attachments *only* developed in the context of a sexual relationship, and in fact they argued that the distinguishing feature of adult attachment – relative to infant/caregiver attachment – was the fact that adult attachments *integrated* attachment with sexuality (Shaver et al., 1988). Certainly, it seemed to be true that most adults *usually* only "fell in love" with individuals to whom they were sexually attracted (after all, this was why the intense platonic friendships in my study seemed so unusual), but I now wondered whether this *had* to be the case. Sexual desire was usually involved, but it no longer seemed to be a necessary precursor. Could this be the case? This was the question that I posed to Cindy Hazan when I met with her (the first of what would become thousands of fascinating conversations over the next several decades, as she became one of my most influential and treasured mentors). I shared with her the data that I was collecting on my respondents' friendships: Were my respondents basically "falling in love" in the absence of sexual desire? Were these *attachment bonds*? Her answer was a resounding yes.

The next question was more complicated: For some of these women, brand-new same-sex desires seemed to "bubble up" out of these intense friendships, often after many years. Was it possible that the attachment bond was *giving rise* to these new feelings? We normally think that romantic relationships *begin* with sexual desire, and that deeper feelings of love come later. But could the opposite happen? Could powerful feelings of romantic love and attachment *create* new sexual desires that did not exist before? "Well, why not?" she responded with excitement. She reminded me that in adults, the attachment system becomes *integrated* with the sexuality system. Perhaps, then, relationships that start out in the attachment domain can come to incorporate sexuality as well.

This sent me off and running, my mind reeling. Prior to this point, I had made the same assumption about sexual orientation and romantic love that practically everyone makes: If you are sexually oriented to a particular gender, you must also be *romantically* oriented to that gender. Lesbians are sexually attracted to women and therefore they should only fall in love with women. Gay men are sexually attracted to men and therefore they should only fall in love with men. Love and sex were simply two sides of the same coin. But now I was no longer sure about this truism. If otherwise heterosexual women could fall passionately in love with their best female friends, and if otherwise lesbian women could fall in love with their best male friends, then love and sex were not two sides of the same coin. They were *separate systems*, pushing and pulling on one another, but fundamentally distinct. Although individuals *usually* only fell in love with partners to whom they were sexually attracted (and hence, partners who "matched" their sexual orientation), this was not necessarily so. The fact that we typically only fall in love with potential sexual partners might simply be due to the fact that we typically only seek intense adult attachment bonds with individuals who are actual or potential sexual partners.

This made perfect sense to me when I revisited Hazan's thinking on adult attachment. In her formulation, adult attachment was an adult "version" of infant–caregiver attachment, and subsequent research (much of it conducted with animals) had confirmed that the fundamental neural circuits underlying these two types of attachment bonds were the same. Research on oxytocin provides a particularly powerful example. Oxytocin is a neuropeptide hormone produced in the hypothalamus that is released into circulation from the posterior pituitary. Studies of animals (typically rats and prairie voles) have identified direct effects of oxytocin on maternal feeding behavior, maternal/infant bonding, and kin recognition (Carter & Keverne, 2002; Keverne & Curley, 2004). Oxytocin has powerful conditioning effects that appear to be an important mechanism through which mammals form stable, intrinsically rewarding bonds to specific social partners, most importantly, the mother. Researchers such as Uvnäs-Moberg (Uvnäs-Moberg, 1998, 2004) have postulated that the physiologically and psychologically soothing and rewarding effects of infant–caregiver attachment would initially be conferred through direct physical contact and mediated by the release of oxytocin and other neurochemicals. The same oxytocinergic mechanisms have also been found to underlie adult pair-bonding. There is extensive evidence from animal studies that this is the case. Much of this research has focused on prairie voles, which are one of the few species of rodents to form enduring pair-bonds. As with infant/caregiver attachments, pair-bonds between monogamous mammals are facilitated by the oxytocin release that is triggered by physical contact (Cho, DeVries, Williams, & Carter, 1999; Mason & Mendoza, 1998; J. R. Williams, Insel, Harbaugh, & Carter, 1994). It is on the basis of such findings that researchers working in this area now generally agree that adult pair-bonding and infant/caregiver attachment share the same neurobiological substrate – a conclusion that supports the notion of a shared evolutionary origin for these two processes (Carter & Keverne, 2002; Keverne & Curley, 2004; Panksepp, 1998; Panksepp, Nelson, & Bekkedal, 1997).

But if this is the case, then romantic love *cannot* be a "gender-oriented" system in the same way that sexual desire is "gender-oriented," and it cannot *require* sexual desire for its formation. After all, "gender of partner" is completely irrelevant in the context of infant-caregiver attachment, as is the experience of sexual desire. Infants do not preferentially attach to other-gender or same-gender caregivers, and sexual desire is obviously irrelevant for attachment formation. Rather, according to Bowlby's research, the driving force behind attachment formation is the caregiver's *responsiveness and availability*. Hence, infant/caregiver attachment is a gender-blind system. Infants can "fall in love" with *any* caregiver.

This fact has profound implications for romantic love: If the infant–caregiver attachment system is fundamentally "gender blind," and if it does not require a substrate of sexual desire, then *the same must be true for adult romantic attachment*. Because the neural architecture underlying both types of attachment is the same, there is no way to "build" gender and sexual desire into one system without building it into both. In essence, just as infants can attach to *any* caregiver, regardless of gender, adults are essentially capable of falling in love with anyone, regardless of gender (and regardless of sexual desire). By "falling in love," I refer to the intense feelings that characterize adult attachment (and which were described to me over and over by my participants): intense desires to be with the attachment figure; preferentially seeking out the attachment figure (over everyone else) for comfort and security when upset; experiencing distress and agitation when separated from the attachment figure for extended periods of time. Although contemporary culture often assumes that sexual desire provides the "energy" behind these powerful feelings, none of these feelings require sexual attraction. As a result, a person's sexual orientation does not limit his or her capacity for adult attachment: Heterosexuals are capable of falling in love with same-sex friends, and lesbian/gay/bisexual individuals are capable of falling in love with other-sex friends. Our sexual orientations do not orient our romantic feelings, contrary to popular belief.

Other Evidence for Platonic Romantic Attachment

If this is true, I thought, then I should be able to find more evidence – other than my own interviews – of passionate, romantic friendships developing between heterosexual same-sex friends. It did not take me long to discover such evidence, across many different cultures and vast historical epochs, dating back to ancient Greece. In some cultures, these friendships were granted a prized status, and friends would exchange gifts and vows of loyalty and devotion. These friendships went by a variety of different names in different cultures, such as "romantic friendships" (Smith-Rosenberg, 1975), "Boston Marriages" (Faderman, 1981), "smashes" (Sahli, 1979), "mummy–baby" relationships (Gay, 1985), "motsoalle" friendships (Kendall, 1999), "camaradia" (Reina, 1966), and "bagburu" relationships (Blackwood, 1985). Descriptions of these friendships revealed many common features – extensive time spent together, close physical affection (such as bed sharing), and verbal expressions of love and devotion. Although at first I thought that these friendships were more common among women than among men, I soon found extensive evidence of similarly intense friendships among heterosexual men.

Williams (1992) documented powerful friendships between North American Indian men that early Western explorers often described as being emotionally reminiscent of romantic love (Parkman, 1969; Trumbull, 1894). Similarly, Brain (1976) documented passionate male–male friendships in the Cameroon, and reviewed reports of comparable male–male ties in Melanesia (Malinowski, 1929), Samoa (Mead, 1943), the

Polynesian islands (Firth, 1967), and Guatemala (Reina, 1966). According to these accounts, such relationships involved "affection of an extreme kind which ... resembles more the passion of heterosexual lovers than the calm friendship of equals" (Brain, 1976, pp. 39–40).

Because we are so accustomed to seeing such emotional passion only between lovers, it is not surprising that many historians and anthropologists assumed that these powerful bonds were "secretly sexual," and that if the participants had simply lived in a more permissive environment, they would have pursued openly sexual relationships with one another. However, those who have studied and documented such relationships argue against this view: In some cases, the bonds appear to have involved some sexual behavior, but in many cases they did not (Faderman, 1981; Blackwood, 2000), and our assumption of a necessary link between romantic and sexual passion comes from our own cultural norms (D'Emilio & Freedman, 1988).

Working Toward a New Model of Love and Desire

On the basis of my research, I reached three conclusions (summarized in Diamond, 2003): First, the evolved processes underlying romantic love and sexual desire were *functionally independent* (allowing individuals to experience sexual desire without love, and to experience love without sexual desire). Second, the processes underlying romantic love (i.e. adult attachment) were essentially *"gender-neutral,"* such that individuals could fall in love with anyone, regardless of that person's gender. This meant that sexual orientation did *not* orient one's capacity for romantic love. Third, the biobehavioral links between the systems of love and desire were *bidirectional*, meaning that individuals could sometimes develop novel sexual desires for a person after developing a romantic attachment to that person.

Perhaps the most novel and controversial aspect of this view is the third premise, which suggests that we can form novel sexual desires, desires that sometimes run counter to our general sexual orientation, *as a result* of forming a powerful emotional attachment to another person. Other than my own interview data, was there any evidence for this? In fact, there is. Some of the evidence comes from neurobiological research on oxytocin (the same hormone that plays such a critical role in both infant–caregiver attachment and adult romantic attachment). Oxytocin-based links between love and desire are of particular interest. In addition to mediating attachment-related feelings and behaviors, oxytocin also plays an important role in *sexual* behavior. Animal research has found that exogenous administration of moderate amounts of oxytocin stimulates females to seek out sexual activity (Argiolas, Melis, Mauri, & Gessa, 1987; Floody, Cooper, & Albers, 1998) and to show receptivity to sexual requests (Arletti & Bertolini, 1985; Caldwell, Prange, & Pedersen, 1986). In fact, the highest circulating levels of oxytocin *in humans* are detected during sexual activity, and oxytocin has been implicated in the experience of orgasm and feeling of satiety that follows sexual activity (Carmichael, Warburton, Dixen, & Davidson, 1994; Riley, 1988). Hence, it is reasonable to suspect that oxytocin might play a role in the *linkage* between love and desire that we typically experience in adulthood. There is no reason to expect that this linkage is unidirectional. Hence, although we usually "start" with sexual desire and progress to romantic love, the neurobiological pathways described above suggest that one might be able to "start" with the oxytocin-mediated process of romantic love and progress to sexual desire.

In addition to the neurobiological evidence, there is also behavioral evidence for this possibility. I combed the scientific and popular literature on sexual orientation to see if there were other individuals who described the same types of experiences reported by my own respondents – that they fell in love with *one specific person*, and started experiencing same-sex desires in that specific context. Sure enough, there are many such accounts (Cass, 1990; Cassingham & O'Neil, 1993; Golden, 1987; Pillard, 1990; Whisman, 1996). As far back as the late 1970s, Philip Blumstein and Pepper Schwartz had pointed out that traditional models of sexual orientation failed to account for individuals "whose fundamental sexual desire seems to be produced within the context of a relationship, rather than by an abstract preference for women or men" (Blumstein & Schwartz, 1990, p. 346). Later in the 1980s, a group of researchers studying bisexuality in San Francisco interviewed numerous men and women who described themselves as attracted to "the person" and not "the gender" (Weinberg, Williams, & Pryor, 1994). They described these individuals as possessing an "open gender schema," meaning that they had *disconnected* gender from sexual desire. As a result, they could respond sexually to a broad range of traits and characteristics, regardless of gender. In many cases these "open gender schemas" revolved around falling in love with particular individuals, similar to the reports of the women in my study.

How common is this phenomenon? It is impossible to say for sure, since data on this type of experience is rarely collected. My own research suggests that for some people, the links between romantic love and sexual desire are stronger than for others. Some of the women in my study reported that they frequently developed sexual desires for people they were emotionally bonded to, whereas others reported that this rarely happened (Diamond, 2008). Hence, perhaps the most important conclusion is that this is a possibility for all individuals, but may be more likely for some than for others.

Implications

What does this tell us about the nature of love and desire, and about the larger phenomenon of sexual orientation? I think that one of the larger lessons has to do with the powerful nature of attachment. One of Bowlby's original claims about the attachment system was that it *superseded* other powerful drives in cases of danger or distress. When a child is distressed, the drive to seek solace from the arms of the caregiver is stronger than hunger or thirst. Our brains are literally "wired" to prioritize our basic needs for love and emotional security. In this context, the ability of intense emotional attachments to potentiate novel sexual desires is perhaps not so surprising. If, as Bowlby argued, attachment is capable of superseding other drives, then it is also capable of barreling right through an individual's overall sexual orientation. It is as if the attachment system is saying, "I don't *care* if this person is the wrong gender for you … *this* is the *one*!!!" On a broader level, I also think that the phenomena I have described help to explain why so many people fall deeply in love with individuals that are "wrong" for them in other ways (incompatible personality, abusive, different age group, married to someone else, etc.). The attachment drive is powerful, and knowing that someone is not the ideal partner for you may have no effect on your feelings (in some cases, it may even make them stronger). You may think to yourself (or you may hear your friends say) "Why do I keep falling for the wrong person?" Do not blame yourself. You are wired to bond, like all humans, and that system often drives you into the arms of people that you might never expect.

Another implication of the research that I have described has to do with the fluidity of human sexuality. A common question that I have been asked about my research, and about the capacity of individuals to experience powerful shifts in their sexual attractions, is whether sexual orientation even *exists*. After all, if sexual orientation does not "orient" our capacity for romantic love, and if individuals can develop novel sexual desires for people that they fall in love with, then maybe it is ridiculous to continue categorizing people as "gay/lesbian," "bisexual," or "straight." I understand the rationale for that argument (and given the discrimination that lesbian/gay/bisexual individuals face, it is exciting to imagine a world in which society truly *did not care* about an individual's sexual orientation), but the

truth is that sexual orientation is, in fact, a real and meaningful phenomenon, and one that researchers must continue to take into account when
making sense of an individual's romantic and sexual relationships. There
is extensive evidence for genetic contributions to sexual orientation: Twin
studies suggest that the heritability of sexual orientation is somewhere
between 30% and 40% (reviewed in Bailey et al., 2016), which shows that
although sexual orientation is not completely genetically determined (in
which case the heritability would be 100%), it is significantly genetically
influenced.

Hence, people are undoubtedly born with predispositions to experience sexual attractions for one gender or the other (or both). Yet these
predispositions are not as rigid as researchers (and laypeople) have historically assumed. Heterosexuals can fall in love with and experience sexual
desires for same-sex partners, and gay/lesbians can fall in love with and
experience sexual desires for other-sex partners. Furthermore, falling in
love is *not* the only phenomenon that might prompt someone to experience a sexual attraction that runs counter to their overall orientation. My
research has shown that sexual desire is, quite simply, a flexible and adaptable system, and many individuals report shifts over time in the types of
people to whom they are erotically drawn (reviewed in Diamond, 2016).
Again, this does mean that there is "no such thing" as sexual orientation,
it simply means that sexual orientation does not provide the last word on
every sexual attraction you might experience in your life.

What does this mean for your own sexual and romantic experiences?
I think that one of the implications is that you might find yourself, or one
of your friends or relatives, experiencing some of these changes in sexual
desire. If that happens, do not panic! Our culture tends to convey the
message that sexual orientation develops and expresses itself at a very early
age, and that it remains completely fixed over the life course. Accordingly,
when individuals find themselves experiencing desires that seem to run
counter to their overall pattern (whether it is a heterosexual woman
developing same-sex desire or a gay man developing other-sex desire),
society tends to react by saying "Well, you must have been repressed
before! You must have been wrong about your sexual orientation!" But
this is overly simplistic. It is certainly the case that sometimes, these unexpected changes result from individuals who are gradually discovering that
they are bisexual rather than exclusively gay, lesbian, or heterosexual (and,
in fact, bisexual patterns of sexual attraction are actually *more common*
than exclusive patterns of same-sex attraction). Yet in other cases, individuals are simply experiencing fluctuations in their sexual desires that stem

from their own capacity for *sexual fluidity*, which can be described as the capacity for one's desires to change based on different situations, environments, and relationships. Experiencing one of these changes in your own life does not mean that you were "wrong" about your orientation. It simply means that your capacity for love and desire is not as rigidly constrained by your orientation as you might have thought. It might also help to know that these experiences are not uncommon. As researchers have begun to collect more and more data on how individuals experience their sexual attractions over time, we have learned that these sorts of unexpected fluctuations are far more common than we used to think (Diamond, 2016).

This does not mean, however, that individuals can forcibly change their sexual attractions. For decades, many individuals have sought "reparative therapy" in an attempt to eliminate their same-sex attractions (Beckstead, 2012; Bradshaw, Dehlin, Crowell, Galliher, & Bradshaw, 2015). Given that same-sex sexuality continues to be harshly stigmatized around the world, it is understandable that many gay/lesbian/bisexual individuals would try to eliminate their same-sex desires so that they could be exclusively heterosexual.

The growing body of research on *fluidity* in sexual attractions has been interpreted by some individuals as suggesting that these efforts might actually prove successful. After all, if sexuality is fluid, then maybe we can "push" that fluidity in a heterosexual direction. *But there is no evidence that this works.* The American Psychological Association put together a task force to review all the research on "Sexual Orientation Change Efforts" and they found no conclusive evidence that it was possible to "eliminate" same-sex attractions, and they also found that these efforts often produced lasting harm to individuals, provoking higher rates of depression, anxiety, and sometimes suicidality (APA Task Force on Appropriate Therapeutic Responses to Sexual Orientation, 2009). As for sexual fluidity, the existing research on changes in sexual attraction suggests a *broadening* of attractions over time and across situations, not a narrowing. Furthermore, my own research suggests that when women are asked about the contexts in which they have experienced changes in their own sexual desires, they describe these changes as unexpected and uncontrollable (Diamond, 2008). Hence, it is important to keep in mind that your capacity for sexual fluidity does not mean that you can effortfully "push" your sexual feelings in a certain direction. Just as we cannot generally control with whom we fall in love, we cannot generally control to whom we are sexually attracted.

This, perhaps, is the most important lesson I have learned from my own research on love and desire. Humans have evolved immensely powerful drives for physical and emotional connection, and as much as we might like to believe that we have control over where those drives take us, and who we will "end up" with, we often overstate our role in these important feelings and events. Similarly, we often overestimate the importance of any *one* love relationship or any *one* sexual desire in presaging the future. The types of individuals that you have passionately loved in the past might not predict the types of individuals that you will passionately love in the future, and the same goes for sexual desire. The hallmark of human love and mating is *flexibility and adaptability*, and through my own research I have gained immense respect for these traits and their power to shape our lives.

References

APA Task Force on Appropriate Therapeutic Responses to Sexual Orientation. (2009). *Report of the task force on appropriate therapeutic responses to sexual orientation*. Washington, DC: American Psychological Association.

Argiolas, A., Melis, M. R., Mauri, A., & Gessa, G. L. (1987). Paraventricular nucleus lesion prevents yawning and penile erection induced by apomorphine and oxytocin but not by ACTH in rats. *Brain Research, 421*, 349–352.

Arletti, R., & Bertolini, A. (1985). Oxytocin stimulates lordosis behavior in female rats. *Neuropeptides, 6*, 247–253.

Bailey, J. M., Vasey, P. L., Diamond, L. M., Breedlove, S. M., Vilain, E., & Epprecht, M. (2016). Sexual orientation, controversy, and science. *Psychological Science in the Public Interest, 17*, 45–101.

Beckstead, A. L. (2012). Can we change sexual orientation? *Archives of Sexual Behavior, 41*(1), 121–134.

Blackwood, E. (1985). Breaking the mirror: The construction of lesbianism and the anthropological discourse on homosexuality. *Journal of Homosexuality, 11*, 1–17.

(2000). Culture and women's sexualities. *Journal of Social Issues, 56*(2), 223–238.

Blumstein, P., & Schwartz, P. (1990). Intimate relationships and the creation of sexuality. In D. P. McWhirter, S. A. Sanders, & J. M. Reinisch (Eds.), *Homosexuality/heterosexuality: Concepts of sexual orientation* (pp. 307–320). New York: Oxford University Press.

Bowlby, J. (1973a). Affectional bonds: Their nature and origin. In R. W. Weiss (Ed.), *Loneliness: The experience of emotional and social isolation* (pp. 38–52). Cambridge, MA: MIT Press.

(1973b). *Attachment and loss*, Vol. 2: *Separation: Anxiety and anger*. New York: Basic Books.

(1980). *Attachment and loss,* Vol. 3: *Loss: Sadness and depression.* New York: Basic Books.

(1982). *Attachment and loss,* Vol. 1: *Attachment* (2nd ed.). New York: Basic Books.

Bradshaw, K., Dehlin, J. P., Crowell, K. A., Galliher, R. V., & Bradshaw, W. S. (2015). Sexual orientation change efforts through psychotherapy for LGBQ individuals affiliated with the Church of Jesus Christ of Latter-day Saints. *Journal of Sex & Marital Therapy, 41*(4), 391–412. doi:10.1080/0092623X. 2014.915907.

Brain, R. (1976). *Friends and lovers.* New York: Basic Books.

Caldwell, J. D., Prange, A. J. J., & Pedersen, C. A. (1986). Oxytocin facilitates the sexual receptivity of estrogen-treated female rats. *Neuropeptides, 7,* 175–189.

Carmichael, M. S., Warburton, V. L., Dixen, J., & Davidson, J. M. (1994). Relationships among cardiovascular, muscular, and oxytocin responses during human sexual activity. *Archives of Sexual Behavior, 23,* 59–79.

Carter, C. S., & Keverne, E. B. (2002). The neurobiology of social affiliation and pair bonding. In J. Pfaff, A. P. Arnold, A. E. Etgen, & S. E. Fahrbach (Eds.), *Hormones, brain and behavior* (Vol. 1, pp. 299–337). New York: Academic Press.

Cass, V. (1990). The implications of homosexual identity formation for the Kinsey model and scale of sexual preference. In D. P. McWhirter, S. A. Sanders, & J. M. Reinisch (Eds.), *Homosexuality/heterosexuality: Concepts of sexual orientation* (pp. 239–266). New York: Oxford University Press.

Cassingham, B. J., & O'Neil, S. M. (1993). *And then I met this woman.* Freeland, WA: Soaring Eagle.

Cho, M. M., DeVries, A. C., Williams, J. R., & Carter, C. S. (1999). The effects of oxytocin and vasopressin on partner preferences in male and female prairie voles (*Microtus ochrogaster*). *Behavioral Neuroscience, 113,* 1071–1079.

D'Emilio, J., & Freedman, E. B. (1988). *Intimate matters: A history of sexuality in America.* New York: Harper & Row.

Diamond, L. M. (2003). What does sexual orientation orient? A biobehavioral model distinguishing romantic love and sexual desire. *Psychological Review, 110,* 173–192.

(2008). *Sexual fluidity: Understanding women's love and desire.* Cambridge, MA: Harvard University Press.

(2016). Sexual fluidity in males and females. *Current Sexual Health Reports.* doi: 10.1007/s11930-016-0092-z.

Faderman, L. (1981). *Surpassing the love of men.* New York: William Morrow.

Firth, R. W. (1967). *Tikopia ritual and belief.* Boston: Allen & Unwin.

Floody, O. R., Cooper, T. T., & Albers, H. E. (1998). Injection of oxytocin into the medial preoptic-anterior hypothalamus increases ultrasound production by female hamsters. *Peptides, 19,* 833–839.

Gay, J. (1985). "Mummies and babies" and friends and lovers in Lesotho. Special issue: Anthropology and homosexual behavior. *Journal of Homosexuality, 11,* 97–116.

Golden, C. (1987). Diversity and variability in women's sexual identities. In Boston Lesbian Psychologies Collective (Ed.), *Lesbian psychologies: Explorations and challenges* (pp. 19–34). Urbana, IL: University of Illinois Press.

Hazan, C., Hutt, M. J., Sturgeon, M. J., & Bricker, T. (1991). The process of relinquishing parents as attachment figures. Paper presented at the Biennial meetings of Society for Research on Child Development, Seattle, WA.

Hazan, C., & Shaver, P. R. (1987). Romantic love conceptualized as an attachment process. *Journal of Personality and Social Psychology, 52*, 511–524.

Hazan, C., & Zeifman, D. (1994). Sex and the psychological tether. In D. Perlman & K. Bartholomew (Eds.), *Advances in personal relationships: A research annual* (Vol. 5, pp. 151–177). London: Jessica Kingsley.

Kendall, K. L. (1999). Women in Lesotho and the (Western) construction of homophobia. In E. Blackwood & S. E. Wieringa (Eds.), *Female desires: Same-sex relations and transgender practices across cultures* (pp. 157–178). New York: Columbia University Press.

Keverne, E. B., & Curley, J. P. (2004). Vasopressin, oxytocin and social behaviour. *Current Opinion in Neurobiology, 14*(6), 777–783.

Malinowski, B. C. (1929). *The sexual life of savages in northwestern Melanesia.* London: Routledge and Kegan Paul.

Mason, W. A., & Mendoza, S. P. (1998). Generic aspects of primate attachments: Parents, offspring and mates. *Psychoneuroendocrinology, 23*, 765–778.

Mead, M. (1943). *Coming of age in Samoa: A psychological study of primitive youth.* New York: Penguin.

Panksepp, J. (1998). *Affective neuroscience: The foundations of human and animal emotions.* New York: Cambridge University Press.

Panksepp, J., Nelson, E., & Bekkedal, M. (1997). Brain systems for the mediation of social separation-distress and social-reward: Evolutionary antecedents and neuropeptide intermediaries. *Annals of the New York Academy of Sciences, 807*, 78–100.

Parkman, F. (1969). *The Oregon trail.* Madison, WI: University of Wisconsin Press.

Pillard, R. C. (1990). The Kinsey scale: Is it familial? In D. P. McWhirter, S. A. Sanders, & J. M. Reinisch (Eds.), *Homosexuality/heterosexuality: Concepts of sexual orientation* (pp. 88–100). New York: Oxford University Press.

Reina, R. (1966). *The law of the saints: A Pokoman pueblo and its community culture.* Indianapolis, IN: Bobbs Merril.

Riley, A. J. (1988). Oxytocin and coitus. *Sexual and Marital Therapy, 3*, 29–36.

Sahli, N. (1979). Smashing: Women's relationships before the fall. *Chrysalis, 8*, 17–27.

Shaver, P. R., & Hazan, C. (1988). A biased overview of the study of love. *Journal of Social and Personal Relationships, 5*, 473–501.

(1993). Adult romantic attachment: Theory and evidence. *Advances in Personal Relationships, 4*, 29–70.

Shaver, P. R., Hazan, C., & Bradshaw, D. (1988). Love as attachment: The integration of three behavioral systems. In J. Sternberg & M. L. Barnes (Eds.), *The psychology of love* (pp. 193–219). New Haven, CT: Yale University Press.

Smith-Rosenberg, C. (1975). The female world of love and ritual: Relations between women in nineteenth century America. *Signs, 1,* 1–29.

Trumbull, H. C. (1894). *Friendship the master passion.* Philadelphia, PA: Wattles.

Uvnäs-Moberg, K. (1998). Oxytocin may mediate the benefits of positive social interaction and emotions. *Psychoneuroendocrinology, 23,* 819–835.

(2004). *The oxytocin factor: Tapping the hormone of calm, love, and healing* (R. W. Francis, Trans.). Cambridge, MA: Da Capo Press.

Weinberg, M. S., Williams, C. J., & Pryor, D. W. (1994). *Dual attraction: Understanding bisexuality.* New York: Oxford University Press.

Whisman, V. (1996). *Queer by choice: Lesbians, gay men, and the politics of identity.* New York: Routledge.

Williams, J. R., Insel, T. R., Harbaugh, C. R., & Carter, C. S. (1994). Oxytocin administered centrally facilitates formation of a partner preference in female prairie voles (*Microtus ochrogaster*). *Journal of Neuroendocrinology, 6,* 247–250.

Williams, W. L. (1992). The relationship between male-male friendship and male-female marriage. In P. Nardi (Ed.), *Men's friendships* (pp. 187–200). Newbury Park, CA: Sage.

CHAPTER 8

Everyday Conceptions of Love

Beverley Fehr

Nearly fifty years ago, Knox (1970) commented that, "Research regarding conceptions of love is lacking. Many writers offer plausible opinions and contentions regarding love attitudes, but provide little empirical data" (p. 151). In the decades that have followed, writers still offer "plausible opinions and contentions," but, as shall be seen, they can no longer be accused of not providing empirical data. Indeed, substantial strides have been made in illuminating how social scientists and ordinary people think about love and the implications of those thoughts for relationship dynamics.

I begin this chapter with the fundamental question: What is love? Experts' answers to this question are presented, followed by research on lay conceptions of love. (The latter is the focus of this chapter.) Next, I present scales that have been developed to assess everyday views of love, followed by a discussion of gender and cultural similarities and differences in conceptions of love. I then turn to the relationship implications of conceptions of love. The chapter ends with a discussion of future directions for research.

Conceptions of Love

In social psychology, the topic of love did not receive conceptual or empirical attention until the 1970s, when Zick Rubin (1970) and Ellen Berscheid and Elaine Hatfield (1974) blazed the trail. Their definitions and taxonomies inspired other social scientists to follow suit. The views of these experts are presented next in order to provide a framework for interpreting research on lay people's conceptions of love.

Experts' Definitions and Taxonomies

Rubin (1970, 1973) was one of the first social psychologists to scientifically study love. His goal was to differentiate the concepts of love and liking.

He defined love as an attitude that predisposes a person to think, feel, and act in particular ways toward the loved one. Liking was conceptualized as a positive evaluation of another person in terms of qualities such as likability, competence, and respect. Rubin also delineated three components of love, namely intimacy, need/attachment, and caring. Years later, Steck, Levitan, McLane, and Kelley (1982) showed that people regard caring as more indicative of love than need/attachment.

Berscheid and Hatfield (1974; Hatfield & Walster, 1978) argued that love is not a single entity, but rather is best conceptualized in terms of two basic kinds: passionate love and companionate love. Passionate love is defined as "a wildly emotional state" that is characterized by emotional extremes, physiological arousal, and sexual attraction. Companionate love is defined as "friendly affection and deep attachment to someone" (Hatfield & Walster, 1978, p. 2). Companionate love is characterized by caring, trust, honesty, and respect and can be experienced for a number of people in one's life, such as close friends, family members, or a romantic partner.

This early work paved the way for a large number of theories and models of love. Based on the work of sociologist John Lee (1973), Hendrick and Hendrick (1986) generated a typology of six different love styles: eros (romantic, passionate love), storge (friendship-based love), agape (altruistic, selfless love), ludus (game-playing love), mania (obsessive, dependent love) and pragma (practical love; see Hendrick & Hendrick, 2006, for a review). Around the same time, Sternberg (1986) developed a theory in which love is conceptualized as a triangle, with passion, intimacy, and decision/commitment as its vertices. The various combinations of these elements produce eight different kinds of love (e.g. companionate love is the combination of the intimacy and decision/commitment components). Another impactful development in this period was Hazan and Shaver's (1987) application of attachment theory to adult romantic relationships. They provided evidence that adults' patterns of attachment to their romantic partners resemble infant attachment styles (secure, anxious-ambivalent, and avoidant) documented much earlier by developmental psychologists. Although attachment theory is not specifically a theory of love, there is a massive body of research on how people with different attachment orientations approach love and relationships (see, e.g., Mikulincer & Shaver, 2016; Pietromonico & Beck, 2015; Simpson & Rholes, 2012, for reviews).

More recently, Berscheid (2006, 2010) expanded the original passionate/companionate love typology to include two additional kinds of love, namely compassionate love and attachment love. In this quadrumvirate model, romantic love is regarded as synonymous with passionate love, eros, and "being in love." Companionate love refers to friendship love, storge, and strong liking. Compassionate love encompasses altruistic love, selfless love, agape, and communal responsiveness. Attachment love is defined as a strong bond with an attachment figure. (Berscheid regards attachment love as different from individual differences in attachment styles.)

In Berscheid's view, these four are basic, fundamental kinds of love that subsume all of the other types, in the same way that the plethora of personality traits that have been identified "boil down" to the Big Five. She points out that these kinds of love are likely to co-occur in romantic relationships, but argues that they can, and should, be distinguished. More specifically, Berscheid articulates the antecedents or causal conditions, associated behaviors, and temporal course of each of these kinds of love. For example, romantic/passionate love is triggered by positive qualities in the other (e.g. physical attraction), sexual desire, and the perception that one is liked by the other. The antecedents of companionate love are proximity, familiarity, and similarity – variables that facilitate the formation of friendships (see Fehr, 1996). Compassionate love is activated by the perception that the loved one is in distress or in need; the key antecedent of attachment love is a threatening situation. Turning to behaviors, the pursuit of sexual relations distinguishes romantic/passionate love from the others. Companionate love is exemplified in behaviors that make interactions enjoyable. These include spending time together so that familiarity can develop, pursuing similar interests, and expressing liking. The behaviors that are characteristic of compassionate love depend on the nature of the distress that is perceived. Finally, attachment love is evidenced in behaviors that promote proximity.

Thus, psychologists have constructed a number of definitions, models, and taxonomies of love. In an attempt at integration, several researchers have factor analyzed scales that assess the constructs identified in these models (e.g. Fehr, 1994; Graham, 2011; Hendrick & Hendrick, 1989; Tzeng, 1993). There is some evidence for a passionate love factor and a companionate love factor, although the findings vary from study to study (see Fehr, 2013a, 2013b for reviews). One problematic issue is that there is not a standard measure of companionate love. In Masuda's (2003) meta-analysis of studies on the relation between passionate love, companionate love, and satisfaction, the various measures of companionate love produced very different results, raising the concern that they are not tapping the same construct. In Graham's (2011) factor analysis, most of the love scales loaded on a single factor. Thus, he found evidence of a general love factor rather than measures of different kinds of love loading on separate factors. Clearly there is a need for further refinement of measures and models of love.

Laypeople's Conceptions of Love

The most extensive analyses of lay people's answers to the "What is love?" question have been conducted from a prototype perspective. As shall be seen, lay conceptions of love also have been explored based on the theory that love is a story and using a social categorization approach. More recently, ordinary people's views of love also have been examined from essentialist and cultural consensus perspectives.

The prototype approach. Eleanor Rosch (1973a, 1973b), a cognitive psychologist, made the bold claim that many natural language concepts are not amenable to classical definition (i.e. cannot be defined in terms of singly necessary and jointly sufficient criterial features). Rather, such concepts are organized around their clearest cases, or best examples, which she referred to as prototypes. Members of a category can be ordered in terms of their degree of resemblance to the prototypical cases, with members shading gradually into non-members. Boundaries between categories, therefore, are blurry, rather than clearly demarcated. In empirical tests of the theory, Rosch focused on object categories such as vegetables, fruit, furniture, and birds (see Mervis & Rosch, 1981, for a review). She demonstrated that some instances of these concepts were considered prototypical, whereas others were regarded as less representative. For example, people saw apples as prototypical of the concept of fruit; avocados were seen as nonprototypical. Moreover, this internal structure affected the cognitive processing of category-relevant information. In a reaction-time study, for example, the category membership of prototypical cases was confirmed more quickly than that of nonprototypical cases (e.g. apples were verified as a kind of fruit more quickly than were avocados; Rosch, 1973b).

Fehr and colleagues (Fehr, 1988; Fehr & Russell, 1984, 1991; see Fehr, 2001, 2006, 2013a, 2013b for reviews) examined whether more abstract concepts that had defied classical definition in the past, such as love, might be amenable to a prototype conceptualization. To test this possibility, Fehr and Russell (1991) conducted a prototype analysis of types of love. In a series of studies, they found that companionate kinds of love (e.g. familial love, parental love, friendship love) were considered prototypical of the concept; passionate kinds of love (e.g. romantic love, passionate love, sexual love) were considered nonprototypical. This prototype structure was validated using various methodologies. For example, in a reaction-time study, participants were faster to verify that maternal love is a kind of love than that infatuation is a kind of love.

In a subsequent series of studies, Fehr (1994) conducted a cluster analysis of fifteen types of love taken from Fehr and Russell's (1991) research. Types of companionate love formed one cluster (e.g. familial love, friendship love, maternal love) while types of passionate love (e.g. romantic love, passionate love, sexual love) formed another. It was concluded that lay conceptions of types of love are best summarized in terms of Berscheid and Hatfield's (1974) distinction between passionate love and companionate love.

The prototype approach was taken one step further by Fehr (1988), who hypothesized that the attributes or features of concepts also might be organized as prototypes, such that some features would be considered more representative of the concept than others. In her first study, participants were asked to list features of the concept of love (as well as the features of commitment; those findings are not presented here). These open-ended responses were coded, resulting in a final set of sixty-eight features listed by more than one participant. Characteristics such as honesty, trust, and caring were listed with the highest frequency. Features such as dependency, sexual passion, and physical attraction were listed less frequently. A new group of participants then rated these features in terms of prototypicality. Features such as trust, caring, intimacy, and friendship were considered central to love, whereas sexual passion, gazing at the other, and heart rate increases were considered peripheral.

This prototype structure was confirmed using a variety of methods. In a study of natural language use, it sounded peculiar to "hedge" prototypical, but not nonprototypical, features. For example, given information that Pat loved Chris, the statement that "Pat sort of trusts Chris" was rated as peculiar-sounding, whereas the statement that "Pat is sort of dependent on Chris" sounded more natural to participants. Prototypical features of love also were more salient in memory than were nonprototypical features. Overall, the findings converged with those in the analysis of types of love: People considered companionate love to capture the meaning of love, whereas passionate love was considered peripheral.

In subsequent research, Aron and Westbay (1996) factor analyzed the sixty-eight features of love identified by Fehr (1988). Their analysis yielded three factors, which they interpreted as corresponding to the passion, intimacy, and commitment components of Sternberg's triangular love. Regardless of whether participants were asked to provide prototypicality ratings or the applicability of these features to their own relationship, the intimacy factor was rated highest, followed by the commitment factor, with the passion factor receiving the lowest ratings.

Following Fehr's (1988) prototype analysis of features of love, relationship scientists conducted prototype analyses of the features of specific kinds of love. For example, Regan, Kocan, and Whitlock (1998) conducted a prototype analysis of the concept of romantic love (treated as synonymous with "being in love"). They extracted 119 features from participants' open-ended responses. The most frequently generated features were as follows: trust, sexual attraction/desire, acceptance and tolerance, spend time together, and share thoughts and secrets. Features that were produced with the lowest frequency were as follows: adoration, caress, submission/obedience to the other, and controlling. When these features were rated in terms of prototypicality, the highest ratings were assigned to trust, honesty, happiness, caring, and intimacy. These features also were rated as most prototypical of love (in general) in Fehr's (1988) analysis. Intermediate typicality ratings were given to features such as sexual attraction/desire, spend time together, touching/holding, passion, miss other/want to be together. It is interesting to note that these are the qualities that are emphasized in experts' definitions of romantic love. Finally, the features that received the lowest prototypicality ratings portrayed the "dark side" of romantic love (e.g. selfishness, controlling, depression, lies/deception).

Recently, Kito (2016) conducted a prototype analysis of seven concepts, including love and passion (the others were trust, commitment, intimacy, satisfaction, and relationship quality). For the concept of love, the highest prototypicality ratings were assigned to the following features: trust, honesty, respect, and faithfulness. The features that received the lowest ratings were lust, obsession, and butterflies (in stomach). For the concept of passion, the features that received the highest typicality ratings were as follows: love, intimacy, happiness, sense of connection, desire, and loyalty. The lowest ratings were given to features such as butterflies, holding hands, lust, and infatuation. It is interesting to note that features that are generally associated with companionate love, namely caring, honesty, loyalty, and communication, were generated for all seven concepts. To give another recent example, Manoharan and de Munck (2017) conducted a prototype analysis of the concepts of love, romantic love, and sex. The features of love that received the highest prototypicality ratings were similar to those identified in Fehr's (1988) prototype analysis of love. The features of romantic love were very similar to those identified by Regan et al. (1998) in their prototype analysis of romantic love. Love and romantic love had many features in common, with the greatest overlap for those features that received the highest prototypicality ratings in studies of love (e.g. honesty, trust, caring).

Fehr and Sprecher (2009) hypothesized that compassionate love also is structured as a prototype concept. In their first study, participants were asked to list the features or characteristics of compassionate love. Conceptions of compassionate love included feelings and emotions (e.g. feel happiest when with the person), cognitions (e.g. think about the other all the time), motivation (e.g. want to make the other happy), and behaviors (e.g. do anything for the other). In the next study, these features were rated in terms of prototypicality. The features that received the highest prototypicality ratings were trust, honesty, caring, understanding, and support. Once again, these are features that are central to the concept of love itself (Fehr, 1988). The features that were designated as lowest in prototypicality were features such as do anything for the other, put other ahead of self, and make sacrifices for the other. These are the kinds of features that experts use to define compassionate love (see Shacham-Dupont, 2003). This prototype structure was confirmed using a variety of methods (e.g. reaction time, memory biases).

It is remarkable that in the prototype analyses of romantic love, compassionate love, and even passion, the features that received the highest ratings are those that are considered most prototypical of the concept of love in general (Fehr, 1988). This suggests that, in the minds of ordinary people, romantic/passionate love and compassionate love are, first and foremost, kinds of love. The less prototypical features seem to serve the diagnostic function of identifying which specific kind of love it is. In the case of romantic/passionate love, the less prototypical features specify that this is the kind of love that involves sexual attraction, wanting to spend time with the other, touching/holding, and so on. In the case of compassionate love, the nonprototypical features, such as sacrifice and put the other first, indicate that this is a kind of love that involves giving of oneself for the good of another.

Other prototype-based approaches. Several other researchers have conducted prototype-based analyses of love. Buss (1988) conducted a prototype analysis of the behavioral indicators of love. In this research, participants were asked to list acts or behaviors that exemplify love. These behaviors then were rated for prototypicality by a new sample. Behaviors that were indicative of commitment (e.g. "She agreed to marry him") received high prototypicality ratings. Behaviors that referred to sexuality or passion (e.g. "He made love to her") received low ratings.

Another approach that has been taken in the prototype literature is to assess lay people's accounts of particular experiences of love (rather than asking them to describe the meaning of the concept, as in Fehr's research). For example, Shaver, Schwartz, Kirson, and O'Connor (1987) asked participants to describe an experience of love (and other emotions). Features were extracted from these accounts and classified as antecedents (e.g. feeling wanted/needed by the other, finding the other attractive), responses (e.g. wanting to be physically close to the other, kissing, sex), physiological reactions (e.g. high energy, fast heartbeat), behaviors (e.g. gazing, smiling), and so on. A variation of this method was used by Fitness and Fletcher (1993) in their analysis of love (and other emotions) as experienced in the context of a marital relationship. More specifically, they asked married couples to describe the most typical incident that would elicit feelings of love for one's spouse. Love experiences were triggered by events such as thinking about one's partner, receiving support from him or her, sharing happy times, and so on. The accounts also included low-arousal physiological responses such as feelings of warmth and relaxed muscles. The behaviors listed included the desire to be physically close to one's partner, giving presents, hugging and kissing, or doing nothing.

In conclusion, prototype analyses of love have taken different forms. Some researchers have asked participants to list features of the concept of love itself or features of a specific kind of love. Others have asked participants to describe an experience of love. Each of these approaches presumably is accessing a different kind of relational knowledge. As has been suggested elsewhere (e.g. Fehr, 2005; Surra & Bohman, 1991), there probably are different levels, or at least different storehouses, of knowledge for concepts such as love. At the most general level, people hold culturally shared conceptions of love. It seems reasonable to assume that this is the kind of knowledge that is being tapped when people are asked to describe the features of the concept or to list the behaviors that are typical of love. People also are likely to hold relationship-specific representations of love, based on their own experiences. This may well be the kind of knowledge that is accessed when people are asked to describe particular experiences or episodes of love.

Love is a story. According to Sternberg (1994, 1995, 1996, 1997, 1998a, 1998b, 2006), people hold implicit theories of what love is – how it begins, unfolds, and (possibly) ends. These love stories are a product of an individual's own characteristics and the messages about love and relationships that the person has extracted from the media, observation of other people's experiences, and his or her own past experiences. Sternberg maintains that these stories are not necessarily consciously held, but, nevertheless play an important role in people choices of partners and in the dynamics of relationships (e.g. whether the relationship is satisfying and fulfilling, whether the relationship survives). In this program of research, twenty-six love stories have been identified (see Sternberg, 1998b, 2006, for reviews). This is not considered to be an exhaustive set, but rather a sampling of the wide range of love stories that people construct. The three most commonly endorsed stories are *travel* ("Love is a journey"), *gardening* ("Relationships need to be continually nurtured and tended to") and *democratic government* ("Two partners share power equally"). The stories that are least endorsed are *horror* ("Relationships become interesting when you terrorize or are terrorized by your partner"), *collector* ("Partner viewed as "fitting in" some overall scheme; partner viewed in a detached way"), *autocratic government* ("One partner dominates or controls the other"), and *game* ("Love is a game or sport").

According to Sternberg, the theory of love is a story falls under the umbrella of prototype approaches, in the sense that not every person's love story necessarily will contain all of the elements of that story (as identified in Sternberg and colleagues' research). Further, people hold multiple stories. These are arranged in a hierarchy such that some stories are dominant or salient, whereas others are lower-level. Potential partners that people encounter will match their story to varying degrees. There is evidence that relationships fare best when both partners have similar love stories (see Sternberg 1998b, 2006).

The social-categorization approach. Myers and Berscheid (1997) developed the social-categorization approach as an indirect way of assessing lay conceptions of love. In this research, the meaning of the terms "love" and "in love" was elucidated by having participants list the names of people in their lives who belonged in each category. Participants also were asked to nominate people toward whom they experienced sexual attraction/ desire. It was found that love is a much broader category (i.e. more names were listed) than the category of "in love." Moreover, the concept of love subsumed the concept of "in love." It was also the case that the people who were listed for the "in love" category generally also were named for the sexual attraction/desire category (but not for "love"), suggesting that the type of love referred to by the term "in love" contains a sexual component. Thus, another approach to understanding love and types of love is ask lay-people to nominate the members of these categories. This approach holds considerable promise as a subtle or indirect method for accessing people's conceptions of love and related constructs.

The essentialist approach. More recently, Bergner and colleagues (Duda & Bergner, 2017, Hegi & Bergner, 2010; see Bergner, Davis, Saternus, Walley, & Tyson, 2013, for a review) have articulated an "essentialist view" of love by which they mean that people define the concept of love in terms of at least one necessary or essential feature. (The essentialist approach is rooted in descriptive psychology; see, e.g., Davis & Todd, 1985.) This view is seen as antithetical to the prototype approach to love, given that the central tenet of prototype theory is that concepts such as love are not definable in terms of necessary and sufficient features. The essentialist feature identified in this model is "investment in the well-being of the other" (also referred to as "caring for the other's well-being for his or her own sake"), a relatively broad term that includes caring, selfless giving, investing effort in promoting the other's happiness, and the like. Hegi and Bergner (2010; see also Bergner et al., 2013) conducted two studies to test the hypothesis that people hold an essentialist view of love. In Study 1, it was found that when "investment in the well-being of the other" was described as missing from romantic love, companionate love, altruistic love, or parental love, people found it contradictory to assert that the two people loved one another. Other features of love that have been identified in the literature (e.g. trust, respect, intimacy, commitment) did not score as high in "essentialness" assessed in this manner. In Study 2, participants were asked to judge how deficient a relationship would be if it were missing these features. Investment in the well-being of the other received high ratings (meaning that a relationship would be seriously deficient if this feature were missing). However, other features of love such as trust, commitment, and emotional intimacy also received high ratings. The authors concluded that their Study 1 findings suggest that people take an essentialist approach to defining love, whereas their Study 2 findings suggest that people switch to prototype approach when asked to evaluate what constitutes a good relationship. It is not clear why human cognition would evolve such that people would organize knowledge of what love means differently from knowledge of what constitutes a good relationship.

Cultural consensus approach. Cultural consensus theory is a statistical framework for the study of individual differences in the knowledge of culturally shared views of a concept or phenomenon. The methodology also allows for the identification of individual differences (e.g. gender, personality) as well as response tendencies such as guessing. Recently, this methodology was used to examine consensus on what makes people feel loved (Heshmati et al., 2017; Oravecz, Muth, & Vandekerckhove, 2016). (Heshmati et al. suggest that this approach can be classified as a prototype approach, but with a broader focus.) The researchers constructed sixty scenarios that portrayed a wide range of love acts (i.e. scenarios pertaining to romantic love, familial and friendship love, and non-interpersonal kinds of love such as love for nature or pets), along with negative behaviors (e.g. controlling behaviors from others) and neutral acts. More specifically, participants received the sentence stem "Most people feel loved when …," followed by phrases intended to capture (1) trust and acceptance (e.g. "when somebody confides with them"), (2) support in needs and goals (e.g. "someone celebrates their accomplishments"), (3) symbolic/physical expressions (e.g. "they get gifts"), (4) sharing time with others (e.g. "they spend time with their friends"), (5) other possible sources of love (e.g. religion, pets, nature, patriotism, gratitude, politeness, etc.), (6) controlling behavior from others (e.g. "someone wants to know where they are at all times"), and (7) neutral scenarios (e.g. "the sun is shining"). Participants in these studies were asked whether *most people* would feel loved in these scenarios (True, False, or Don't Know). The results revealed that people agreed on the indicators of love and that these included both romantic and non-romantic (e.g. friends, family) scenarios. For example, there was a high level of consensus that the following scenarios were indicators of love: someone shows compassion toward them in difficult times, a child snuggles up to them, their pets are happy to see them, and someone tells them "I love you." Moreover, there was evidence of individual differences in how knowledgeable people were about the cultural consensus on the meaning of love. For example, women were more likely to know the cultural consensus on love than men, as were people who were currently in a relationship and those who scored high on agreeableness or neuroticism.

Measurement of Conceptions of Love

Progress in any area of research is dependent on the availability of psychometrically sound measurement instruments to assess the constructs of interest. Research in the close-relationships field has focused overwhelming on romantic/passionate love. The most widely used scales in this area assess the experience of this kind of love. (The focus in this section will be on scales that assess conceptions of, or beliefs about, romantic/passionate love.) Although companionate (friendship-based) love has long been recognized as an important theoretical construct, there is not a standard scale for measuring the experience or conceptions of this kind of love. (The most commonly used measure is the Storge love style scale.) Sprecher and Fehr (2005) developed the Compassionate Love Scale to assess the experience of compassionate love (or the proclivity to experience this kind of love). At this point, no scales have been published to assess attachment as a kind of love.

Romantic/Passionate Love

Attempts to measure people's views of romantic love date back at least to 1944, when Gross developed the Belief Pattern Scale for Measuring Attitudes Toward Romanticism. This eighty-item scale included items such as, "It is important to choose a handsome person with an attractive figure for a sweetheart" and "The impetuous person makes the best kind of sweetheart." A subset of these items was intended to assess a contrasting "realist" view of romantic love (e.g. "A girl should not expect her sweetheart to be chivalrous on all occasions"). A large number of scales to measure romantic beliefs was published in the decades that followed, including the Attitudes Toward Romanticism Scale (Hobart, 1957), the Attitudes Toward Love Scale (Knox & Sporakowski, 1968), the Romantic Love Complex (Spaulding, 1970), the Romantic Idealist Factor (Fengler, 1974), the Attitudes Toward Love Scale (Munro & Adams, 1978) and the Romantic Beliefs Scale (Sprecher & Metts, 1989; see Fehr, 1994, for a review). In general, these scales assess the extent to which a respondent subscribes to romantic beliefs such as true love overcomes all obstacles, there is only one true love for each person, it is possible to fall in love at first sight, and true love lasts forever.

The proliferation of social-psychological models of love in the mid 1980s was accompanied by a surge in scale construction. Most of these scales were developed to assess the experience of love (e.g. PLS, Hatfield & Sprecher, 1986; Triangular Love Scale, Sternberg, 1998a; see Fehr, 2013a, 2013b, for reviews). An exception is Hendrick and Hendrick's Love Attitudes Scale (1986), which measures a combination of people's beliefs about love (e.g. "Genuine love first requires *caring* for a while") and their relationship experiences ("My lover and I were attracted to each other immediately after we first met"). There is a scale for each of the six different approaches that people take to romantic love. The Eros scale assesses a romantic/passionate love style. A relationship-specific scale that focuses exclusively on relationship experiences subsequently was developed (Hendrick & Hendrick, 1990). However, the original Love Attitudes Scale is much more widely used (Fehr, 2013a, 2013b).

Fehr (1994; see also Fehr & Broughton, 2001) developed a prototype-based scale to assess conceptions of love. On this measure, participants are presented with prototypes (i.e. feature lists) depicting twenty kinds of love and are asked to rate how similar the view of love portrayed in each prototype is to their own view of love. A romantic/passionate conception of love is measured by summing ratings of feature lists depicting passionate love, romantic love, infatuation, sexual love, and the like (based on the results of a cluster analysis). Of course, researchers also can use ratings of the individual prototypes if they have a specific interest in a particular variety of romantic/passionate love (e.g. infatuation). The disadvantage of this approach is that participants are required to read a relatively long list of features of each kind of love before making their rating. Moreover, their agreement or disagreement with each individual feature is unknown. Thus, a next step for this line of research would be to gather prototoypicality ratings of the features of each of these kinds of love and construct shorter scales that would include only the most prototypical features.

An inventory also has been developed to assess the extent to which people subscribe to each of the twenty-six stories identified by Sternberg and colleagues (see Sternberg, 1998b). For example, the gardening story is measured with items such as "I believe that relationships need to be nourished constantly in order to survive the ups and downs in life" and "I believe that any relationship that is left unattended will not survive." The love as art story is assessed with items such as "Physical attractiveness is quite honestly the most essential characteristic I look for in a partner."

In short, there are standard scales available to assess people's beliefs about romantic love. Some of the early scales no longer seem relevant to present-day relationships. Scales that were constructed in the 1980s are the most widely used today. However, most of these scales focus on how people experience romantic/passionate love rather than how they think about these concepts. An exception is Sternberg's love stories inventory that assesses the extent to which people subscribe to various beliefs about the course of romantic love.

Companionate Love

Given that companionate love has been "on the table" since the beginning of research on love, it is surprising that no standard scale exists to measure either the experience or conceptions of this kind of love. (Some scales have been constructed for use in individual studies but have not become widely used, validated measures; see Fehr, 2013a, 2013b.) The Storge (friendship-based love) love style scale of Hendrick and Hendrick's (1986) Love Attitudes Scale is most often used to assess companionate love. This scale contains statements such as "The best kind of love grows out of a long friendship" which seems to taps conceptions, along with items that seem to assess the experience of companionate love (e.g. "Our love is really a deep friendship, not a mysterious, mystical emotion"). As mentioned earlier, in a meta-analysis, the Storge love style scale was found to behave differently than other companionate love scales (Masuda, 2003).

Fehr (1994) developed a prototype-based measure of companionate love. In this research, participants rated the extent to which prototypes of various kinds of companionate love captured their own conception of love (e.g. friendship love, familial love, maternal love, affection). The idea was that each of these prototypes could be administered separately or a more global conception of companionate love could be assessed by summing the ratings of these prototypes (based on a cluster analysis). This measure has the same limitations as those noted above when describing the romantic/passionate love prototype-based measure.

Thus, despite the importance of the construct of companionate love in both experts' and lay conceptions of love, there is still a need for a psychometrically sound scales. Ideally, measures would be created to assess both conceptions and the experience of this kind of love.

Compassionate Love

As mentioned earlier, social scientists are beginning to turn their attention toward compassionate love. The Agape love style scale of Hendrick and Hendrick's (1986) Love Attitudes Scale depicts an altruistic, sacrificial kind of love that is akin to compassionate love. This scale contains items such as: "I would rather suffer myself than let my lover suffer" and "I would endure all things for the sake of my lover." Thus, these items appear to refer to a specific person rather than beliefs or conceptions of altruistic love. (Indeed, the Agape items are identical on the Love Attitudes Scale and on the Relationship Specific version.)

Sprecher and Fehr (2005) created a twenty-one-item self-report instrument to measure people's dispositional tendency to experience compassionate love. In developing the Compassionate Love Scale, research on lay conceptions of compassionate love (see Fehr & Sprecher's 2009 prototype analysis) was the starting point. Items also were taken from Underwood (2002), who assessed compassionate love with two items (e.g. "I feel a selfless caring for others"), from the Agape love scale (e.g. Hendrick & Hendrick, 1986), and from standard romantic love scales that contained items referring to sacrifice or selflessness (e.g. Rubin's [1970] Love Scale). This scale is focused on people's proclivity to experience compassionate love toward others, rather than assessing their conceptions per se. (Information on the psychometric properties of this scale can be found in a compendium of compassion and compassionate love scales compiled by Sprecher and Fehr, in press.)

Gender Similarities and Differences in Conceptions of Love

"Thoughtful men, and probably all women, have speculated on the nature of love" (Harry Harlow, 1958, p. 673). Are men and women in agreement when speculating on the nature of love? The answer to that question depends on whether the question is asked with respect to the concept of love in general or with respect to specific kinds of love.

Love in general. In studies of the prototype of love in general, gender differences typically are not found when women's and men's prototypicality ratings are compared. Researchers who have correlated women's and men's prototypicality ratings and consistently have found very high correlations (see Kito, 2016 for a recent example; see Fehr, 2013a, 2013b, for reviews of earlier studies).

Romantic/passionate love. There is a longstanding stereotype that women are more likely than men to hold a romantic view of love. In a recent study, Ackerman and colleagues (2011) approached women and men "on the street" and asked them two questions: "Who normally says they are in love *first* in romantic relationships?" and "In a new relationship, who thinks about getting serious first?" Nearly two-thirds of participants (64.4%) responded "women" to the first question; 84.4% of participants responded "women" to the second question. In a follow-up study, the researchers asked participants (undergraduates) to recall a romantic relationship in which love was expressed and to indicate who had done so first and at what point in the relationship. Nearly two-thirds (61.2%) of the sample reported that the man had expressed love first. Men also reported having thought about confessing love significantly earlier in the relationship (forty-two days earlier on average) than women (Ackerman, Griskevicius, & Li, 2011).

Is this gender difference also reflected in women's and men's conceptions of love? When focusing on romantic beliefs, it is quite clear that men are the more romantic sex. For example, men are more likely than women to subscribe to romantic beliefs such there is only one "true love" for a person, that true love lasts forever, and that it is possible to fall in love at first sight (e.g. Rubin, Peplau, & Hill, 1981; Sprecher & Metts, 1989). In contrast, women see love in more practical, pragmatic terms, believing that socioeconomic resources should be considered when choosing a partner, that a satisfying relationship can be had with a number of potential partners and that partner choices should be based on similarity in terms of backgrounds (see Hendrick & Hendrick, 1997, for a review). Consistent with these gender differences, Fehr and Broughton (2001) found that men rated prototypes of various kinds of passionate kinds of love (e.g. romantic love, passionate love, sexual love) as capturing their own view of love to a greater extent than did women.

There are some exceptions. For example, men generally do not score higher than women when romantic/passionate love is assessed with the Eros (romantic, passionate) love style scale (see Hendrick & Hendrick, 1997, for a review). Sprecher and Toro-Morn (2002) found that Chinese men scored higher than Chinese women on the Romantic Beliefs Scale (Sprecher & Metts, 1989), but there was not a significant gender difference in an American sample.

In Sternberg and colleagues' research on love as a story, men score higher than women for the art (choosing a partner based on physical attractiveness), pornography (love involves degrading or being degraded by the other), sacrifice (love is defined in terms of giving of oneself), and science fiction stories (the feeling that one's partner is an alien or strange incomprehensible). Women score higher than men for the travel story (love is a journey; see Sternberg, 1998b, 2006, for reviews).

Companionate love. There is evidence that women hold a more companionate, friendship-based conception of love compared with men. For example, women usually score higher than men on the Storge (friendship based) love style scale (see, e.g., Hendrick & Hendrick, 1990, 1997; Worobey, 2001). But, again, there are exceptions. In a study conducted in Australia, women scored higher than men on this scale, but this difference did not reach statistical significance (Heaven, Silva, Carey, & Holen, 2004). Sprecher and Toro-Morn (2002) did not find a gender difference on the Storge scale in an American sample, but found that men scored higher than women in a Chinese sample.

Fehr and Broughton (2001) found that women rated the prototype of friendship love as capturing their view of love to a greater extent than did men. However, there was no gender difference on ratings of a companionate love cluster that included prototypes of various kind of companionate love (familial kinds of love, affection, friendship love).

Compassionate/altruistic love. Fehr and Sprecher's (2009) prototype analysis of compassionate love revealed that women and men hold similar conceptions of compassionate love. More specifically, women's and men's prototypicality ratings of features of compassionate love did not differ significantly. Similarly, gender differences generally have not been found on the Agape (altruistic) love style scale (see Hendrick & Hendrick, 1997). However, in more recent studies, men have scored higher on this scale than women. This gender difference has been found in American (Sprecher & Toro-Morn, 2002; Worobey, 2001) Australian (Heaven et al., 2004) and Chinese samples (Sprecher & Toro-Morn, 2002). The reason for this shift is unclear.

Overall, the evidence suggests that men have a more passionate, romantic orientation to love, whereas women have a more companionate orientation. Consequently, it has been concluded that, when it comes to love, women and men inhabit different worlds or even different planets (e.g. Gray, 1992). Such a conclusion seems unwarranted, however, given that researchers generally assess only romantic/passionate love or only companionate love, but not both. Those who have measured both kinds of love typically have conducted between, and not within, gender analyses. Thus, the relative emphasis that women and men place on each of these kinds of love generally is not investigated. In a series of studies designed to address this issue, Fehr and Broughton (2001) presented women and men with prototypes depicting passionate and companionate love. Participants were asked to rate the extent to which the view of love depicted in each prototype corresponded to their own view of love. It was found that both women and men assigned significantly higher ratings to companionate love than to passionate love. In other words, by assessing both companionate and passionate love and comparing ratings of these kinds of love within each gender, a rather different picture emerged – one in which the sexes appear to exhibit much greater agreement than disagreement.

Cultural Similarities and Differences in Conceptions of Love

Fehr's (1988) research on the prototype of love was conducted on the West Coast of Canada. Other social scientists subsequently tested whether this prototype would be replicable in other regions of North America (see Fehr, 1993, for a review). For example, Button and Collier (1991) replicated Fehr's prototype of love with samples of university student and community participants living on the East Coast of Canada. Luby and Aron (1990) replicated Fehr's prototype analysis with Americans living on the West Coast of the United States. Their research was conducted with students at the University of California, Santa Cruz, as well as with members of the public enrolled in music appreciation classes. The findings across these studies were remarkably consistent which is noteworthy, given that in all studies, participants provided open-ended accounts which were then summarized using coding schemes independently constructed by each set of researchers. Consensus across data sets was especially strong for the features of love identified as prototypical by Fehr (1988). More specifically, five features of love were listed frequently and received the highest prototypicality ratings in each of these data sets: trust, caring, honesty, friendship, and respect. Intimacy also received high ratings in each study.

More recently Kito (2016) replicated Fehr's (1988) prototype of love in samples of university students and the community in central Canada. Thus, at least within North America, among university students and nonstudents alike, there appears to be consensus on the prototype of love and agreement that it is the companionate features of love that capture the meaning of the concept.

Turning to non-North American contexts, Lamm and Wiesmann (1997) asked university students in Germany to answer this question: "How can you tell that you love someone?" Other participants were asked about liking and still others about being in love. Although this research was not portrayed as a prototype analysis, the methodology was very similar in that participants' responses were coded and feature lists were derived for each concept. For love, the most frequent responses were as follows: positive mood when thinking about, or being with, the other, trust, desire to be with the other, altruistic behavior toward other, and self-disclosure. For the concept of "being in love" (which was treated as synonymous with romantic and passionate love), the most frequent responses were as follows: arousal when thinking about, or being with, the other, positive mood, thinking about the other, desire for the other's presence, and the like. The researchers concluded that there was considerable overlap between the indicators of love identified in this research and the features generated with the highest frequency in Fehr's (1988) prototype analysis.

Finally, Kline, Horton, and Zhang (2008) asked American university students and Asian students attending university in the United States to report on their attitudes and beliefs about love in marriage. The responses were highly similar in the two samples, particularly those listed with the highest frequency. For example, in the American sample, features such as trust, going out together, respect, and honesty were generated with high frequency. In the Asian sample, trust, caring, and respect were among the most frequently listed responses. As these examples illustrate, in both samples, the features that were paramount reflected a companionate conception of love more so than a passionate conception. The authors conclude that, "These findings parallel and validate Fehr's (1988) prototype analysis of love ... and extend the prototype findings to East Asians" (Kline et al., 2008, p. 211).

Another approach has been to examine the hierarchical structure of different emotions, including love. Shaver and colleagues conducted a prototype analysis of love and other emotions in the United States (Shaver, Schwartz, Kirson, & O'Connor, 1987) and in Indonesia (Shaver, Murdaya, & Fraley, 2001). Specifically, participants were given a large number of emotion terms and asked to sort them into categories. Similar emotion hierarchies were found in both countries, such that positive and negative emotion were higher-order, superordinate categories and love was situated at the middle, basic level. However, cultural differences emerged at the finer-grained, subordinate level. For example, Indonesian participants had a much broader concept of types of love. They identified twenty-six love terms as subcategories of the concept whereas American participants selected sixteen terms. In both countries, terms referring to sexual desire/arousal and affection/liking/fondness were classified as sub-categories of love. However, the Indonesian concept of love also included subcategories referring to yearning or longing. The researchers conclude that the superordinate and basic levels of emotion concepts may be universal, but that cultures may vary considerably in terms of the finer-grained categories that are seen as comprising love.

Relational Implications of Conceptions of Love

Kelley (1983) pointed out that the kinds of questions people ask about their own relationships almost invariably involve love and commitment issues (e.g. "How can I be sure my partner loves me?"). He went on to say that people's conceptions of love influence whether they initiate, maintain, or end their relationships. As shall be seen, empirical research, although not plentiful, confirms that the way in which people construe love plays an important role in predicting how satisfied they are in their relationship and, ultimately, whether the relationship endures.

Conceptions of Love and Relationship Satisfaction

The outcome variable that has most frequently been correlated with conceptions of love is satisfaction. As shall be seen, conceptions of romantic/passionate love, companionate love, and compassionate love are all linked to the level of satisfaction in a relationship.

Romantic/passionate love. The Eros love style scale is the measure of romantic/ passionate love that most often has been correlated with relationship satisfaction (see Fehr, 2013a, 2013b; as noted earlier, the items on this scale refer to a particular partner and therefore this scale may not actually capture *conceptions* of love). In the studies reviewed by Fehr (2013a, 2013b) correlations varied widely (from –.00 to.75), with most correlations falling in the .40–.60 range. (Some studies obtained higher correlations for men than for women; others found the opposite; researchers generally did not test whether these correlations differed significantly.)

Sternberg and colleagues found that endorsement of positive, adaptive love stories was unrelated to satisfaction, but that endorsement of maladaptive love stories was significantly negatively correlated with relationship satisfaction. The latter stories included love as horror, science fiction, business, and love is a game, to name a few.

Companionate love. The measure of companionate love that has been most frequently correlated with relationship satisfaction is the Storge love style scale. Conceptions of companionate love assessed in this way are largely unrelated to relationship satisfaction. In most studies, correlations fall in the range of 0 to.26, with the majority hovering around the low end of this range (see Fehr, 2013a, 2013b). Thus, it would appear that whether or not one agrees with statements such as "It is hard to say exactly where friendship ends and love begins" has little bearing on how happy one is in one's romantic relationship.

Compassionate love. The relation between conceptions of compassionate love (assessed by the Agape love style scale) and satisfaction also has been explored. Correlations vary widely, ranging from .07 to .57 (see Fehr, 2013a, 2013b), with most correlations falling in the .20s. When coefficients vary by gender, generally there is a stronger link between agape and satisfaction for women than for men.

Thus, there is some evidence that the way in which people construe love is associated with relationship happiness. People who endorse a romantic, passionate love style tend to be satisfied in their romantic relationships, although there is considerable variability in the strength of this association. Those who hold an altruistic, compassionate conception also are likely to be satisfied, although this relation is not particularly strong. So far there is little evidence that a companionate conception of love is associated with relationship satisfaction. The Storge love style scale was never intended to be a measure of conceptions of companionate love, but rather a measure of a friendship-based orientation to love. Thus, the question about whether people's conceptions of companionate love predict satisfaction remains an open one.

Conceptions of Love and the Deterioration and Dissolution of Relationships

People's beliefs about, and conceptions of, love play a role in relational decline. For example, Simpson and colleagues (1986) asked respondents whether the disappearance of love was a sufficient reason for ending a marriage. The question was posed to participants at two time points – 1976 and 1984. In 1976, nearly two-thirds of women and men agreed that loss of love was valid grounds for marital dissolution. In 1984, the numbers were lower, but even so, nearly half of the participants agreed with this view. Levine, Sato, Hashimoto and Verma (1995) conducted a cross-cultural replication of this research. They found that people in Western cultures were more likely to hold this belief than people in Eastern cultures, although the differences between cultures were not particularly clear or strong.

Other researchers have focused on whether people's beliefs about decline and dissolution depend on the kind of love that is waning. For example, Fehr (1988) conducted a scenarios study to explore the implications of conceptions of companionate and passionate love for the deterioration and dissolution of relationships. Violations of companionate features of love (e.g. failures of trust or respect) were seen as undermining the level of love in a relationship more so than violations of passionate features (e.g. no longer experiencing sexual attraction). In line with these findings, Sprecher and Toro-Morn (2002) found that the disappearance of passionate love was not regarded by American university students as grounds for ending a marriage if the relationship was still high in companionate love.

Thus, the loss of love is seen as a reason to end a relationship. People are especially likely to regard the loss of companionate love as leading to relationship deterioration and dissolution.

Future Directions

There is little doubt that progress has been made in the quest to uncover lay conceptions of love itself as well as different kinds of love. However, there are still miles to go before love researchers can sleep. One important area for future research is to elucidate lay conceptions of the understudied types of love in Berscheid's typology. Conceptions of companionate love have not been studied extensively, nor have lay conceptions of attachment love. (There has been one prototype analysis of compassionate love; Fehr & Sprecher, 2009.) Prototype analyses would be especially useful for fleshing out what these kinds of love mean to ordinary people.

Once social scientists have documented the meaning of these four basic kinds of love for laypeople, it will be critical to explore empirically the implications of this knowledge for "real world" relationships. This is a glaring omission in current work on lay conceptions of love. As stated earlier, Kelley (1983) pointed out that people's conceptions of love influence whether they regard themselves to be in love currently and decisions such as whether to remain in a relationship. If relationship partners hold differing views of love, the stage is set for miscommunication, misunderstandings, and potentially, the demise of the relationship itself.

Relationship science also would benefit from further investigations of individual differences (e.g. personality, Fehr & Broughton, 2001) and cultural differences in conceptions of love. In Western cultures, decisions about marriage are based on individuals' perceptions of whether or not they love the other person (usually meaning romantic/passionate love; see Fehr, 2013a, 2013b). In contrast, in more collectivist cultures, people place a higher value on companionate love (e.g. Dion & Dion, 1996; see Fehr, 2013a, 2013b). One might also expect more compassionate conceptions of love in non-individualistic cultures. Conversely, attachment love might be stronger in individualist cultures than in collectivist cultures, given that in individualist cultures, romantic partners often serve as the primary attachment figure. Research that includes all of the kinds of love in Berscheid's typology would be invaluable in fleshing out universals and cultural nuances in conceptions of love.

Analyses of individual and cultural differences in love stories also merits further research. According to Sternberg's theory, love stories are a function of people's dispositions and lessons learned from observation and experience. For example, it would be interesting to examine the relation between love stories and the Big Five personality traits. One would expect that those who score high on nurturance, for example, would be more likely to endorse the "love is a garden" story. In cultures in which women are afforded few of the same rights as men, autocratic government might be a love story that is more likely to be learned compared to more egalitarian societies.

To conclude, in his seminal paper, "The nature of love," Harry Harlow (1958) wrote that "Psychologists … not only show no interest in the origin and development of love or affection, but they seem to be unaware of its very existence" (p. 673). Fortunately, half a century later, psychologists can no longer be accused of blitheful unawareness of love. There is now a substantial body of work on both relationship scientists' and lay people's conceptions of love. However, much more needs to be done before relationship scientists fully understand how everyday people conceive of love and the implications of those conceptions for the formation, continuation, and termination of intimate relationships.

References

Ackerman, J. M., Griskevicius, V., & Li, N. P. (2011). Let's get serious: Communicating commitment in romantic relationships. *Journal of Personality and Social Psychology, 100*(6), 1079–1094. doi:10.1037/a0022412.

Aron, A., & Westbay, L. (1996). Dimensions of the prototype of love. *Journal of Personality and Social Psychology, 70*(3), 535–551. doi:10.1037/0022-3514.70.3.535.

Beck, L. A., Pietromonaco, P. R., DeBuse, C. J., Powers, S. I., & Sayer, A. G. (2013). Spouses' attachment pairings predict neuroendocrine, behavioral, and psychological responses to marital conflict. *Journal of Personality and Social Psychology, 105*(3), 388.

Bergner, R., Davis, K., Saternus, L., Walley, S., & Tyson, T. (2013). Romantic love: An empirically based essentialist account. In R. Bergner, K. Davis, F. Lubuguin, & W. Schwartz (Eds.), *Advances in descriptive psychology*, Vol. 10. Ann Arbor, MI: Descriptive Psychology Press.

Berscheid, E. (2006). Searching for the meaning of "love". In R. J. Sternberg & K. Weis (Eds.), *The new psychology of love* (pp. 171–183). New Haven, CT: Yale University Press.

(2010). Love in the fourth dimension. *Annual Review of Psychology, 61,* 1–25. doi:10.1146/annurev.psych.093008.100318.

Berscheid, E., & Walster [Hatfield], E. (1974). A little bit about love. In T. L. Huston (Ed.),*Foundations of interpersonal attraction* (pp. 356–381). New York: Academic Press.

Buss, D. M. (1988). Love acts: The evolutionary biology of love. In R. J. Sternberg, M. L. Barnes, R. J. Sternberg, & M. L. Barnes (Eds.), *The psychology of love* (pp. 100–118). New Haven, CT: Yale University Press.

Button, C. M., & Collier, D. R. (1991). A comparison of people's concepts of love and romantic love. Paper presented at the Canadian Psychological Association Conference, Calgary, Alberta.

Davis, K. E., & Todd, M. J. (1985). Assessing friendship: Prototypes, paradigm cases and relationship description. In S. Duck & D. Perlman (Eds.),*Understanding personal relationships: An interdisciplinary approach* (pp. 17–38). Thousand Oaks, CA: Sage.

Dion, K. K., & Dion, K. L. (1996). Cultural perspectives on romantic love. *Personal Relationships, 3,* 5–17.

Duda M. L., & Bergner, R. M. (2017). Sustaining versus losing love: Factors discriminating the two. *Journal of Marriage and Family Review, 53*(2), 166–184.

Fehr, B. (1988). Prototype analysis of the concepts of love and commitment. *Journal of Personality and Social Psychology, 55,* 557–579.

(1993). How do I love thee…? Let me consult my prototype. In S. Duck (Ed.), *Understanding personal relationships,* Vol. 1: *Individuals in relationships* (pp. 87–120). Newbury Park, CA: Sage.

(1994). Prototype-based assessment of laypeople's views of love. *Personal Relationships, 1*(4), 309–331. doi: 10.1111/j.1475–6811.1994.tb00068.x.

(1996). *Friendship processes.* Thousand Oaks, CA: Sage.

(2001). The status of theory and research on love and commitment. In G. J. O. Fletcher & M. S. Clark (Eds.), *Blackwell handbook of social psychology: Interpersonal processes* (pp. 331–356). Oxford, UK: Blackwell.

(2005). The role of prototypes in interpersonal cognition. In M. Baldwin (Ed.), *Interpersonal cognition* (pp. 180–206). New York: Guilford Press.

(2006). A prototype approach to studying love. In R. J. Sternberg, K. Weis, R. J. Sternberg, & K. Weis (Eds.), *The new psychology of love* (pp. 225–246). New Haven, CT: Yale University Press.

(2013a). Love: Conceptualization and experience. In J. A. Simpson & J. Dovidio (Eds.), *Handbook of personality and social psychology,* Vol. 2: *Interpersonal relationships and group processes* (pp. 495–522). Washington, DC: APA Press.

(2013b). The social psychology of love. In J. A. Simpson & L. Campbell (Eds.), *The Oxford handbook of close relationships* (pp. 201–233). New York: Oxford.

Fehr, B., & Broughton, R. (2001). Gender and personality differences in conceptions of love: An interpersonal theory analysis. *Personal Relationships, 8,* 115–136.

Fehr, B., Harasymchuk, C., & Sprecher, S. (2014). Compassionate love in romantic relationships: A review and some new findings. *Journal of Social and Personal Relationships, 31*(5), 575–600.

Fehr, B., & Russell, J. A. (1984). Concept of emotion viewed from a prototype perspective. *Journal of Experimental Psychology: General, 113*, 464–486.

(1991). The concept of love viewed from a prototype perspective. *Journal of Personality and Social Psychology, 60*, 425–438.

Fehr, B., & Sprecher, S. (2009). Prototype analysis of compassionate love. *Personal Relationships, 16*, 343–364.

(in press). Compassionate love: What we know so far. In M. Hojjat & D. Cramer (Eds.), *Positive psychology of love* (pp. 106–120). New York: Oxford Press.

Fehr, B., Sprecher, S., & Underwood, L. (Eds.) (2009). *The science of compassionate love: Theory, research, and applications.* Malden, MA: Wiley-Blackwell.

Fengler, A. P. (1974). Romantic love in courtship: Divergent paths of male and female students. *Journal of Comparative Family Studies, 5*(1), 134–139.

Felmlee, D. H., & Sprecher, S. (2006). Love. In J. Stets and J. H. Turner (Eds.), *Handbook of the sociology of emotions* (pp. 389–409). Boston, MA: Springer.

Fitness, J., & Fletcher, G. J. (1993). Love, hate, anger, and jealousy in close relationships: A prototype and cognitive appraisal analysis. *Journal of Personality and Social Psychology, 65*, 942–958.

Graham, J. M. (2011). Measuring love in romantic relationships: A meta-analysis. *Journal of Social and Personal Relationships, 28*(6), 748–771. doi: 10.1177/0265407510389126.

Gray, J. (1992). *Men are from Mars, women are from Venus: A practical guide for improving communication and getting what you want in relationships.* New York: HarperCollins.

Gross, L. (1944). A belief pattern scale for measuring attitudes toward romanticism. *American Sociological Review, 9*(5), 463–472.

Harlow, H. F. (1958). The nature of love. *American Psychologist, 13*(12), 673–685. doi: 10.1037/h0047884.

Hatfield, E., & Sprecher, S. (1986). Measuring passionate love in intimate relationships. *Journal of Adolescence, 9*(4), 383–410. doi: 10.1016/S0140-1971 (86)80043-4.

Hatfield, E., & Walster, G. W. (1978). *A new look at love.* Lantham, MA: University Press of America.

Hazan, C., & Shaver, P. (1987). Romantic love conceptualized as an attachment process. *Journal of Personality and Social Psychology, 52*(3), 511–524. doi: 10.1037/0022-3514.52.3.511.

Heaven, P. L., Da Silva, T., Carey, C., & Holen, J. (2004). Loving styles: Relationships with personality and attachment styles. *European Journal of Personality, 18*(2), 103–113. doi: 10.1002/per.498.

Hegi, K. E., & Bergner, R. M. (2010). What is love? An empirically-based essentialist account. *Journal of Social and Personal Relationships, 27*(5), 620–636. doi: 10.1177/0265407510369605.

Hendrick, C., & Hendrick, S. (1986). A theory and method of love. *Journal of Personality and Social Psychology, 50*(2), 392–402. doi: 10.1037/0022-3514.50.2.392.

(1989). Research on love: Does it measure up? *Journal of Personality and Social Psychology, 56*(5), 784–794. doi: 10.1037/0022-3514.56.5.784.

(1990). A relationship-specific version of the Love Attitudes Scale. *Journal of Social Behavior and Personality, 5*(4), 239–254.

Hendrick, S. S., & Hendrick, C. (1997). Love and satisfaction. In R. J. Sternberg, M. Hojjat, R. J. Sternberg, & M. Hojjat (Eds.), *Satisfaction in close relationships* (pp. 56–78). New York: Guilford Press.

(2006). Styles of romantic love. In R. J. Sternberg & K. Weis (Eds.), *The new psychology of love* (pp. 149–170). New Haven, CT: Yale University Press.

Heshmati, S., Oravecz, Z., Pressman, S., Batchelder, W. H., Muth, C., & Vandekerckhove, J. (2017). What does it mean to feel loved: Cultural consensus and individual differences in felt love. *Journal of Social and Personal Relationships*. doi: 10.1177/0265407517724600.

Hobart, C. W. (1957). The incidence of romanticism during courtship. *Social Forces, 36*, 362.

Hwang, J., Plante, T., & Lackey, K. (2008). The development of the Santa Clara Brief Compassion Scale: An abbreviation of Sprecher and Fehr's Compassionate Love Scale. *Pastoral Psychology, 56*(4), 421–428. doi: 10.1007/s11089-008-0117-2.

Kelley, H. H. (1983). Love and commitment. In H. Kelley, E. Berscheid, A. Christensen, J. H. Harvey, T. L. Huston, et al. (Eds.), *Close relationships* (pp. 20–76). New York: W.H. Freeman.

Kito, M. (2016). Shared and unique prototype features of relationship quality concepts and their role in relationship functioning. *Personal Relationships, 23*, 759–786.

Kline, S. L., Horton, B., & Zhang, S. (2008). Communicating love: Comparisons between American and East Asian university students. *International Journal of Intercultural Relations, 32*(3), 200–214.

Knox, D. R., & Sporakowski, M. J. (1968). Attitudes of college students toward love. *Journal of Marriage and the Family, 30*(4), 638–642. doi: 10.2307/349508.

Knox Jr, D. H. (1970). Conceptions of love at three developmental levels. *Family Coordinator, 19*, 151–157.

Lamm, H., & Wiesmann, U. (1997). Subjective attributes of attraction: How people characterize their liking, their love, and their being in love. *Personal Relationships, 4*(3), 271–284. doi: 10.1111/j.1475-6811.1997.tb00145.x.

Lee, J. A. (1973). *The colours of love: An exploration of the ways of loving.* Don Mills, ON: New Press.

Levine, R., Sato, S., Hashimoto, T., & Verma, J. (1995). Love and marriage in eleven cultures. *Journal of Cross-Cultural Psychology, 26*(5), 554–571. doi: 10.1177/0022022195265007.

Luby, V., & Aron, A. (1990, July). A prototype structuring of love, like, and being-in-love. Paper presented at the Fifth International Conference on Personal Relationships, Oxford, UK.

Manoharan, C., & de Munck, V. (2017). The conceptual relationship between love, romantic love, and sex: A free list and prototype study of semantic association. *Journal of Mixed Methods Research*, *11*(2), 248–265.

Masuda, M. (2003). Meta-analyses of love scales: Do various love scales measure the same psychological constructs? *Japanese Psychological Research*, *45*(1), 25–37. doi: 10.1111/1468-5884.00030.

Mervis, C. B., & Rosch, E. (1981). Categorization of natural objects. *Annual Review of Psychology*, *32*, 89–115. doi: 10.1146/annurev.ps.32.020181.000513.

Meyers, S. A., & Berscheid, E. (1997). The language of love: The difference a preposition makes. *Personality and Social Psychology Bulletin*, *23*(4), 347–362. doi: 10.1177/0146167297234002.

Mikulincer, M., & Shaver, P. R. (2009). An attachment and behavioral systems perspective on social support. *Journal of Social and Personal Relationships*, *26*(1), 7–19.

(2016). *Attachment in adulthood: Structure, dynamics, and change*. New York: Guilford Press.

Munro, B., & Adams, G. R. (1978). Love American style: A test of role structure theory on changes in attitudes toward love. *Human Relations*, *31*(3), 215–228. doi: 10.1177/001872677803100302.

Oravecz, Z., Muth, C., & Vandekerckhove, J. (2016). Do people agree on what makes one feel loved? A cognitive psychometric approach to the consensus on felt love. *PLoS ONE*, *11*(4), e0152803.

Pietromonaco, P. R., & Beck, L. A. (2015). Attachment processes in adult romantic relationships. In M. Mikulincer, P. R. Shaver, J. A. Simpson, & J. F. Dovidio (Eds.), *APA handbook of personality and social psychology, Vol. 3: Interpersonal relations* (pp. 33–64). Washington, DC: American Psychological Association.

Regan, P. C., Kocan, E. R., & Whitlock, T. (1998). Ain't love grand! A prototype analysis of the concept of romantic love. *Journal of Social and Personal Relationships*, *15*(3), 411–420. doi: 10.1177/0265407598153006.

Rosch, E. H. (1973a). On the internal structure of perceptual and semantic categories. In T. E. Moore (Ed.), *Cognitive development and the acquisition of language* (pp. 111–144). New York: Academic Press.

(1973b). Natural categories. *Cognitive Psychology*, *4*(3), 328–350. doi: 10.1016/0010-0285(73)90017-0.

Rubin, Z. (1970). Measurement of romantic love. *Journal of Personality and Social Psychology*, *16*(2), 265–273. doi: 10.1037/h0029841.

(1973). *Liking and loving*. New York: Holt, Rinehart and Winston.

Rubin, Z., Peplau, L. A., & Hill, C. T. (1981). Loving and leaving: Sex differences in romantic attachments. *Sex Roles*, *7*(8), 821–835.

Shacham-Dupont, S. (2003). Compassion and love in relationships – Can they coexist? *Relationship Research News*, *2*, 13–15.

Shaver, P. R., Murdaya, U., & Fraley, R. (2001). Structure of the Indonesian emotion lexicon. *Asian Journal of Social Psychology*, 4(3), 201–224. doi: 10.1111/1467-839X.00086.

Shaver, P., Schwartz, J., Kirson, D., & O'Connor, C. (1987). Emotion knowledge: Further exploration of a prototype approach. *Journal of Personality and Social Psychology*, 52(6), 1061–1086. doi: 10.1037/0022-3514.52.6.1061.

Simpson, J. A., Campbell, B., & Berscheid, E. (1986). The association between romantic love and marriage: Kephart (1967) twice revisited. *Personality and Social Psychology Bulletin*, 12(3), 363–372. doi: 10.1177/0146167286123011.

Simpson, J. A., & Rholes, S. W. (2012). Adult attachment orientations, stress, and romantic relationships. *Advances in Experimental Social Psychology*, 45, 279.

Spaulding, C. B. (1970). The romantic love complex in American culture. *Sociology and Social Research*, 55(1), 82–100.

Sprecher, S., & Fehr, B. (2005). Compassionate love for close others and humanity. *Journal of Social and Personal Relationships*, 22(5), 629–651. doi: 10.1177/0265407505056439.

Sprecher, S., & Fehr, B. (in press). Compassionate Love Scale. In N. N. Singh & O. N. Medvedeve (Eds.), *Handbook of assessment in mindfulness*. New York: Springer.

Sprecher, S., & Metts, S. (1989). Development of the 'Romantic Beliefs Scale' and examination of the effects of gender and gender-role orientation. *Journal of Social and Personal Relationships*, 6(4), 387–411.

Sprecher, S., & Toro-Morn, M. (2002). A study of men and women from different sides of earth to determine if men are from Mars and women are from Venus in their beliefs about love and romantic relationships. *Sex Roles*, 46(5), 131–147.

Steck, L., Levitan, D., McLane, D., & Kelley, H. H. (1982). Care, need, and conceptions of love. *Journal of Personality and Social Psychology*, 43(3), 481–491. doi: 10.1037/0022-3514.43.3.481.

Sternberg, R. J. (1986). A triangular theory of love. *Psychological Review*, 93(2), 119–135. doi: 10.1037/0033-295X.93.2.119.

(1994). Love is a story. *The General Psychologist*, 30(1), 1–11.

(1995). Love as a story. *Journal of Social and Personal Relationships*, 12(4), 541–546.

(1996). Love stories. *Personal Relationships*, 3, 1359–1379.

(1997). Construct validation of a triangular love scale. *European Journal of Social Psychology*, 27(3), 313–335.

(1998a). *Cupid's arrow: The course of love through time*. New York: Cambridge University Press.

(1998b). *Love is a story*. New York: Oxford University Press.

(2006). A duplex theory of love. In R. J. Sternberg & K. Weis (Eds.), *The new psychology of love* (pp. 184–199). New Haven, CT: Yale University Press.

Surra, C. A., & Bohman, T. (1991). The development of close relationships: A cognitive perspective. In G. O. Fletcher & F. D. Fincham (Eds.), *Cognition in close relationships* (pp. 281–305). Hillsdale, NJ: Lawrence Erlbaum.

Tzeng, O. S. (1993). *Measurement of love and intimate relations: Theories, scales, and applications for love development, maintenance, and dissolution.* Westport, CT: Praeger/Greenwood.

Underwood, L. G. (2002). The human experience of compassionate love: Conceptual mapping and data from selected studies. In S. G. Post, L. G. Underwood, J. P. Schloss, & W. B. Hurlbut (Eds.), *Altruism and altruistic love: Science, philosophy, and religion in dialogue* (pp. 72–88). New York: Oxford University Press.

Worobey, J. (2001). Sex differences in associations of temperament with love-styles. *Psychological Reports, 89*(1), 25–26.

CHAPTER 9

Passionate Love

Cyrille Feybesse and Elaine Hatfield

Passionate love is a universal emotion (Jankowiak, 1995). Yet despite its universality, culture has a profound impact on people's definitions of love, and on the way they think, feel, and behave in romantic settings. Cross-cultural studies provide a glimpse into the complex world of emotion and allow us to gain an understanding of the extent to which people's emotional lives are written in their cultural and personal histories, as well as their evolutionary history, and in the interaction of the two (Tooby & Cosmides, 1992).

The Nature of Passionate Love

Poets, novelists, and social commentators have proposed numerous definitions of love. Scholars usually distinguish between two kinds of love: passionate love and companionate love (Hatfield, Purvis, & Rapson, 2018).

> Sweat pours down me, I shake all over, I go pale as green grass. I'm that close to being dead. —Sappho (630–580 BCE, an ancient Greek poet)

Passionate Love

Passionate love (sometimes called "obsessive love," "infatuation," "lovesickness," or "being-in-love") is a powerful emotional state. In this chapter we will focus on this kind of love. We will define such love as follows:

> A state of intense longing for union with another. Passionate love is a complex whole including appraisals of the situation, one's subjective feelings, expressions, patterned physiological processes, action tendencies, and instrumental behaviors. Reciprocated love (union with the other) is associated with ecstasy and a sense of fulfillment. Unrequited love (separation) is associated with feelings of emptiness, anxiety, and despair. (Hatfield et al., 2018, p. 5)

Usually, it is easy to identify people who have been hit by Cupid's arrow. Lovers are usually are usually aware of their emotions. Researchers have found that passionate love can occur at any age, even in young children (Hatfield, Schmitz, Cornelius, & Rapson, 1988), although passion is likely to be experienced in all its complexity after puberty (Hatfield & Rapson, 1993). Falling in love is more frequent among adolescents than young adults (Hill, Owen, Blakemore, & Drumm, 1997). Elderly individuals experience love, too, but they are plagued with fewer obsessional thoughts than are younger people (Wang & Nguyen, 1995).

Passionate love brings down a whirlwind of emotions. Lovers can tumble from delight to despair in a moment, depending on the progress of their relationship. They often experience a confusing array of ecstasy and happiness as well as fear and pain. Lovers may find it difficult to adjust to this plethora of emotions (Marazziti & Baroni, 2012). It is interesting to note that passionate love can emerge from the anxiety of daily life. Children and adolescents who are high in anxiety have been found to be more susceptible to the lure of passionate love (Hatfield & Rapson, 1996).

How Tightly Linked Are Passionate Love and Sexual Desire?

In the Victorian era, romantic love was considered to be a delicate, spiritual feeling – the antithesis of crude, animal lust. Freudians, of course, mocked such pretensions. They irritated romantics by insisting that chaste love was simply a sublimated form of carnal love, which lay bubbling just below the surface.

What about today? In the West, most college students make a sharp distinction between "being in love" (which embodies sexual feelings) and "loving" someone (which is not necessarily associated with sexual desire). Ellen Berscheid and her colleagues (Meyers & Berscheid, 1995) found that most students assumed that although you could "love" someone platonically, you could only be "in love" with someone you were sexually attracted to and desired sexually. They concluded: "Thus, our findings suggest that although sexuality may not be a central feature of love, it is most definitely a central feature of the state of being in love" (p. 24). In a national survey, Andrew Greeley (1991) interviewed newly married couples who said they were still in the "falling in love" stage of marriage. He found that passionate love is a highly sexual state. He described the falling in love stage of marriage this way: "When one is in love, one is absorbed, preoccupied, tense and intense, and filled with a sexual longing which permeates the rest of existence, making it both glorious and exhausting ... Those who are falling in love seem truly to be by love possessed." (Greeley, 1991, pp. 122–124)

In the end, Hatfield and Rapson (1987) concluded that passionate love and sexual desire were "kissing cousins." Passionate love was defined as "a longing for union" while sexual desire was defined as "a longing for sexual union."Today, among social psychologists this debate seems settled. As Susan and Clyde Hendrick (1987. pp. 282 and 293) noted:

> It is apparent to us that trying to separate love from sexuality is like trying to separate fraternal twins: they are certainly not identical, but, nevertheless, they are strongly bonded … Love and sexuality are strongly linked to each other and to both the physical and spiritual aspects of the human condition. For romantic personal relationships, sexual love and loving sexuality may well represent intimacy at its best.

There is abundant social-psychological evidence in support of the contention that in most people's minds, love and sex are tightly related – in fact, most people find it hard to imagine passionate love in the absence of sexual desire (Hatfield & Rapson, 2005; Regan et al., 1999, 2004; Regan & Berscheid, 1999; Ridge & Berscheid, 1989). (Naturally, men and women can easily imagine the converse – sexual desire without passionate love.) As Pamela Regan (2004, p. 115) observes:

> Theoretical discourse from a number of disciplines suggest that sexual desire is a distinguishing feature of the passionate love experience … Empirical research substantiates this hypothesis. People believe that sexual desire is part and parcel of the state of being in love, assume that couples who desire each other sexually are also passionately in love, and report a similar association when reflecting on their own dating relationships.

Of course, culture surely has a powerful impact on how likely young couples are to link passionate love, sexual desire, and sexual *expression* (Hatfield & Rapson, 2005). Many men, for example, are taught to separate sex and love, whereas many women are taught to connect the two. The different meanings attributed to sexual activity have been known to cause lovers much distress (Hatfield & Rapson, 2006). Age seems to play a role in the relationship sex has with love, since it has been demonstrated that the perception of the importance of sex to love decreases with age (Neto, 2012).

Neuroscientists and evolutionary psychologists, however, are still in sharp disagreement as to whether love and lust are very different systems, activating somewhat different brain systems (Cacioppo et al., 2013;

Diamond, 2003, 2004; Gonzaga et al., 2006) or are tightly linked (Bartels & Zeki, 2000). These neuroscientists do agree, however, that all of the brain systems for passionate love, sexual desire, and attachment do in fact communicate and coordinate with one another.

When the dust settles, we suspect neuropsychologists will come to acknowledge that although love and lust may possess a few distinct features, they are tightly linked. It is hard to imagine that two phenomena so linked in the public mind could be such disparate entities. Thus, the contention that love and sexual desire are "kissing cousins" seems to be an appropriate one.

One important aspect of passionate lovers is the fact that lovers are unable to stop thinking about their beloved. People in love often spend most of their waking time thinking uncontrollably about the loved one and the relationship (Fisher, 2004; Hill, Blakemore, & Drumm, 1997). One neuroscientific study found that the obsessive thoughts of passionate lovers are as intense as are the obsessive thoughts of people suffering from OCD (Marazziti, Akiskal, Rossi, & Cassano, 1999). These ruminations provoke a significant loss of cognitive control, reducing one's ability to engage in analytic or convergent thinking.

No surprise then that people in love have more difficulty in performing daily tasks, such as studying or working (Steenbergen, Langeslag, Band, & Hommel, 2013). Cyrille Feybesse and Todd Lubart (Feybesse, 2015) found that college students in love were less creative than were students who were not in love. Their creative productions tended to get even worse when the authors asked them to think about the beloved before performing a creative task.

On the other hand, romantic love has been positively associated with daydreaming, global thinking, and imagination (Griskevicius, Cialdini, & Kenrick, 2006; Poerio, Totterdell, Emerson, & Miles, 2015). This research indicates that lovers' attention and cognitions are focused on the loved one and the relationship. People in love focus more attention on their partner than on other people – be they friends or strangers (Langeslag, Jansma, Ingmar, Franken, & Strien, 2007) – stealing their minds from any other seductive alternative (Gonzaga, Haselton, Smurda, Davies, & Poore, 2008).

Scanned brains of those experiencing passion indicate that the neocortex (the brain region associated with critical thinking) shuts down when we are contemplating our beloved (Bartels & Zeki, 2000). Some authors suggest that the emotional imbalance and obsessive aspects of passionate love are the first elements to disappear if a romantic relationship prevails (Acevedo

& Aron, 2009; Graham, 2011). This fact leads to feelings of dependence and facilitates anxious attachments.

Feelings of passionate love generally occur most strongly at the beginning of a romantic relationship. As the attachment grows stronger, couples will experience a great deal of sexual interest and attraction without having so many emotional ups and downs. Others suggested that passionate love and intimacy keep interacting, fueling each other. Feelings of passion will facilitate higher levels of intimacy. If levels of intimacy remain stabilized, passion will decrease in its intensity. When intimacy is well cemented in a romantic affair, passionate feelings will become a friendlier type of love (Baumeister & Bratalavisky, 1999). This idea suggests that passion is a function of changes in intimacy, as it is hard to imagine passionate love will prevail when one person's love is unrequited.

Measuring Passionate Love

The *Passionate Love Scale* (PLS) was designed to tap into the cognitive, emotional, and behavioral indicants of passionate longings (Hatfield & Sprecher, 1986). The PLS has been found to be a useful measure of passionate love with men and women of all ages, in a variety of cultures, be they heterosexual or homosexual (Graham & Christiansen, 2009). This measure is very reliable and stable across different cultures and groups, especially among participants who are in love or in a relationship. Usually, there are no gender or cultural differences on the PLS scores among people that are in love (Hatfield & Rapson, 1996). This measure can be an interesting way of exploring cross-cultural differences by analyzing the scales factorial solutions. The PLS can be seen as a list of "symptoms" (traits) of passionate love that can have different residual factors with different samples (Landis & O'Shea, 2000).

In order to investigate passionate love, psychologists have created several scales to assess this captivating emotion (Hatfield, Benson, & Rapson, 2012). The PLS (Hatfield & Sprecher, 1986) is the most commonly used of these scales. It was designed to tap the cognitive, emotional, and behavioral components of passionate love (see Table 9.1). (The PLS comes in two versions – a fifteen-item scale and a comparable thirty-item scale, for use by researchers.) This instrument has been translated for use in many countries, such as France, Germany, India, Indonesia, Iran, Italy, Japan, Korea, Peru, Poland, Spain, Sweden, and Switzerland. Cyrille Feybesse tried to collect all international studies and articles he could find of the PLS, The Hendricks' Love Attitude

Table 9.1 *The Passionate Love Scale*

We would like to know how you feel (or once felt) about the person you love, or have loved, most *passionately*. Some common terms for passionate love are romantic love, infatuation, love sickness, or obsessive love.

Please think of the person whom you love most passionately *right now*. If you are not in love, please think of the last person you loved. If you have never been in love, think of the person you came closest to caring for in that way. Try to describe the way you felt when your feelings were most intense. Answers range from (1) Not at all true to (9) Definitely true.

	Not True	Definitely True
I would feel deep despair if _____ left me.		1 2 3 4 5 6 7 8 9
Sometimes I feel I can't control my thoughts; they are obsessively on _____.		1 2 3 4 5 6 7 8 9
I feel happy when I am doing something to make _____ happy.		1 2 3 4 5 6 7 8 9
I would rather be with _____ than anyone else.		1 2 3 4 5 6 7 8 9
I'd get jealous if I thought _____ were falling in love with someone else.		1 2 3 4 5 6 7 8 9
I yearn to know all about _____.		1 2 3 4 5 6 7 8 9
I want _____ physically, emotionally, and mentally.		1 2 3 4 5 6 7 8 9
I have an endless appetite for affection from _____.		1 2 3 4 5 6 7 8 9
For me, _____ is the perfect romantic partner.		1 2 3 4 5 6 7 8 9
I sense my body responding when _____ touches me.		1 2 3 4 5 6 7 8 9
_____ always seems to be on my mind.		1 2 3 4 5 6 7 8 9
I want _____ to know me – my thoughts, my fears, and my hopes.		1 2 3 4 5 6 7 8 9
I eagerly look for signs indicating _____'s desire for me.		1 2 3 4 5 6 7 8 9
I possess a powerful attraction for _____.		1 2 3 4 5 6 7 8 9
I get extremely depressed when things don't go right in my relationship with _____.		1 2 3 4 5 6 7 8 9
		Total: _____

Now add up all your points. The total will tell you how much in love you are compared to your peers.

Results:
- 106–135 points = Wildly, even recklessly, in love.
- 86–105 points = Passionate, but less intense.
- 66–85 points = Occasional bursts of passion.
- 45–65 points = Tepid, infrequent passion.
- 15–44 points = The thrill is gone.

Scale (Hendrick & Hendrick, 1986), and Sternberg's Triangular Love Scale (Sternberg, 1997). He discovered that these three measures were used in at least fifty different countries. Romantic love crosses national borders.

In recent fMRI studies (functional magnetic resonance imagery studies) of brain activity, the PLS has been found to correspond well with certain well-defined patterns of biochemical and neural activation. For example, Aron and his colleagues (2005) discovered that PLS scores are tightly linked with activation in a region of the *caudate* associated with reward (see Cacioppo & Cacioppo, 2015, and Hatfield & Rapson, 2009, for a review of recent neuroscience research correlating the PLS with participants' fMRI reactions.) The PLS has also been found to be highly correlated with a variety of measures of love, intimacy, and sexuality (see Feybesse, 2015 for a summary of this voluminous research).

Other Definitions of Love. Scientists have proposed a variety of definitions and typologies of other forms of love, including altruistic love, parental love, companionate love, consummate love, and so on (see Hendrick & Hendrick, 1989; Shaver & Hazan, 1988; Sternberg, 1988). Luckily, because these forms of love are discussed throughout this book, we need not address them further here.

History of Scholarly Work on Passionate Love

For more than 5,000 years, poets, writers, and troubadours have sung of the delights and sufferings of love and lust. When the Sumerians invented writing around 3500 BCE, one of the first topics they wrote about was passionate love. Buried among the Sumerians' clay tablets was history's oldest known love letter – a poem dedicated to King Shu-Sin by one of his chosen brides. She wrote: "Bridegroom, let me caress you. My precious caress is more savory than honey" (Arsu, 2006). Speculations about passionate love and sexual desire possess a very long and distinguished lineage.

Beginning in the 1940s, social scientists began attempting to understand this phenomenon and crafting ways to measure this emotion (Hatfield et al., 2012). Over the next sixty years, numerous scales of romantic and passionate love were created. Most of the pioneering measures were casually constructed. They read a bit like the slap-dash "scales" readers confront in the magazines *Cosmopolitan* or *Glamour*. (The creators of these scales provided little or no theoretical rationale for the inclusion of scale items or the scales' reliability and validity). A few scales were well-conceived and utilized sophisticated psychometric techniques in their construction – at least by the standards of the time. What has become of these measures? Alas, many of them have been lost in the mists of time.

Until the 1960s and 1970s, discussions of passionate love were almost completely absent from textbooks and journals. When briefly touched upon, love was assumed to be equivalent to "intense linking" or "strong sexual attraction, associated with feelings of affinity" (Reis, Aron, Clark, & Finkel, 2013). Naturally enough, scholars of that era tended to adopt their own point of view when discussing the phenomenon: Cognitive psychologists assumed love was a cognition, biologists focused on the biology of love, behaviorists on the behavior of lovers, and the like. In the late 1960s, for example, Berscheid and Hatfield (1969) treated passionate love as an "attitude" – primarily because they knew a great deal about attitudes and very little about love. Today, such a view is very naive. (Only when evolutionary approaches gained favor, did scholars begin to conceive of emotions as *clusters* of cognitions, physiology, and behavior.)

Scholars had to wait until the 1970s in order to find theorists, mostly social psychologists, proffering well-crafted theories and testing their hypotheses with scientific rigor. The place of love in the social sciences utterly shifted during the 1980s. By this time, scientists were posing true theories of love and treating love as a multidimensional construct. Now their theories were buttressed by compelling empirical data (e.g. Hendrick & Hendrick, 1989).

The success of these attempts became clear in the 1990s, with a large number of fields adopting social-psychological perspectives on love in the furtherance of their own research. By then, love had become a respected field of scientific study. It was also the moment of the emergence of cross-cultural and historical studies of love, and the realization that this new psychology of love was relevant to cultures outside the West.

Today, romantic love is a respected academic topic throughout the world. Translations and psychometric measures of love can be found on all continents. This plethora of research has made it possible to explore the universality and commonalities of love, as well as cultural differences. Passionate love has been found to have a powerful impact on a host of variables important in daily life. What academia still lacks is the integration of this wide-ranging cultural research into the world's scientific literature. Sadly, most theorists of love, generally working in the United States, are not yet aware of the existence of this flood of international studies. Awareness, however, is increasing fast.

Cross-cultural Perspectives on Passionate Love

Passionate love is a universal emotion experienced by all peoples, in all cultures and in all historical eras (see Fischer, Shaver, & Carnochan, 1990; Shaver, Morgan, & Wu, 1996). Yet, despite its universality, culture may have a significant impact on the way in which people define love and on the way they think, feel, and behave in romantic settings. Cross-cultural studies provide a glimpse into the complex world of emotion and allow us to gain an understanding of the extent to which people's emotional lives are shaped by their cultural and personal histories, as well as "writ in their genes" and evolutionary history. The big story, unsurprisingly, is in the interaction between the two (Tooby & Cosmides, 1992).

> With love, bitter turns into sweetness.
> With love, dregs turn into honey.
> With love, pains turn into healing.
> With love, they revive the dead.
> With love, the king becomes a servant.
> With love, thorns become flowers.
> With love, vinegar becomes wine.
> With love, gallows become thrones.
> With love, misery turns into happiness
> With love, prison becomes a rose garden.
> With love, the house becomes a home
> With love, thorns become lilies
> Without love, wax turns into iron.
> With love, fire becomes light.
> With love, the devil becomes an angel.
> With love, stones turn into dust.
> Without love, the garden turns into a desert.
> With love, sorrow becomes joy.
> With love, monsters become divine.
> With love, sting becomes pleasure.
> With love, lions become tamed.
> With love, sickness leads to health.
> With love, fury turns into mercy.
> With love, the dead turn into living
> —Persian poet and mystic
> Jalal al-Din Rumi (1207–1273)

Love Is a Universal Emotion

Passionate love is as old as humankind. The Sumerian love fable of Inanna and Dumuzi, for example, was spun by tribal storytellers in 2,000 BCE (Wolkstein, 1991). Today, most anthropologists argue that passionate love is a universal experience, transcending culture and time (Buss, 1994; Hatfield & Rapson, 1996; Jankowiak, 1995; Tooby & Cosmides, 1992).

Jankowiak and Fischer (1992) drew a sharp distinction between "romantic passion" and "simple lust." They proposed that both passion and lust are universal feelings. Drawing on a sampling of tribal societies from the *Standard Cross-Cultural Sample*, they found that in almost all of these far-flung societies, young lovers talked about passionate love, recounted tales of love, sang love songs, and spoke of the longings and anguish of infatuation. When passionate affections clashed with the wishes of parents or elders, young couples often eloped.

Social anthropologists have explored folk conceptions of love in such diverse cultures as the People's Republic of China, Indonesia, Turkey, Nigeria, Trinidad, Morocco, the Fulbe of North Cameroun, the Mangrove (an aboriginal Australian community), the Mangaia in the Cook Islands, Palau in Micronesia, and the Taita of Kenya (see Jankowiak, 1995, for a review of this research). In all these studies, they found that people in the various cultures possessed surprisingly similar views of love and other "feelings of the heart" (for a review of this research, see Fischer, Wang, Kennedy, & Cheng, 1998; Jankowiak, 1995; Karandashev, 2015; Kim & Hatfield, 2004; Shaver, Murdaya, & Fraley, 2001).

Psychometricians provide additional support for this contention that lovers worldwide fall in love and tend to love with equal intensity. Cyrille Feybesse is currently conducting a cross-cultural meta-analysis of the scores of people from around fifty countries on the most popular measures of passionate and companionate love. He found that among lovers, the mean scores on the PLS were startlingly similar. (Respondents' scores tended to hover around $M = 7.0$ and the PLS possessed "an equivalent high reliability.") Passionate love does not appear to care about one's gender, sexual orientation, or even one's birthplace. Psychometricians have failed to find any cultural or gender differences in the intensity of lovers' feelings or in the dimensions of passionate love (on the PLS scale; Hatfield & Rapson, 1996; Kim & Hatfield, 2004; Neto et al., 2000; Sprecher et al., 1994). One recent study even failed to find any differences in the intensity of passionate love between Indian couples whose marriages had been arranged versus those couples who married for love (Regan, Lakhanpal, & Anguiano, 2012).

Never let your heart open
With the Spring Flowers;
One week of love
Is an inch of ashes.
—Li Shang-yin, a ninth-century Chinese poet

Cultural Variations in Passionate Love

Recently, though, cultural researchers have begun to investigate the impact (if any) of culture on people's definitions of love, what they desire in romantic partners, their likelihood of falling in love, the intensity of their passion, and their willingness to acquiesce in arranged marriages *versus* insisting on marrying for love. From this preliminary research, it appears cultures turn out to be more similar than one might expect. Nonetheless, a few cultural differences seem to exist.

Most scholars who have explored the impact of social conditions on love have compared lovers in individualist versus collectivist cultures. The world's cultures differ profoundly in the extent to which they emphasize individualism or collectivism (although some cross-cultural researchers focus on related concepts: independence or interdependence, modernism or traditionalism, urbanism or ruralism, affluence or poverty).

Individualistic cultures such as the United States, Britain, Australia, Canada, and the countries of Northern and Western Europe tend to focus on personal goals. Collectivist cultures such as China, many African and Latin American nations, Greece, southern Italy, and the Pacific Islands, on the other hand, press their members to subordinate personal interests to those of the group (Markus & Kitayama, 1991; Triandis, McCusker, & Hui, 1990). Triandis and his colleagues point out that, in individualistic cultures, young people are allowed to "do their own thing"; in collectivist cultures, the group comes first.

On the basis of such speculations, cross-cultural researchers proposed that romantic love would be common only in modern, industrialized societies (Goode, 1959; Rosenblatt, 1967). It should be less valued in traditional cultures with strong, extended family ties (Simmons, Vom Kolke, & Shimizu, 1986). In recent years, cultural researchers have begun to test these provocative hypotheses, let alone the individualistic/collectivist model itself. Some researchers have found a few cultural differences in *attitudes* toward love. They speculate that cultural values may, indeed, have an impact on the subtle shadings of meaning assigned to the construct of "love" (Cohen, 2001; Kim & Hatfield, 2004; Kitayama, 2002; Luciano,

2003; Nisbet, 2003; Oyserman, Kemmelmeier, & Coon, 2002; Weaver & Ganong, 2004).

Shaver, Wu, and Schwartz (1991) interviewed young people in the United States, Italy, and the People's Republic of China about their emotional experiences. These nations were chosen for contrast because the United States is generally considered to be an individualistic culture, where romance is valued, while China is thought to be a collectivist culture, where people are expected to sacrifice their desires for the good of their families and friends. Thus, the authors thought, young people should have different views of love.

They found that Americans and Italians tended to equate love with happiness and to assume that both passionate and companionate love were intensely positive experiences. Students in Beijing, China, possessed a darker view of love. In the Chinese language, there are few "happy-love" words; love is associated with sadness.

Not surprisingly, then, the Chinese men and women interviewed by Shaver and his colleagues tended to associate passionate love with ideographic symbols such as infatuation, unrequited love, nostalgia, and sorrow love. Fehr (1988) found that in the West, falling in love is looked on favorably, as it is associated with the expectation of a deep romantic relationship and happiness. In more traditional, Eastern societies, falling in love is generally viewed in a different light. Here, romantic love is experienced in a social context. Even if a young couple has freely chosen to be with one another, they must seek social and familial approval. The major source of intimacy comes from the individual bonds to the family (Gao, 2001). Falling in love is also considered to be a dangerous choice that can be labeled as sad and painful and likely to lead to a negative outcome (Dion & Dion, 1996).

Feelings of love may be universal but they will be expressed very differently according to the land from which they come. Northern Europeans sometimes view people from tropical and Latin societies as exaggerated and promiscuous in their expressions of love, full of lust and not love. One African man, when he sees them interacting in public, might consider a Japanese couple empty of love and emotion. The tendency is to think that love is more real or true in one's own society, since one's own people surely react to it as they "should" and as love "requires." But, in fact, all lovers of the world are experiencing the same butterflies in the stomach, the same uncontrollable attraction and emotional frenzy. fMRI researchers found consistencies across different samples and studies of people experiencing feelings of passionate love (Ortigue, Bianchi-Demicheli, Patel, Frum, &

Lewis, 2010). All participants presented the same brain activation when they saw a picture of their beloved (Xu et al., 2011). The only exception was that the Chinese participants appeared to engage the critical thinking area of the brain a bit more than did the Americans. This kind of research, of course, is in its early stages, and one must be careful not to overgeneralize from the data.

Cyrille Feybesse (2017) administered the Passionate Love Scale and other love measures to college students in very different societies: Brazil, France, Nigeria, Vietnam and Portugal, and collaborated with researchers from other countries. Regardless of their nationality, all participants were familiar with the meaning of passionate love and were comfortable indicating whether or not they were in love at the time they completed the survey. Although all the lovers fell prey to the same passions, participants from Western cultures claimed to fall in love more often than did participants from all the other continents. The majority of the Western students claimed to be in love, and half of them declared they were involved in a romantic relationship at the time of the survey. These numbers drop when we look at the frequencies of lovers' answers on the other continents. It is hard to explain why this difference exists. Western students might be more aware of their romantic feelings or have slightly more freedom to embark on love affairs. We don't know. Maybe love "isn't all you need."

So, to sum up: scientists still don't have a clear picture on how common passionate love is throughout the world. That it exists everywhere, we know. What is still in contention is how common passionate love is, how intensely people experience it, and whether or not people expect to marry for love. As we have seen, some cultural theorists find differences in people view love. Others do not (Fehr, 2015). Many cultural psychologists, for example, found no cultural differences in whether or not people were currently in love (Aron & Rodriguez, 1992; Doherty et al., 1994; Sprecher et al., 1994). Nor were there differences in the intensity of their passionate love, as measured by the PLS (Doherty et al., 1994; Hatfield & Rapson, 1996).

In Conclusion

Fifty years of cross-cultural research suggest that the large differences that once existed between Westernized, modern, urban, industrial societies and Eastern, modern, urban industrial societies may be fast disappearing. Those interested in emphasizing large cross-cultural differences may be forced to focus their studies on only the most underdeveloped (or developing), rural, and collectivist of societies – such as in Africa or Latin America, in China or the Arab countries.

It may well be, however, that even there, the winds of Westernization, individualism, and social change are blowing. Despite the censure of their elders, in a variety of traditional societies, young people are increasingly adopting "Western" patterns – placing a high value on "falling in love," pressing for less gender inequality in love and sex, and insisting on marrying for love (as opposed to arranged marriages). Such changes have been documented in Finland, Estonia, and Russia (Haavio-Mannila & Kontula, 2003), as well as among Australian aboriginal people of Mangrove and a Copper Inuit Alaskan Indian tribe (see Jankowiak, 1995, for an extensive review of this research).

Even in Africa and the Middle East, young people are searching for love on the Web, according to a study by Hatfield and colleagues (unpublished data).

Naturally, cultural differences still exert a profound influence on attitudes, emotions, and behavior, young and old, and such differences are not likely to disappear in our lifetime. In Morocco, for example, marriage was once an alliance between families (as historically it was in most of the world before the eighteenth century), in which the spouses-to-be had little or no say. Today, although parents can no longer simply dictate whom their children will marry, parental approval remains critically important in many places. Nonetheless, young men and women are becoming increasingly permitted to have more say in the matter (see Davis & Davis, 1995).

Many have observed that today two powerful forces – globalization versus nationalism – are battling it out for men's and women's souls around the world. True, to some extent, the people of the world may be becoming "one," but in truth the delightful (and divisive!) cultural variations that have made our world such an interesting, and simultaneously dangerous, place, are likely to add spice to that heady brew of love and sexual practices for some time to come. The convergence of cultures around the world may be reducing the differences in the ways passionate love is experienced and expressed in our world, but tradition can be tenacious, and the global future of passionate love cannot be predicted with any certainty.

The Origins of Love

Two questions that everyone asks but no one can answer are the following: Why does passionate love exist? When did it begin? A few scholars (anthropologists and evolutionary psychologists) have speculated that love may be even older than humankind. They propose that in the course of hominid evolution, romantic love evolved to support a monogamous pair-bonding system (Mercado & Hibel, 2017). It functioned to ensure that couples will stay together long enough to enable their offspring to survive until they could make it on their own (Fisher, 2004); presumably that increased the survival of the species (Fletcher, Simpson, Campbell, & Overall, 2015). They argued that passionate love supported fidelity, the accumulation of resources (such as food, shelter, and protection), and a willingness to provide parental investment and self-sacrifice (Buss, 2006). According to this view, passionate love does not need to last forever; it simply has to long enough for offspring to become independent. After this, a couple could stay together or find a new romantic mate and restart the whole process.

It obviously is impossible to provide evidence for such a contention, but there is some. When investigating our closest ancestor, *homo erectus*, scholars studying brain fossils noticed that the brains of *homo erectus* were large and demanded a constant high-energy intake, just as human brains do. The infant *homo erectus* would then also need a parental support and some insurance of bi-parental care for a long period of time during their development (Cofran & Silva, 2015). Scholars already pose the possibility that couples developed deep attachments in order to stay together and therefore experience passionate love feelings. This circumstantial evidence suggests that *homo erectus* lived in small hunter-gathering bands, centered on monogamous pair-bonding (Fletcher et al., 2015). Other archeological research inferred that this species performed rituals and customs promoting social relationships and sharing of emotional expression (Massey, 2002), so they may have also had some kind of couple union activities Other evidence that passionate love is older than our own species can be found in our brains. The brain circuitry and the regions associated with passionate love have existed for a very long time in hominid evolution, so the thrills of romantic passion could have been operative long before the arrival of our kind (Fisher, 2004). Such speculations are fascinating, but are a slender reed on which to base a theory as to the origins of love.

For a very long time, scholars considered romantic love to be an aristocratic European invention arising from the courtiers in the Middle Ages (Denis de Rougemont, 1983.) This assumption is wrong. Accounts of romantic love in the East and the West can be found as long as 5,000 years ago (Fletcher, Simpson, Campbell, & Overall, 2015; Hatfield, Bensman, & Rapson, 2012). One thing that is new, even in the West, is the notion of marriage for love.

It was not until the nineteenth century that this notion began to spread throughout the world. Most of the great Victorian novels focused on the question of whether women should marry for love or for more practical reasons. Before this, love and marriage were considered to be very different entities. Marriage was assumed to have a political, material, and social function (Lindholm, 1995). Passionate love was generally only expected in couples living forbidden or undisclosed relationships (Karandashev, 2015). And the story of Romeo and Juliet, of course, did not end happily.

Today, marriage or unions for love seem to be increasing throughout the world, perhaps because people are becoming more individualistic as they seek to live with more freedom, and as they seek *happiness* in marriage. A successful romantic relationship today is one that can encompass both passionate and companionate love. People may also utilize both short- and long-term strategies designed to fulfill their mating goals (Buss & Schmitt, 1993). In modern society, sex and love have many purposes.

The Future of Love

Trying to anticipate sweeping historical trends is a daunting task. It is difficult enough to attempt to predict Tomorrow – that is, the state of the world in the next twenty years. But in the world of Tomorrow, say the year 3000, will Earth have been reduced to cinders in a nuclear fireball, global warming, or disease and famine? Will Earth dwellers be vacationing on our sister planets of Mars, Jupiter, or Kepler 186f? It is impossible to know. But let us, in a playful and modest spirit, make the effort. In this section, we will consider futurists' predictions as to the social, economic, and behavioral advances we might expect to see in the next fifty years.

Guesses About the Future of Love, Sex, and Marriage: AD 2068

The global village created by worldwide communication, computers, satellites, information exchange, travel, and trade will most certainly continue to reduce cultural differentiation and augment homogenization. While we can anticipate that the world of the future might combine something of East and West, there can be little doubt that in the areas of passionate love and sexual desire – at least in the short run – the influence of the West on the East will be far greater than the reverse. For some that is an appealing vision. (They equate Westernization with freedom, women's rights, equality, democracy, and higher living standards.) For others, that is a nightmare vision, an image of selfishness, rampant greed and materialism – all made in the West. In the next section, we divide our predictions into three categories: anticipated technological transformations, economic and practical changes, and cultural alterations (see Hatfield, Purvis, & Rapson, 2018, for a comprehensive discussion of these predictions). Since we think technology is the major driver of change in history, we start there.

Technological

There are eight technological changes that we foresee: *First, it is inevitable that people will continue to search for love, sex, and fulfilling relationships on the Web.* We see that happening now. Even in countries such as most African nations and in the Islamic states, where such activity is forbidden, the number of Web users are increasing dramatically (Hatfield, unpublished data). Will social media provide tools for authorities to increase their control over captive populations, or will the availability of social media result in increased freedom for those users? It could go either way.

Second, there will be increased availability of pornography and technological sex. Right now, an amazing number of children have been exposed to pornography by eleven years of age. What will be the consequences of this? Will it change young people's views of sex? Will they expect more from their partners?

Third, there will be increased availability of new partners from social media and dating apps. Will this make it difficult to maintain long-term relationships? Currently, when one encounters problems in a relationship one is motivated to work at it – knowing how difficult to find a more suitable mate. Soon, people may think that they need only to click some buttons and a new, better mate can be ordered up.

Fourth, there is likely to be a cure for AIDS, SRIs, and impotence. Will this prefigure lesser emphasis on monogamy?

Fifth, there will be advances in reproductive technology, including birth control and abortion technology. Will there be more Boutique/Designer babies?

Sixth, there will be improvements in cosmetic surgery. What will be considered beautiful/handsome when everyone matches the ideal?

Seventh, and this may turn out to be as important as the new technologies: robots and sex dolls will be perfected. Will machines surpass humans in appeal? How will this affect relationships?

Finally, people will be living healthier lives for longer periods of time. Much, much longer? Surely this will have a dramatic impact on relationships.

Economic/Practical

Increasingly, we will see both spouses working. This will surely affect power in relationships.

As a consequence, this will contribute to the epical movement toward gender/economic equality. What affect will this have on love and romance? There will be more consensual unions. There will be more long-distance relationships. There will be more cyberspace relationships.

What effect will all these social changes have on love, sex, and relationships?

Cultural

There will be continued acceptance of homosexuality and interracial relationships. There will be increasing acceptance of hookups and sex before dating. There will be increasing acceptance of multiple definitions of "family." The meaning of "family" will be ever-changing. Finally, the norm will be change – probably very rapid change.

History and Change

Of all our predictions, the linchpin is this one: *The norm will be change – probably very rapid change.*

We began this chapter with a discussion of the fact that passionate love and sexual desire are universal desires. Feybessse (2015) found that passionate love appears to take the same form in almost all the countries. But if the eight anticipated changes we have just detailed were to occur, how would that affect the nature of love? We cannot discuss the implications that the changes we predict will have on love and sex. That would require a book, not just a chapter. But to give an indication of the discussion, let us consider just one of the changes we have proposed: "Robots will become ever more lifelike. They may well become superior to real Earthlings. How will that affect people's romantic choices in 2068? Will people fall in love with robots? Prefer them to real people?"

> Continuing advances in computers and robotics will make legal marriages between *Homo* and *Robo* feasible by mid-century. —David Levy

Once manufacturers craft robots that simulate love (and eventually actually feel love), will people purchase and fall in love with such perfect machines? The bet is "yes." In David Levy's (2007) fascinating book, *Love + Sex with Robots,* he makes a compelling case for that proposition. His logic proceeds as follows:

> People love their pets. They attribute all sorts of ideas, feelings, and intentions to them. "But my dog loves me," they insist. Many young children can't get to sleep without cuddling their favorite teddy bear or blanket. A 2007 AP-AOL Autos poll found that 44% of women and 30% of men

say they think of their car as having a personality of its own (Heretic TOC, 2015). Many cars are given pet names.

But what about romantic robots? What if your bot knows your name? Appears fully human? Can interact with you? What if your bot not only whispers "I love you" but seems to pass every test that you can devise to test his or her affection? What then? What if he or she actually *feels* love? Will you love him or her back?

People have a great capacity for love and the best bet is that many will come to love their robots. As any user of Tinder or Match.com can tell you, it is hard to find a suitable mate ... or sometimes any mate at all. As alternatives such as sex robots become more and more realistic and affordable, many individuals may simply come to prefer this non-traditionally partnered sex to the "old-fashioned" way. This may already be occurring; futurists such as Levy (2007) predict that by 2050 robots will transform human notions of love and sexuality.

> What *does* seem to me to be entirely reasonable and extremely likely – nay, inevitable – is that many humans will expand their horizons of love and sex, learning, experimenting, and enjoying new forms of relationship that will be made possible, pleasurable, and satisfying through the development of highly sophisticated humanoid robots ... Love and sex with robots on a grand scale are inevitable. (p. 22.)

Levy also believes that humans will fall in love with robots, marry robots, and have sex with robots, all as (what will be regarded as) "normal" extensions of our feelings of love and sexual desire (2007, p. 22). He also contends that by 2050, human-on-robot love/sex will be more common than human-on-human love/sex.

One is left to ponder:

> What kind of robot personality will be desired when anyone can have anything they want ... for a price? Is it ethical to allow people to engage in sadomasochism with a sentient robot? To participate in child sexuality?

That remains to be seen.

Some scholars are fascinated by the impact of our evolutionary heritage on passionate love and by continuities in human love and mate selection. Given the wildly rapid changes occurring in our world – representative of a tale of *discontinuity*, no less true and valuable than the one about continuity – it is no surprise that many focus on the cultural and technological changes that are occurring in this, one of the most powerful of emotions – love – and its corollaries of sex, mate selection, and the family.

References

Acevedo, B. P., & Aron, A. (2009). Does a long-term relationship kill romantic love? *Review of General Psychology, 13*, 59–65.

Acevedo, B. P., Aron, A., Fisher, H. E., & Brown, L. L. (2011). Neural correlates of long-term intense romantic love. *Social Cognitive and Affective Neuroscience, 7*, 145–149.

Aron, A, Fisher, H. E., Mashek, D.J., Strong, G., Li, H., & Brown, L. L. (2005). Reward, motivation, and emotion systems associated with early-stage intense romantic love. *Journal Neurophysiology, 94*, 327–337.

Aron, A., & Rodriguez, G. (1992, July 25). Scenarios of falling in love among Mexican-, Chinese-, and Anglo-Americans. Paper presented at the Sixth International Conference on Personal Relationships, Orono, ME.

Arsu, S. (2006, February 14). The oldest line in the world. *New York Times*, p. 1.

Bartels, A., & Zeki, S. (2000). The neural correlates of maternal and romantic love. *Neuroimage, 21*, 1155–1166.

Baumeister, R. F., & Bratslavsky, E. (1999). Passion, intimacy, and time: Passionate love as a function of change in intimacy. *Personality and Social Psychology Review, 3*(1), 49–67.

Berscheid, E., & Hatfield, E. (1969). *Interpersonal attraction.* New York: Addison-Wesley.

Buss, D. M. (1994). *The evolution of desire.* New York: Basic Books.

(2006). Strategies of human mating. *Psychological Topics, 15*, 239–260.

Buss, D. M., & Schmitt, D. P. (1993). Sexual strategies theory: An evolutionary perspective on human mating. *Psychological Review, 100*, 204–232.

Cacioppo, S., & Cacioppo, J. T. (2015). Author reply: Demystifying the neuroscience of love. *Emotion Review.* doi: 10.1177/1754073915594432.

Cacioppo, S., Couto, B., Bolmont, M., Sedeno, L., Frum, C., Lewis, J. W., Manes, F., Ibanez, A., & Cacioppo, J. T. (2013). Selective decision-making deficit in love following damage to the anterior insula. *Current Trends in Neurology, 7*, 15–19. [PMC free article] [PubMed].

Cofran, Z., & DeSilva, J. M. (2015). A neonatal perspective on Homo erectus brain growth. *Journal of Human Evolution, 81*, 41–47.

Cohen, D. (2001). Cultural variation: Considerations and implications. *Psychological Bulletin, 127*, 451–471.

Davis, D. A., & Davis, S. S. (1995). Possessed by love: Gender and romance in Morocco. In W. Jankowiak (Ed.), *Romantic passion: A universal experience?* (pp. 219–238). New York: Columbia University Press.

De Rougemont, D. (1983). *Love in the Western World.* Princeton,NJ: Princeton University Press.

Diamond, L. M. (2003). What does sexual orientation orient? A biobehavioral model distinguishing romantic love and sexual desire. *Psychological Review, 110*, 73–192.

(2004). Emerging perspectives on distinctions between romantic love and sexual desire. *Current Directions in Psychological Science, 13*, 116–119.

Dion, K. K., & Dion, K. L. (1996). Cultural perspectives on romantic love. *Personal Relationships, 3*(1), 5–17.

Doherty, R. W., Hatfield, E., Thompson, K., & Choo, P. (1994). Cultural and ethnic influences on love and attachment. *Personal Relationships, 1*, 391–398.

Fehr, B. (1988). Prototype analysis of the concepts of love and commitment. *Journal of Personality and Social Psychology, 55*(4), 557–579.

(2015). Love: Conceptualization and experience. In M. Mikulincer & P. R. Shaver (Eds), *APA handbook of personality and social psychology*, Vol. 3: *Interpersonal relations* (pp. 495–522). Washington, DC: The American Psychological Association.

Feybesse, C. (2015). The adventures of love in the social sciences: Social, psychometric evaluations and cognitive influences of passionate love. Dissertation completed in partial fulfillment of the doctor of philosophy Université Paris Descartes. Paris, France.

(2017). L'amour romantique dans 6 cultures différentes, Talk presented at the *Laboratory "Adaptation, Travail, Individu."* Université Paris Descartes (Paris, France). 9–19.

Fischer, K. W., Shaver, P. R., & Carnochan, P. (1990). How emotions develop and how they organize development. *Cognition and Emotion, 4*, 81–127.

Fischer, K. W., Wang, L., Kennedy, B., & Cheng, C-L. (1998). Culture and biology in emotional development. In D. Sharma & K. W. Fischer (Eds.), *Socioemotional development across cultures. New directions for child development, No. 82)* (pp. 20–43). San Francisco, CA: Jossey-Bass.

Fisher, H. (2004). *Why we love: The nature and chemistry of romantic love.* New York: Macmillan.

Fletcher, G. J., Simpson, J. A., Campbell, L., & Overall, N. C. (2015). Pairbonding, romantic love, and evolution the curious case of homo sapiens. *Perspectives on Psychological Science, 10*(1), 20–36.

Gao, G. (2001). Intimacy, passion, and commitment in Chinese and US American romantic relationships. *International Journal of Intercultural Relations, 25*(3), 329–342.

Gonzaga, G. C., Haselton, M. G., Smurda, J., sian Davies, M., & Poore, J. C. (2008). Love, desire, and the suppression of thoughts of romantic alternatives. *Evolution and Human Behavior, 29*(2), 119–126.

Gonzaga, G. C., Turner, R. A., Keltner, D., Campos, B., & Altemus, M. (2006). Romantic love and sexual desire in close relationships. *Emotion, 6*, 163–179.

Goode, W. J. (1959). The theoretical importance of love. *American Sociological Review, 24*, 38–47.

Graham, J. M. (2011). Measuring love in romantic relationships: A meta-analysis. *Journal of Social and Personal Relationships, 28*, 748–771.

Graham, J. M., & Christiansen, K. (2009). The reliability of romantic love: A reliability generalization meta-analysis. *Personal Relationships, 16*(1), 49–66.

Greeley, A. (1991). *Faithful attraction: Discovering intimacy, love, and fidelity in American marriage.* New York: St. Martin's Press.

Griskevicius, V., Cialdini, R. B., & Kenrick, D. T. (2006). Peacocks, Picasso, and parental investment: The effects of romantic motives on creativity. *Journal of Personality and Social Psychology, 91*, 52–66.

Haavio-Mannila, E., & Kontula, O. (2003). Single and double sexual standards in Finland, Estonia, and St. Petersburg. *The Journal of Sex Research, 40*, 36–49.

Hatfield, E., Bensman, L., & Rapson, R. L. (2012). A brief history of social psychologists' attempts to measure passionate love. *Journal of Personality and Social Psychology, 29*, 143–164. doi: 10.1177/0265407511431055.

Hatfield, E., Purvis, J., & Rapson, R. L. (2018). *What's next in love and sex: Psychological and cultural perspectives.* Oxford, UK: Oxford University Press.

Hatfield, E., & Rapson, R. L. (1987). Passionate love/sexual desire: Can the same paradigm explain both? *Archives of Sexual Behavior, 16*, 259–277.

  (1993). *Love, sex, and intimacy: Their psychology, biology, and history.* New York: HarperCollins.

  (1996). Stress and passionate love. In C. D. Spielberger & I. G. Sarason (Eds.), *Stress and emotion: Anxiety, anger, and curiosity* (pp. 29–50). Washington, DC: Taylor & Francis.

  (2005). *Love and sex: Cross-cultural perspectives.* Needham Heights, Lanham, MD: University Press of America.

  (2006). Love and passion. In I. Goldstein, C. M. Meston, S. R. Davis, & A. M. Traish (Eds.), *Women's sexual function and dysfunction: Study, diagnosis and treatment* (pp. 93–97). London: Taylor and Francis.

  (2009). The neuropsychology of passionate love. In E. Cuyler & M. Ackhart (Eds.), *Psychology of relationships* (pp. 519–543). Hauppauge, NY: Nova Science.

Hatfield, E., Schmitz, E., Cornelius, J., & Rapson, R. L. (1988). Passionate love: How early does it begin? *Journal of Psychology & Human Sexuality, 1*(1), 35–51.

Hatfield, E., & Sprecher, S. (1986). Measuring passionate love in intimate relations. *Journal of Adolescence, 9*, 383–410.

Hendrick, C., & Hendrick, S. (1986). A theory and method of love. *Journal of Personality and Social Psychology, 50*, 392–402.

Hendrick, S. S., & Hendrick, C. (1987). Love and sexual attitudes, self-disclosure, and sensation-seeking. *Journal of Social and Personal Relationships, 4*, 281–297.

Hendrick, C., & Hendrick, S. S. (1989). Research on love: Does it measure up? *Journal of Personality and Social Psychology, 56*, 784–794.

Heretic TOC. (2015, October 26). [The personal blog of Thomas O'Carroll.] Holy hots, why not child sex robots. *Heretic TOC: Not the dominant narrative.* Retrieved from https://tomocarroll.wordpress.com/2015/10/.

Hill, C. A., Owen, J., Blakemore, J. E. O., & Drumm, P. (1997). Mutual and unrequited love in adolescence and young adulthood. *Personal Relationships, 4*(1), 15–23. Retrieved from https://doi.org/10.1111/j.1475-6811.1997.tb00127.x.

Jankowiak, W. (Ed.). (1995). *Romantic passion: A universal experience?* New York: Columbia University Press.

Jankowiak, W. R., & Fischer, E. F. (1992). A cross-cultural perspective on romantic love. *Ethnology, 31*(2), 149–155.

Karandashev, V. (2015). A cultural perspective on romantic love. *Online Readings in Psychology and Culture, 5*(4). Retrieved from https://doi.org/10.9707/2307-0919.1135.

(2017). *Romantic love in cultural contexts.* New York: Springer.

Kim, J., & Hatfield, E. (2004). Love types and subjective well-being: A cross-cultural study. *Social behavior and personality: An international journal, 32*(2), 173–182.

Kitayama, S. (2002.) Culture and basic psychological processes – Toward a system view of culture: Comment on Oyserman et al. (2002). *Psychological Bulletin, 128*, 89–96.

Landis, D., & O'Shea, W. A. (2000). Cross-cultural aspects of passionate love an individual differences analysis. *Journal of Cross-Cultural Psychology, 31*(6), 752–777.

Langeslag, S. J., Jansma, B. M., Franken, I. H., & Van Strien, J. W. (2007). Event-related potential responses to love-related facial stimuli. *Biological Psychology, 76*(1), 109–115.

Levy, D. (2007). *Love + sex with robots: The evolution of human-robot relationships.* New York: Harper Perennial.

Lindholm, C. (1995). Love as an experience of transcendence. In W. Jankowiak (Ed.), *Romantic passion: A universal experience* (pp. 57–71). New York: Columbia University Press.

Luciano, E. M. C. (2003). Caribbean love and sex: Ethnographic study of rejection and betrayal in heterosexual relationships in Puerto Rico. Paper presented at the twenty-ninth annual meeting of the International Academy of Sex Research meetings, Bloomington, IN.

Marazziti, D., Akiskal, H. S., Rossi, A., & Cassano, G. B. (1999). Alteration of the platelet serotonin transporter in romantic love. *Psychological Medicine, 29*(3), 741–745.

Marazziti, D., & Baroni, S. (2012). Romantic love: The mystery of its biological roots. *Clinical Neuropsychiatry, 9*(1), 14–19.

Markus, H. R., & Kitayama, S. (1991). Culture and self: Implications for cognition, emotion, and motivation. *Psychological Review, 98*, 224–253.

Massey, D. (2002). Editorial: Time to think. *Transactions of the Institute of British Geographers, 27*, 259–261. Retrieved from https://doi.org/10.1111/1475-5661.00054.

Mercado, E., & Hibel, L. C. (2017). I love you from the bottom of my hypothalamus: The role of stress physiology in romantic pair bond formation and maintenance. *Social and Personality Psychology Compass, 11*(2), e12298.

Meyers, S., & Berscheid, E. (1997). The language of love: What a difference a preposition makes. *Personality and Social Psychology Bulletin, 23*, 347–362.

Neto, F. (2012). The perceptions of love and sex across the adult life span. *Journal of Social and Personal Relationships, 29*(6), 760–775.

Neto, F., Mullet, E., Deschamps, J. C., Barros, J., Benvindo, R., Camino, L., Falconi, A., Kagibanga, V., & Machado, M. (2000). Cross-cultural variations in attitudes towards love. *Journal of Cross-Cultural Psychology, 30*, 626–635.

Nisbett, R. (2003). *The geography of thought: How Asians and Westerners think differently ... and why.* New York: The Free Press.

Ortigue, S., Bianchi-Demicheli, F., Patel, N., Frum, C., & Lewis, J. W. (2010). Neuroimaging of love: fMRI meta-analysis evidence toward new perspectives in sexual medicine. *The Journal of Sexual Medicine, 7*(11), 3541–3552.

Oysermann, D., Kemmelmeier, M., & Coon, H. M. (2002). Cultural psychology, a new look: Reply to Bond (2002), Fiske (2002), Kitayama (2002), and Miller. *Psychological Bulletin, 128*, 110–117.

Poerio, G. L., Totterdell, P., Emerson, L. M., & Miles, E. (2015). Love is the triumph of the imagination: Daydreams about significant others are associated with increased happiness, love and connection. *Consciousness and Cognition, 33*, 135–144.

Regan, P. C. (2004). Sex and the attraction process: Lessons from science (and Shakespeare) on lust, love, chastity, and fidelity. In J. H. Harvey, A. Wenzel, & S. Sprecher (Eds.), *The handbook of sexuality in close relationships* (pp. 115–133). Mahwah, NJ: Lawrence Erlbaum.

Regan, P. C., & Berscheid, E. (1999). *Lust: What we know about human sexual desire.* London: Sage.

Regan, P. C., Kocan, E. R., & Whitlock, T. (1999). Ain't love grand! A prototype analysis of the concept of romantic love. *Journal of Social and Personal Relationships, 15*, 411–420.

Regan, P. C., Lakhanpal, S., & Anguiano, C. (2012). Relationship outcomes in Indian-American love-based and arranged marriages. *Psychological Reports, 110*(3), 915–924.

Reis, H. T., Aron, A., Clark, M. S., & Finkel, E. J. (2013). Ellen Berscheid, Elaine Hatfield, and the emergence of relationship science. *Perspectives on Psychological Science, 8*(5), 558–572.

Ridge, R. D., & Berscheid, E. (1989, May). On loving and being in love: A necessary distinction. Paper presented at the annual convention of the Midwestern Psychological Association, Chicago, IL.

Rosenblatt, P. C. (1967). Marital residence and the function of romantic love. *Ethnology, 6*, 471–480.

Shaver, P. R., & Hazan, C. (1988). A biased overview of the study of love. *Journal of Social and Personal Relationships, 5*, 474–501.

Shaver, P. R., Morgan, H. J., & Wu, S. (1996). Is love a "basic" emotion? *Personal Relationships, 3*, 81–96.

Shaver, P. R., Murdaya, U., & Fraley, R. C. (2001). Structure of the Indonesian emotion lexicon. *Asian Journal of Social Psychology, 4*, 201–224.

Shaver, P. R., Wu, S., & Schwartz, J. C. (1991). Cross-cultural similarities and differences in emotion and its representation: A prototype approach. In M. S. Clark (Ed.), *Review of personality and social psychology*, Vol. 13 (pp. 175–212). Newbury Park, CA: Sage.

Simmons, C. H., Vom Kolke, A., & Shimizu, H. (1986). Attitudes toward romantic love among American, German, and Japanese students. *Journal of Social Psychology, 126,* 327–337.

Sprecher, S., Aron, A., Hatfield, E., Cortese, A., Potapova, E., & Levitskaya, A. (1994). Love: American style, Russian style, and Japanese style. *Personal Relationships, 1*(4), 349–369.

Steenbergen, H., Langeslag, S. J., Band, G. P., & Hommel, B. (2013). Reduced cognitive control in passionate lovers. *Motivation and Emotion, 38*(3), 444–450.

Sternberg, R. J. (1988). *The triangle of love.* New York. Basic Books.

    (1997). Construct of a triangular love scale. *European Journal of Psychology, 27,* 313–335.

Tooby, J., & Cosmides, L. (1992). The evolutionary and psychological foundations of the social sciences. In J. H. Barkow, L. Cosmides, & J. Tooby (Eds.), *The adapted mind: Evolutionary psychology and the generation of culture* (pp. 19–136). New York: Oxford University Press.

Triandis, H. C., McCusker, C., & Hui, C. H. (1990). Multimethod probes of individualism and collectivism. *Journal of Personality and Social Psychology, 59,* 1006–1020.

Wang, A. Y., & Nguyen, H. T. (1995). Passionate love and anxiety: A cross- generational study. *The Journal of Social Psychology, 135*(4), 459–470.

Weaver, S. E., & Ganong, L. W. (2004). The factor structure of the Romantic Belief Scale for African Americans and European Americans. *Journal of Social and Personal Relationships, 21,* 171–185.

Wilkins, R., & Gareis, E. (2006). Emotion expression and the locution "I love you": A cross cultural study. *International Journal of Intercultural Relations, 30*(1), 51–75.

Wolkstein, D. (1991). *The first love stories.* New York: Harper Perennial.

Xu, X., Aron, A., Brown, L., Cao, G., Feng, T., & Weng, X. (2011). Reward and motivation systems: A brain mapping study of early-stage intense romantic love in Chinese participants. *Human Brain Mapping, 32*(2), 249–257.

Young, L. J., & Wang, Z. (2004). The neurobiology of pair bonding. *Nature Neuroscience, 7*(10), 1048–1054.

CHAPTER 10

Slow Love: Courtship in the Digital Age

Helen E. Fisher and Justin R. Garcia

Love and Courtship

Today, some 66% of single Americans have had a one-night-stand at some point in their dating life; 34% have had sex with a potential partner before their first date; 54% have had a friends-with-benefits relationship (in which the couple meet for uncommitted, socially hidden sexual activity); and 56% of singles have lived together before their wedding. Americans tend to believe this is reckless behavior. But data collected as part of an annual cross-sectional demographically representative sample of over 5,000 single adults in the United States, polled between 2010 and 2017 (35,000-plus in total and referred to throughout as the *Singles in America* or SIA study), suggests this pattern is not recklessness but caution. Today's singles appear to want to know everything about a potential partner before they invest their time, money, and energy into initiating a formal commitment to him or her (Fisher, 2015, 2016).

We hypothesize that the *pre-commitment* stage of courtship is currently expanding in the United States. Singles today are taking time to find a partner who is highly emotionally and physically compatible with them. With hanging out as "just friends," with friends-with-benefits, with sex before the first date, with codified (and more serious) "official" first dates, and with living together before marriage, today's singles are slowly transforming their informal, uncommitted sexual and romantic relationships into long-term, formally committed partnerships – what Fisher calls *slow love* (Fisher, 2015, 2016). Where marriage was traditionally the beginning of a partnership, today it is the finale.

Current advances in technology are changing *how* singles court; but technology cannot – and will not – alter the innate human disposition to love. Indeed, 83% of men and 89% of women in America will marry by age forty-nine; many will divorce and remarry too (Fisher, 1992, 2016). In this chapter, we first discuss the biology of romantic love to illustrate its durability; we then explore changing courtship patterns in today's Digital Age.

Technology Cannot Change Love

Around the world people love. They compose songs, poems, novels, plays, ballets, and operas about romantic love. They have myths and legends about love, and they create love charms, love magic, and love holidays. Anthropologists have now found evidence of romantic love in well over 150 societies; indeed, everywhere they have looked, they have found evidence of this passion (Jankowiak & Fischer, 1992; Jankowiak & Paladino, 2008). Romantic love is characterized by a constellation of traits. These include: focused courtship attention on a *specific* partner; intense energy; ecstasy; mood swings; anxiety; bodily reactions including butterflies in the stomach; sexual possessiveness; emotional dependence; separation anxiety; frustration-attraction; obsessive thinking about the beloved; craving for emotional union with the beloved; and extreme motivation to win this *preferred* mating partner (Fisher, 1992, 2004, 2016). People pine for love, live for love, kill for love, and die for love. Romantic love is one of the most powerful brain systems humanity has evolved.

Several brain-scanning studies using functional magnetic resonance imaging (fMRI) have shown that the primary neural circuits associated with romantic love lie subcortically, near the base of the brain in regions associated with motivation or "drive" (Aron et al., 2005; Fisher et al., 2003) and addiction (Fisher, 2014; Fisher et al., 2010; Fisher et al., 2016). In fact, the primary circuits for this passion lie near neural mechanisms that orchestrate thirst and hunger. Thirst and hunger enable you to live another day; romantic love enables you to form a reproductive partnership and send your DNA into tomorrow. Thus, romantic love has been called a "survival mechanism" (Frascella et al., 2010). It may have evolved over four million years ago in conjunction with the evolution of social monogamy as our hominin forbearers emerged from the disappearing forests of ancient Africa and adapted to the expanding woodland/savannah econiche (Fisher 1992, 2011, 2016). So despite widespread concern about the influence of modern technology on human motivation to love, this passion cannot be extinguished as singles swipe left or right on Tinder or use any other internet dating platform. Romantic love is a system in the brain.

In fact, romantic love is one of three primary brain systems that together orchestrate human mating and reproduction (Fisher, 1998, 2004, 2016); all are associated with specific brain systems, and none can be extinguished by technology in our Digital Age. The *sex drive* (orchestrated primarily by the testosterone system in both men and women) evolved to enable our ancestors to seek sexual union with a range of mating partners. *Romantic love* (associated primarily with the dopamine reward system in the brain) evolved to motivate ancestral males and females to focus their mating energy on a single individual at a time, thereby conserving courtship time and metabolic energy. *Attachment* to a mating partner (associated primarily with the oxytocin and vasopressin systems in the brain) evolved to motivate our first forebears to form a pair and sustain this affiliative connection at least long enough to raise a single child through infancy as a team, expressed as pair-bonding or social monogamy.

This human predisposition for pair-bonding (or social monogamy) plays an important role in how we court. In every society on record, the primary human reproductive strategy is pair-bonding, regardless of sex/gender, age, or sexual orientation. Even in polygynous societies, most men form a pair-bond to conceive and rear their young, as few can acquire enough resources to entice and retain a harem (Fisher, 2016). Moreover, humans bear highly altricial young with an extended childhood and adolescence – requiring many years of parenting. Thus, men and women are obliged to invest considerable time, metabolic energy, and resources to judiciously assess and select effective mating and *parenting* partners during reproductive years. Courtship often does not end with one's reproductive years either. Adultery is common cross-culturally, as is divorce and remarriage – serial monogamy (Fisher, 1992, 2016; Tsapelas, Fisher, & Aron, 2010). This has led some to theorize that our basic human reproductive strategy is *serial social monogamy and clandestine adultery* (Fisher, 1992, 2004, 2011, 2016). Like the other 3% of mammals and 15% of primates that engage in pair-bonding, humans regularly express social monogamy, but not always sexual monogamy (Gray & Garcia, 2013). Thus, as a result of this flexible, unstable, multi-part mating scheme, men and women of the past and present are likely to court throughout their lives.

Technology in the Digital Age cannot change this human predisposition to woo and woo again. But it can change how, when, and where we seek romance.

How Technology Changes Courtship

Courtship customs vary considerably from one culture to the next, in tandem with each society's specific cultural and physical environments, including their technology. For example, women in hunting/gathering societies collect over 50% of daily food with digging sticks and baskets. Most likely in conjunction with this economic power, they tend to be socially and sexually powerful too; and courtship in these cultures tends to be casual. For example, among the Kung! Bushmen of the Kalahari Desert of Botswana and the Mehinaku of the Amazon basin, premarital sex is commonplace, arranged marriages are insignificant, and both sexes tend to select partners for reasons of attraction.

With the invention of the plow, in use from around 5,000 BP (before present) in ancient Mesopotamia and the concomitant proliferation of agrarian societies, women lost their ancestral role as foragers; their economic, social, and sexual lives became curtailed; and a host of new credos emerged along with the technology of the plow. Included were strictly arranged marriages (for the upper classes), virginity at marriage, the belief that the father was the head of household, and that marriage must last till death (Fisher, 1992. 1999, 2016).

As the Industrial Age developed and the modern job market emerged after World War I, a host of new technological inventions reduced some of women's domestic labor in the home, women began to move back into the paid labor force. And with their increasing economic power, women began to regain their social and sexual power as well. Then in the late 1940s and early 1950s, the automobile became widely accessible in America, a technological invention that gave singles a rolling bedroom and motels. By 1960, "parking" was a common path to sex, romance, and attachment. Then the introduction of the hormonal birth control pill in the 1960s and 1970s (legalized for all in 1972) unleashed female sexuality, enabling more sexual freedom for both sexes prior to wedding.

The current proliferation of digitally mediated platforms are altering courtship once again. Online dating sites, phone apps, text messaging, email, Facebook, and other internet forums offer new ways to assess and select appropriate (or at least desirable) mating partners. Today, 51% of singles research a date on Facebook and 34% use Google to investigate a potential partner (SIA); 51% of singles have used an emoji to give their written interactions more personality and 37% have used these icons to express their feelings (Gesselman, Ta, & Garcia, 2018); 48% of singles have posted selfies on the Internet to attract a mate; 36% have sent a sexy photo for courtship purposes (Garcia et al., 2016); and singles now use Instagram, Snapchat, and other internet forums to flirt, connect, and arrange courtship meet-ups. New courtship taboos are emerging too. Among them, 66% of singles are turned off if a potential partner texts during a date; and 57% are upset if a date reads an occasional text during a courtship get-together.

Some of the mechanisms for assessing potential partners are likely to change as well. For example, when meeting via the Internet, it is impossible to hear, smell, or touch a potential partner, so other cues to health are likely to become more important, particularly those most visible in a photograph. And with no knowledge of a potential partner's background, family, and social networks, a single's written descriptions on internet platforms of themselves, their friends, their kin, their interests, and their occupation, are likely to become essential courtship tools.

But researching a potential date via Google, as well as texting, emailing, expressing oneself with emoticons or emojis in a written message, and all the other modern technological mechanisms used to court are just the newest way to do the same old thing – assess and court potential candidates for love and commitment. In fact, dating sites are not dating sites; they are introducing sites (Fisher, 2016). When potential partners meet in person, their ancient human brains snap into action and they smile, laugh, watch, listen, and parade the ways our forebears did long before the Internet existed. Technology is not changing the capacity or desire for love. In tandem with internet introductions, however, technology is providing new ways to assess and build a partnership.

Three Paths to Romance

In collaboration with the internet introducing site Match.com, we polled 5,000-plus singles annually between 2010 and 2018 (study ongoing), using a demographically representative opt-in panel sample of single adults, based on national demographic distributions reported in the US census. Participants were all unmarried and single at the time of survey. Some were casually dating; some were never-married; others were divorced, separated, or widowed; none of these participants were recruited through the dating site Match.com or its subsidiaries; instead we used a third-party data collection company. Participants were all between eighteen and seventy-plus years of age, with a variety of backgrounds and experiences. Individuals of all sexual orientations were queried, as well as men and women from every major ethnic group and every region of the country.

The majority of singles polled in 2017 were looking for a serious relationship (69%). Yet, these data indicated that today's singles are pursuing four distinct paths to romance: (1) 40% of singles had had a *just friends* relationship during their lives, also known as *hanging out*; (2) 55% of singles had had a *friends-with-benefits* relationship during their dating experiences; (3) 44% of singles have gone out on an *official first date* in 2017; and (4) over 50% had engaged in a casual hook-up or one-night stand, possibly to trigger instant feelings of romance and/or attachment in a partner or themselves. Each of these paths appear to be a form of uncommitted courtship associated with a specific set of social rules.

Just Friends. Singles in our 2017 SIA study easily distinguished the differences between what they considered to be appropriate behavior when hanging out with "just a friend" as opposed to those behaviors appropriate when on an official first date. Included were the following: "Asking you out the day of the date": 48% of singles approved of this when hanging out versus 27% who regarded this as appropriate for a "first date." "Splitting the bill" was more permissible when "just friends": 48% approved of this when hanging out versus 29% who approved of this on an official first date. "Drinking 3–5 drinks" and "fast food" were also regarded as more appropriate when "just friends." Last, only 37% of singles regarded kissing as appropriate when "hanging out," whereas 64% believed this was appropriate on an "official first date." Just Friends get to know each other prior to making any emotional, sexual, or financial commitments.

Most importantly, almost 40% of singles report that they have fallen madly in love with someone they didn't initially find attractive. And 29% of singles reported that at least one of these "just friends" relationships had turned into a committed partnership. Beginning a relationship as "just friends" appears to be a current (perhaps ancient) mating strategy.

Friends-with-Benefits. In this courtship arrangement, a couple has coitus when convenient; but they do not appear in public as a committed pair. In our 2017 *Singles in America* study, 55% of singles reported that they had had a friends-with-benefits relationship at some point in their dating lives, whereas in 2013, 58% of men and 50% of women reported that they had had a friends-with-benefits relationship, including one in three people in their seventies (SIA). When queried in 2017 on how this friends-with-benefits relationship started, 71% of men and 80% of women reported that they were friends first, before they embarked on a sexual relationship; whereas only 19% of singles actively sought a friends-with-benefits relationship (27% of men and 12% of women). And 88% of women and 73% of men said, "it just happens."

This form of relationship also has specific rules. In 2017, 59% of men and 74% of women believed that their friends-with-benefits relationship should be exclusive; neither partner should have more than one of these relationship at a time. Moreover, 69% of adult singles believed that close friends should not be told about the relationship; 62% of singles believed that the close friends of your friends-with-benefits partner should be off limits to date; and 92% believed that birth control or condoms must be used.

Most relevant to this chapter, in 2017, 48% of the men and 42% of women who had engaged in a friends-with-benefits relationship reported that at least one of these relationships had turned into a committed partnership. Hence, for many, friends-with-benefits and seemingly casual sex is also a path to romance, attachment, and commitment (Garcia & Fisher, 2015).

The First "Official" Date. In past decades (and centuries), the first date was primarily a "look-see," an opportunity to assess the possibility of romantic interest with a relatively unknown individual. Today the first date is often preceded by a lengthy period of friendship instead, with or without "benefits." So it appears that the "first date" has now taken on a significant new meaning – as an "official" first step toward commitment. Suggesting this are the strict codes of behavior that singles now regard as appropriate for a "first date": 54% of singles regard "asking you out 2–3 days in advance" as appropriate first-date behavior, whereas only 27% approve of asking someone out on the same day. Moreover, 59% of singles regard it as appropriate to take a first date to a nice restaurant, whereas only 22% believe it is acceptable to take a first date for fast food. Further, 56% of men and 48% of women report that they had imagined a long-term future with someone during a first date (SIA).

Layman and academics lament the decline of dating, with some labeling it a crisis. Indeed, only 44% of singles went on a first date in 2017. But today dates can be expensive and time-consuming. In fact, singles contribute billions of dollars to the US economy as a result of their dating and courtship-related activities, perhaps partially explaining why singles report more stress than married people across a variety of domains of living (Ta, Gesselman, Perry, Fisher, & Garcia, 2017). However, as the first date becomes designated as an official first step toward commitment, fewer men and women are likely to invite or accept a first date unless they find someone who truly interests them.

"Casual Sex." In 2014, 66% of single men and 50% of single women reported that they had engaged in a one-night stand at some point in their dating lives. Although casual sex is in itself not necessarily risky, it can potentially lead to sexually transmitted infections, unwanted pregnancy, and/or emotional anguish. Yet the number of men and women who have engaged in one-night stands has varied little over the past eight years of *Singles in America* studies. Moreover, in 2016, 34% of singles reported that they had had sex with a potential partner at least once before the first date. Even those who have begun to date a specific other do not generally develop any form of commitment with this partner before they engage in sexual activity: 28% of adult singles have had sex with a dating partner by the third date; and 46% have had sex with a dating partner by the sixth date.

Are these sexual escapades a form of sex interview? Possibly. Five of the twelve cranial nerves are triggered when kissing; and during coitus a host of biological and psychological processes become activated as well. Sexual activity provides extensive data on a partner's smell, taste, touch, and sounds, as well as valuable information about a partner's degree of kindness, empathy, patience, ability to listen, their physical health and mental stability, and perhaps even their sense of humor. Singles learn a lot about a potential partner between the sheets.

Rather than a sex interview, some singles may, instead, be using casual sex to trigger feelings of romantic love and attachment in themselves and/or their partner. Genital stimulation and arousal produce elevated activity in the dopamine system, potentially triggering romantic passion. Pre-commitment sex can potentially trigger feelings of attachment too, because pleasing touch and orgasm activate oxytocin and vasopressin, which are neuropeptides associated with attachment and bonding. And although the correlation between orgasm and the promotion of socio-sexual pair-bonds is controversial among evolutionary behaviorists (Lloyd, 2005; Gray & Garcia, 2013), over 31% of singles (39% of men and 26% of women) have had a one-night stand turn into a long-term romantic partnership (SIA; Garcia & Fisher, 2015).

Like relationships that begin as "just friends" or friends-with-benefits, or an "official" first date, casual sex can initiate a romance and/or a committed partnership (Garcia & Reiber, 2008; Garcia & Fisher, 2015).

Living Together. This phenomenon, cohabitation, became popular in the 1970s; and today what had been scandalous has become routine. In 2012, 58% of singles reported that they have lived with one to five partners outside of wedlock. And 64% of Americans believe this living arrangement is regularly a step toward wedding (Pew Research Center, 2008).

Marriage Contracts. But even marriage is no longer a firm commitment. In 2013, 36% of singles in our annual *Singles in America* study said they wanted a prenuptial agreement (SIA). Moreover, alternate forms of marriage are becoming popular. Civil partnerships in England, civil unions in the United States, and de facto partnerships in Australia enable a couple to end a partnership relatively easily. France's *pacte civil de solidarité*, or PACS, is particularly indicative of this trend. Enacted in 1999 primarily to enable gay men and lesbian women to obtain a legal means of attachment without conventional matrimony, it immediately became popular among heterosexuals. All you do is go to a federal office with your partner and sign some papers to initiate a legal relationship; then if you want to end it, you send in a form. If divorce were made easier in America, many might avail themselves of it – because 33% of American singles believe that it is acceptable to leave a "satisfactory marriage" if you are no longer passionately in love.

Slow Love

We are a romantic species. Historical and anthropological literature confirms this (see Fisher, 2016), and our predisposition for romance hasn't changed in the modern era. Over 54% of American singles believe in love at first sight; 86% seek a committed partner with whom they can spend their life whereas only 14% would marry for financial security (SIA); 56% believe laws should make it easier to wed; and 89% believe you can stay married to the same person forever. In America today, as in much of the post-industrial world, romantic love is in full bloom. Yet 43% to 50% of US marriages are projected to fail. And 67% of American cohabiting couples report that they are terrified of the social, legal, emotional, and economic consequences of divorce (Miller, Sassler, & Kusi-Appouh, 2011).

So it is hypothesized that today's singles seek to know everything they can about a potential partner before they spend the metabolic energy, time, and money to build a committed partnership; hence the *pre-commitment stage* of the courtship process is expanding (Fisher, 2015, 2016). "Just friends," friends-with-benefits, codified "official" first dates, casual sex, living together before wedding, and prenuptial agreements are all core components of today's courtship trajectory – slow love.

Conclusion

Marriage has long been a hallmark of human social and family life. But today, with little pressure to marry soon after puberty and more permissive attitudes toward sex before dating, cohabiting, and wedding, new norms for courtship and mating have emerged. Will dating sites, dating apps, and new means of communication, including texting, emailing, Facebook, Snapchat, and other innovative forms of technology change romance? No, they cannot. The brain circuitry for romantic love lies in primitive factories and pathways near the base of the brain that evolved millions of years ago to drive our ancestors to focus their mating energy on *preferred* partners. Romantic love is a motivation to find one of life's greatest prize, a mating and parenting partner. Even if one does not want to reproduce or parent, the vast majority of men and women cross-culturally still seek to form a pair-bond by middle age. The brain circuitry for romantic love (and attachment) will be central to humanity if our species manages to survive a million years from now.

Nevertheless, technology is changing how single Americans woo, including adding some problems to our courting lives. Foremost is cognitive overload, owing to too many options on internet introducing sites and apps. The brain is not well built to select between hundreds, sometimes thousands of potential mating partners. In fact, scientists suggest that the optimal number of options the brain can process effectively is between five and nine (Iyengar & Lepper, 2000; Miller, 1955; Schwartz 2016). But like any new technology, effective use of the Internet must be learned. For example, after meeting nine potential mates, one might stop and get to know one or more of these individuals better. Data show that the more you get to know someone, the more you like them (Fisher, 2016).

Pundits and scientists warn of another problem with internet introductions: with the widespread use of computer-mediated communication, some say we are losing our ability to communicate, interact, and connect in real time. But there is now a host of data that those who use the Internet the most also have the most social interactions (Chayko, 2014; Hampton et al., 2016). In fact, today Americans send over 15,000 emails annually; Americans appear hyper-connected. And these introducing sites enable singles to seek like-minded partners, as well as provide older singles, gay men, lesbian women, minority groups, and all other singles of diverse demographics with access to a wider range of potential mates. Singles are using these introducing sites, too. In 2017, 40% of American singles met their last first date on the Internet, whereas only 25% meet through a friend and 6% met in a bar. And internet introducing sites have now been correlated with two positive outcomes: interracial partnerships have increased (Ortega & Hergovich, 2017); and marriages between people who met via the Internet are incrementally, yet statistically significantly, more stable (Cacioppo et al., 2013).

But the overarching current trend is slow love. Around the world men and women are marrying later (*The Economist*, 2017); and with this, the courtship process is slowing down, owing to the expansion of the pre-commitment courtship phase associated with mate assessment and selection. One-night stands; "just friends"; friends-with-benefits; codified dating; living together; prenuptial agreements; and civil unions: these all spell caution.

In addition, from the evolutionary perspective, slow love is likely adaptive – because the human brain is soft-wired to attach to a partner slowly. Men and women who have fallen madly in love within the past eight months show activity in brain regions associated with energy, focus, motivation, craving, and intense romantic passion; whereas those who have been passionately in love for eight to seventeen months also show activity in an additional brain region associated with feelings of attachment (Aron et al., 2005). Thus romantic love can be triggered rapidly; however, feelings of deep attachment take time to develop. Society's expanding phases of pre-committed courtship and commitment "lite" is in alignment with our primordial brain circuits for romance and attachment. Slow love is within our evolved human biology.

With this trend toward slow love, partnerships may become more stable too –because men and women are marrying later. Data on eighty societies culled from the Demographic Yearbooks of the United Nations between 1947 and 2011 indicate that the later you marry, the more likely you are to remain married (Fisher, 2016). Likewise, a study of over 3,000 married people in the United States found that, compared to those who dated less than a year, couples who dated for one to two years were 20% less likely to later get a divorce, and couples who dated for three years or longer were 39% less likely to later get a divorce (Francis-Tan & Mialon, 2015). Another indication of this possible trend toward marital stability comes from a related investigation of 1,095 married Americans, done as part of a supplement to our 2012 *Singles in America* study with Match. Among the questions posed to them was: "Knowing what you now know about your spouse, would you marry the same person again?" 81% said "yes." Moreover, 76% of these married men and 73% of these married women said they were still "very much in love." A 2013 survey of more than 12,000 adults in fifteen countries also suggests that today's marriages are more stable; in this study, 78% of married men and women reported that they were "happy" (Ipsos, 2014). Slow love may give singles time to gain experience and select a truly appropriate mating partner, enabling the brain circuitry for romance and attachment to flourish in the long term. Indeed, we can remain "in love" in the long term. A recent fMRI study of seventeen men and women married an average of twenty-one years – who maintained that they were still madly in love with their long-term spouse – has shown that the primary brain regions for romantic love and attachment can remain active for decades (Acevedo et al., 2011; Acevedo et al., 2012).

During our long agrarian past, our forebears married to please their God, the local community and their extended family; spouses were tied to the land and to one another; and singles married young, fast, and for eternity. Unchained from the constraints of farm living, however, today's singles are turning inward, choosing partners for themselves and taking time to court, pair, and wed. In fact, rapidly committing to a new partner may be riskier to long-term happiness than getting to know a potential partner slowly via casual sex, hanging out, friends-with-benefits, assiduous dating and living together prior to wedding.

Love is not dead; courtship is not ruined; and sex has not replaced emotional intimacy. Our romantic and sexual lives are simply adapting to our new environments. In fact, with the current marriage revolution toward slow love, we may see more happy and enduring partnerships in the Digital Age.

References

Acevedo, B., Aron, A., Fisher, H. E., & Brown, L. L. (2011). Neural correlates of long-term intense romantic love. *Social Cognitive and Affective Neuroscience*, doi: 10.1093/scan/nsq092.

(2012). Neural correlates of marital satisfaction and well-being: Reward, empathy, and affect. *Clinical Neuropsychiatry*, *9*(1), 20–31.

Aron, A., Fisher, H. E., Mashek, D. J., Strong, G., Li, H. F., & Brown, L. L. (2005). Reward, motivation and emotion systems associated with early-stage intense romantic love: An fMRI study. *Journal of Neurophysiology*, *94*, 327–337.

Cacioppo, J. T., Cacioppo, S., Gonzaga, G. C., Ogburn, E. L., & VanderWeele, T. J. (2013). Marital satisfaction and break-ups differ across on-line and off-line meeting venues. *Proceedings of the National Academy of Sciences*, *110*(25), 10135–10140.

Carter, C. S. (1992). Oxytocin and sexual behavior. *Neuroscience and Biobehavioral Reviews*, *1*, 131–144.

(1998). Neuroendocrine perspectives on social attachment and love. *Psychoneuroendocrinology*, *23*, 779–818.

Chayko, M. (2014). Techno-social life: The internet, digital technology, and social connectedness. *Sociology Compass*, *8*(7), 976–991.

The Economist. (2017). A looser knot: Special report on marriage. November 25.

Fisher, H. E. (1992). *Anatomy of love* (1st ed.). New York: W.W. Norton.

    (1998). Lust, attraction, and attachment in mammalian reproduction. *Human Nature, 9*, 23–52.

    (1999). *The first sex: The natural talents of women and how they are changing the world*. New York: Random House.

    (2004). *Why we love: The nature and chemistry of romantic love*. New York: Henry Holt.

    (2011). Serial monogamy and clandestine adultery: Evolution and consequences of the dual human reproductive strategy. In S. C. Roberts (Ed.), *Applied evolutionary psychology* (pp 96–111). New York: Oxford University Press.

    (2014). The tyranny of love: Love addiction – An anthropologist's view. In K. P. Rosenberg & L. C. Feder (Eds.), *Behavioral Addictions: Criteria, evidence and treatment* (pp 237–260). London: Elsevier Press/Academic Press.

    (2015). Slow love: How casual sex may be improving marriage. *Nautilus*, online March 5.

    (2016). *Anatomy of love: The natural history of monogamy, adultery, and divorce* (2nd ed.). New York: Norton.

Fisher, H. E., Aron, A., & Brown, L. L. (2006). Romantic love: A mammalian brain system for mate choice. *Philosophical Transactions of the Royal Society: Biological Sciences, 361*, 2173–2186.

Fisher, H., Aron, A., Mashek, D., Strong, G., Li, H., & Brown, L. L. (2003). Early stage intense romantic love activates cortical-basal-ganglia reward/motivation, emotion and attention systems: An fMRI study of a dynamic network that varies with relationship length, passion intensity and gender. Poster presented at the Annual Meeting of the Society for Neuroscience, New Orleans, November 11.

Fisher, H. E., Brown, L. L., Aron, A., Strong, G., & Mashek, D. (2010). Reward, addiction, and emotion regulation systems associated with rejection in love. *Journal of Neurophysiology, 104*, 51–60.

Fisher, H. E., Xu, X., Aron, A., & Brown, L. L. (2016). Intense, passionate romantic love: A natural addiction? How the fields that investigate romance and substance abuse can inform each other. *Frontiers in Psychology*. Retrieved from https://doi.org/10.3389/fpsyg.2016.00687.

Francis-Tan, A., & Mialon, H. M. (2015). "A diamond is forever" and other fairy tales: The relationship between wedding expenses and marriage duration. *Economic Inquiry, 53*(4), 1919–1930.

Frascella, J., Potenza, M. N., Brown, L. L., & Childress, A. R. (2010). Shared brain vulnerabilities open the way for non-substance addictions: Carving addiction at a new joint? *Annals of the New York Academy of Sciences, 1187*(1), 294–315.

Garcia, J. R., & Fisher, H. E. (2015). Why we hook up: Searching for sex or looking for love? In S. Tarrant (Ed.), *Gender, sex, and politics: In the streets and between the sheets in the 21st century* (pp. 238–250). New York: Routledge.

Garcia, J. R., Gesselman, A. N., Siliman, S. A., Perry, B. L., Coe, K., & Fisher, H. E. (2016). Sexting among singles in the USA: Prevalence of sending, receiving, and sharing sexual messages and images. *Sexual Health*, *13*(5), 428–435.

Garcia, J. R., & Reiber, C. (2008). Hook-up behavior: A biopsychosocial perspective. *Journal of Social, Evolutionary, and Cultural Psychology*, *2*(4), 192–208.

Gesselman, A. G., Ta, V. P., & Garcia, J. R. (in review). Worth a thousand words: Emojis as affective signals for relationship-oriented communication.

Gray, P. B., & Garcia, J. R. (2013). *Evolution and human sexual behavior.* Cambridge, MA: Harvard University Press.

Hampton, W. H., Unger, A., Von Der Heide, R. J., & Olson, I. R. (2016). Neural connections foster social connections: A diffusion-weighted imaging study of social networks. *Social Cognitive and Affective Neuroscience*, *11*(5), 721–727.

Heussner, K. M. (2010). Is technology taking its toll on our relationships? *Technology Review.* Retrieved from abcnews.go.com.

Ipsos. (2014). *Valentine's Day: Correlations between relationship status and happiness, financial situation.* Ipsos: A Global Independent Market Research Company. February 12. Retrieved from www.ipsos.com/en-us/valentines-day-correlations-between-relationship-status-and-happiness-financial-situation.

Iyengar, S. S. & Lepper, M. R. (2000). When choice is demotivating: Can one desire too much of a good thing? *Journal of Personality and Social Psychology*, *79*(6), 995–1006.

Jankowiak, W. R., & Fischer, E. F. (1992). A cross-cultural perspective on romantic love. *Ethnology*, *31*(2), 149–155.

Jankowiak, W. R., & Paladino, T. (2008). Desiring sex, longing for love: A tripartite conundrum. In W. R. Jankowiak (Ed.), *Intimacies: Love and sex across cultures* (pp. 1–36). New York: Columbia University Press.

Lloyd, E. A. (2005). *The case of the female orgasm: Bias in the science of evolution.* Cambridge, MA: Harvard University Press.

Miller, A. M., Sassler, S., & Kusi-Appouh, D. (2011). The specter of divorce: Views from working- and middle-class cohabitors. *Family Relations*, *60*, 602–616.

Miller, G. A. (1955). The magical number seven, plus or minus two: Some limits on our capacity for processing information. *Psychological Review*, *101*(2), 343–352.

Ortega, J., & Hergovich, P. (2017). The strength of absent ties: Social integration via online dating. *arXiv preprint arXiv:1709.10478.*

Pew Research Center. (2008). Social and demographic trends. "The decline of marriage and rise of new families." November 18. Retrieved from http://pewsocialtrends.org/2010/11/18.

Schwartz, B. (2016). *The paradox of choice: Why more is less* (rev. ed.). New York: Harper Perennial.

Ta, V. P., Gesselman, A. N., Perry, B. L., Fisher, H. E., & Garcia, J. R. (2017). Stress of Singlehood: Marital status, domain-specific stress, and anxiety in a national US sample. *Journal of Social and Clinical Psychology*, *36*(6), 461–485.

Tsapelas, I., Fisher, H. E., & Aron, A. (2010). Infidelity: Who, when, why. In W. R. Cupach & B. H. Spitzberg (Eds.), *The dark side of close relationships II*, (pp. 175–196). New York: Routledge.

Xu, X., Brown, L. L., Aron, A., Cao, G., Feng, T., Acevedo, B., & Weng, X. (2012). Regional brain activity during early-stage intense romantic love predicted relationship outcomes after 40 months: An fMRI assessment. *Neuroscience Letters, 526*(1), 33–38.

Xu, X., Aron, A., Brown, L. L., Cao, G., Feng, T., & Weng, X. (2011). Reward and motivation systems: A brain mapping study of early-stage intense romantic love in Chinese participants. *Human Brain Mapping, 32*(2), 249–257.

CHAPTER II

Styles of Romantic Love

Clyde Hendrick and Susan S. Hendrick

To understand why we view love as we do, it is necessary (or at least useful) to understand how we came to our viewpoints. When we first began our research on love, we were newlyweds (beginning a second marriage with some life experience and heaps of idealism). In addition, we were a counseling psychologist (Susan) and a social psychologist (Clyde), trying to find an area of work that would be practical (Susan conducted couple therapy in her private practice) and empirically rigorous (Clyde was a seasoned scholar). We converged on love as something we experienced, saw in other couples, saw missing in other couples, and seemed to us to be incredibly important to humanity. We had also each read Lee's (1973) book on the love styles and found it intriguing. Thus began our journey into studying the love styles.

Sociologist John Alan Lee (1973) proposed the concept of love styles – the idea that romantic love could be changeable across persons, across time, and across partners. His original and engaging research involved a complex interview procedure called the Love Story Card Sort. People sorted green cards with phrases on them such as "The night after I met X ..." and then matched the green card to phrases on one or more white cards that completed a sentence, such as "I could hardly get to sleep"; "I wanted to ask X a lot more questions"; "I wanted to call X in the middle of the night," and so on. After working through a card sort for several hours, that person's love story with a particular partner became clear. The results of Lee's painstaking work appeared in books such as *The Colours of Love* (Lee, 1973) and *Styles of Loving* (Lasswell & Lobsenz, 1980).

Lee used an analogy of a color wheel as a way to visualize his styles of love. There were three primary "colors," mapped onto three primary love styles: eros, ludus, and storge. A mixture of the three primaries yielded three secondaries: pragma, mania, and agape. Other mixtures are possible, but Lee and succeeding researchers have focused overwhelmingly on these six types of love. A summary of the meanings is: eros (passionate, erotic), ludus (game-playing, uncommitted), storge (friendship), pragma (practical, calculating), agape (altruistic, giving), and mania (obsessional).

Although love stories can differ in many ways, they may also have consistencies across time, particularly with the same partner. Lee described his card sort results as ideologies of love but also as styles of loving. We have always referred to love "styles," viewing them as six attitude/belief systems that encompass an emotional core that has both variability and stability and may be linked to personality traits. The love styles were appealing to us as an approach to romantic love because they allowed wide latitude in personal definitions and experiences of love, plus they map onto some "commonsense" views of what romantic love might be. A fuller description of the six love styles is given below.

EROS: Strong physical attraction, emotional intensity, a preferred physical appearance, and a sense of inevitability of the relationship define the central core of eros. Eros can "strike" suddenly in a revolution of feeling and thinking.

LUDUS: Love is a game to be played with a diverse set of partners over time. Deception of the partner and lack of disclosure about the self and other partners are prime attributes of ludus. Because of ludus's lack of honesty, college students often have disagreed with items for this love style. However, Lee (1973) noted that this approach reflects a desirable reality for many people. In fact, substantial numbers of college students behave ludically during some phases of their partner selection process.

STORGE: This style is love as friendship. It is quiet and companionate. The fire of eros is unfamiliar to storge. Storge has been described as love by "evolution" rather than love by "revolution."

PRAGMA: With this style, love is a shopping list of desired attributes (e.g. fitting into one's family, being a good parent in the future, and so on). Computer matching is a good contemporary way for pragma lovers to proceed.

MANIA: This style might be called "symptom" love. Mania is intense, alternating between ecstasy and agony. Manic love, when felt strongly, usually does not end well.

AGAPE: This style is giving and sacrificial, placing the loved person's welfare above one's own. In romantic love, pure agape is shown rarely. In settled relationships, agape can be reduced by the demands of equity/fairness in long-term relationships and increased by life events such as a partner's illness.

These descriptions appear to tap six different "styles" of romantic love. But naming these differing love styles does not mean that they actually exist. Giving reality to the descriptions requires some way to measure them with some precision. Developing that precision of measurement occupied us for several years. The result was the Love Attitudes Scale. Its development is described in the next section.

Measuring the Six Love Styles

Our initial attempt at measuring the six love styles (C. Hendrick, Hendrick, Foote, & Slapion-Foote, 1984) used a set of fifty true/false items developed by Lasswell and Lasswell (1976), plus four additional items. We transformed all items to five-point rating scales rather than use a true/false format. Many items showed gender differences, and statistical analyses were only partially supportive of the six styles proposed by Lee. In our next attempt at rating-scale building (C. Hendrick & Hendrick, 1986), we revised and standardized a set of forty-two items (seven items for each of the six love styles). In two studies at each of two different universities (four studies in all), the statistical procedure called factor analysis of the forty-two items revealed six subsets of items that closely matched the definitions of the six love styles. We concluded that Lee's definitions could be measured by a rating scale. On the basis of this initial validation of what we named the Love Attitudes Scale (LAS), we began a decades-long research program.

Over the years, there were some criticisms of the LAS. Johnson (1987) noted that the items were a mix of general and specific relationship statements and that the relative proportions of such items differed across the six scales of the LAS. In response, we rewrote nineteen general items to create a completely relationship-specific version of the LAS (C. Hendrick & Hendrick, 1990). Results with the new version were completely consistent with the original version, and because of the substantial number of studies already completed, we continued to use the 1986 version.

Over time, we noticed that other researchers were "borrowing" subsets of the seven-item scales to create even briefer scales. We finally decided we had no choice but to join the revisionists ourselves, so we set to work to extract the best four-item version from each seven-item scale. The results exceeded our expectations (C. Hendrick, Hendrick, & Dicke, 1998). The statistical properties for this twenty-four-item version of the LAS were excellent, and in some cases they were better than for the original longer version.

It is important to note why we went through all this work for several years to make sure we had a psychometrically solid scale (meaning that it measured what we said it measured). If you answer items on a given scale, whether a love scale, a personality scale, or something else, you should want to know that your answers "mean something." You want a scale that truly measures what it says it measures so that you know you are getting accurate information about your own love style or your own personality style. That is why you need to know how a scale has been developed. Before we describe our research with the LAS and LAS: Short Form, it will be useful to distinguish the six love styles from the phenomenon of "falling in love."

The Love Styles and Falling in Love

"Falling in love" is a widely recognized cultural phenomenon. It is also complex. Shaver and colleagues (Shaver, Morgan, & Wu, 1996) argued that love is a basic emotion. We have also argued that love in general has a strong emotional component (C. Hendrick & Hendrick, 2003). Perhaps Hatfield's (1988) concept of passionate love most closely reflects falling in love.

A side issue involves whether or not passionate love involves sexual desire. Some (e.g. Regan, 1998; Regan & Berscheid, 1999) view sexual desire as an important component of romantic love. Hatfield (1988) is more wary of such an automatic linkage. For example, young children may fall passionately in love even before they have any understanding of sexual love. We tend to agree with Hatfield, and we also subscribe to Fisher's (2000) view that sex and passionate love evolved as separate, but loosely linked, emotion systems.

So how is the intense emotional experience of falling in love related to the six love styles? Each of the six love styles is, at minimum, an attitude/belief complex with more or less of an emotion component. The amount of emotion attached to each love style should depend on the attitudes/beliefs that characterize that style. For example, eros and mania each have a strong "emotion switch," whereas storge, pragma, and ludus have less emotion. People high on the latter three love styles may not experience the emotional "rush" of falling in love. Those high on mania, especially, may experience it all too easily. Of course we must remember that we are talking here about emotion in the context of romantic love. Other kinds of love – for example, love for children and grandchildren – may be powerfully emotional (e.g. Hrdy, 2009).

This approach is converging on the notion of falling in love as an "emotional storm" leading to at least temporary changes in a range of beliefs and attitudes, including some of the love styles. Such thinking led us to predict wide-ranging differences on many relational constructs/variables for college students "in love" as compared to students "not in love." Our general thesis was that "lovers wear rose colored glasses" (C. Hendrick & Hendrick, 1988). Indeed, we found differences on many variables that supported our predictions. With regard to the love styles, college students who were in love were more erotic and agapic, and less ludic, than students who were not in love. Students in love were less permissive and instrumental in their sexual attitudes than students not in love. Being in love also gave a boost to self-esteem yet lowered self-monitoring and sensation seeking.

We concluded that the six love styles are relatively independent attitude/belief systems about love that have likely developed for the last two thousand or more years (e.g. Singer, 1984). Falling in love is best construed as a global emotional experience that has wide-ranging attitudinal and bodily effects, including at least temporary changes in three of the six love styles. The love styles and falling in love are thus related, but are conceptually distinct constructs. Falling in love may well be experienced differently, depending on whether an individual is high on a single love style, and which one, or moderate on several of them. For example, someone high on eros should experience the classic full-blown syndrome of falling in love, as should someone high on mania. In contrast, someone high on pragma would probably have only a mild experience of falling in love. Someone high on ludus would not fall in love. Thus the love styles, along with other variables, undoubtedly moderate the experience of falling in love.

Clearly, multiple factors influence (and are influenced by) falling in love and perhaps even by the average level of some of the love styles themselves (C. Hendrick & Hendrick, 1988). We believe that the love styles are substantially attitude-based, though personality may also come into play. However, one's age, life stage, particular partner, the interaction of the self and the partner, as well as social network and sociodemographic factors could all be expected to influence some of the love styles to a degree.

Individual Factors

Early in our love research program, we found that self-esteem, considered as an aspect of personality, was related to two love styles: positively to eros (greater passionate love means higher self-esteem) and negatively to mania (greater dependent, possessive love means lower self-esteem) (C. Hendrick & Hendrick, 1986). Self-disclosure, another aspect of personality, has been related to the love styles. For example, self-disclosure was related positively to eros (greater passionate love means more disclosure) and negatively to ludus (greater game-playing love means less disclosure) (S. Hendrick & Hendrick, 1987b).

Exploring links between the love styles and more traditional aspects of personality, White and colleagues (White, Hendrick, & Hendrick, 2004) found that the love attitudes were related to several personality dimensions as measured by the *NEO Personality Inventory – Revised* (Form S; Costa & McCrae, 1985, 1992). The *NEOPI-R* is a widely used personality instrument and measures the personality factors of agreeableness, conscientiousness, extraversion, neuroticism, and openness to experience (informally known as the Big Five). Passionate eros was related positively to agreeableness, conscientiousness, and extraversion, and related negatively to neuroticism. Friendship-oriented storge was not related to agreeableness, but was otherwise similar to eros in its relationships with the other personality variables. Game-playing ludus showed almost the opposite pattern, relating negatively to agreeableness and conscientiousness, but positively to neuroticism. Practical pragma was related positively to conscientiousness and negatively to openness to experience, whereas possessive mania and neuroticism were related positively. Altruistic agape was not related to any of the five factors.

In research similar to that of White et al. (2004), Heaven, Da Silva, Carey, and Holen (2004) explored personality, attachment, and the love styles and also found extensive relationships between the Big Five and the love styles. Their results were fairly consistent with those of White et al. For example, eros was related positively to conscientiousness and extraversion and was related negatively to neuroticism. They also found that anxious attachment mediated the relationship between neuroticism and the love styles to which it was related. White et al. (2004) found that mania mediated the relationship between neuroticism and relationship satisfaction, so it appears that neuroticism, in particular, is complexly related to relational constructs such as the love styles.

More recently, Zadeh and Bozorgi (2016) used the NEOPI (Costa & McCrae, 1985), the LAS (C. Hendrick & Hendrick, 1986), and a measure of marital adjustment/quality, in assessing married students at an Iranian university. They found significant relationships between personality factors, love styles, and marital quality. Regression analyses indicated that the eros and storge love styles, as well as several facets of personality (e.g. agreeableness, openness to experience) were strong predictors of marital quality.

Just as love styles are related to *individual* phenomena (factors within persons), so they are also related to *interpersonal* phenomena (factors between persons).

Interpersonal Factors

Although romantic love and sexuality are not the same, we have proposed that they "are inextricably linked, with love as the basis for much of our sexual interaction, and sex as the medium of expression for much of our loving" (S. Hendrick & Hendrick, 1987a, p. 159).

To explore love styles in conjunction with sexuality, specifically sexual attitudes, we developed the Sexual Attitudes Scale (S. Hendrick & Hendrick, 1987c), a forty-three-item scale with subscales measuring permissiveness (casual sexuality); sexual practices (responsible, tolerant sexuality); communion (idealistic sexuality); and instrumentality (biologically focused sexuality). We correlated the Sexual Attitudes Scale and the LAS across several studies, finding some consistent relationships between the subscales of the two measures. Casual sexuality (permissiveness) and game-playing love were related positively – a logical finding for a lover who likes a variety of partners, not wanting to get too close to any particular one. In addition, passionate love was related consistently to both idealized sexuality (communion) and responsible sexuality (sexual practices) (S. Hendrick & Hendrick, 1987a).

We continued to conduct research with both the love and sex scales and eventually decided that the factor structure of the Sexual Attitudes Scale had shifted a bit (e.g. Le Gall, Mullet, & Riviere-Shafighi, 2002). In addition, we wanted to tighten the scale and have it reflect changing sexual behavior. Thus, conducting one new study and using two existing data sets, we worked with a colleague to shorten the scale (Hendrick, Hendrick, & Reich, 2006). The new scale, entitled the Brief Sexual Attitudes Scale consisted of 23 items (contrasted with the 43 items), with four subscales: permissiveness (10 items); birth control (3 items); communion (5 items); and instrumentality (5 items). The brief measure was used by Katz and Schneider (2013), who found that permissive and instrumental sexual attitudes were related positively to positive attitudes and behavior of college students' involvement in hook-up sex. Although individual and interpersonal qualities are important to attitudes about romantic love, social structural factors (sometimes called demographic factors), are important also.

Social Factors: Love Styles and Demographic Characteristics

Gender, a characteristic of the individual, has tremendous influence on society in general. Gender is a master status variable, meaning that it is an inherent characteristic of the person (e.g. Laumann, Gagnon, Michael, & Michaels, 1994), perhaps even more powerful than race/ethnicity. We found a number of gender differences in several of the love styles (C. Hendrick et al., 1984), causing us to question whether women and men might actually "love differently." For example, men have been consistently more endorsing of (or at least less in agreement with) game-playing love, whereas women have agreed more with friendship and practical love. Using the shortened form of the scale (C. Hendrick et al., 1998), men also more consistently agreed with agape (altruistic love) than women did. More recently, Cramer and colleagues (Cramer, Marcus, Pomerleau, & Gillard, 2015) used the longer form of the love scale with approximately 365 men and 580 women and found that the basic structures of the scales (meaning which items were on which scales) differed somewhat for women and men. The authors rightly concluded that before it can be concluded that men and women really "love differently," it is important that women and men are interpreting the items (and thus the scales) in the same way. We found that although the genders may differ in average scores on some of the love styles, when the styles are correlated with other relationship constructs, women's and men's correlation patterns are very similar (S. Hendrick & Hendrick, 1995).

Ethnicity/culture is another demographic variable that has relevance to the love styles. Love is neither a recent nor a Western phenomenon. Basing their discussion on Chinese literature up to 3,000 years old, Cho and Cross (1995) proposed that forms of love such as passionate love, obsessive love, devoted love, and casual love, as well as freedom to choose one's mate, were known in earlier time periods. Using the LAS, these authors assessed the love styles of Taiwanese students living currently in the United States, finding that while the six factors they obtained did not map exactly onto the six subscales of the LAS, there were many similarities. Consistent with these findings, Sprecher et al. (1994) explored Russian, Japanese, and US love styles. Although these groups differed on certain dimensions, "the young adults from the three countries were similar in many love attitudes and experiences" (Sprecher et al., 1994, p. 363). Murstein, Merighi, and Vyse (1991) found French college students more endorsing of agape, and US students reporting more storgic and manic love attitudes. However, Gana, Saada, and Untas (2013) found that only the love style of eros was related to marital satisfaction in French married couples. This finding was consistent with research by Contreras, Hendrick, and Hendrick (1996), who found that Mexican American and Anglo married couples differed only modestly on love attitudes (showing no differences on passionate, friendship, or altruistic love). Regan (2016) encompassed several demographic domains by focusing on age, gender, and ethnicity to assess endorsement of agape (altruistic love). Her sample included men and women who comprised a community sample of nearly 700 persons of varying ages and ethnicities/race, including Latino/a; African American; Asian/Pacific Islander; and non-Hispanic white. Men endorsed agape significantly more than did women, and African Americans endorsed it less than did other groups. Such findings are interesting but not surprising, given that society is always changing to some degree, and also, with a large sample, even small differences can be significant. Finally, Shahrazad, Mohd, and Chong (2012) found that the factor structure of the twenty-four-item form of the LAS was suitable for research with Malaysian samples. Similarities across groups appear to be more pronounced than differences. For additional findings of the love attitudes across cultures, see Smith and Klases (2016) and Zeng and colleagues (Zeng, Pan, Zhou, Yu, & Liu, 2016).

Although most love styles research has been conducted with young persons, some research has explored love and love styles in older persons, especially couples. Grote and Frieze (1994) assessed love predictors of relationship satisfaction for middle-aged married couples, finding that passionate love and friendship love were positive predictors of satisfaction, whereas game-playing love was a negative predictor. Such findings are consistent (at least for eros) with those of other scholars (Gana et al., 2013; Contreras et al., 1996).

A direct comparison of college students and their parents (Inman-Amos, Hendrick, & Hendrick, 1994) found no similarities in love styles between students and their own parents. When comparing means for the student group as a whole with the parent group as a whole, however, love styles were very similar for the generations. Montgomery and Sorell (1997) compared love styles and other relationship constructs in the following groups: (a) young, college-age persons; (b) married persons under thirty years of age without children; (c) married persons aged from twenty-four to fifty with children at home; and (d) married persons aged from fifty to seventy with no children at home. The greatest differences between the groups occurred between the married and non-married persons, whereas the other groups differed little. Based on these research findings, although age does not seem to be a great demarcation factor for love attitudes, marital status may be more important.

Sexual orientation is also a demographic characteristic of interest in relationships. Adler and colleagues (Adler, Hendrick, & Hendrick, 1986) assessed gay males and heterosexual males in both the New York city area and in West Texas. Men were asked about their love attitudes (and other relationship variables) and for the most part, no sexual orientation differences emerged. For location, however, New York respondents were less manic than were Texas respondents, and gay men in New York endorsed agapic love significantly less than did gay men in Texas or heterosexual men in either location. More recently, Zamora, Winterowd, Koch, and Roring (2013) assessed seventy-two gay men in various relationship statuses, assessing love styles and other relationship constructs. Gay men in love were more likely to endorse mania and pragma, but were less endorsing of eros. There seemed to be a strong emphasis on needing reassurance from the partner (thus the mania). There is considerable need to explore love styles in the LGBT community, though as Peplau and Spaulding (2000) noted, "Efforts to apply basic relationship theories to same-sex couples have been largely successful. There is much commonality among the issues facing all close relationships, regardless of the sexual orientation of the partners" (p. 123).

Talking about commonalities among issues and relationships offers an opportunity to discuss commonalities among scholars regarding one type of love. In our research and that of others, the importance of eros (passionate love) has been very clear. As an example, Hatfield and Sprecher (1986) developed the Passionate Love Scale (PLS), consisting of thirty rating items focusing solely on the passion aspect of romantic love.

Another strong example was provided by Sternberg (1986), who proposed his triangular theory of love. In this theory, love is a varying mix of three components: passion, intimacy, and commitment. As examples, a person high on passion and intimacy is romantically in love. A person high on passion only is infatuated. A person who is high on all three components is experiencing consummate love. A person who is low on all three components is not experiencing love. From these three "tips of the triangle" (passion, intimacy, and commitment), Sternberg derived eight types of love, including the three types just mentioned.

In summary, although theories and research on love diverge widely, there is nevertheless wide agreement that passion (we would say eros) is an indispensable element of romantic love.

Love Styles and Relationship Satisfaction

An aspect of our love research has been a focus on how love correlates with relationship satisfaction. In some of our earliest work (S. Hendrick, Hendrick, & Adler, 1988), we focused on two primary themes: partner similarity and prediction of both satisfaction and staying together/breaking up. In assessing fifty-seven college dating couples, we found relationship partners to be similar on eros, storge, mania, and agape. We also found eros to be a positive predictor, and ludus a negative predictor of relationship satisfaction for both women and men, with mania an additional negative predictor for women. After two months, we recontacted a subsample of thirty couples to determine which ones were still together. Some twenty-three couples were still together, whereas seven had broken up. Based on their earlier responses to the relationship measures, we determined that the "together" couples had been more passionate (eros) and less game playing in their love styles than had the breakup couples. The similarity findings of this study were replicated by Morrow, Clark, and Brock (1995), who found partners to be similar in love styles.

In additional research discussed earlier, Contreras et al. (1996) found that passionate love was "the most consistent predictor of marital satisfaction for both wives and husbands, across all ethnic categories" (p. 412). Gana et al. (2013) also found that passionate love was related to satisfaction for French married couples.

In a study of relational quality in dual-career couple and family work issues, Sokolski and Hendrick (1999) surveyed 160 married couples in which one or both spouses were law, medical, or graduate students. Spouses showed significant similarity on the love styles of eros, ludus, storge, and pragma. Also, eros, storge, and agape were associated positively with satisfaction for both wives and husbands (ludus was negatively associated for both).

Meeks, Hendrick, and Hendrick (1998) surveyed love styles and several additional relationship constructs in 140 dating college couples. Partners were similar on four of the six love styles (as well as several other constructs), and in the final predictive analysis, positive love (a combination of eros, storge, and agape) was one of the positive predictors of relationship satisfaction, whereas game-playing ludus was one of the negative predictors.

Thus, based on a variety of research findings from young dating couples, young married couples, and older married couples, partners are typically similar on several of the love styles. And several of the love styles are significantly and positively related to relationship satisfaction, with eros always a positive predictor of satisfaction.

Although most of our research has been on love and its many facets, we broadened out from love and its influence on satisfaction to include a relationship construct that is both understudied and important: respect.

Respect, Love, and Relationships

Our research on respect arose in response to the narrative biographical work of Lawrence-Lightfoot (2000). In her book on respect, she detailed accounts of persons whom she believed lived their lives in such a way as to exemplify varied aspects of respect. Her accounts profiled a nurse-midwife, pediatrician, high-school teacher, photographer, law professor, and chaplain/counselor to dying patients. These persons crossed gender and racial/ethnic lines. The elements of respect that they exemplified include empowerment, healing, dialogue, attention, curiosity, and self-respect.

Based on Lawrence-Lightfoot's concepts, we developed a brief measure of respect (S. Hendrick & Hendrick, 2006) used to assess persons' respect for their romantic partner. The six-item measure was statistically strong and related in a predictable fashion to several relationship variables, including the love styles. Second only to passionate love in its power to predict relationship satisfaction, the respect scale also shows potential as a generic measure of respect for others. Because respect was also found by Feeney, Noller, and Ward (1997) to be a consistent element of marital quality, and because we believe that a truly mature love has mutual respect as one of its foundational properties, the study of respect seems to us to be a logical extension of our study of love and of others' study of romantic relationships. Respect is important beyond romantic relationships, however, and has also been shown to be foundational in the family, with adults and children respecting both themselves and each other (e.g. S. Hendrick, Hendrick, & Logue, 2010).

Love Styles Come of Age

Love and love styles in particular have been the major (though not the only) focus of our research across decades. And the love styles have found audiences beyond our work or our borders, as we noted in an earlier section of this chapter. For example, love styles are important to psychotherapists, and we contributed a brief article to a British publication, explaining how the love styles can be useful in couple counseling/therapy (C. Hendrick

& Hendrick, 2012). The love styles are also relevant to the area of psychology called "positive psychology," which focuses on human strengths and the qualities that contribute positively to individuals and to humanity in general. Love is one such quality. Thus, we have contributed to current volumes on positive psychology and how positive psychology is assessed (C. Hendrick & Hendrick, in press; S. Hendrick & Hendrick, in press). Requests to use the love scales (both forms) have come from a number of countries over the past couple of years (e.g. China, Germany, Holland, Hungary, India, Indonesia, Italy, Malaysia, Pakistan, the Philippines, Russia, Serbia, and Slovenia). Thus, people everywhere are interested in love. A high-end fashion company has even named one of its fragrances for women "eros." Love rules!

So how does all this information relate to you? How might it be useful to your love life?

Have you ever been in a romantic relationship with someone you really liked (or even loved), but who just did not feel completely "trustworthy" when it came to cheating on you? If so, how did you handle the situation? Did you drive by your partner's apartment to see if his or her car was there, knowing your partner was supposed to be at home "studying?" Or did you call/text your partner until you finally got an answer (no matter how long it took)? If you have done any of these behaviors, then you were being a Mania lover at the time. In contrast, are you in a romantic relationship with someone who has been your friend for a while? And somehow the friendship just grew into more – into love? If yes, then you are a Storge lover. Do you have a romantic partner with whom you "just knew" that you were meant to be together. The first time you met (at a party) you left the party and went to a coffee shop where you hung out and talked until the shop closed. You told each other everything about yourselves. You felt like you were home. Then you are an Eros lover.

Of course, no one is just one type of lover with just one love style. We are all some mixture of some of the styles, with different styles coming to the forefront at different times: Eros during romantic times; Storge when helping each other move from one apartment to another and cleaning both the one you are leaving and the one to which you are moving; and Agape when one of you is ill. But certain styles predominate in certain relationships, and we recommend that you know yourself and your partner and "how" you love. We hope that we have made love styles a bit more understandable and tangible. If we have made love sound easy, do not believe us, but if we have made it sound as if it is worth all the trouble, then we have done our job.

References

Adler, N. L., Hendrick, S. S., & Hendrick, C. (1986). Male sexual preference and attitudes toward love and sexuality. *Journal of Sex Education and Therapy, 12* (2), 27–30.

Cho, W., & Cross, S. E. (1995). Taiwanese love styles and their association with self-esteem and relationship quality. *Genetic, Social, & General Psychology Monographs, 121,* 283–309.

Contreras, R., Hendrick, S. S., & Hendrick, C. (1996). Perspectives on marital love and satisfaction in Mexican American and Anglo-American couples. *Journal of Counseling and Development, 74,* 408–415.

Costa, P. T., Jr., & McCrae, R. R. (1985). *The NEO personality inventory manual.* Odessa, FL: Psychological Assessment Resources.

(1992). *Revised NEO personality inventory (NEO PI-R) and NEO five-factor (NEO-FFI) professional manual.* Odessa, FL: Psychological Assessment Resources.

Cramer, K., Marcus, J., Pomerleau, C., & Gillard, K. (2015). Gender invariance in the love attitudes scale based on Lee's color theory of love. *TPM, 22,* 403–413.

Feeney, J. A., Noller, P., & Ward, C. (1997). Marital satisfaction and spousal interaction. In R. J. Sternberg & M. Hojjat (Eds.), *Satisfaction in close relationships* (pp. 160–189). New York: Guilford Press.

Fisher, H. E. (2000). Lust, attraction, attachment: Biology and evolution of three primary emotion systems for mating, reproduction, and parenting. *Journal of Sex Education and Therapy, 25,* 96–104.

Gana, K., Saada, Y., & Untas, A. (2013). Effects of love styles on marital satisfaction in heterosexual couples: A dyadic approach. *Marriage and Family Review, 49,* 754–772.

Grote, N. K., & Frieze, L. H. (1994). The measurement of friendship-based love in intimate relationships. *Personal Relationships, 1,* 275–300.

Hatfield, E. (1988). Passionate and companionate love. In R. J. Sternberg & M. L. Barnes (Eds.), *The psychology of love* (pp. 191–217). New Haven, CT: Yale University Press.

Hatfield, E., & Sprecher, S. (1986). Measuring passionate love in intimate relationships. *Journal of Adolescence, 9,* 383–410.

Heaven, P. C. L., Da Silva, T., Carey, C., & Holen, J. (2004). Loving styles: Relationships with personality and attachment styles. *European Journal of Personality, 18,* 103–113.

Hendrick, C., & Hendrick, S. S. (1986). A theory and method of love. *Journal of Personality and Social Psychology, 50,* 392–402.

(1988). Lovers wear rose colored glasses. *Journal of Social and Personal Relationships, 5,* 161–183.

(1990). A relationship-specific version of the Love Attitudes Scale. *Journal of Social Behavior and Personality, 5,* 239–254.

(2003). Romantic love: Measuring Cupid's arrow. In S. J. Lopez & C. R. Snyder (Eds.), *Positive psychological assessment: A handbook of models and measures* (pp. 235–249). Washington, DC: American Psychological Association.

(2012). Six ways to love. *The Psychotherapist, 52*, 18–20.

(in press). Love. In C. R. Snyder, S. J. Lopez, L. M. Edwards, & S. Marques (Eds.), *Handbook of positive psychology* (3rd ed.). New York: Oxford University Press.

Hendrick, C., Hendrick, S. S., & Dicke, A. (1998). The Love Attitudes Scale: Short form. *Journal of Social and Personal Relationships, 15*, 147–159.

Hendrick, C., Hendrick, S. S., & Reich, D. A. (2006). The Brief Sexual Attitudes Scale. *The Journal of Sex Research, 43*, 76–86.

Hendrick, C., Hendrick, S. S., Foote, F. H., & Slapion-Foote, M. J. (1984). Do men and women love differently? *Journal of Social and Personal Relationships, 1*, 177–195.

Hendrick, S. S., & Hendrick, C. (1987a). Love and sex attitudes: A close relationship. In W. H. Jones & D. Perlman (Eds.), *Advances in personal relationships*, Vol. 1 (pp. 141–169). Greenwich, CT: JAI Press.

(1987b). Love and sex attitudes and religious beliefs. *Journal of Social and Clinical Psychology, 5*, 391–398.

(1987c). Love and sexual attitudes, self-disclosure, and sensation seeking. *Journal of Social and Personal Relationships, 4*, 281–297.

(1995). Gender differences and similarities in sex and love. *Personal Relationships, 2*, 55–65.

(2006). Measuring respect in close relationships. *Journal of Social and Personal Relationships, 23*, 881–899.

(in press). Measuring love. In S. J. Lopez & M. Gallagher (Eds.), *Positive psychological assessment* (2nd ed.). Washington, DC: American Psychological Association Press.

Hendrick, S. S., Hendrick, C., & Adler, N. L. (1988). Romantic relationships: Love, satisfaction, and staying together. *Journal of Personality and Social Psychology, 54*, 980–988.

Hendrick, S. S., Hendrick, C., & Logue, E. M. (2010). Respect and the family. *Journal of Family Theory & Review, 2*, 126–136.

Hrdy, S. B. (2009). *Mothers and others: The evolutionary origins of mutual understanding*. Cambridge, MA: Belknap Press of Harvard University Press.

Inman-Amos, J., Hendrick, S. S., & Hendrick, C. (1994). Love attitudes: Similarities between parents and between parents and children. *Family Relations, 43*, 456–461.

Johnson, M. P. (1987, November). Discussion of papers on love styles and family relationships. In K. E. Davis (chair), *New directions in love style research*. Symposium conducted at the Preconference Theory Construction and Research Methodology Workshop. Atlanta, GA: National Council on Family Relations.

Katz, J., & Schneider, M. E. (2013). Casual hook up sex during the first year of college: Prospective associations with attitudes about sex and love relationships. *Archives of Sexual Behavior, 42*, 1451–1462.

Lasswell, T. E., & Lasswell, M. E. (1976). I love you but I'm not in love with you. *Journal of Marriage and Family Counseling, 38*, 211–224.

Lasswell, M., & Lobsenz, N. M. (1980). *Styles of loving: Why you love the way you do.* Garden City, NY: Doubleday.

Laumann, E. O., Gagnon, J. H., Michael, R. T., & Michaels, S. (1994). *The social organization of sexuality: Sexual practices in the United States.* Chicago, IL: University of Chicago Press.

Lee, J. A. (1973). *The colors of love: An exploration of the ways of loving.* Don Mills, ON: New Press.

LeGall, A., Mullet, E., & Riviere-Shafighi, S. (2002). Age, religious beliefs, and sexual attitudes. *The Journal of Sex Research, 39,* 207–216.

Lawrence-Lightfoot, S. (2000). *Respect: An exploration.* Cambridge, MA: Perseus Books.

Meeks, B. S., Hendrick, S. S., & Hendrick, C. (1998). Communication, love, and relationship satisfaction. *Journal of Social and Personal Relationships, 15,* 755–773.

Montgomery, M. J., & Sorell, G. T. (1997). Differences in love attitudes across family life stages. *Family Relations, 46,* 55–61.

Morrow, G. D., Clark, E. M., & Brock, K. F. (1995). Individual and partner love styles: Implications for the quality of romantic involvement. *Journal of Social and Personal Relationships, 12,* 363–387.

Murstein, B. I., Merighi, J. R., & Vyse, S. A. (1991). Love styles in the United States and France: A cross-cultural comparison. *Journal of Social and Clinical Psychology, 10,* 37–46.

Peplau, L. A., & Spaulding, L. R. (2000). The close relationships of lesbians, gay men, and bisexuals. In C. Hendrick & S. S. Hendrick (Eds.), *Close relationships: A sourcebook* (pp. 111–123). Thousand Oaks, CA: Sage.

Regan, P. C. (1998). Romantic love and sexual desire. In V. C. de Munck (Ed.), *Romantic love and sexual behavior: Perspectives from the social sciences* (pp. 91–112). Westport, CT: Praeger.

(2016). Loving unconditionally: Demographic correlates of the agapic love style. *Interpersona, 10,* 28–35.

Regan, P. C., & Berscheid, E. (1999). *Lust: What we know about human sexual desire.* Thousand Oaks, CA: Sage.

Shaver, P. R., Morgan, H. J., & Wu, S. (1996). Is love a "basic" emotion? *Personal Relationships, 3,* 81–96.

Shahrazad, W. S., Mohd, S., & Hoesni, C. S. T. (2012). Investigating the factor structure of the Love Attitude Scale (LAS) with Malaysian samples. *Asian Social Science, 8*(9), 66–73.

Singer, I. (1984). *The nature of love,* Vol. 1: *Plato to Luther* (2nd ed.). Chicago, IL: University of Chicago Press.

Smith, R., & Klases, A. (2016). Predictors of love attitudes: The contribution of cultural orientation, gender attachment style, relationship length and age in participants from the UK and Hong Kong. *Interpersona, 10,* 90–108.

Sokolski, D. M., & Hendrick, S. S. (1999). Fostering marital satisfaction. *Family Therapy, 26,* 39–49.

Sprecher, S., Aron, A., Hatfield, E., Cortese, A., Potapova, E., & Levitskaya, A. (1994). Love: American style, Russian style, and Japanese style. *Personal Relationships 1*, 349–369.

Sternberg, R. (1986). A triangular theory of love. *Psychological Review, 93*, 119–135.

White, J. K., Hendrick, S. S., & Hendrick, C. (2004). Big five personality variables and relationship constructs. *Personality and Individual Differences, 37*, 1519–1530.

Zadeh, S. S., & Bozorgi, Z. D. (2016). Relationship between the love styles, personality traits, and the marital life of married students. *International Journal of Humanities and Cultural Studies, 3*, 746–756.

Zamora, R., Winterowd, C., Koch, J., & Roring, S. (2013). The relationship between love styles and romantic attachment styles in gay men. *Journal of LGBT Issues in Counseling, 7*, 200–217.

Zeng, X., Pan, Y., Zhou, H., Yu, S., & Liu, X. (2016). Exploring different patterns of love attitudes among Chinese college students. *PLoS ONE, 11*(11), e0166410.

CHAPTER 12

An Anthropologist Goes Looking for Love in All the Old Places: A Personal Account

William Jankowiak

In 1986, I returned to Inner Mongolia, having lived there between 1981 and 1983. I wanted to understand how Mongolian youth were adapting to what was then becoming a new discourse in their lives – one in which the criteria for selecting a mate was changing. There was a shift away from social attributes as the dominant factors in mate selection to new criteria that saw love as an important consideration. Although "love," the term itself, was rarely mentioned or infrequently referred to, I was struck by how many individuals felt that it was something to be valued, even cherished. The more I looked, the more I found that the youth of Mongolia hoped that love would be present when it became time to choose a life partner. At the time, I was preparing a paper about how the current political opening of China was bringing with it a wide-ranging social transformation. One indicator was the growing interest in 'becoming modern,' an interest that was purposefully, even self-consciously affirmed. To my eyes, this interest, far from superficial, expressed itself as a desire – from the adoption of obvious badges of modernity such as Western dress and car ownership to a deeper assimilation of Western ideas of beauty and the idealization of the love marriage.

As a break from the exhaustiveness of data collection, I began to read stories from the Tang Dynasty (AD 600 to 900). One was about a fox who would take the form of a beautiful woman to attract men. They quickly developed a love crush, whereas she, the fox woman, fell unexpectedly in love with the men she had attracted. After reading a few more stories, it struck me that love as a literary theme predated Western contact. I wondered how widespread or present this predating might be in other cultures. I came to realize, over the course of my reading, that a culture's literature is one of the best ways, if not the best one, to learn what is on the mind of a culture.

When I returned to the United States, I called an old friend, Professor Barry Hewlett, and asked him if he had ever found evidence of romantic love among the Aka forgers of Central Africa. "Absolutely not," he answered. I then asked if he knew or had heard of any of the Aka forgers feeling upset, disappointed, sad, or otherwise unsettled, when experiencing a personal rejection. After some thought, he told me of two cases in which a youth, despondent from being rejected, climbed a huge tree in the forest canopy, placed a vine around his neck and then jumped to his death. I asked Barry what he thought the young man's motive might have been? Why did he jump? Could it have been because the youth anticipated having great sex with the beloved and it was not going to happen? I was in effect asking Barry to consider the youth's state of mind, something I found myself doing when I was reading the stories. Barry replied: "No way." "Then why?" I asked. He slowly responded: "He loved her."

In both the various intellectual disciplines and the media at large, men commit suicide far more often out of frustrated love than out of frustrated sexual desire. This is true in literature across the world. Myths, legends, and fictional stories about suicide, male or female, resulting from frustrated sexual desire are extremely rare. The overwhelming majority depicted suicide as an outcome of frustrated or failed love.

Anthropology of Love: An Overview

While in graduate school during the 1980s, I had assumed like most other people that romantic love was a Western idea that became Euro-America's contribution to world culture. Between 1981 and 1983, during my research in China, I overheard on numerous occasions individuals noting that this or that marriage was not a love match. The mere fact that love was used as a way to describe a marriage was telling in itself. Each time I heard that love was not present, I thought to myself, "well, maybe, it is not something you have ever experienced." It struck me that the constant statement of love's absence might be to pass as modern.

When I returned in 1987, I was determined to listen, with close attention, to what the young people were saying and to stop doubting their motivations. I started with the assumption that they did love their boyfriend or girlfriend. But I did not think that love was a human universal. I believed that love's presence in China was only evidence of cultural diffusion; that is, it had come from other cultures and that China's college-educated people had slowly embraced it. I also felt it possible that what I was observing was a mere attitude or posture. It was only after reading the literature of Imperial China that I saw that love had been present for more than 2,000 years. Still, I assumed that China was a special case. But how special? In what way? It was then that I decided to embark on a cross-cultural investigation to see if love as a private experience, and not a cultural expression, could be documented. Most anthropologists were doubtful. The conventional wisdom held that sexual desire could be documented because it was a behavior. But love could not be because it was an internal experience, an emotional one, that is, a human experience too subjective to truly document. In effect, the conventional wisdom in anthropology at the time held that sexual desire, a subjective experience, is often expressed through sexual intercourse, which can be more readily described than love, which is an intensely private experience that does not lend itself to a straightforward description. In short, sex is a real universal, while love is not, with few willing to challenge the truth of this claim. However, as a result of twenty years or so of research, the conventional wisdom holds far less sway now.

The discipline's conventional wisdom stood in sharp contrast to the view of American psychologists. By the late 1950s most of them had accepted Harlow's primate research documenting the importance for good health of affection-based relationships. With the assumption that love is a common human experience, psychologists sought to understand the life-course factors that promoted, modified, and shaped an individual's love experience. Yet anthropologists assumed that love is context-dependent, and thus not a human universal. Most anthropologists, like everyone else, assumed that romantic love was a European contribution to world culture. Some, with little actual data, supposed that it might be present in societies that encouraged economic and social mobility and individual decision making, and absent in those that did not and prioritized identity within a wider kinship unit. As a result, anthropologists habitually overlooked or ignored behaviors that did not conform to the discipline's prevailing wisdom. The attitude was, after all, why try to study something that is not there?

In 1992, I, together with Ted Fischer, published a cross-cultural study of romantic love that created something of a cognitive shock to anthropology's collective consciousness: It was the first empirical study to document the presence of romantic love, at the very least as a private experience, in almost every culture. The study presented concrete instances of romantic love in 151 of 166 cultures, or 91%. The finding stood in direct contradiction to the popular idea that romantic love is essentially limited to, or the product of, Western culture, or is found only in smaller, highly mobile, hunter-gathering societies. Moreover, our finding suggests that passionate love constitutes a human universal or, at the least, a near universal (Brown 1992).

Given the widespread presence of passionate love, why did so many anthropologists overlook for so long its existence? One reason is the dominance of the Western folk notion that depicts love as an experience that is detached from, or indifferent to, material concerns or ordinary discourse, or both. But this detachment or indifference is not typical of other societies that use material displays to signal a variety of feeling states that can range from straightforward utilitarian exchanges to unvoiced, deep-seated emotional attachments. Although women in many cultures expect to receive material resources, they also expect, as Jennifer Cole and Lynn Thomas (2011) pointed out, to form some form of affection-based union – in short, a love connection. I found that many Chinese women were unwavering in their insistence that love and material realities are not in contradiction. For most, a concern with material realities did not indicate or reflect an absence of love. A twenty-four-year-old Chinese woman highlighted the point, telling me that: "I do not see the problem, you can have both. One without the other is incomplete."

It is a common dilemma: How can a subjective state be expressed without a material referent? Western cultures tend to idealize subjective feelings that are devoid of material realities in favor of some form of spirituality that is entirely subjective. This is especially so in cultures that have been influenced by Christianity, a religion that actively promoted "spiritual" love as the highest form of love. In this way, historian William Reddy is correct: the spiritualization of romantic love is a uniquely Western contribution to world culture.

This is not the case in other cultures. For example, South and East Asian cultures never prioritize the importance of a spiritual bond between spouses. A number of other considerations have been promoted and prioritized. Lynn Pan's (2012) historical investigation found that, for much of Imperial China's history, sexual desire and affection readily flowed together. Because the Chinese did not conceptualize the mind as separate from the body, they readily recognized the connection between sexual desire and affection. Sonia Ryang (2006) sees the connection in medieval Japan, where love "meant holism: it included bodily fusion usually taking the form of sexual consummation" (p. 5). Clearly, separating spiritual love from sexual or physical love was more prevalent in Christianized Europe but was either less idealized or not present at all in other societies.

Pan's and Ryang's critiques of the Western Europe's spiritualization of love are not only informative, but useful because they contribute to our understanding of the significance of the changes taking place amongst Chinese and Japanese youth. On my return to China in 2000, I saw an increased emphasis on the formation of a more spiritual love bond. Although material needs and related social factors remained important for mate selection, there was a noticeable increase in the value given to subjective factors that reordered the importance of a feeling of love preceding marriage. In the 1980s, many urban Chinese tended to fall in love *after* agreeing to marry rather than before. They typically began their self-arranged marriage discussions with a skeptical detachment and in clear calculation of each other's negative and positive social and material attributes. Once an agreement was reached, however, engaged men and women tended to fantasize about their future spouse and their forthcoming marriage with an idealization of passion (Jankowiak, 1993, 2013). For example, in 1982, a thirty-three-year-old male intellectual recalled fondly the early stages of his informal dating:

> At first it was terrible: I didn't know what to do. I thought my wife was the most beautiful girl I'd ever seen and that she wouldn't want me. I worried and worried about this. Then I asked her if she wanted to see me again. I truly believed she would refuse. But she did not. I was so happy for days and days and thought of nothing else but how much I loved her.

In romantic love, the line separating anxiety and excitement is thin and easily crossed, sometimes suddenly. A twenty-eight-year-old female worker, who had admired her future husband from a distance for some time, readily recalled the initial phases of her formal courtship:

> After being introduced, I was not disappointed but feared that I wasn't pretty enough for him. When he didn't call on me for several days, I sunk into a deep depression that only lifted when he asked to see me again. After a few more encounters, we were all but married. It was a wonderful time. Everything was easy and happy. Although I am satisfied with my marriage, we seem more distant and busy." (Jankowiak, 1993)

In the beginning of the new century, researchers found evidence that China's single-child generation had altered some of its mate selection criteria. Unlike their parents' generation, most thought it was essential to be in love before agreeing to marry. Moreover, there was a clear readiness characterized by a striking lack of shame in discussing love's attributes or what it felt like once one was "in love." For example, a 2008 focus group gave the following attributes or feelings in a romantic love experience: "It is maddening." "A hot feeling." "Crazy feeling." "Amazing feeling." "It makes us happy." "It makes us worried." "It makes us excited and you do not want to share." As a follow-up, I asked: "Then how do you know you are in love?" The following responses were given: "You feel a hurt in your heart when he is not around." "He is my only one, without him I cannot live." "Love is determined. I will obey this arrangement till I die." "I cannot sleep without her." "I miss her, I think about her constantly."

How should one behave when in love? Members in the focus group said: "You show you care," "You do everything for the person," "You help one another," and "You want your lover to be happy." A twenty-two-year-old, who was not a member of the focus group, added: "When I feel in love, I want a lot of affection and want to give a lot of affection. It involves simple things like holding hands, sitting close together, snuggling up on the sofa to watch a late-night movie. It also means speaking and acting kindly and with respect to one another."

To date in this century, love, as it did in the 1980s, inspires an idealization of the beloved. However, in the 1980s, youth were more circumspect in voicing their love. Often it was made tersely and awkwardly, and in non-individualized phrases such as "I miss you," and "I love you," or "I think she loves me." In the 2000s there were fewer generic phrases and descriptions, and more self-assurance, combined with greater boldness in a willingness to affirm and express love. The Chinese youth in the two separate generations are remarkably similar in the way they define the essence of love, the way they understand it. They differ only in the confidence and self-assurance with which they disclose and talk about their love relationships.

For contemporary Chinese, romantic love, as an idiom, is perceived as a deep-seated subjective experience that carries with it understood social obligations. It has become a desired experience, one that many want to embrace but, once experienced, does not necessarily lead to a decision about marriage. The singleton generation, like the generation of their parents, continues to value a strong commitment to the ideal of family — one that is seen as greater, more powerful, than the immediate and personal notion of "coupleness." In this way, the family, and not the conjugal dyad, remains China's basic social unit. To this end, the Chinese have two understandings of what makes for a good marriage. One is grounded in a romantic ideal of transcendence that is experienced by the couple, and the other is rooted in the ordinary life of family practicalities. The romantic ideal holds that husband and wife should have conversational intimacy, feel close, and enjoy warm feelings of being together. In the other less-personal understanding, there is a belief that marriage begins as a pure love, but must be transformed by other more-pressing practicalities of career demands, housework requirements, childcare duties, and the schooling of offspring. In effect, couples recognize the need for a certain amount of privacy and individual space to accomplish different things. This produces a border between husband and wife as each person lives in separate, albeit overlapping, behavioral spheres (Jankowiak & Li, 2017).

My Chinese research (Jankowiak & Li, 2017) also found a gradual transformation in the meaning and expectation of what makes for a satisfying love marriage. Whereas previous generations settled into either a "dead marriage" or, at best, something like a companionship marriage (i.e. spouses develop affectionate friendship for each other), China's single-child generation has increasingly embraced a heightened expectation that romantic love or emotional passion does not end with marriage, but rather is something that should be a continuous part of every satisfying marriage. For example, a twenty-six-year-old Chinese woman admitted that a "good marriage is based in harmony. When we are together, I hope we have many good times, such as cuddling up to go to sleep, holding hands while watching the sunrise and sunset, chasing each other on the beach, walking beside rivers, watching TV and movies together. Love needs tolerance, understanding, and trust. We need not promise each other too much – our behavior will prove that what we feel is true love" (Jankowiak & Li, 2017, p. 153).

Under the halo of intimacy, however, equality and independence must be ensured as well as privacy and individual space to accomplish different things. The emphasis of the border between husband and wife in their separate but overlapping spheres varies according to the couple and by various individual partners. A twenty-three-year-old female acknowledged that "we will have nice moments together, but I will not be controlled by the person I love …and yet I know I am also a submissive woman. I will sacrifice everything for him. I will make a full commitment to him. I will believe in and trust him." When asked if she was a genuine (*Zhen*) submissive, she smiled and stressed that "there are limits to what I will tolerate" (Jankowiak & Li, 2017, p. 154). Her qualification is significant. The word *sacrifice* is a metaphor for the value that she places on the importance not only of family harmony but also of emotional unity. Unstated is the expectation that her husband has similar values and will also reciprocate emotionally. Another female seconded this, speculating about what may have been wrong with her first marriage:

> I spoiled my husband and made him very comfortable being with me, and he stopped reciprocating. This was a mistake. A husband must appreciate his wife's actions and be willing to reciprocate. He too must be willing to dedicate his life to the family and be a responsible husband and father. Cooperation and mutuality are not only expected in the everyday life of a

couple but also deemed essential. This is especially so when the marriages are organized around continuous expressions of loving sentiment. (Jankowiak & Li, 2017, p. 160)

What is striking is that the subtleties in behavior and expectations, and degrees of the essential qualities of the good marriage are becoming layered, as they continue to develop and deepen.

The value placed on creating a passionate love marriage continues to wear a gendered face. When marriage was defined as a faithful performance of customary familial and marital roles, a man's emotional reserve or detachment was tolerated. When the customary lessens, and women gain new resources of power, there can be a totalizing change in the meaning of marriage and the expectation of what constitutes a good spouse. I found that during China's Reform (1979 to the present) a pervasive shift in the terms of marriage in that men no longer have the institutionalized authority to advance their self-interests, but must adjust and strive to meet their wives' expectations. For example, a forty-six-year-old woman aptly summarized the opinion of the majority of mature women interviewed in stating that

> all humans have love in their hearts. The difference is that some would like to use words to express their love, while others use another way to express love. I think nowadays most Chinese prefer to express their feelings and talk about their love. As for me, I prefer to speak to my husband and show my feelings. Love comes from both of us, and we need to show our feelings.

When men refuse to change and adjust, women increasingly use divorce as a means of sanctioning and rejecting male behavior. In this way, women are not only redefining the standards for good marriages but also actively shaping men's notions of how to be both a good man and good husband through their more considered and deliberate mate selection decisions and clear justifications for changes in relationship status (Jankowiak & Li, 2017, pp. 151–152).

To more fully understand love as a cognitive phenomenon, with its implications for understanding how love-based marriages develop and are sustained, I became involved in a collaborative study that compared how Chinese, American, Russian, and Lithuanian youths conceptualized what it meant to be in love (DeMunck, Korotayev, & Khaltourina, 2009, 2010; Jankowiak, Shen, Wang, & Yao, 2015). Our study found similarities in the Chinese, European, and American responses. The study also found five core attributes that all individuals in the four cultures, regardless of gender, experience when "in love." These attributes are given with both a statement that epitomizes the individual responses and a term that define the attributes:

1. "I will do anything for the person I love" (or altruism);
2. "I constantly think about the person I am in love with" (or intrusive thinking);
3. "romantic love is the supreme happiness of life" (or self-actualization);
4. my "love makes my partner stronger and a better person," (or emotional fulfillment); and
5. "sexual attraction is necessary for love" (biology).

I do not mean to say that the five attributes are universal. I think that what is now required is replication of these findings in other types of societies such as foraging and horticultural cultures.

In probing the psychological foundation of love as a cultural and psychological phenomenon, I also discovered, almost by accident, that most societies consider passionate love to be dangerous. This more than intrigued me. To this end, I undertook a cross-cultural study that looked primarily at whether or not a society's folklore contained stories of sexual and/or love relationships that resulted in harm to the participants. It is a given that romantic love, a complex emotion, can and often does disrupt social relations. It is romantic passion's ability to provoke reflective and non-reflective behavior that makes it such a turbulent and complex human emotion. Given this propensity, I found that in arranged marriage societies, the senior generation almost always viewed romantic love as a dangerous emotion because it involved some form of personal choice and thus was best ignored, denied, or rejected. Nonetheless, societies that value personal choice in mate selection and idealize romantic love also find love can be dangerous. The chief reason is that those societies recognize that love does not have to be reciprocated. They see that the love of one person does not necessarily lead to the return of that love, and that such a return is not obligated. Given this unpredictability, most cultures provide warnings or offer some form of guidance on how to avoid being misled, seduced, or harmfully used. The possibility of harmful seduction is at its most dangerous when the lover possesses the desired physical attributes and the preferred social traits. In the sexual encounter, it usually happens that men place higher value on female physical attraction, whereas women greater value on social and material factors (Buss, 2015).

To better assess the frequency of cultures that regard these preferred traits as potentially dangerous, I conducted a cross-cultural examination of folk tales that depicted the anxieties of men and woman that arose from wanting yet fearing the attributes they most desired: beauty or status. The examination found of the seventy-eight cultures sampled, seventy-three, or 94%, had stories that warn men of the dangerous of becoming involved with a beautiful woman (in some cases, presented in behaviors that we associate with a femme fatale). In contrast, only twenty out of seventy-eight, or 26%, had stories about the dangers of male beauty, whereas the dangers of status were present in the stories of twenty-five out of fifty cultures, or 50% (Jankowiak & Ramsey, 2000, p. 62). Significantly, the tales portrayed the seducer as incapable of love; yet these seducers demonstrated signs of affection and emotional commitment that allowed harmful manipulation of their lover. My examination suggested human beings around the world do fear the prospect of becoming emotionally involved with someone who does not share or reciprocate their love sentiments. For example, there are well-known stories in the Chinese literature where a fox fairy or spirit assumes the form of a beautiful woman in order to seduce and then kill her lover. Today, Chinese men still tease one another that a particular beautiful woman might be a fox fairy (Jankowiak, 1993, p. 183). In contemporary Chinese society, newspaper and magazine stories warn men about "falling in love" with a mistress who may have no interest in reciprocatin g because she might bankrupt her lover and then abandon him. These modern-day stories make for cautionary tales reminding men that beautiful women can be dangerous. At the level of individual psychology, the commonality of these tales suggests that anxiety about being manipulated is a frequent concern (see expanded overview in Jankowiak & Ramsey, 2000, p. 67).

The theme of disappointment in love can be found around the world and it has given rise to competing explanations and philosophies on how to best avoid it. The thematic emphasis ranges from rejecting love completely to embracing it not as dyadic, but as a pluralistic phenomenon. My working hunch was that humans as a species are not so much sexually monogamous as they are emotionally monogamous. It is very difficult to love two people at the same time. To determine if the hunch was correct, I embarked on a six-year investigation into a Mormon polygamous family that believes plural, not romantic love, is the highest form of love. In plural love, wives, children, and husband hold a high mutual regard for each other and actively work, and often struggle to build a harmonious love bond that will unite them in this world and in the next. The plural family is held together as much by a collective will or communal effort to maintain a strong image of a harmonious family as it is by individual actions and decisions. The community's own belief that this harmonious love bond can be accomplished has received support from few anthropologists. For Bohannan, (1995) and Harrell (1997), the pair-bond is a culturally constructed ideal, more a byproduct of a specific type of social organization and thus not a cultural universal. In this way, it is not inconceivable that communal efforts at complex family living can be successful. Others disagree, arguing that an impulse to form a pair-bond is present in every known society, even in those that strive to deny its existence (Feybesse & Hatfield, this volume).

Conflicted Love Inside a Mormon Fundamentalist Polygamous Community

The Mormon Fundamentalist community that I studied is organized around a notion of harmonious or familial love that encourages the development of a spiritual love bond between all family members. The bond includes co-wives and their children who collectively learn to love and care for each other. In effect, it is an idealized state that is neither individualized nor dyadic in orientation. Harmonious love, unlike a dyadic love bond, is akin to communitas in being unbounded in its potential for forging, strengthening, and sustaining affectionate bonds. It is somewhat equivalent to Reddy's (2012) idea of "longing for association." Because it encourages respect, empathy, helpfulness, and lasting affection, harmonious love often serves as the principal means to bind and unite the polygamous family. Its non-dyadic focus stands, however, in sharp contrast to romantic love, a tolerated but seldom openly affirmed emotional experience. Although harmonious love is fervently stressed as the ideal, it is vulnerable to personal sexual desires and romantic preferences.

In spite of the religious doctrine that harmonious love is superior to romantic love, advanced most adamantly by men, women regularly use the quality of their husband's affection as the primary basis to assess the quality of their marriage. Women are not powerless servants to the prevalent patriarchal ethos that elevates male status above theirs. In contrast, I found many women to be a formidable resistance that acts as a clear check on their husband's behavior. This is especially evident in the actions of a "favorite wife" who knows that her husband cannot tolerate any emotional withdrawal or distancing of interactions with him. Her ability to withhold emotional intimacy is a sharp, practical "resource of power," as evident in this middle-aged woman's account of how to guide her husband to do the right thing:

[H]e wants the Principle [that is, living in a polygamous family] and talks a good philosophy. But he does not live the Ten Commandments and the Gospel of Jesus Christ. Those doctrines are more important and difficult than living the Principle. I accept the Principle, so I am not jealous of the lack of attention as long as he is fair in the time spent with all of his wives.

In point of observation, she seemed to have been one of the more jealous women in the community. However, in stressing her commitment to the ideal of polygynous marriage, while simultaneously helping to encourage her husband to develop and sustain a united plural family, she was able to obtain more emotional and material resources for herself and her children. Over the course of the six years, I found her behavior highly representative of most of the community's favorite wives (Jankowiak & Allen, 1995, pp. 282–284). It is the desire for romantic intimacy that intensifies a woman's yearning for emotional exclusivity. This poses a dilemma: If emotional exclusivity is always dyadic, it can never be present in a plural or harmonious love family. For most fundamentalists, the paradox is often ignored and seldom addressed, explored or commented upon. It is understood, for example, that on a wife's wedding anniversary and birthday, she will be taken on an outing to see a theater show such as Phantom of the Opera or to attend a local rodeo, go on a river trip, or dine at an upscale restaurant. Whatever the selection, everyone knows that this is a dyadic event that reaffirms the presence of a special relationship. Community leaders have suggested that this practice be modified. Instead of bringing only one wife, a husband should bring all his wives. The council stresses that the arrival of a new wife is just as much about her marrying into the entire family as it is about her taking a husband. The council reminded everyone that the wedding ceremony (a highly secretive and exclusive ritual) is organized around the belief that marriage is essentially a pluralistic institution, not a dyadic one.

A fundamentalist Mormon wedding requires the presence of all the husband's wives who, at the appropriate moment in the ceremony, place their hands over the incoming bride's hands when she agrees to marry her husband (as well as all his other wives). In this way, the recommendation of the priesthood council was not a foreign notion. After the church service, a twenty-seven-year-old man, who has only one wife, seconded the council's recommendation. He stressed that their religion "teaches us to put our natural desires at bay and live a spirit life." To this a middle-aged man, who had two wives, responded: "Okay, a good goal. But let's be realistic here. A woman needs to have time alone with her man. It is difficult or impossible to prevent this from happening. A woman wants to develop a special relation with her husband." To which the younger man said: "I agree, but I think we should strive for perfection." Yet the fact that the community continues to ignore the council's recommendation underscores the persistent difficulty and internal conflict. The vast majority of fundamentalist men find it easier to honor each wife's request to be treated special or unique, if only for one day. This approach stands in sharp contrast to the religious ideal that marriage is primarily a procreative institution organized around an ethos of the plural family's harmonious love. (See the expanded overview in Jankowiak & Allen, 1995, pp. 282–284.)

Because social relations in the polygamous Mormon family, like many other polygamous societies (Jankowiak et al., 2005), revolve around personal sentiment as much as duty, there is a twin pull of almost equal force – the personal pushing against the societal and doctrinal. Whenever a conflict arises, an individual's response is unpredictable, threatening the social order. The tension hovers: Which partner will uphold family harmony and which one will seek to satisfy personal gratification? The threat is dominant in the case of romantic love, which, more than any other emotional experience, can not only overwhelm a person's judgment, but also reorder his or her priorities; the duration of the priorities is unpredictable.

For Mormon women, romantic love's presence or absence – much more than role equity – constitutes the primary measure of the quality of their relationship. That primacy is movingly revealed in the following personal report of what happens when a husband's love is lost. A man, who had two wives, remarked that "my wives are not upset over sex, but they are over the amount of time I spend with each wife. They seem to count the time and measure it. It is the source of many of our family disagreements." In this way, the present-day community is similar to nineteenth-century Mormon polygamists whose love letters were filled with expressions of romantic yearnings, descriptions of emotional turmoil, and heart-rending disclosures (Young, 1954). At a bio-psychological level, these expressions of passionate love resemble those found not only in mainstream America, but also those reported in other cultures around the world.

After completing my polygamous research, I was more convinced that humans are fundamentally a pair-bond species with a desire to form deep affectionate bonds with one specific person. I still wondered, however, whether individuals who come from a less religiously based cultural background could create, prosper in, and sustain a non-dyadic love bond. After all, popular Western media regularly provides an alternative to the dyadic love model on TV, and in films and novels; one presents the possibility of simultaneously loving two people at the same time (see the expanded over-view in Jankowiak & Gerth, 2012).

Moreover, advocates of the benefits of a "polyamour marriage" argue for the possibility that some individuals can maintain a strong concur-rent love relationship (Anapol, 1997; Kipnis, 2000). Robert Sternberg (2006) remains more skeptical, asserting the real difficulty of maintaining a concurrent love. If it does occur, he notes, that kind of love will be sustained by individuals creating separate and distinctive narratives of how it was formed and what it means to be involved. It is through psycho-logical bracketing that the phenomenon of twin loves operates. It allows one to create different roles in the relationship for both oneself and one's partner, and thus can fulfill different desires. Sternberg speculates that these narratives will be hierarchically arranged to help individuals manage their often conflicting emotions that arise in a concurrent love relation-ship from competing resources. If concurrent love is possible, Sternberg suggests, it would seldom be intentional, planned, or expected. Moreover, it would always result in a painful internal conflict (Jankowiak & Gerth, 2012, p. 96).

The two competing models of love combined with polygamous com-munity research made me intensely interested in understanding exactly what it meant to be involved in a concurrent love. I began, therefore, a new investigation among Las Vegas urbanities who reported that they had at one time or other loved more than one person at the same time. I began with skepticism, but open to finding out what these urbanites thought they had experienced, who they understood it.

If passionate or romantic love is indeed organized around emotional exclusivity, which also includes the reordering of an individual's motiv-ational priorities, what then is the effect of becoming emotionally (as opposed to sexually) involved with more than one person? Our research found, as Sternberg predicted, that individuals who were in love with more than one person struggled to balance both lovers in a manageable arrangement. For many, there was, at the beginning of the relationship, little or no tension or conflict. In our sample, these individuals tried to manage the relationships, like some bisexuals do in a concurrent relation-ship – through the establishment of boundaries, either with actual geo-graphical distance or by psychological bracketing, a cognitive technique that helps them to close-off or isolate, however short-lived, their involve-ment with another (Jankowiak & Gerth, 2012, pp. 95–96).

In striving to produce a rationale of their ideal lover, respondents look to attain a counter-balancing of complementary needs within the two relationships. A number of individuals reported, as concurrent love advocates claim, experiencing a deeper, richer, and more meaningful satisfaction being involved with multiple lovers. Their satisfaction, however, appears to be relatively brief (Jankowiak & Gerth, 2012, pp. 98–99). All of the respondents upon further reflection told me that it was the worst time of their lives and they would not wish the experience of "loving two at the same time" on anyone.

The problematic nature of concurrent love may stem from the dyadic nature of love. It is telling that no one reported experiencing happiness or emotional satisfaction or nourishment in their concurrent love relationships. This strongly underscores the burdens of departing from a pair-bond relationship that is organized around emotional exclusivity. It raises the question: would the experience of the individuals in our small sample have been any different if they lived in a community that supported plural or concurrent loves? In spite of optimistic expectations and enthusiastic hopes, other researchers have shown that concurrent love is inherently fragile, unstable, and seldom long lasting (Jankowiak & Gerth, 2012, pp. 102–103). I suspect that, while there may be occasional, and, thus, highly idiosyncratic concurrent love relationships that are successful, ethnographic and historical studies have consistently documented that these relationships are not feasible on a larger community scale. For example, Benjamin Zablocki's (1980) comprehensive sociological research into plural or group love arrangements among, for example, the Oneida, Kerista, New Buffalo found that group love arrangements presented insurmountable difficulties for its members. In fact, the arrangements are often abandoned in a relatively short time for some type of pair-bond relationship.

Clearly, some humans have a capacity for deep-seated concurrent or simultaneous loves, but it seems that these seldom endure for any significant length of time. In time, they tend to move toward a more companionship based love. Whenever that occurs, cognitive dissonance arises, as the two lovers who had been situated in a person's mind at different endpoints on the love spectrum can no longer easily separate them (Jankowiak & Gerth, 2012, p. 99).

A concurrent love requires a strong dedication, or even a conscious determination, to maintain simultaneous, albeit separate, life histories or narratives that for most are simply too trying to sustain. Moreover, the construction of separate personae can lead into various behaviors and attitudes associated with "a dual personality." Regardless of how we might describe the behaviors, separate personae can result in inner turmoil. In effect, such personae can be sustained for a time, but predictably at some emotional cost. The very nature of what these individuals hoped to achieve will produce stress on their sense of self, if not substantially fragment it. In the process, the stress on hopes can weaken the very foundation of the bond they seek with another individual. What may have begun as a need to satisfy passion and secure companionship eventually turns into an acute psychological dilemma that is experienced as intensely dissatisfying and ultimately personally destructive. The inability to resolve the dilemma of merging both types of love – passionate and companionship – into a sustainable whole underscores the primacy of the dyadic bond which is based more on emotional exclusivity than on sexual exclusivity (Jankowiak & Gerth, 2012, pp. 99–100). In the end, love's pull toward dyadic exclusiveness conquers most polygamous and other triadic arrangements such as those found in the polyamour movement.

This raises a related question: Is there a disadvantage to seeking a dyadic love bond? My Chinese research is instructive. I found that the family organization in urban China has shifted away from a social unit organized around duty and toward an emergent preference for a love-based marriage. My research also found that it is Chinese women who encourage their husbands to become more emotionally involved, not through action, but through the development and increase in love talk. As much as men try to comply, however, it seems, at least from their spouse's perspective, the result is insufficient.

Women and men can become impatient, anxious and, at times, angry, with the shift in cultural norms, making it difficult to interpret another's intentions. This new environment of ethical and emotional focus leads some women and men to delay marriage, as their needs can easily be met in alternative social arenas. This poses something of a paradox. On the one hand, both genders have benefited from the opportunity to explore their inner lives and perhaps achieve a deeper sense of fulfillment. On the other hand, they may remain anxious about the inability to find suitable mates who can fulfill their idea of "what makes life worth living." Their search for life partners, who will also be their ideal soul mates, is rooted in a widespread cultural aspiration, one that is consistently articulated by women and sometimes by men, in both public and private conversation. Yet the aspiration is typically not realized in ordinary life.

For China's single-child generation, the marital ideals and relationship values that were common to their parents' generation no longer thrive. Rather they are questioned and challenged. Today what remains is a tense knot of alternative paths often clearly at odds with each other. Individuals are more or less on their own (that is, without a clear and certain ethos) in their efforts to find life satisfaction in a culture that is no longer sure of itself (Jankowiak & Li, 2017, pp. 159–160).

For some there is a growing feeling of being on one's own, which is acutely felt when making critical life choices such as choosing a marital partner. This change has led to a new openness among younger people in more closed-off countries such as China to talks about the tensions and challenges. The benefit for anthropology is significant: an opportunity to gain a better understanding of a culture in transition. The benefit is greatest in those cultures where ethical mores and social expectations that prohibited or discouraged personal disclosures in favor of reticence and restraint are losing their power. In any event, the growth in popularity around the globe of the "forever love marriage" is raising expectations that few couples can achieve. With it an increase in life dissatisfaction is likely. Totalizing the pursuit of a love-pleasure relationship carries with it the real possibility of undermining other values and personal interests that can make life worth living.

Because most cultural anthropologists are more concerned with the question of why cultural meanings change over time, they tend to minimize or even ignore, however, the psychological research that examines the more universal aspect of the love experienced. Anthropologists' observations of ordinary life have been superb in their recognition and description of daily behavior. Their analytical explanations, however, have often been undermined by limitations implicit in their models of human motivation that guide their research. This is especially evident in the domain of love. In the last twenty years, research has produced excellent studies of love around the word. We can no longer regard love's presence as a byproduct of Westernization or globalization. We are fully aware that love is not Europe's contribution to world culture. It has its own local history and forms of expression, but not necessarily its own unique cultural psychology. Love is a rich phenomenon that requires renewed scholarly investigation, so that we can better distinguish, and appreciate, what is universal to the human experience and what has been historically constructed.

Acknowledgments

I would like to thank Robert J. Sternberg and Karin Sternberg for their kind invitation to summarize my body of work on the topic of love as it exists around the world and my reflections on that work. In doing so, I would also like to acknowledge the contributions of my co-collaborators and fellow authors who diligently participated in the gathering, analyzing, and writing up of the data. Without their earnest efforts and insights, many of the articles and chapters discussed and cited above would never have been published.

References

Anapol, D. (1997). *Polyamory, the new love without limits: Secrets of sustainable intimate relationships*. San Rafael, CA: IntiNet Resource Center.

Bohannan, P. (1985). *All the happy families*. New York: McGraw-Hill.

Brown, D. (1992). *Human universals*. New York: McGraw-Hill.

Buss, D. (2015). *Evolutionary psychology: The new science of the mind*. New York: Routledge.

Cole, J., & Thomas, L. (Eds.). (2009). Introduction. In J. Cole & L. Thomas (Eds.), *Love in Africa* (pp. 1–30). Chicago, IL: University of Chicago Press.

(2011). *Love in Africa*. Chicago, IL: University of Chicago Press.

De Munck, V., Korotayev, A., & Khaltourina, D. (2009). A comparative study of the structure of love in the US and Russia: Finding a common core of characteristic and national and gender differences. *Ethnology*, *48*, 337–357.

DeMunck, V., Korotayev, A., Khaltourina, D., & deMunck, J. (2010). The structure of love: Cross-cultural analysis of models of romantic love among US residents, Russians and Lithuanians. *Cross-Cultural Research*, *20*(10), 1–27.

Harrell, S. (1999). *Human families*. Boulder, CO: Westview Press.

Hewlett, B., & Hewlett, B. (2008). A biocultural approach to sex, love, and intimacy in central African forgers and farmers. In W. Jankowiak (Ed.), *Intimacies: Between love and sex* (pp. 37–34). New York: Columbia University Press.

Jankowiak, W. (1993). *Sex, death, and hierarchy in a Chinese city*. New York: Columbia University Press.

(2013). From courtship to dating culture: China's emergent youth. In P. Link, R. P. Madsen, & P. G. Pickowicz (Eds.), *Restless China* (pp. 191–212). Lanham, MD: Rowman and Littlefield.

Jankowiak, W., & Allen, E. (1995). The balance of duty and desire in an American polygamous community. In W. Jankowiak (Ed.), *Romantic passion* (pp. 277–296). New York: Columbia University Press.

Jankowiak, W., & Gerth, H. (2012) Can you love two people at the same time? A research report. *Anthropologica* [Canadian Anthropological Journal], *4*(1), 78–89.

Jankowiak, W., & Li, X. (2017). Emergent conjugal love, male affection, and female power. In S. Harrell & G. Santos (Eds.), *Is Chinese patriarchy over? The decline and transformation of a system of social support* (pp. 146–162). Seattle: Washington University Press.

Jankowiak, W., & Paladino, T. (2008). Introduction. In W. Jankowiak (Ed.), *Intimacies: Between love and sex* (pp. 1–36). New York: Columbia University Press.

Jankowiak, W., & Ramsey, A. (2000). Femme fatale and status fatale: A cross-cultural perspective. *Cross Cultural Research, 34*(2), 57–69.

Jankowiak, W., Shen, Y., Wang, C., & Yao, Y. (2015). Investigating love's universal attributes: A research report from China. *Cross-Cultural Research, 49*(44), 422–436.

Jankowiak, W., Sudakov, M., & Wilreker, B. (2005). Co-wife conflict and co-operation. *Ethnology, 44*(1), 81–98.

Jankowiak, W., Volsche, S., & Garcia, J. (2015). Romantic kiss: Another human universal? *American Anthropologist, 117*(3), 535–539.

Kipnis, L. (2000). Adultery. In L. Berlant (Ed.), *Intimacy* (pp. 9–47). Chicago, IL: University Chicago Press.

Pan, L. (2016). *When true love came to China.* Hong Kong: University of Hong Kong Press.

Reddy, W. (2012). *The making of romantic love: Longing sexuality in Europe, South Asia and Japan: 900–1200 CE.* Chicago, IL: University of Chicago Press.

Ryang, S. (2006). *Love in modern Japan.* New York: Routledge.

Sternberg, R. (2006). A duplex theory of love. In R. Sternberg & K. Weis, (Eds.), *The new psychology of love* (pp. 184–199). New Haven, CT: Yale University Press.

Young, K. (1954). *Isn't one wife enough? The story of Mormon polygamy.* New York: Henry Holt.

Zablocki, B. (1980). *Alienation and charisma: A study of contemporary American communes.* New York: Free Press.

CHAPTER 13

A Behavioral Systems Approach to Romantic Love Relationships: Attachment, Caregiving, and Sex

Mario Mikulincer and Phillip R. Shaver

Over thirty years ago, Shaver and his colleagues (Hazan & Shaver, 1987; Shaver & Hazan, 1988; Shaver, Hazan, & Bradshaw, 1988) suggested that Bowlby's (1973, 1979, 1980, 1982) attachment theory, which was designed to characterize human infants' love for and attachment to their caregivers, is also highly relevant to romantic love and adult couple relationships. The core assumption was that romantic relationships – or pair-bonds, as evolutionary psychologists call them – involve a combination of three innate behavioral systems described by Bowlby (1982): attachment, caregiving, and sex. Each of these behavioral systems has its own evolutionary functions, and although the systems affect each other in various ways, they are distinct. Viewed from this theoretical perspective, love is a dynamic state involving both partners' needs and capacities for attachment, caregiving, and sex.

Although this perspective is necessarily abstract when stated scientifically, it is evident in any powerful romantic attachment. A letter written by Nobel-prize-winning physicist Richard Feynman to his deceased spouse provides a poignant example:

> I want to tell you I love you. I will always love you. I find it hard to understand what it means to love you after you are dead – but *I still want to comfort you and take care of you – and I want you to love me and take care of me* ... I've met some very nice girls – but in two or three meetings they all seem ashes ... You only are left to me. You are real ... You, dead, are so much better than anyone else alive ... P.S. Please excuse me for not mailing this, but I don't know your new address. [emphasis added]

Although not mentioned in this letter, discovered by Feynman's daughter in a box of his correspondence after he died (Feynman, 2005), the third behavioral system, sexuality, was a central part of the two spouses' correspondence while both were still alive.

The main goal of the present chapter is to provide an updated review of literature related to an attachment-theoretical perspective on love, focusing on the interplay of the three behavioral systems in the creation of individual differences in patterns of romantic love and in the cognitions, emotions, and behaviors of adult romantic partners.

We begin with a brief summary of Bowlby's (1982) primary motivational construct, the *behavioral system*, and describe the normative and individual-difference components of the attachment, caregiving, and sexual behavioral systems. Next, we present ideas and findings concerning the interplay of the three systems. Finally, we present a brief review of studies examining the implications of these behavioral systems for the quality of love relationships.

A Behavioral Systems Perspective on Attachment and Caregiving

In explaining human behavior, Bowlby (1973, 1980, 1982) borrowed from ethology the concept of behavioral system, a species-universal neural program that organizes an individual's behavior in ways that increase the likelihood of survival and reproductive success. Each behavioral system is organized around a particular goal (e.g. attaining a sense of security, providing support to a needy other) and includes a set of interchangeable, functionally equivalent behaviors that constitute the *primary strategy* of the system for attaining its goal (e.g. proximity seeking, empathically understanding another person's needs). These behaviors are automatically "activated," or triggered, by stimuli or situations that make a particular goal salient (e.g. loud or unusual noises that signal danger). The behaviors are "deactivated" or "terminated" by other stimuli or outcomes that signal attainment of the desired goal. Each behavioral system also includes cognitive operations that facilitate goal attainment and excitatory and inhibitory neurological links with other systems.

Bowlby (1973) believed that although behavioral systems are innate, life experiences shape their parameters and strategies in various ways, resulting in systematic individual differences. According to Bowlby, the residues of such experiences are stored in the form of mental representations, or *working models of the self and others,* that guide future attempts to attain a behavioral system's goal. With repeated use, these models become automatic and are important sources of within-person continuity in behavioral system functioning throughout development.

The Attachment Behavioral System

According to Bowlby (1982), the biological function of the attachment system is to protect a person (especially during infancy and childhood, but later in life as well) from danger by assuring that he or she maintains proximity to loving and supportive others (*attachment figures*). The proximal goal of the system is to attain a subjective sense of protection or security (called "felt security" in an influential paper by Sroufe & Waters, 1977), which normally terminates the system's activation (Bowlby, 1982). The goal of attaining security becomes salient when threats or dangers are encountered, causing the threatened person to seek actual or symbolic proximity to attachment figures (Bowlby, 1982). According to Ainsworth, Blehar, Waters, and Wall (1978), during infancy, activation of the attachment system includes nonverbal expressions of need and desire for proximity, as well as observable behavior aimed at restoring and maintaining actual proximity. According to our extension of the theory to adult relationships (Mikulincer & Shaver, 2016), attachment-system activation in adulthood also involves heightened accessibility to soothing, reassuring mental representations of supportive attachment figures.

The consolidation of an inner sense of attachment security during interactions with supportive attachment figures promotes general faith in other people's good will; a sense of being loved, esteemed, and accepted by relationship partners; and optimistic beliefs about one's ability to cope with stress and manage distress. Bowlby (1988) considered attachment security to be a mainstay of mental health and social adjustment throughout life. A host of cross-sectional and longitudinal studies supports this view (see Mikulincer & Shaver, 2016, for a review).

However, when attachment figures are not reliably available, responsive, and supportive, a sense of attachment security is not attained, negative working models are constructed, worries about self-protection and lovability are heightened, and strategies of affect regulation (that Cassidy & Kobak, 1988, called *secondary attachment strategies*) other than appropriate proximity seeking are adopted. Attachment theorists (e.g. Cassidy & Kobak, 1988; Mikulincer & Shaver, 2016) emphasize two such secondary strategies: *hyperactivation* and *deactivation* of the attachment system. Hyperactivation is manifested in energetic attempts to gain greater proximity, support, and protection, combined with a lack of confidence that it will be provided. Deactivation of the system involves inhibition of proximity-seeking tendencies, denial of attachment needs, maintenance of emotional and cognitive distance from others, and compulsive reliance on oneself as the only reliable source of comfort and protection.

When studying these secondary strategies during adolescence and adulthood, attachment researchers have focused mainly on a person's *attachment orientation* – the chronic pattern of relational cognitions and behaviors that results from a particular history of attachment experiences (Fraley & Shaver, 2000). Initially, attachment research was based on Ainsworth et al.'s (1978) three-category typology of attachment patterns in infancy – secure, anxious, and avoidant – and on Hazan and Shaver's (1987) conceptualization of similar adult styles in the romantic relationship domain. Subsequent studies (e.g. Brennan, Clark, & Shaver, 1998) revealed, however, that attachment styles are more appropriately conceptualized as regions in a two-dimensional space. The first dimension, *attachment-related avoidance*, reflects the extent to which a person distrusts a relationship partner's good will, deactivates his or her attachment system, and strives to maintain behavioral independence and emotional distance from his or her partner. The second dimension, *attachment anxiety*, reflects the degree to which a person worries that a partner will not be available in times of need and therefore engages overzealously in proximity seeking. People who score low on both insecurity dimensions are relatively secure with respect to attachment. The two dimensions can be measured with reliable and valid self-report scales (e.g. Experiences in Close Relationships Scale, ECR; Brennan et al., 1998) and are associated in theoretically predictable ways with emotion regulation, mental health, adjustment, and interpersonal functioning (see Mikulincer & Shaver, 2016, for a review).

The Caregiving Behavioral System

According to Bowlby (1982), human beings are born with a capacity to provide protection and support to others who are either chronically dependent or temporarily in need. Bowlby (1982) claimed that these behaviors are organized by a *caregiving behavioral system* that emerged over the long course of evolution because it increased the inclusive fitness of humans by increasing the likelihood that children, siblings, and tribe members with whom a person shared genes would survive to reproductive age and succeed in producing and rearing offspring (Hamilton, 1964). Today, through educational elaboration, the caregiving system can include genuine concern for anyone in need. Although most of us probably care more, and more easily, for people to whom we are closely related, either psychologically or genetically, we can experience empathy for and direct caregiving efforts to all suffering human beings.

The goal of the caregiving system is to reduce other people's suffering, protect them from harm, and foster their healthy growth and development (e.g. Feeney & Woodhouse, 2016; Mikulincer & Shaver, 2015; Shaver, Mikulincer, & Shemesh-Iron, 2010). Two main triggers activate the caregiving system (Feeney & Woodhouse, 2016). First, realizing that another person is confronting danger, stress, or discomfort and is either openly seeking help or would clearly benefit from it. Second, realizing that another person has an opportunity to achieve important goals and either needs help in taking advantage of the opportunity or seems eager to talk about it or to receive validation for making an effort. In either case, effective caregiving involves what Batson (2010) called empathic concern — taking the other's perspective in order to help him or her reduce suffering or pursue growth. Collins, Guichard, Ford, and Feeney (2006) described optimal caregiving in terms of the two parenting qualities (sensitivity and responsiveness) that have been emphasized as contributing to a child's secure attachment (Ainsworth et al., 1978). Sensitivity includes attunement to, and accurate interpretation of, another's signaled or communicated needs (Mikulincer & Shaver, 2015). Responsiveness includes validating a troubled person's needs and feelings; respecting his or her beliefs and values; and helping the person feel understood and cared for (Reis, 2014; Reis & Shaver, 1988).

When the caregiving system functions well, it not only benefits the person being cared for, but also benefits the support provider, even though its primary goal is to benefit the other. It promotes an inner sense of what Erikson (1993) called "generativity" – a sense that one is more than an isolated self and is able to contribute importantly to others' welfare. This sense tends to enhance positive feelings about one's own efficacy and goodness as well as the quality of dyadic or group relationships (e.g. Collins & Feeney, 2000; Mikulincer, Shaver, & Gillath, 2009).

Although Bowlby (1982) assumed that everyone is born with the potential to provide care, the functioning of the caregiving system can be impaired by self-focused worries and doubts (Collins, Ford, Guichard, Kane, & Feeney, 2010). It can also be impaired by problems in emotion regulation, which can cause a caregiver to be overwhelmed by what Batson (2010) called personal distress. In addition, caregiving can be disrupted by social skill deficits, depletion of psychological resources, lack of a desire to help, and egoistic motives that interfere with accurate empathy and genuine other-oriented concern (Collins et al., 2010).

As with the attachment system, dysfunctions of the caregiving system can involve either hyperactivation or deactivation (Shaver et al., 2010). Hyperactivated caregiving is intrusive, poorly timed, and effortful and may be motivated by a wish to make oneself indispensable to a relationship partner or a wish to feel competent and admirable as a caregiver. These goals are sometimes served by exaggerating others' needs, coercing others to accept one's help, or focusing on others' needs to the neglect of one's own. In contrast, strategies associated with deactivation of the caregiving system involve insufficient empathy, lack of a desire to help, withdrawal from caregiving, offering only half-hearted assistance, and insisting on emotional distance when someone wants care and comfort. These two caregiving dysfunctions can be measured with a reliable and valid self-report scale, the Caregiving System Functioning scale (CSFS, Shaver et al., 2010). A person's scores on this scale are systematically associated with caregiving-related cognitions, emotions, and actual behaviors.

The Sexual Behavioral System

Following Bowlby's (1982) reasoning, we view individual differences in sexual motives, feelings, attitudes, and behaviors as reflecting, in part, the functioning of the sexual behavioral system (Birnbaum, 2015). From an evolutionary perspective, the major function of the sexual system is to pass genes from one generation to the next, and its main goal is to have sexual intercourse with an opposite-sex partner and either become pregnant oneself (in the case of women) or impregnate a partner (in the case of men). As evolutionary psychologists have explained, however, the proximal motivation for an act (i.e. wishing to have sex with an attractive person) need not be the same as the evolutionary reason for the existence of the motives involved. People can seek sexual pleasure without the goal of reproduction, and modern methods of birth control, as well as homosexuality, make it possible to separate the two goals. Nevertheless, many aspects of sexual behavior (e.g. being attracted to people whose qualities suggest fertility or "good genes"; Gangestad, Simpson, Cousins, Garver-Apgar, & Christensen, 2004) are governed by neural systems that evolved for reproductive purposes.

The sexual system is automatically activated by noticing and appraising an attractive, sexually interested, and (in the case of heterosexual attraction) presumably fertile partner (Birnbaum, 2015). Once the system is activated, its primary strategy is typically to approach the desirable partner, entice her or him to have sex, and engage in sexual intercourse (Fisher, 1998; Fisher, Aron, Mashek, Li, & Brown, 2002). The behaviors that constitute this primary strategy involve asserting one's sexual interest while being sensitive to the desired partner's signals. Optimal functioning of the sexual system requires coordination of the two partners' desires and responses and typically involves a gradual rise in physical and emotional intimacy (Rubin & Campbell, 2012). Such mutually coordinated sexual interactions may promote feelings of love and affection, thereby contributing to the quality of romantic relationships and the strength of attachment (see Impett, Muise, & Peragine, 2014, for a review).

Despite its considerable potential for gratification and delight, human sexuality is sometimes constrained by aversive feelings (e.g. Brauer et al., 2012) and negative mental representations of sexual experiences (e.g. Birnbaum & Reis, 2006). Such negative reactions can result from either partner's sexual worries and inhibitions, problems in coordinating sexual interests and behavior, or lack of sexual desire. Moreover, these negative responses can interfere with the primary strategy of the sexual system – enhancing mutual attraction and sexual gratification – and the adoption of secondary hyperactivating or deactivating strategies (Birnbaum, Mikulincer, Szepsenwol, Shaver, & Mizrahi, 2014).

Hyperactivation of the sexual system includes effortful, mentally preoccupying, sometimes intrusive, and sometimes even coercive attempts to persuade a partner to have sex or to acknowledge one's own sexual value (Birnbaum et al., 2014). It is characterized by exaggerated emphasis on the importance of sex, hypervigilance to a partner's signals of sexual arousal, attraction, or disinterest or rejection, and heightened anxiety and concerns about one's own sexual attractiveness and potency (Birnbaum et al., 2014). In contrast, deactivation of the sexual system is characterized by inhibiting or deemphasizing sexual desire and attempting to avoid sex (Birnbaum et al., 2014). It may include dismissal of sexual needs, distancing from or disparaging a partner when he or she expresses interest in sex, suppressing sexual thoughts and fantasies, and blocking sexual arousal and discounting or evading orgasmic pleasure. These two sexual dysfunctions can be measured with a reliable and valid self-report scale – the Sexual System Functioning Scale (SSFS, Birnbaum et al., 2014), scores on which are systematically associated with a broad array of sex-related cognitions, emotions, physiological responses, and actual behaviors.

Interplay among the Attachment, Caregiving, and Sexual Systems

Following Bowlby's (1982) theoretical writings about the interactions of behavioral systems, Shaver et al. (1988) formulated explicit hypotheses about how individual differences in the functioning of the attachment system might bias the functioning of the caregiving and sexual systems. In this section, we present a brief review of the accumulating evidence concerning these hypotheses.

Attachment and Caregiving

According to Bowlby (1982), activation of the attachment system interferes with non-attachment activities, which are conceptualized as products of other behavioral systems. This interference was demonstrated in Ainsworth et al.'s (1978) research on the inhibition of children's exploration of a laboratory Strange Situation when an attachment figure was asked to leave the room. The same kind of inhibition occurs in romantic relationships (Kunce & Shaver, 1994) when a person who is asked to act as a caregiver for his or her needy partner also feels insecure, distressed, or in need of support and comfort. Under such conditions, the person generally turns to others for support rather than thinking first about providing support for a partner. Only when the person restores his or her sense of attachment security and repairs his or her negative mood, can the person easily direct attention and energy to caregiving activities and perceive a partner as someone who needs and deserves comfort and support.

Reasoning along these lines, Shaver et al. (1988) hypothesized that people who were more secure with respect to attachment would be more likely than insecure people to provide effective care to a needy partner, because experiencing a sense of security is related to holding optimistic beliefs about distress management and maintaining a sense of self-efficacy when coping with distress. Furthermore, Shaver et al. (1988) hypothesized that attachment anxiety and avoidance would lead to different problems in caregiving. Specifically, avoidant people, who distance themselves from emotional partners and dismiss signals of need, should be less willing to feel compassionate toward a needy partner and less willing to provide care. In contrast, anxiously attached people, who seek closeness to romantic partners and are often preoccupied with their own needs, should react to others' suffering with personal distress rather than empathy, which is likely to produce insensitive, intrusive, ineffective care.

There is now considerable evidence that self-reports of attachment security (lower anxiety or avoidance scores) are associated with higher scores on measures of responsiveness to a relationship partner's needs and support provision (e.g. Davila & Kashy, 2009; Julal & Carnelley, 2012; Péloquin, Brassard, Lafontaine, & Shaver, 2014). Similarly, more secure people have actually been observed to be more responsive and to provide more support when they were videotaped while their partner waited to undergo a stressful experience or disclosed a personal problem or future plans (e.g. Collins & Feeney, 2000; Feeney & Trush, 2010; Feeney, Collins, van Vleet, & Tomlinson, 2013; Monin, Feeney, & Schulz, 2012). In addition, we (Mikulincer, Shaver, Bar-On, & Sahdra, 2014; Mikulincer, Shaver, Sahdra, & Bar-On, 2013) found that experimental priming of security-enhancing mental representations increased behavioral responsiveness (as scored by external judges) toward a distressed partner or toward a partner who was exploring his or her personal plans. Security priming also overrode the negative effects that mental fatigue otherwise had on responsiveness. Finally, using the CSFS, Shaver et al. (2010) found correlations between attachment insecurities and hyperactivation or deactivation of the care-giving system.

Attachment and Sex

Following Bowlby's (1982) ideas about the attachment system's apparent dominant influence in many cases of inter-system conflict, Shaver et al. (1988) hypothesized that anxiously attached people, who focus mainly on their own protection and security, would have trouble attending accurately to their partner's sexual needs and preferences. Anxious people were expected to have difficulty in maintaining the relatively relaxed and secure state of mind that fosters mutual sexual satisfaction (Shaver et al., 1988). Avoidant attachment was also expected to interfere with or distort the sexual system (Shaver et al., 1988), but in this case the interference would derive from lack of care or desire for emotional closeness. Moreover, the heightened physical and emotional closeness inherent in sex can cause people scoring high on avoidant attachment to feel uncomfortable during sexual intercourse and to inhibit sexual arousal and behavior.

There is now extensive evidence that attachment orientations shape sexual motives, experiences, and behaviors (see Birnbaum, 2015, for a review). For example, more secure people express more love for their partner during sex, experience more positive emotions during sexual interactions, and engage in more positive sexual fantasies (e.g. Birnbaum, Mikulincer, &

Gillath, 2011; Birnbaum, Reis, Mikulincer, Gillath, & Orpaz, 2006; Butzer & Campbell, 2008; Khoury & Findlay, 2014; Little, McNulty, & Russell, 2010). There is also evidence that people scoring high on attachment-related avoidance are less likely to have and to enjoy mutually intimate sex. They are also more likely to engage in sex to manipulate their partner or achieve other non-romantic goals, such as reducing stress or increasing their prestige among peers (e.g. Birnbaum & Reis, 2012; Brassard, Shaver, & Lussier, 2007; Davis, Shaver, & Vernon, 2004; Tracy, Shaver, Albino, & Cooper, 2003). People scoring high on attachment anxiety tend to use sex as a means of achieving personal reassurance and avoiding abandonment, even when particular sex acts are otherwise unwanted (e.g. Davis et al., 2004; Schachner & Shaver, 2004; Tracy et al., 2003). Using the SSFS, Birnbaum et al. (2014) found that whereas attachment anxiety was related to both deactivation and hyperactivation of sexual desires and feelings, avoidant attachment was exclusively related to sexual avoidance and inhibition of sexual desire.

Potential Recurring Effects of Caregiving and Sex on Attachment

All of the findings reviewed so far illustrate various ways in which individual differences in attachment-system functioning can affect other behavioral systems. Bowlby (1982) began his theorizing by portraying attachment security as a "secure base for exploration," which suggested that the attachment system is primary, comes first in development, and forms either a solid or a shaky foundation for the functioning of other behavioral systems. However, changes in the functioning of the other systems (e.g. having positive sexual experiences and then having confidence in one's sexual attractiveness and potency; volunteering to help others and becoming more self-confident as a result) can feed back on attachment security. At present, we know little about the extent to which other behavioral systems affect the attachment system, but Gillath, Mikulincer, Birnbaum, and Shaver (2008) provided initial evidence for the effects of sexual arousal on attachment security and caregiving inclinations. In four studies, heterosexual adults were subliminally primed with either neutral pictures or photographs of naked members of the opposite sex and were asked to describe their willingness or unwillingness to self-disclose, become psychologically intimate, deal constructively with interpersonal conflicts, and sacrifice for a partner. The results indicated that activating the sexual system moved people, on average, in the direction of greater self-disclosure and intimacy – tendencies usually associated with attachment security. Moreover, subliminal sexual priming, as compared with neutral priming, produced a stronger tendency to sacrifice for a partner and more constructive handling of conflicts, presumably reflecting a more caring attitude toward close relationship partners.

Following up these findings, Mizrahi, Hirschberger, Mikulincer, Szepsenwol, and Birnbaum (2016) conducted a prospective, longitudinal dyadic study examining the extent to which expressions of sexual desire affect relationship-specific attachment orientations. Specifically, they asked the two partners of couples that had been dating for three to four months to rate the extent to which they felt attachment anxiety and avoidance in their current relationship (using the ECR scale) and videotaped partners' conversation about sexual aspects of their relationship. Judges then coded their displays of sexual desire and emotional intimacy during the conversation. Four and eight months later, participants again completed the ECR scale. Findings indicated that women whose partner expressed heightened sexual desire toward them became more secure during the eight-month study period. However, this effect was not evident among men. In fact, men showed a decline in attachment insecurities mainly when their partner expressed signs of emotional intimacy. That is, sex-related processes can affect attachment insecurities but these effects seem to depend on gender.

We also have preliminary evidence that a heightened sense of caring for others might increase attachment security – for example, by strengthening a person's sense of connectedness. Specifically, we have found that anxious people become more secure as a result of volunteering to help others (Gillath et al., 2005). In a direct examination of the caregiving–sex link, Birnbaum and Reis (2012) found that perceiving a partner as more responsive was associated with higher interest in sex with this partner. Following these initial findings, Birnbaum et al. (2017) used experimental designs, behavioral observations, and diary methods to examine the effects of empathic responsiveness on sexual desire within romantic relationships. The authors found that men's empathic responsiveness to a female partner's needs was associated with increases in the women's sexual desire. That is, women felt more special and more sexually desirable when their partner reacted in a more empathic and responsive manner.

Future research should explore more systematically the ways in which other behavioral systems shape the functioning of the attachment system and should further consider potential reciprocal relations between caregiving and sex. We also need more research on the mediators of these effects. The preliminary findings reviewed here suggest that, at least in adults, different behavioral systems are intertwined, such that activation of one has effects on the others, and individual differences in one tend to be correlated with individual differences in the others. But there is still a great deal we do not understand about the mechanisms.

Attachment, Caregiving, and Sex within Romantic Relationships

In this section, we present ideas and research concerning how individual differences in the attachment, caregiving, and sexual systems affect the quality of romantic love. We believe that these three systems are important for understanding romantic love, because their smooth functioning brings relationship partners together, increases physical and emotional closeness, and heightens feelings of love and gratitude toward the partner as well as feelings of being loved and esteemed by the partner. The smooth operation of these three systems is crucial for forming and maintaining intimate, satisfying, and long-lasting romantic relationships.

With respect to Sternberg's (1986) triangular theory of love, optimal functioning of the attachment, caregiving, and sexual systems enlarges the area of the "love triangle" by increasing the intensity of its three components – intimacy, commitment, and passion. As explained earlier, smooth functioning of the three behavioral systems tends to create feelings of communion, connectedness, and togetherness with a relationship partner, thereby sustaining the "intimacy" component of romantic love. The attachment and caregiving systems strengthen the "commitment" component of romantic love as conceptualized by Sternberg. Positive interactions with a partner who is available and responsive in times of need generate not only a sense of security but also feelings of gratitude and love toward this sensitive and responsive person, which in turn motivates the secure person to stay in the relationship and commit himself or herself to maintain it and promote the partner's welfare. Moreover, positive interactions in which a person is effective in promoting a partner's welfare strengthen the caregiver's emotional involvement in the relationship, thereby sustaining the "commitment" component of romantic love. Finally, the "passion" component of romantic love is closely related to the activation and functioning of the sexual behavioral system, which creates feelings of attraction, arousal, vitality, and excitement within the relationship.

Attachment researchers have been successful in generating a large body of theory-consistent results, showing that secure attachment is associated with higher levels of relationship stability and satisfaction in both dating and married couples (see Mikulincer & Shaver, 2016, for a review). Studies have also linked secure attachment with higher scores on measures of relationship intimacy and commitment (e.g. Brock & Lawrence, 2014; Impett & Gordon, 2010; Randall & Butler, 2013; Vicary & Fraley, 2007). More secure people tend to engage in more positive, engaging, and satisfactory patterns of dyadic communication (e.g. Mohr, Selterman, & Fassinger, 2013; Roisman et al., 2007) and to react more constructively to a partner's transgressions (e.g. Arriaga, Capezza, Reed, Wesselman, & Williams, 2014; Overall, Girme, Lemay, & Hammond, 2014). Moreover, attachment security is positively associated with forgiveness – one of the most effective responses for reestablishing relational harmony following a partner's hurtful behavior (e.g. Ashy, Mercurio, & Malley-Morrison, 2010; Martin, Vosvick, & Riggs, 2012).

Research also indicates that attachment security facilitates a person's adaptive handling of relational conflicts. Specifically, lower scores on attachment anxiety and avoidance are associated with appraising relational conflicts in less threatening terms, relying more on compromise and integrative conflict-management strategies, and generating fewer cases of conflict escalation and leaving a conflict unresolved (e.g. Cann, Norman, Welbourne, & Calhoun, 2008; Dominique & Mollen, 2009). In addition, more secure people are more likely to express affection toward a relationship partner during conflicts and are less likely to use coercive or withdrawal strategies or to engage in verbal or physical aggression during conflicts (e.g. La Valley & Guerrero, 2012; Wood, Werner-Wilson, Parker, & Perry, 2012).

In the domain of caregiving, relational episodes in which an individual sensitively attends to and empathically responds to a romantic partner's attachment behaviors and signals of need lead to enhanced relationship satisfaction in both the caregiver and the care recipient (e.g. Collins & Feeney, 2000; Feeney & Collins, 2001, 2003). In addition, studies have shown that empathic responsiveness to a partner's disclosure of distress or sharing of positive experiences is associated with heightened trust and commitment (e.g. Finkenauer & Righetti, 2011; Simpson, 2007) and stronger feelings of connectedness and intimacy (e.g. Gable, Gonzaga, & Strachman, 2006; Gable, Reis, Impett & Asher, 2004). According to Reis (2014), responsiveness plays a critical role in facilitating what Wieselquist, Rusbult, Foster, and Agnew (1999) called *mutual cyclical growth* – a process by which partners in a close relationship support each other's goals and aspirations and enhance both personal and relational growth. Specifically, people learn to trust their partner mainly when they learn that the partner is sensitive and responsive to their needs and disclosures. This heightened trust, in turn, leads people to be more committed to the relationship and more benevolent, sensitive, and responsive to a partner's needs and signals, thereby facilitating a chain-like sequence of mutual cyclical growth and relational quality. Dysfunctions in the caregiving system of one of the partners can disrupt this mutual cyclical growth, erode trust, commitment, and intimacy, and gradually destroy the relationship.

As we would expect, sexual interactions in which both partners gratify their sexual needs contribute to relationship satisfaction and stability (see Birnbaum, 2015, for an extensive review). Phenomenological (non-quantitative) studies have shown that people tend to believe that sex fosters closeness, intimacy, and love (e.g. Birnbaum, 2003; Birnbaum & Gillath, 2006; Meston & Buss, 2007). And studies using quantitative methods have shown that positive sexual experiences and open expressions of sexual interest and desire within romantic relationships promote intimacy and pro-relational behaviors (e.g. Birnbaum et al., 2006; Rubin & Campbell, 2012). These experiences and expressions also buffer against the detrimental consequences of a partner's hurtful behaviors or of relationship conflicts (e.g. Birnbaum et al., 2006; Litzinger & Gordon, 2005; Russell & McNulty, 2011). In a recent study, Birnbaum et al. (2017) experimentally enhanced participants' sexual desire and found that this manipulation increased self-disclosure and interest in future interactions with a new acquaintance. In another study (Szepsenwol, Mizrahi, & Birnbaum, 2015), deactivation of the sexual system (as measured by the SSFS) was associated with relationship dissatisfaction in newly dating couples, and it predicted further decline in relationship satisfaction over an eight-month period.

Concluding Remarks

Over thirty years ago, Shaver et al. (1988) proposed that romantic love can be fruitfully conceptualized in terms of three behavioral systems that were identified by Bowlby (1982): attachment, caregiving, and sex. This approach to romantic love was unique at the time in placing romantic love within an evolutionary and developmental framework, viewing it as a human universal rather than a culturally constructed artifact, and measuring some of its aspects in terms of individual differences noted by Ainsworth and her colleagues (1978) in studies of infant-caregiver attachment. Over the years, this once-speculative approach to love has generated a huge body of empirical evidence and has made contact with the expanding literature on evolutionary psychology. It has also begun to influence clinical work with individuals and couples (e.g. Brassard & Johnson, 2016; Daniel, 2015; Holmes, 2014; Johnson, 2012; Obegi & Berant, 2009).

There is still a great deal of work to be done. We need to learn more about how and why each of the three behavioral systems develops either optimally or non-optimally. We need to explore ways to intervene clinically or educationally to correct non-optimal development, not only in the domain of attachment but also in the domains of sex and caregiving. We need more studies, using more methods, of the reciprocal dynamic links of the attachment, caregiving, and sexual systems, including studies of physiological and neurological underpinnings. In the present chapter, we provide a small example of the interactions and integration of these three behavioral systems in the context of romantic relationships. We hope that as we continue to explore love's complexities, we will generate more useful ideas for a broader, more humane, and more applicable psychology of love relationships.

References

Ainsworth, M. D. S., Blehar, M. C., Waters, E., & Wall, S. (1978). *Patterns of attachment: Assessed in the strange situation and at home.* Hillsdale, NJ: Lawrence Erlbaum.

Arriaga, X. B., Capezza, N. M., Reed, J. T., Wesselmann, E. D., & Williams, K. D. (2014). With partners like you, who needs strangers? Ostracism involving a romantic partner. *Personal Relationships, 21,* 557–569.

Ashy, M., Mercurio, A. E., & Malley-Morrison, K. (2010). Apology, forgiveness and reconciliation: An ecological world-view framework. *Individual Differences Research, 8,* 17–26.

Batson, C. D. (2010). Empathy-induced altruistic motivation. In M. Mikulincer & P. R. Shaver (Eds.), *Prosocial motives, emotions, and behavior: The better angels of our nature* (pp. 15–34). Washington, DC: American Psychological Association.

Birnbaum, G. E. (2003). The meaning of heterosexual intercourse among women with female orgasmic disorder. *Archives of Sexual Behavior, 32,* 61–71.

(2015). On the convergence of sexual urges and emotional bonds: The interplay of the sexual and attachment systems during relationship development. In J. A. Simpson & W. S. Rholes (Eds.), *Attachment theory and research: New directions and emerging themes* (pp. 170–194). New York: Guilford Press.

Birnbaum, G. E., & Gillath, O. (2006). Measuring subgoals of the sexual behavioral system: What is sex good for? *Journal of Social and Personal Relationships, 23,* 675–701.

Birnbaum, G. E., Mikulincer, M., & Gillath, O. (2011). In and out of a daydream: Attachment orientations, daily relationship quality, and sexual fantasies. *Personality and Social Psychology Bulletin, 37,* 1398–1410.

Birnbaum, G. E., Mikulincer, M., Szepsenwol, O., Shaver, P. R., & Mizrahi, M. (2014). When sex goes wrong: A behavioral systems perspective on individual differences in sexual attitudes, motives, feelings, and behaviors. *Journal of Personality and Social Psychology, 106,* 822–842.

Birnbaum, G. E., Mizrahi, M., Kaplan, A., Kadosh, D., Kariv, D., Tabib, D., Ziv, D., Sadeh, L., & Burban, D. (2017). Sex unleashes your tongue: Sexual priming motivates self-disclosure to a new acquaintance and interest in future interactions. *Personality and Social Psychology Bulletin, 43,* 706–715.

Birnbaum, G. E., & Reis, H. T. (2006). Women's sexual working models: An evolutionary-attachment perspective. *The Journal of Sex Research, 43,* 328–342.

(2012). When does responsiveness pique sexual interest? Attachment and sexual desire in initial acquaintanceships. *Personality and Social Psychology Bulletin, 38,* 946–958.

Birnbaum, G. E., Reis, H. T., Mikulincer, M., Gillath, O., & Orpaz, A. (2006). When sex is more than just sex: Attachment orientations, sexual experience, and relationship quality. *Journal of Personality and Social Psychology, 91,* 929–943.

Birnbaum, G. E., Reis, H. T., Mizrahi, M., Kanat-Maymon, Y., Sass, O., & Granovski-Milner, C. (2017). Intimately connected: The importance of partner responsiveness for experiencing sexual desire. *Journal of Personality and Social Psychology, 111,* 530–546.

Bowlby, J. (1973). *Attachment and loss,* Vol. 2: *Separation: Anxiety and anger.* New York: Basic Books.

(1979). *The making and breaking of affectional bonds.* London: Tavistock.

(1980). *Attachment and loss,* Vol. 3: *Sadness and depression.* New York: Basic Books.

(1982). *Attachment and loss,* Vol. 1: *Attachment* (2nd ed.). New York: Basic Books. (Original ed. 1969).

(1988). *A secure base: Clinical applications of attachment theory.* London: Routledge.

Brassard, A., & Johnson, S. (2016). Couples and family therapy: An attachment perspective. In J. Cassidy & P. R. Shaver (Eds.), *Handbook of attachment: Theory, research, and clinical applications* (3rd ed., pp. 805–825). New York: Guilford Press.

Brassard, A., Shaver, P. R., & Lussier, Y. (2007). Attachment, sexual experience, and sexual pressure in romantic relationships: A dyadic approach. *Personal Relationships, 14,* 475–494.

Brauer, M., van Leeuwen, M., Janssen, E., Newhouse, S. K., Heiman, J. R., & Laan, E. (2012). Attentional and affective processing of sexual stimuli in women with hypoactive sexual desire disorder. *Archives of Sexual Behavior, 41,* 891–905.

Brennan, K. A., Clark, C. L., & Shaver, P. R. (1998). Self-report measurement of adult romantic attachment: An integrative overview. In J. A. Simpson & W. S. Rholes (Eds.), *Attachment theory and close relationships* (pp. 46–76). New York: Guilford Press.

Brock, R. L., & Lawrence, E. (2014). Intrapersonal interpersonal and contextual risk factors for overprovision of partner support in marriage. *Journal of Family Psychology, 28,* 54–64.

Butzer, B., & Campbell, L. (2008). Adult attachment, sexual satisfaction, and relationship satisfaction: A study of married couples. *Personal Relationships, 15,* 141–154.

Cann, A., Norman, M. A., Welbourne, J., & Calhoun, L. G. (2008). Attachment styles, conflict styles, and humor styles: Interrelationships and associations with relationship satisfaction. *European Journal of Personality, 22,* 131–146.

Cassidy, J., & Kobak, R. R. (1988). Avoidance and its relationship with other defensive processes. In J. Belsky & T. Nezworski (Eds.), *Clinical implications of attachment* (pp. 300–323). Hillsdale, NJ: Lawrence Erlbaum.

Collins, N. L., & Feeney, B. C. (2000). A safe haven: An attachment theory perspective on support seeking and caregiving in intimate relationships. *Journal of Personality and Social Psychology, 78,* 1053–1073.

Collins, N. L., Ford, M. B., Guichard, A. C., Kane, H. S., & Feeney, B. C. (2010). Responding to need in intimate relationships: Social support and caregiving processes in couples. In M. Mikulincer & P. R. Shaver (Eds.), *Prosocial motives, emotions, and behavior: The better angels of our nature* (pp. 367–389). Washington, DC: American Psychological Association.

Collins, N. L., Guichard, A. C., Ford, M. B., & Feeney, B. C. (2006). Responding to need in intimate relationships: Normative processes and individual differences. In M. Mikulincer & G. S. Goodman (Eds.), *Dynamics of romantic love: Attachment, caregiving, and sex* (pp. 149–189). New York: Guilford Press.

Daniel, S. I. F. (2015). *Adult attachment patterns in a treatment context: Relationship and narrative.* London: Routledge.

Davila, J., & Kashy, D. (2009). Secure base processes in couples: Daily associations between support experiences and attachment security. *Journal of Family Psychology, 23,* 76–88.

Davis, D., Shaver, P. R., & Vernon, M. L. (2004). Attachment style and subjective motivations for sex. *Personality and Social Psychology Bulletin, 30,* 1076–1090.

Dominique, R., & Mollen, D. (2009). Attachment and conflict communication in adult romantic relationships. *Journal of Social and Personal Relationships, 26,* 678–696.

Erikson, E. H. (1993). *Childhood and society.* New York: Norton. (Original work published 1950.)

Feeney, B. C., & Collins, N. L. (2001). Predictors of caregiving in adult intimate relationships: An attachment theoretical perspective. *Journal of Personality and Social Psychology, 80,* 972–994.

(2003). Motivations for caregiving in adult intimate relationships: Influence on caregiving behavior and relationship functioning. *Personality and Social Psychology Bulletin, 29,* 950–968.

Feeney, B. C., Collins, N. L., van Vleet, M., & Tomlinson, J. M. (2013). Motivations for providing a secure base: Links with attachment orientation and secure base support behavior. *Attachment & Human Development, 15,* 261–280.

Feeney, B. C., & Thrush, R. L. (2010). Relationship influences on exploration in adulthood: The characteristics and function of a secure base. *Journal of Personality and Social Psychology, 98,* 57–76.

Feeney, B. C., & Woodhouse, S. S. (2016). Caregiving. In J. Cassidy & P. R. Shaver (Eds.), *Handbook of attachment: Theory, research, and clinical applications* (3rd ed., pp. 827–851). New York: Guilford Press.

Feynman, R. P. (2005). *Perfectly reasonable deviations from the beaten track: The letters of Richard P. Feynman* (M. Feynman, Ed.). New York: Basic Books.

Finkenauer, C., & Righetti, F. (2011). Understanding in close relationships: An interpersonal approach. *European Review of Social Psychology, 22,* 316–363.

Fisher, H. E. (1998). Lust, attraction, and attachment in mammalian reproduction. *Human Nature, 9,* 23–52.

Fisher, H. E., Aron, A., Mashek, D., Li, H., & Brown, L. L. (2002). Defining the brain systems of lust, romantic attraction, and attachment. *Archives of Sexual Behavior, 31,* 413–419.

Fraley, R. C., & Shaver, P. R. (2000). Adult romantic attachment: Theoretical developments, emerging controversies, and unanswered questions. *Review of General Psychology, 4,* 132–154.

Gable, S. L., Gonzaga, G. C., & Strachman, A. (2006). Will you be there for me when things go right? Supportive responses to positive event disclosures. *Journal of Personality and Social Psychology, 91,* 904–917.

Gable, S. L., Reis, H. T., Impett, E. A., & Asher, E. R. (2004). What do you do when things go right? The intrapersonal and interpersonal benefits of sharing positive events. *Journal of Personality and Social Psychology, 87,* 228–245.

Gangestad, S. W., Simpson, J. A., Cousins, A. J., Garver-Apgar, C. E., & Christensen, P. N. (2004). Women's preferences for male behavioral displays. *Psychological Science, 15,* 203–206.

Gillath, O., Mikulincer, M., Birnbaum, G., & Shaver, P. R. (2008). When sex primes love: Subliminal sexual priming motivates relationship goal pursuit. *Personality and Social Psychology Bulletin, 34,* 1057–1069.

Gillath, O., Shaver, P. R., Mikulincer, M., Nitzberg, R. A., Erez, A., & van IJzendoorn, M. H. (2005). Attachment, caregiving, and volunteering: Placing volunteerism in an attachment-theoretical framework. *Personal Relationships, 12,* 425–446.

Hamilton, W. D. (1964). The genetic evolution of social behavior. *Journal of Theoretical Biology, 7,* 1–52.

Hazan, C., & Shaver, P. R. (1987). Romantic love conceptualized as an attachment process. *Journal of Personality and Social Psychology, 52,* 511–524.

Holmes, J. (2014). *The search for the secure base: Attachment theory and psychotherapy.* London: Routledge.

Impett, E. A., & Gordon, A. M. (2010). Why do people sacrifice to approach rewards versus to avoid costs? Insights from attachment theory. *Personal Relationships, 17,* 299–315.

Impett, E. A., Muise, A., & Peragine, D. (2014). Sexuality in the context of relationships. In D. L. Tolman, L. M. Diamond, J. A. Bauermeister, W. H. George, J. G. Pfaus, & L. M. Ward (Eds.), *APA handbook of sexuality and psychology*, Vol. 1: *Person-based approaches* (pp. 269–315). Washington, DC: American Psychological Association.

Johnson, S. M. (2012). *The practice of emotionally focused couple therapy: Creating connection*. London: Routledge.

Julal, F., & Carnelley, K. (2012). Attachment, perceptions of care and caregiving to romantic partners and friends. *European Journal of Social Psychology, 42*, 832–843.

Khoury, C. B., & Findlay, B. M. (2014). What makes for good sex? The associations among attachment style, inhibited communication and sexual satisfaction. *Journal of Relationships Research, 5*, Article ID e7.

Kunce, L. J., & Shaver, P. R. (1994). An attachment-theoretical approach to caregiving in romantic relationships. In K. Bartholomew & D. Perlman (Eds.), *Advances in personal relationships* (Vol. 5, pp. 205–237). London: Jessica Kingsley.

La Valley, A. G., & Guerrero, L. K. (2012). Perceptions of conflict behavior and relational satisfaction in adult parent–child relationships: A dyadic analysis from an attachment perspective. *Communication Research, 39*, 48–78.

Little, K. C., McNulty, J. K., & Russell, V. M. (2010). Sex buffers intimates against the negative implications of attachment insecurity. *Personality and Social Psychology Bulletin, 36*, 484–498.

Litzinger, S., & Gordon, K. C. (2005). Exploring relationships among communication, sexual satisfaction, and marital satisfaction. *Journal of Sex & Marital Therapy, 31*, 409–424.

Martin, L. A., Vosvick, M., & Riggs, S. A. (2012). Attachment, forgiveness, and physical health quality of life in HIV + adults. *AIDS Care, 24*, 1333–1340.

Meston, C. M., & Buss, D. M. (2007). Why humans have sex. *Archives of Sexual Behavior, 36*, 477–507.

Mikulincer, M., & Shaver, P. R. (2015). An attachment perspective on prosocial attitudes and behavior. In D. A. Schroeder & W. Graziano (Eds.), *The Oxford handbook of prosocial behavior* (pp. 209–230). New York: Oxford University Press.

(2016). *Attachment in adulthood: Structure, dynamics, and change* (2nd ed.). New York: Guilford Press.

Mikulincer, M., Shaver, P. R., Bar-On, N., & Sahdra, B. K. (2014). Security enhancement, self-esteem threat, and mental depletion affect provision of a safe haven and secure base to a romantic partner. *Journal of Social and Personal Relationships, 31*, 630–650.

Mikulincer, M., Shaver, P. R., & Gillath, O. (2009). A behavioral systems perspective on compassionate love. In B. Fehr, S. Sprecher, & L. G. Underwood (Eds.), *The science of compassionate love: Research, theory, and application* (pp. 225–256). Malden, MA: Wiley-Blackwell.

Mikulincer, M., Shaver, P. R., Sahdra, B. K., & Bar-On, N. (2013). Can security-enhancing interventions overcome psychological barriers to responsiveness in couple relationships? *Attachment & Human Development, 15*, 246–260.

Mizrahi, M., Hirschberger, G., Mikulincer, M., Szepsenwol, O., & Birnbaum, G. E. (2016). Reassuring sex: Can sexual desire and intimacy reduce relationship-specific attachment insecurities? *European Journal of Social Psychology*, *46*, 467–480.

Mohr, J. J., Selterman, D., & Fassinger, R. E. (2013). Romantic attachment and relationship functioning in same-sex couples. *Journal of Counseling Psychology*, *60*, 72–82.

Monin, J. K., Feeney, B. C., & Schulz, R. (2012). Attachment orientation and reactions to anxiety expression in close relationships. *Personal Relationships*, *19*, 535–550.

Obegi, J. H., & Berant, E. (Eds.). (2009). *Attachment theory and research in clinical work with adults*. New York: Guilford Press.

Overall, N. C., Girme, Y. U., Lemay, E. P., Jr., & Hammond, M. D. (2014). Attachment anxiety and reactions to relationship threat: The benefits and costs of inducing guilt in romantic partners. *Journal of Personality and Social Psychology*, *106*, 235–256.

Péloquin, K., Brassard, A., Lafontaine, M.-F., & Shaver, P. R. (2014). Sexuality examined through the lens of attachment theory: Attachment, caregiving, and sexual satisfaction. *Journal of Sex Research*, *51*, 561–576.

Randall, A. K., & Butler, E. A. (2013). Attachment and emotion transmission within romantic relationships: Merging intrapersonal and interpersonal perspectives. *Journal of Relationships Research*, *4*, Article ID e10.

Reis, H. T. (2014). Responsiveness: Affective interdependence in close relationships. In M. Mikulincer & P. R. Shaver (Eds.), *Mechanisms of social connection: From brain to group* (pp. 255–271). Washington, DC: American Psychological Association.

Reis, H. T., & Shaver, P. R. (1988). Intimacy as an interpersonal process. In S. Duck (Ed.), *Handbook of research in personal relationships* (pp. 367–389). London: Wiley.

Roisman, G. I., Holland, A., Fortuna, K., Fraley, R. C., Clausell, E., & Clarke, A. (2007). The Adult Attachment Interview and self-reports of attachment style: An empirical rapprochement. *Journal of Personality and Social Psychology*, *92*, 678–697.

Rubin, H., & Campbell, L. (2012). Day-to-day changes in intimacy predict heightened relationship passion, sexual occurrence, and sexual satisfaction: A dyadic diary analysis. *Social Psychological and Personality Science*, *3*, 224–231.

Russell, V. M., & McNulty, J. K. (2011). Frequent sex protects intimates from the negative implications of their neuroticism. *Social Psychological and Personality Science*, *2*, 220–227.

Schachner, D. A., & Shaver, P. R. (2004). Attachment dimensions and sexual motives. *Personal Relationships*, *11*, 179–195.

Shaver, P. R., & Hazan, C. (1988). A biased overview of the study of love. *Journal of Social and Personal Relationships*, *5*, 473–501.

Shaver, P. R., Hazan, C., & Bradshaw, D. (1988). Love as attachment: The integration of three behavioral systems. In R. J. Sternberg & M. Barnes (Eds.), *The psychology of love* (pp. 68–99). New Haven, CT: Yale University Press.

Shaver, P. R., Mikulincer, M., & Shemesh-Iron, M. (2010). A behavioral-systems perspective on prosocial behavior. In M. Mikulincer & P. R. Shaver (Eds.), *Prosocial motives, emotions, and behavior: The better angels of our nature* (pp. 73–91). Washington, DC: American Psychological Association.

Simpson, J. A. (2007). Foundations of interpersonal trust. In A. W. Kruglanski & E. T. Higgins (Eds.), *Social psychology: Handbook of basic principles* (2nd ed., pp. 587–607). New York: Guilford Press.

Sroufe, L. A., & Waters, E. (1977). Attachment as an organizational construct. *Child Development, 48*, 1184–1199.

Sternberg, R. J. (1986). A triangular theory of love. *Psychological Review, 93*, 119–135.

Szepsenwol, O., Mizrahi, M., & Birnbaum, G. E. (2015). Fatal suppression: The detrimental effects of sexual and attachment deactivation within emerging romantic relationships. *Social Psychological and Personality Science, 6*, 504–512.

Tracy, J. L., Shaver, P. R., Albino, A. W., & Cooper, M. L. (2003). Attachment styles and adolescent sexuality. In P. Florsheim (Ed.), *Adolescent romance and sexual behavior: Theory, research, and practical implications* (pp. 137–159). Mahwah, NJ: Lawrence Erlbaum.

Vicary, A. M., & Fraley, R. C. (2007). Choose your own adventure: Attachment dynamics in a simulated relationship. *Personality and Social Psychology Bulletin, 33*, 1279–1291.

Wieselquist, J., Rusbult, C. E., Foster, C. A., & Agnew, C. R. (1999). Commitment, pro-relationship behavior, and trust in close relationships. *Journal of Personality and Social Psychology, 77*, 942–966.

Wood, N. D., Werner-Wilson, R. J., Parker, T. S., & Perry, M. S. (2012). Exploring the impact of attachment anxiety and avoidance on the perception of couple conflict. *Contemporary Family Therapy, 34*, 416–428.

CHAPTER 14

When Love Goes Awry (Part 1): Applications of the Duplex Theory of Love and Its Development to Relationships Gone Bad[*]

Robert J. Sternberg

What is love and how does it develop? How does it go awry? A duplex theory of love captures two essential components of the nature of love – first, its structure (a triangular model); and second, its development (a model of love as a story). The model of love as a story is an attempt to specify how various kinds (triangles) of love develop. Together, the two parts of the duplex theory – the triangular theory and the theory of love as a story – can help us understand many of the causes of failed relationships.

The Triangular Theory of Love

The triangular theory of love (Sternberg, 1986, 1988a, 1988b, 1997, 1998a, 2007; Weis & Sternberg, 2008) holds that love can be understood in terms of three components that together can be viewed as forming the vertices of a triangle. The triangle serves as a metaphor, not as a strict geometric model. The three components of the theory are intimacy (metaphorically, the top vertex of the triangle), passion (metaphorically, the left-hand vertex of the triangle), and decision/commitment (metaphorically, the right-hand vertex of the triangle). (Which component serves as which vertex is arbitrary.) These three components have appeared in various other theories of love (see Aron & Tomlinson, this volume), and moreover, appear to correspond rather well to people's implicit theories, or folk theories, of love (Aron & Westby, 1996).

Three Components of Love

The three components comprising love in the triangular theory of love are intimacy, passion, and decision/commitment. Each component refers to a different aspect of love.

---

[*] This chapter is an update and expansion of my chapter in the first edition of this book (Sternberg, 2006).

Intimacy. Intimacy comprises feelings of closeness, bondedness, and connectedness in loving relationships. It involves those feelings that give rise, essentially, to the experience of warmth and caring in love. Intimacy comprises the following: (a) desire to promote the welfare of the loved one; (b) experienced happiness with the loved one; (c) high regard for the loved one; (d) being able to count on the loved one in times of need; (e) mutual understanding with the loved one; (f) sharing of one's self and one's possessions with the loved one; (g) receipt of emotional support from the loved one; (h) giving of emotional support to the loved one; (i) intimate communication with the loved one; and (j) valuing of the loved one in one's life (Sternberg & Grajek, 1984).

Passion. Passion refers to the drives that lead to romance, physical attraction, sexual consummation, and related phenomena in loving relationships (Feybesse & Hatfield, this volume; Hatfield & Walster, 1981). The passion component involves sources of motivational and other forms of arousal that produce the sensation of passion in love. In a relationship between loving partners, sexual needs may tend to predominate in this experience. It is possible, however, that other needs, including those for self-esteem, nurturance, succorance, dominance, submission, affiliation, and self-actualization, may also contribute to the experience of passion.

Decision/commitment. Decision/commitment characterizes, in the short term, the decision that an individual loves a certain other individual, and in the long term, one's commitment to maintain that love indefinitely. The decision and commitment aspects of the decision/commitment component do not always occur together. One may decide that one loves someone without at the same time feeling committed to the love in the long term. Conversely, one can feel committed to a relationship without experiencing that commitment as love toward the other in the relationship.

The three components of love interact with each other. For instance, greater intimacy may lead to greater passion or thoughts of greater commitment; similarly, more serious commitment may result in greater intimacy, or less likely, greater passion. Although all three components are significant in loving relationships, their relative importance may vary from one relationship to the next, or over a period of time within a given relationship. Different kinds of love can result from limiting cases of different combinations of the components.

Table 14.1 *Taxonomy of kinds of triangles of love*

Type of love	Intimacy	Passion	Commitment
Non-love	No	No	No
Friendship	Yes	No	No
Infatuated love	No	Yes	No
Empty love	No	No	Yes
Romantic love	Yes	Yes	No
Companionate love	Yes	No	Yes
Fatuous love	No	Yes	Yes
Consummate Love	Yes	Yes	Yes

Kinds of Love

The three components of love generate eight possible kinds of love when considered in combination (Sternberg, 1988a, 1988b). No relationship in the real world is apt to be a pure case of any of the components. They are shown in Table 14.1.

Non-love occurs in the absence of all three components of love. Liking comes about when an individual experiences only intimacy in the absence of the passion and decision/commitment components. Infatuated love results from the experiencing of passion without the simultaneous experiencing of the other components of love. Empty love comes from the decision that one feels loves toward another and is committed to that love in the absence of the intimacy and passion components. Romantic love comes from a combination of intimacy and passion. Companionate love comes from a combination of intimacy and decision/commitment. Fatuous love comes from the combination of passion and decision/commitment in the absence of intimacy. Consummate, or complete love, comes from the combination of all three components: intimacy, passion, and commitment.

Geometry of the Love Triangle

The geometry of the "love triangle" depends upon two factors: the amount of love and the balance of love. Differences in amounts of love are shown by differing areas of the respective love triangles: the greater the amount of love, the greater the area of the corresponding triangle. Differences in balances among the three kinds of love are characterized by differing shapes of triangles. For instance, balanced love (roughly comparable amounts of each of the three components) is represented by an equilateral triangle.

Multiple Triangles of Love

Love does not involve just a single triangle. Rather, it involves a variety of different triangles. For instance, one can contrast real with ideal triangles. An individual has not only a triangle that represents his or her love for a partner, but also a triangle representing an ideal partner for that relationship (see Sternberg & Barnes, 1985). The ideal may be derived in part from experiences in previous relationships of a similar kind (Thibaut & Kelley, 1959), and in part on ideals for what the particular close relationship can be. One also can distinguish between self- and other-perceived triangles. In other words, one's feelings of love in a given relationship do not always correspond to how the partner perceives one to feel. Finally, it is possible to differentiate between triangles of feelings and triangles of action. One's actions, of course, do not always match the feelings of one's partner.

Each of the three components – intimacy, passion, and commitment – has a set of actions associated with it. For instance, intimacy might be displayed in action through sharing one's time and possessions, expressing empathy and care for another, communicating honestly and fully with another, and so forth. Passion might be shown through gazing, embracing, making love, and so forth. Commitment might be shown through verbal expressions of commitment, sexual fidelity, engagement, marriage, and so forth. The particular actions that demonstrate a particular component of love can vary somewhat from one person to another, from one relationship to another, or from one situation to another.

Data

For comprehensive reports of data, see Sternberg (1997, 1988a, 1998b). All individuals were heterosexual and over the age of eighteen. All subjects were either involved in a current close relationship or recently had been in a close relationship.

All participants received the Triangular Love Scale (Sternberg, 1997, 1998a). The scale comprises twelve Likert-scale items (on a scale from one to nine) measuring each of intimacy, passion, and commitment. An example of an item measuring intimacy would be "I have a warm and comfortable relationship with _____." An example of an item measuring passion would be "I cannot imagine another person making me as happy as _____ does." An example of an item measuring commitment would be "I view my relationship with _____ as permanent." Other scales also were administered, including the Rubin Liking and Love Scales, among others.

Subjects rated (between subjects) either how *important* or how *characteristic* each of the statements was for each of six different love relationships (mother, father, sibling closest in age, lover/spouse, best friend of the same sex, and ideal lover/spouse). Importance is essentially a value judgment, whereas characteristicness is essentially a judgment of the actual state of an existing relationship.

If the triangular theory and the scale based on it are viable, then there should be a significant interaction between a particular relationship and component: In other words, different relationships (father, mother, etc.) ought to show different blends of intimacy, passion, and commitment. Such a significant interaction was obtained, and showed the highest F value (58.25) with the most variance accounted for of any of the two-, three-, or four-way interactions studied.

The mean ratings for the various relationships made sense in terms of the triangular theory. For example, one would anticipate that the mean characteristicness ratings for the lover relationship would vary less for passion, as opposed to either intimacy or commitment, where passion seems crucial, than for the other relationships, where passion does not seem crucial. For lover, the mean passion rating came out at 6.91. The second highest rating was for mother at 4.98, a difference of 1.93. In contrast, the mean rating for lover on intimacy was 7.55, and the next highest mean, for friend was 6.78, a smaller difference of only .77. Similarly, for commitment, the difference between the mean for lover and the next highest mean, for mother, was a mere 1.07. The importance ratings showed much the same pattern, but more strongly.

Internal-consistency analysis of the triangular scale revealed that all but four of the thirty-six test items served their appropriate functions. In addition, the subscale reliabilities, which ranged in the .80s and .90s, and the overall scale reliabilities, which were in the high .90s, were quite favorable.

Analyses of correlational patterns showed that although means for actions were lower than means for feeling, the two kinds of ratings – for feelings and actions – were highly correlated with each other (generally in the .90s); as a result, action ratings were disregarded in subsequent analyses. The correlational analyses also showed that, for characteristicness ratings, intimacy and commitment were more highly correlated than were either intimacy and passion, on the one hand, or passion and commitment, on the other. For ratings of importance, the correlation between intimacy and passion was lower than the correlation between intimacy and commitment, on the one hand, and passion and commitment, on the other.

Principal-component analyses yielded three rotated principal components for the characteristicness ratings, corresponding to intimacy, passion, and commitment in the triangular theory, and four principal components for the importance ratings, with decision/commitment splitting off into decision and commitment as separate principal components. In general, then, the principal-components analyses were supportive of the theory.

External validation showed moderate to substantial correlations with the Rubin (1970) scale, although there was no compelling convergent-discriminant pattern with regard to liking and loving. The intimacy, passion, and commitment subscales of the Sternberg Triangular Love Scale correlated at a higher level with satisfaction ratings than did either scale of the Rubin Liking and Loving Scales.

In a follow-up study, the correlations of individual items to scales other than their own (e.g. intimacy items with passion and commitment subscale scores) were substantially lower, and correlations among subscales were also lower, especially for characteristicness ratings. As in the earlier work, both characteristicness and importance ratings revealed a structure with three principal components corresponding to intimacy, passion, and commitment. Correlations with overall relationship satisfaction were again very high (with a median of .76 for the three subscales).

Overall, the data were supportive of the triangular account of love, although the Sternberg Triangular Love Scale was less than a perfect measure of intimacy, passion, and commitment.

Where Love Goes Wrong According to the Triangular Theory of Love

In the triangular theory, love can go awry in at least eight different ways.

- *Empty love.* A partner realizes that whatever intimacy and passion he or she might have once had is gone. All that is left is the commitment of the marriage or relationship, and that is faltering too. Often when one realizes that all that is left is the commitment, the commitment begins to go too. This is *not* the case in arranged marriages, which may start rather than end with empty love.

- *Insufficient love.* The triangle of love is just too small to sustain a relationship.
- *Mismatching actual triangles.* The partners both love each other, but their triangles are different. For example, one partner feels a high level of commitment while the other does not, or one partner emphasizes intimacy greatly while the other partner is mostly interested in passion.
- *Mismatch between actual triangle and ideal triangle.* The triangle of love one has with another person is not a good match to one's ideal triangle: One may have a reasonably good relationship, but it is not close enough to what one ideally is seeking in order to satisfy oneself.
- *Mismatch between actual triangle and action triangle.* The partner does not perceive one's actions as consistent with one's professed feelings. For example, one claims to feel intimacy, but then refuses to confide in the partner.
- *Mismatch between other-experienced and other-perceived triangle.* One partner truly does feel intimacy, passion, and/or commitment, but the other partner does not experience it. Either the first partner is unable to communicate his or her feelings or the second partner is unable to receive the communication.
- *Changing triangles.* One had a satisfactory triangle of love with one's partner, but one feels it changing in a direction that does not suit one. Even though the change may not have reached a critical point, the experiencing of change (usually, diminution) makes one uncomfortable and on guard for looming failure. Or one partner seeks a change in the triangle that the other partner rejects.
- *Competitive triangles.* One has a triangle of love with one's partner, but another individual has entered the picture and the triangle of love the partner experiences toward the third individual is a better match to his or her needs than is the triangle with the first partner.

In sum, there are at least eight ways in which love relationships can go wrong in terms of the triangular theory of love. All of them are based in some way on flawed comparisons of some sort – between the triangle one wants and the triangle one has or thinks one has vis-à-vis the other partner.

The Theory of Love as a Story

Triangles of love grow out of stories. We all are exposed to many diverse stories that portray varied conceptions of ways in which love can be experienced and understood. Some of these stories may be intended to be love stories; other stories may be more general, but may have love stories embedded within them. Either way, all of us have diverse opportunities – through our own experience, through literature, through media, and through whatever else – to observe diverse conceptions of what love is and can be. As a consequence of our exposure to these stories of love, we create, over time, our own stories of what love is, can be, or should be for us personally.

The interaction of our personal traits with the environmental context, which we in part create, leads to the formation of love stories that we then try to fulfill, as much as we can, in our own lives (Sternberg, 1994, 1995, 1996, 1998b; Sternberg, Hojjat, & Barnes, 2001). Different potential partners fit into these stories in different degrees. We are more likely to have success in close relationships with partners whose stories are a better match to our own.

Kinds of Stories

Although the number of possible different love stories is certainly very large, certain genres of stories seem to continue to appear again and again. Because the stories my colleagues and I have analyzed were from people living in the United States, the stories currently in the theory are likely to show some degree of cultural bias.

The stories overlap to some extent. Particularly common stories are shown in Table 14.2. This non-exhaustive list of stories is based on three main sources: (a) an analysis of love stories in literature; (b) previous psychological research; and (c) interpretations of informally gathered case material.

Aspects of Love Stories

Several aspects of the stories are common across them.

First, the list of twenty-six kinds of stories shown in Table 14.2 represents a broad range of conceptions of what love can be for different people and for different relationships. Some of the stories of love are more common (e.g. a garden story) than are others (e.g. a pornographic story).

Second, each of the stories has typical modes of thought and behavior. For example, an individual with a game-based story of love (see the "Ludus" love style as described by Hendrick & Hendrick, 1986, and Lee, 1977) will think and act differently toward a partner than will an individual

Table 14.2 *Taxonomy of some love stories*

---

1. *Addiction*. Strong anxious attachment to a partner; clinging behavior; anxiety at prospect of losing one's partner.

2. *Art*. Love of partner for physical appearance; importance to person of partner's always looking immaculate.

3. *Business*. Relationships viewed as business deals; money is viewed as power; partners in close relationships act as business partners.

4. *Collection*. A partner is viewed as "fitting in" to some overall collection scheme; the partner is viewed in a distant and detached way.

5. *Cookbook*. Doing things a certain way (i.e. following a recipe) results in the relationship being more likely to succeed; departure from the particular recipe for success leads to increased likelihood of failure.

6. *Fantasy*. One expects to be saved or at least aided by a knight in shining armor or to marry a princess and then to live happily ever after.

7. *Game*. Love is viewed as a game or sport.

8. *Gardening*. The view that relationships need to be continually nurtured and tended to.

9. *Government*. (a) *Autocratic*. One partner comes to dominate or even control the other. (b) *Democratic*. The two partners equally share power.

10. *History*. Events of a relationship over time come to form an indelible record; the person tends to keep a lot of records, which can be mental or physical.

11. *Horror*. Relationships become interesting and even exciting when you terrorize or are terrorized by your romantic partner.

12. *House and Home*. Relationships have their core in the home, through its maintenance and development.

13. *Humor*. Love is both funny and sometimes strange.

14. *Mystery*. Love is a mystery. You shouldn't let too much of yourself be known because then the mystery is gone.

15. *Police*. You have to keep close watch of your partner to make sure he or she behaves properly, or you need to be under close surveillance to make sure you behave properly.

16. *Pornography*. Love is dirty. To love is to degrade or to be degraded.

17. *Recovery*. This story involves a survivor mentality; it is the view that after past trauma, a person can get through practically anything.

18. *Religion*. The partner either views love as a religion, or love as feelings, thoughts, and activities dictated by religion.

19. *Sacrifice*. To love is to give of oneself or for a partner or else for the partner to give of him or herself to you.

20. *Science*. Love can be understood, scientifically analyzed, and even carefully dissected, just like any other natural phenomenon.

21. *Science Fiction*. The partner is like an alien–incomprehensible, very strange, and possibly very different from anything you might have imagined before.

22. *Sewing*. Love is whatever you stitch it into.

23. *Theater*. Love is like a theater script, with predictable lines, scenes, and acts.

24. *Travel*. Love is a journey through time and space.

25. *War*. Love is a series of hard-fought battles in a continuing war.

26. *Student-teacher*. Love is a close relationship between a student and a teacher.

---

with a religion-based story (see the anxious-ambivalent attachment style as proposed by Hazan & Shaver, 1987; Mikulincer & Shaver, this volume; and Shaver, Hazan, & Bradshaw, 1988).

Third, as mentioned in the paragraph, there is an overlap between the theory of love as a story and other theories of love. Thus, the story of love as a game is related to Lee's (1977) Ludus love style; the religion story may lead to an anxious-ambivalent attachment style (Shaver, Hazan, & Bradshaw, 1988); the fantasy story is related to conventional conceptions of romantic love (e.g. Hatfield & Walster, 1981; Sternberg, 1986); and so forth. A difference in the theory of love as a story from other theories is that the love-story theory attempts to capture the richness of stories as they lead to different structural love relations, as characterized by the triangular theory.

Fourth, having a particular kind of love story can lead to certain ideas about what a loving relationship is, almost in the same way that Beck and his colleagues have spoken of "automatic thoughts" in cognitive therapy (e.g. Beck, 1976; Beck & Beck, 2011; Ellis, 1973; Ellis & Doyle, 2016). We may not even know that we have these automatic thoughts, or that the thoughts are particularly relevant to the particular story we hold about love. Rather, we often will view the stories as accurate characterizations of what love is or should be, and as a result, we will view partners who fail to fulfill the requirements of a given story as being somehow not up to standard. Alternatively, we may look at ourselves as not up to standard if we cannot meet the demands of the story we have about love relationships. Therefore, if a person views love as a business, but is unable, after several attempts, to form a business-based relationship, the person may view him- or herself as a "failure" in love.

Fifth, stories of love involve complementary roles. These roles may or may not be symmetrical. We seek out a partner who shares our story or story profile, or at least who has a story or set of stories compatible with our own. But we do not necessarily seek out someone who is exactly like ourselves. Rather, we may seek out a partner who shares a story or similar story, but who is complementary to us with respect to the role the partner plays within that story. Thus, individuals seek out others who are, in one way, similar, but in another way, different. Looked at this way, neither similarity theory (Byrne, 1971) nor complementarity theory (Kerckhoff & Davis, 1962) is correct in its assertions about love. Rather, we seek similarity of stories but, in many instances, complementarity of roles.

Sixth, any given story may have both adaptive advantages and disadvantages. How adaptive a story is may depend on the demands of a given cultural milieu.

Seventh, some stories have better potential for success than do other stories. Some stories, such as an art story, may have a "short shelf life" and thus lack sustainability over the long term, whereas other stories, such as a travel story, are more likely to last a lifetime.

Eighth, stories serve as both causes and effects: The stories interact with the rest of our lives. Stories may cause us to behave in certain ways, but also to bring out certain kinds of behavior in others. At the same time, our life experience may modify the stories we have. Our stories are so inextricably intertwined with everything else in our lives that we cannot easily point to what is cause and what is effect.

All of us prefer some stories over others. We are likely to find partners differentially satisfying as a function of the extent to which those stories match our more-preferred rather than less-preferred stories.

Stories can be understood, in part, in terms of prototypical conceptions of meaning (Rosch, 1973, 1978), which have been applied in studies of love and have been shown to yield useful models of how people understand love (e.g. Barnes & Sternberg, 1997; Fehr, 1988; Fehr & Russell, 1991). For example, a prototypical feature of love would be intimacy. On the prototypical view, conceptions of love do not have defining features, but rather characteristic features that, although not necessary and sufficient, are more or less suggestive of a construct. For example, if someone has a "mystery story," there may be no defining features that uniquely identify that story as a mystery story, but rather prototypical features that are characteristic of mysteries (e.g. a mystery in need of a solution, a detective attempting to solve the mystery, a mysterious figure whom the detective is trying to understand).

The theory of love as a story is consistent within a tradition of attempting to understand the role of narrative in people's lives (Bruner, 1990; Cohler, 1982; Josselson & Lieblich, 1993; McAdams, 1993; Murray & Holmes, 1994; Sarbin, 1986; Taylor, 1989). Stories also have some relation to other psychological constructs, such as scripts (Schank & Abelson, 1977) and schemas, whether adaptive (Piaget, 1972) or maladaptive (Young & Klosko, 1993).

Data

My colleagues and I performed two validation studies testing some aspects of the theory of love as a story (Sternberg, Hojjat, & Barnes, 2001). We devised a Likert-scale-based questionnaire to assess people's stories. We used such a questionnaire for narratives because preliminary qualitative data revealed that people do not know their own stories and because a scale more easily provides quantitative tests of the theory.

Participants were all college students aged seventeen years and older. All participating individuals either were presently in a close relationship or had been in one in the near past. All participants were primarily heterosexual.

All participants received a scale based on the theory of love as a story. Examples of items included the following:

1. *Addiction:* "If my partner were to leave me, my life would be completely empty."
2. *Art:* "Physical attractiveness is quite honestly the most essential characteristic that I look for in a partner."
3. *Business:* "I believe close relationships are partnerships, just like most business relationships."
4. *Fantasy:* "I think people owe it to themselves to wait for the partner they have always dreamed about."
5. *Game:* "I view my relationships as games; the uncertainty of winning or losing is part of the excitement of the game."
6. *Garden:* "I believe a good relationship is attainable only if you are willing to spend the time and energy to care for it, just as you need to care for a garden."

Participants also received other scales, such as the Triangular Love Scale.

In the first study, we investigated the reliability of the love-stories scale and validated the scale, looking in two different ways (hierarchical cluster analysis and principal-components analysis) at representations of the latent structure that underlies love stories. In the second study, we correlated scores on the love-stories scale to scores obtained for measures derived from other theories. We also tested the prediction that members of couples will be more happy with, and successful in, their intimate relationships if their profiles of stories better match each other's (see also Byrne, 1971). Of course, many other elements besides stories also enter into satisfaction in close relationships (see Gottman, 1994; Gottman & Silver, 2015; essays in Sternberg & Hojjat, 1997).

Stories were found to differ widely in popularity. The most popular stories in the theory, from most to least popular, were travel, gardening, democratic government, and history. The least popular stories were horror, collectors, autocratic government, and game (in order from least popular to more popular). There were significant sex differences: Men had a preference for art, pornography, sacrifice, and science fiction stories. Women showed a preference for the travel story.

Although all three components of the triangular theory of love – intimacy, passion, and commitment – were positively correlated with satisfaction, those stories that showed statistically significant correlations with satisfaction all showed *negative* correlations with the satisfaction ratings. The stories showing significant negative correlations with satisfaction were business, collector, game, governor, governed, horror (both terrorist and victim), humor (comedian), mystery (mystery figure), police (officer), recovery (helper), science fiction, and theater (both actor and audience). It thus appears that maladaptive stories are associated with dissatisfaction, but that adaptive stories are not associated with satisfaction. What matters is the match to the partner rather than the particular adaptive story.

Similarity theory holds that romantic partners who are more similar will be more likely to be attracted to each other and will be more likely to be satisfied in their close relationships. But similarity with respect to what attributes? In the second study, we examined similarity with respect to love stories, as well as other aspects of love in relationships. Overall, the results supported the prediction that having more similar stories (as well as triangular profiles of love) is related to greater happiness and satisfaction in close relationships. There was a sizable correlation (.65) between the story profiles of men and women involved in close relationships. In addition, as predicted by the theory, the degree of discrepancy (or difference) in couples' profiles of stories was negatively correlated with ratings of satisfaction (−.45).

Where Love Goes Wrong According to the Theory of Love as a Story

A number of things can go wrong in a loving relationship according to the theory of love as a story.

- *Maladaptive stories.* Although no stories in particular are associated with success, certain stories tend to fail. These are business, collector, game, governor, governed, horror (both terrorist and victim), humor (comedian), mystery (mystery figure), police (officer), recovery (helper), science fiction, and theater (both actor and audience).
- *Mismatching profiles of stories.* The two partners' profiles of stories mismatch. What they are looking for out of love in a relationship is simply different.
- *Mismatched top story in the profile.* Although the partners may have similar profiles, the story at the top of each partner's hierarchy of stories is different, resulting in friction as each partner tries to fulfill a different story.

- *Actions failing to match stories.* The actions of one or both partners do not match the stories underlying them. For example, the partners have a fairy-tale story but one partner turns out to be an indifferent prince (or princess), or worse, an evil prince (or princess).
- *Failure to adapt to a partner's stories.* No two partners are likely to have identical profiles of stories. So each partner ultimately has to adapt to the stories of a partner. One partner may not be able to adapt and so love in the relationship falters.
- *One adapts to the partner's stories, but does not like who one becomes.* One may adapt to a partner's stories but then find, usually over a period of time, that one no longer likes who one has become. One may not even recognize oneself anymore. One decides that one does not want to continue being the person one has become in the relationship as an adaptation to the partner's stories.
- *Changing stories no longer work.* Stories can change over periods of time. For example, a partner who originally had a fairy-tale story may decide that the fairy tale was nice in a courtship, but that in an actual marriage a business story is more appropriate. The other partner, however, feels cheated with the change of story and wants to stick with the original one.
- *A third person is a better profile match than one's partner.* A third person comes between the two individuals in a relationship, and however good the match may be for the original two partners, the third person provides an even better match than does the original partner.

Love Gone Awry: When Love Turns to Hate

It is interesting to note that hate can be characterized in the same way as love, with related triangular and story components (Sternberg, 2003; Sternberg & Sternberg, 2008).

The Triangular Theory

The triangular theory of hate has three components.

Negation of intimacy (distancing) in hate: Repulsion and disgust. The first component of hate is negation of intimacy. Intimacy involves creating closeness and connection; negation of intimacy involves the creation of distance. Distance is sought from a targeted individual because that individual arouses feelings of repulsion, disgust, and revulsion in the person who feels hate. At times, one may be in a loving relationship and then discover something about the partner that one did not initially know, usually because the information was kept under wraps, purposely or otherwise. In such cases, intimacy can change into repulsion and revulsion. For example, one may find that one's lover is cheating or that one's lover has a sordid past that he or she failed to reveal.

Passion in hate: Anger/fear. A second component of hate is passion. Passion expresses itself as intense fear or anger, typically in response to a threat. For example, love may transform itself into hate if one feels wronged by a partner (or by a member of one's family or by close neighbors). Crimes of passion committed toward individuals often arise from the sudden experiencing of hate because one feels wronged, perhaps by a family member. Most often, such wrongs are committed against those one has loved (and, oddly enough, may still love). Sometimes, love and hate may be experienced at the same time, as conflicting emotions.

Decision/commitment in hate: Devaluation/diminution through contempt. The third component of hate is decision/commitment. This is characterized by thoughts of devaluation and diminution of, as well as contempt for, the target. The target individual or group may seem barely human or even subhuman.

The Theory of Hate as a Story

Just as there are stories of love, so are there stories of hate. Because there are numerous stories (see Sternberg & Sternberg, 2008), only some will be described here.

- *The Stranger Story.* The hated partner is a stranger. One thought one knew one's partner, and now discovers that the partner one thought one knew either no longer exists or never existed in the first place. One is in a relationship with someone who now seems like a stranger.
- *The Impure Other Story.* The partner is now viewed as impure. In some countries, when a partner is raped, instead of feeling compassion, an individual (usually a male) feels that the partner is now impure and unworthy. The individual may feel that the partner actually invited the rape or otherwise was somehow colluding with the rapist – indeed, that perhaps it was not a rape after all. Or if a partner has an affair, that partner may now seem impure.
- *The Controller Story.* One comes to perceive that one's partner is not truly a loving partner, but rather is in the relationship in order to control one's life. One feels trapped by and then comes to hate the controller.

- *The Moral-Bankruptcy Story.* One discovers that one's partner is morally bankrupt. Perhaps one has discovered that the partner is involved in criminal activity, or espionage activity for money, or treasonous behavior.
- *The Enemy-of-God Story.* One comes to believe, indeed likely becomes convinced by others, that one's partner is actually an Enemy of God. In the case of cults, when one partner leaves a cult, the other members of that cult may try to convince the remaining partner that the partner who is leaving is an enemy of God. Or if one is married to someone of a different religion or group within a religion, others may try to convince one that believers in the other religion or religious doctrine are enemies of God.

There are a number of other stories. But the point in each one is that love quite rapidly can go awry if it turns into hate. Unfortunately, this is not infrequently the case, as can be confirmed by anyone who has watched nasty divorce battles.

Toxic Love for Leaders

The world has exhibited, in the past but also in current times, how toxic leaders can come to be beloved by followers (see Lipman-Blumen, 2006; Sternberg, in press). Usually, these toxic leaders are highly charismatic – at least to their followers – and love for these leaders can lead to moral disengagement on the part of their followers (Bandura, 2016; Sternberg, 2012).

At present, there are toxic leaders in charge of countries in every continent of the world. These leaders are often beloved by their followers, and often held in contempt by those who do not count themselves among their followers. The leaders are often sociopathic and commit flagrant moral transgressions, which are then excused or even condoned on the part of followers, including religious followers who may view them as modern-day "saviors" of some sort in a warped religion or addiction story. The flawed toxic leaders come to be viewed as heroes, when in fact their only concern is with themselves. Many in the world thought that such toxic love had ended with the toxic leaders of the twentieth century – Hitler, Stalin, Mussolini, and the like. But not only is the world witnessing a rebirth of toxic leaders, but also a rebirth of movements to re-idolize the highly flawed toxic leaders of the past, such as Stalin. Love for these toxic leaders is perhaps the most baneful current example of love having gone awry.

In every case I have been able to locate, toxic leaders feed on a sense of grievance. They appeal to the worst instincts in people, convincing their followers that their grievances are justified and that, moreover, they are caused by an identifiable group of people, who must now be punished (or killed) to make up for the sins they have committed. The story of toxic leaders appealing to grievances is so old that it is surprising in some ways that it still works, but apparently it works as well in the twenty-first century as it ever has before. People are ready to be taken in today, just as they were in the twentieth century and in ancient times.

Conclusion

Love comprises triangles and stories. The triangles characterize the structure of love. They are formed from three distinct but interrelated components: intimacy, passion, and commitment. Different combinations of these three components yield different kinds of love. Each of the three components is strongly associated with happiness and satisfaction in relationships. Partners tend to be happier when the amounts of love (sizes of triangles) and types of love (shapes of triangles) correspond.

Stories generate different kinds of triangles. The current version of the theory has twenty-six stories, although doubtless there are many more that could be added, especially if one considers stories across cultures. Each story involves two distinct roles. The roles may or may not be symmetrical. Stories develop through the confluence of personality and experience. No particular stories predict happiness and satisfaction in relationships, although some do predict dissatisfaction. Couples tend to be more satisfied with relationships if they have matching profiles of stories (i.e. agreement with respect to more-preferred and less-preferred stories).

Love can go awry either through flawed triangles or through flawed stories. Once love goes awry, it is a nontrivial task to get it back on track. Most often, love falters because triangles or stories fail to match between partners. A problem that plagues the world of today as the world of yesterday is the toxic leader, who may be beloved by his followers but held in contempt by those who do not follow him (and usually it is a "him").

In sum, we experience love in terms of intimacy, passion, and commitment, and what experience we have depends on the story or stories that give rise to these three components of the triangle of love.

Note

The Triangular Love Scale is in Sternberg (1998a). The Love Stories Scale is in Sternberg (1998b). See also Sternberg (2013).

References

Aron, A., & Tomlinson, J. M. (this volume). Love as expansion of the self. In R. J. Sternberg & K. Sternberg (Eds.), *The new psychology of love* (2nd ed., pp. 1–24). New York: Cambridge University Press.

Aron, A., & Westbay, L. (1996). Dimensions of the prototype of love. *Journal of Personality and Social Psychology, 70*(3), 535–551.

Bandura, A. (2016). *Moral disengagement.* New York: Worth.

Barnes, M. L., & Sternberg, R. J. (1997). A hierarchical model of love. In R. J. Sternberg & M. Hojjat (Eds.), *Satisfaction in close relationships* (pp. 79–101). New York: Guilford Press.

Beck, A. T. (1976). *Cognitive therapy and the emotional disorders.* New York: International Universities Press.

Beck, J. S., & Beck, A. T. (2011). *Cognitive behavior therapy: Basics and beyond.* New York: Guilford Press.

Bruner, J. (1990). *Acts of meaning.* New York: Cambridge University Press.

Byrne, D. (1971). *The attraction paradigm.* New York: Academic Press.

Cohler, B. J. (1982). Personal narrative and the life course. In P. Baltes & O. G. Brim, Jr. (Eds.), *Life span development and behavior* (Vol. 4, pp. 205–241). New York: Academic Press.

Ellis, A. (1973). Rational-emotive therapy. In R. J. Corsini (Ed.), *Current psychotherapies.* Itasca, IL: Peacock.

Ellis, A., & Doyle, K. (2016). *How to control your anxiety before it controls you.* New York: Citadel.

Fehr, B. (1988). Prototype analysis of the concepts of love and commitment. *Journal of Personality and Social Psychology, 55*, 557–579.

(this volume). Everyday conceptions of love. In R. J. Sternberg & K. Sternberg (Eds.), *The new psychology of love* (2nd ed., pp. 154–182). New York: Cambridge University Press.

Fehr, B., & Russell, J. A. (1991). Concept of love viewed from a prototype perspective. *Journal of Personality and Social Psychology, 60*, 425–438.

Feybesse, C., & Hatfield, E. (this volume). Passionate love. In R. J. Sternberg & K. Sternberg (Eds.), *The new psychology of love* (2nd ed., pp. 183–207). New York: Cambridge University Press.

Gottman, J. (1994). *Why marriages succeed or fail.* New York: Simon & Schuster.

Gottman, J., & Silver, N. (2015). *The seven principles for making marriage work: A practical guide from the nation's foremost relationship expert.* New York: Harmony.

Hatfield, E., & Walster, G. W. (1981). *A new look at love.* Reading, MA: Addison-Wesley.

Hazan, C., & Shaver, P. (1987). Romantic love conceptualized as an attachment process. *Journal of Personality and Social Psychology, 52*, 511–524.

Hendrick, C., & Hendrick, S. S. (1986). A theory and method of love. *Journal of Personality and Social Psychology, 50*, 392–402.

(this volume). Styles of romantic love. In R. J. Sternberg & K. Sternberg (Eds.), *The new psychology of love* (2nd ed., pp. 223–239). New York: Cambridge University Press.

Josselson, R., & Lieblich, A. (Eds.) (1993). *The narrative study of lives.* Newbury Park, CA: Sage.

Kerckhoff, A. C., & Davis, K. E. (1962). Value consensus and need complementarity in mate selection. *American Sociological Review, 27*, 295–303.

Lee, J. A. (1977). A topology of styles of loving. *Personality and Social Psychology Bulletin, 3*, 173–182.

Lipman-Blumen, J. (2006). *The allure of toxic leaders.* New York: Oxford University Press.

McAdams, D. P. (1993). *Stories we live by.* New York: Morrow.
    (2013). *The redemptive self: Stories Americans live by.* New York: Oxford University Press.

Mikulincer, M., & Shaver, P. R. (this volume). A behavioral systems approach to romantic love relationships: Attachment, caregiving, and sex. In R. J. Sternberg & K. Sternberg (Eds.), *The new psychology of love* (2nd ed., pp. 259–279). New York: Cambridge University Press.

Murray, S. L., & Holmes, J. G. (1994). Storytelling in close relationships: The construction of confidence. *Personality and Social Psychology Bulletin, 20*, 650–663.

Piaget, J. (1972). *The psychology of intelligence.* Totowa, NJ: Littlefield Adams.

Rosch, E. (1973). On the internal structure of perceptual and semantic categories. In T. E. Moore (Ed.), *Cognitive development and the acquisition of language* (pp. 111–144). New York: Academic Press.
    (1978). Principles of categorization. In E. Rosch & B. B. Lloyd (Eds.), *Cognition and categorization* (pp. 27–48). Hillsdale, NJ: Lawrence Erlbaum.

Rubin, Z. (1970). Measurement of romantic love. *Journal of Personality and Social Psychology, 16*, 265–273.

Sarbin, T. (Ed.) (1986). *Narrative psychology: The storied nature of human conduct.* New York: Praeger.

Schank, R. C., & Abelson, R. A. (1977). *Scripts, plans, goals, and understanding.* Hillsdale, NJ: Lawrence Erlbaum.

Shaver, P. Hazan, C., & Bradshaw, D. (1988). Love as attachment: The integration of three behavioral systems. In R. J. Sternberg & M. L. Barnes (Eds.), *The psychology of love* (pp. 68–99). New Haven, CT: Yale University Press.

Sternberg, R. J. (1986). A triangular theory of love. *Psychological Review, 93*, 119–135.
    (1988a). *The triangle of love.* New York: Basic Books.
    (1988b). Triangulating love. In R. J. Sternberg & M. L. Barnes (Eds.), *The psychology of love* (pp. 119–138). New Haven, CT: Yale University Press.
    (1994). Love is a story. *The General Psychologist, 30*, 1–11.
    (1995). Love as a story. *Journal of Social and Personal Relationships, 12*, 541–546.
    (1996). Love stories. *Personal Relationships, 3*, 59–79.
    (1997). A construct-validation of a Triangular Love Scale. *European Journal of Social Psychology, 27*, 313–335.

(1998a). *Cupid's arrow*. New York: Cambridge University Press.

(1998b). *Love is a story*. New York: Oxford University Press.

(2003). A duplex theory of hate: Development and application to terrorism, massacres, and genocide. *Review of General Psychology, 7*(3), 299–328.

(2006). A duplex theory of love. In R. J. Sternberg & K. Weis (Eds.), *The new psychology of love* (pp. 184–199). New Haven, CT: Yale University Press.

(2007). Triangular theory of love. In R. Baumeister & K. Vohs (Eds.), *Encyclopedia of social psychology* (Vol. 2, pp. 997–998). Los Angeles, CA: Sage.

(2012). A model for ethical reasoning. *Review of General Psychology, 16*, 319–326.

(2013). Measuring love. *The Psychologist, 26*(2), 101.

(in press). Wisdom, foolishness, and toxicity: How does one know which is which? In M. Mumford (Ed.), *Leader skills*. New York: Taylor & Francis.

Sternberg, R. J., & Barnes, M. L. (1985). Real and ideal others in romantic relationships. *Journal of Personality and Social Psychology, 49*, 1586–1608.

Sternberg, R. J., & Grajek, S. (1984). The nature of love. *Journal of Personality and Social Psychology, 55*, 345–356.

Sternberg, R. J., & Hojjat, M. (Eds.) (1997). *Satisfaction in close relationships*. New York: Guilford Press.

Sternberg, R. J., Hojjat, M., & Barnes, M. L. (2001). Empirical aspects of a theory of love as a story. *European Journal of Personality, 15*, 1–20.

Sternberg, K., & Sternberg, R. J. (2013). Love. In H. Pashler (Ed.), *Encyclopedia of the mind*. Thousand Oaks, CA: Sage.

Sternberg, R. J., & Sternberg, K. (2008). *The nature of hate*. New Haven, CT: Yale University Press.

Taylor, C. (1989). *Sources of the self*. Cambridge, MA: Harvard University Press.

Thibaut, J. W., & Kelley, H. H. (1959). *The social psychology of groups*. New York: Wiley.

Weis, K., & Sternberg, R. J. (2008). The nature of love. In S. F. Davis & W. Buskist (Eds.), *21st century psychology: A reference handbook* (Vol. 2, pp. 134–142). Thousand Oaks, CA: Sage.

Young, J. E., & Klosko, J. S. (1993). *Reinventing your life*. New York: Dutton.

CHAPTER 15

When Love Goes Awry (Part 2): Application of an Augmented Duplex Theory of Love to Personal and Situational Factors in Jealousy and Envy

Robert J. Sternberg, Navjot Kaur, and Elisabeth J. Mistur

At sixteen years of age, a co-author of this chapter fell madly and all-consumingly in love – or so he thought – with the student sitting in front of him in his biology class. As it turned out, the love was "infatuated love" (Sternberg, 1986), but he did not know that at the time. To him, she was his "true love." There was a problem, however. The woman – call her "Jane" – had a boyfriend. He was not just any boyfriend, but also the captain of the high-school soccer team. Bob found himself extremely envious of the boyfriend – call him "John" – because of Bob's strong feelings toward Jane; but his envy was tempered by the fact that he knew he could never have Jane as a girlfriend because, he thought, he did not deserve her, whereas John did. Bob not only was not the captain of the soccer team; he actually had flunked out of the team. And there was another tempering factor: Jane did not seem to care at all about Bob. His love was blatantly unrequited. The story of Bob's envy – what created it and what tempered it – is, in the small, the story of this research report.

In the context of romance, we will view jealousy as involving an individual (the jealous romantic partner), a romantic partner (the other romantic partner in what has been a dyadic relationship), and a rival who is perceived as a threat to the romantic relationship between the individual and the other romantic partner. We will view envy as involving an individual (the envious individual), a potential romantic partner, and a rival with whom the potential romantic partner is involved in a dyadic relationship, or perceived to be involved by the envious individual. This distinction roughly follows that of Parrott (1991), Parrott and Smith (1993), and Smith (2008). Thus, as the terms are used here, jealousy involves retention of what one believes one has that is under threat, whereas envy involves the potential acquisition of what one believes one does not have because of an existing threat (typically another romantic partner). Romantic jealousy and envy both consist of social triangles, such as of Bob, Jane, and John. But the triangles for jealousy and envy are different (Miller, 2014). (In this chapter, we will discuss only heterosexual romantic relationships, as those are what we studied, but many of the same principles might apply to other kinds of relationships as well.) Although we make a distinction between jealousy and envy here, we recognize that, in everyday parlance, the terms are sometimes used interchangeably.

Introduction

Background Research on Jealousy

Jealousy typically involves feelings of hurt, anger, and fear (Guerrero, Trost, & Yoshimura, 2005). Envy may involve similar feelings, but in reference to what one wants rather than what one has. In the case of envy, the hurt and anger are because one does not have the desired partner, and the fear is that one never will get the partner. The feelings are presumably not identical, however, because in one case one wishes to retain what one has, and in the other case one wishes to acquire what one does not have.

Romantic jealousy has been far more studied than has been romantic envy, and hence we focus on jealousy in our introduction. Jealousy is sometimes viewed as being of two types, reactive, when one responds to an actual threat, and suspicious, when one is suspicious despite no clear evidence that one's partner has gone astray (Bringle & Buunk, 1991). In practice, the distinction between the two is not always so clear, because often one has only probabilistic information that one's romantic partner is interested in someone else. And a given piece of information often is subject to multiple interpretations. If one's partner, for example, is spending a lot of time with another individual of the opposite sex, is it to get work done, to pursue a harmless friendship, to chat about current issues, to pursue a romantic relationship, or some combination of such factors?

In the four studies reported in this chapter we investigate the relative importances of two kinds of predictors of each of jealousy and envy, personal (internal) and situational (external) ones. We further investigate sex differences in factoring and prediction, but our studies were not designed in particular to explore those variables most likely to elicit sex differences, as described below. Before describing our studies, some review of background literature is in order. This review starts with a consideration of diverse theories and kinds of theories of romantic jealousy. They fall into several distinct categories.

One kind of theory is evolutionary (e.g. Buss, 2016). On this view, selection pressure over long periods of time, combined with certain forms of environmental inputs (such as mate poachers), has resulted in prewired responses to circumstances provoking jealousy. These responses in turn are influenced by selective pressures in the environment. This theory gives rise to the hypothesis that men and women tend to be jealous in differing degrees as a result of different forms of infidelity, in particular, sexual versus emotional infidelity. This view suggests that whereas female jealousy is more likely to be triggered by a mate's emotional infidelity, male jealousy is more likely to be triggered by a mate's sexual infidelity (Buss, 2016; Buss, Larsen, Westin, & Semmelroth, 1992; Edlund & Sagarin, 2017; Harris, 2004; Harris & Darby, 2010). These gender differences are viewed, in this theory, to be a consequence of the different adaptive challenges men and women have faced over evolutionary time that are relevant to the production of viable offspring. In particular, males have had more reason evolutionarily to be concerned about whether they are truly the father, as prior to DNA testing, there was no way to know for sure; women, in contrast, have had more reason evolutionarily to be concerned with whether the father will provide sufficient resources for them to be able to raise the children resulting from the sexual union with the man.

In general, while some studies show more support for jealousy over emotional infidelity regardless of gender and sexual orientation (Harris, 2003), other studies show that, contrary to the evolutionary hypothesis, females actually are more predisposed to jealousy over sexual infidelity, even in sexually open marriages (Buunk, 1981). The preponderance of evidence currently appears to be generally consistent with an evolutionary interpretation (Edlund & Sagarin, 2017).

More recent research on gender differences in jealousy, however, found that men and women sometimes have similar reactions to infidelity. This research does not show a gender difference in predispositions to jealousy over sexual or emotional infidelity (Berman & Frazier 2005). Form of response seems to make a difference. Use of a forced-choice response with a continuous scale measure has seemingly attenuated the sex difference. Contrary to the evolutionary hypothesis, both men and women showed more predisposition toward jealousy over sexual infidelity than over emotional infidelity (DeSteno, Bartlett, Braverman, & Salovey, 2002). Others (Barrett et al., 2006; Buss, 2018; Buss et al., 2000), however, have questioned the validity of this finding and the validity of the methodology underlying it for testing evolutionary hypotheses.

Another approach to understanding jealousy is through attachment styles. This perspective derives from the work of Hazan and Shaver (1987) on attachment styles. Hazan and Shaver proposed that romantic relationships are formed through attachment processes that are similar to the attachment between infants and their caregivers. Three common attachment styles are secure, insecure-avoidant, and anxious. Romantic jealousy arises when this attachment relationship is threatened by a rival or third-party individual. Different attachment styles can produce different reactions to potential relationship threats in individuals (Sharpsteen & Kirkpatrick, 1997). In particular, someone who is anxiously attached is particularly susceptible to jealousy because the individual tends more or less continually to feel that the relationship is under threat, whether it really is or not.

Whereas some research suggests that insecurely attached individuals will show more signs of jealousy (Buunk, 1997), other findings show that securely attached individuals are more likely to show jealous anger (Sharpsteen & Kirkpatrick, 1997). To make sense of these inconsistent findings, Harris and Darby (2010) proposed a two-stage model of attachment and threat suggesting that the stage of threat moderates how an attachment style affects the jealous reactions of an individual. The first stage in this model is the appraisal of the threat to the romantic relationship. Individuals have different propensities in appraising possible threats. Individuals who have low thresholds for threat appraisal are more likely to appraise the presence of an interloper or potential rival as a threat to the relationship, whereas individuals who have high thresholds are less likely to appraise the presence of another interloper or potential rival as a threat to the relationship.

Whereas the first stage of the two-stage model focuses on appraisal of the threat, the second stage focuses on the reaction to the threat. Once a potential rival has passed the threat threshold, he or she is considered an actual threat and individuals start to engage in coping mechanisms to determine how they will react to the threat and deal with their feelings of jealousy. Secure individuals tend to have positive mental models of themselves, their relationships, and others. This security results in high thresholds for appraisal of threat. There are two contradictory hypotheses regarding the jealousy experiences of securely attached individuals. These are the secure/low-reactive hypothesis and the secure/high-reactive hypothesis.

According to the former hypothesis, secure individuals feel less jealous than do others, because they have successful relationships in which both partners are happy and are also invested in the relationship (Harris & Darby, 2010; Kirkpatrick & Hazan, 1994). As a result, secure individuals have less reason to fear potential threats to the relationship. In contrast, the secure/high-reactive hypothesis suggests that because secure individuals place more value on attachment relationships, they will react with more jealousy and may be more prone to jealous anger than are others (Harris & Darby, 2010; Sharpsteen & Kirkpatrick, 1997). According to this hypothesis, secure individuals are more likely to employ jealousy as an emotional tool to protect their valued relationships. This secure/high-reactive hypothesis is consistent with the functional-evolutionary approach, which suggests that jealousy is an evolutionary adaptation to preserve social and romantic attachment relationships.

There is empirical support for both hypotheses. To reconcile these findings, Harris and Darby (2010) suggested that attachment style may impact jealousy based on whether the secure individual is in the process of appraising a potential threat to the relationship or has already deemed a definite threat to the romantic relationship. In the first stage (appraisal of threat), secure individuals are less likely to show bouts of jealousy. In the second stage (reaction to the threat), secure individuals are more likely to react with jealous anger once the threat is established as certain.

Understanding of jealousy also can arise through attribution theory. According to this theory, there are three main types of attributions that can be made about the actions of others – causality, controllability, and intent (Weiner, 1995). Bauerle, Amirkhan, and Hupka (2002) suggested that the attributions an individual makes about his or her romantic partners actions in a jealousy-inducing situation play a large role in whether the individual feels jealous. Their research suggested that people feel more jealous when their partner personally caused, had control over, was responsible for, and intentionally committed actions that induced jealousy. However, when the partner did not cause, had no control over, was not responsible for, and did not intentionally commit the jealousy-inducing action, participants did not feel jealous. Therefore, the appraisals and attributions an individual makes about his or her partner's actions, as opposed to the actions themselves, may lead to differential levels of jealousy, or to no jealousy at all (Harris & Darby, 2010).

Other researchers have looked at the impact of jealousy and other relationship variables on satisfaction in romantic relationships. For example, Barelds and Barelds-Dijkstra (2007) found that partners' levels of reactive jealousy – jealousy in response to one or more specific events – related positively to relationship quality, whereas partners' levels of anxious jealousy – jealousy not tied to specific events – were negatively related to relationship quality.

Afifi and Reichert (1996) studied the effects of relational uncertainty on jealousy. They found that participants who reported high levels of relational uncertainty were *more likely to experience* but *less likely to express* feelings of romantic jealousy than were other subjects. They concluded that there are contrasting patterns for the experience, on the one hand, and the expression, on the other hand, of romantic jealousy. They suggested that partners who felt high levels of relational uncertainty and jealousy were less likely to express their feelings of romantic jealousy because they feared a response of an ultimatum (i.e. an end to the relationship) for doing so.

Although we may look at jealousy as an adverse event, it can have a positive side as well. Mathes (1986, 1991) found that participants who were rated high on jealousy scales in 1978 were more likely to remain with the same partner in 1985. In contrast, those who rated lower on the jealousy scale were less likely to have remained in the same relationship as in 1978. Mathes theorized that jealousy can serve as a safeguard mechanism against relationship threats (i.e. potential rivals). People who are jealous protect what they believe is theirs. Moreover, the fact that they are jealous shows that they have a serious interest in the partner (Buss, 2011).

Relationship uncertainty is also significantly correlated with romantic jealousy. More relationship uncertainty among partners is associated with feelings of suspicion and anxiety over potential relationship threats and rivals (Knobloch, Solomon, & Cruz, 2001). It appears that uncertainty in relationships leads to a low threshold of subjective threat appraisal, which in turn results in high levels of jealousy among partners who are uncertain about the present and/or future status of their romantic relationship.

For many individuals, romantic relationships play an important role in self-esteem and self-worth. As a result, a threat to a valued romantic relationship can serve as a threat to an individual's self-esteem (Salovey & Rodin, 1991; Salovey & Rothman, 1991). According to a "domain-relevance hypothesis," potential rivals pose a greater threat to a romantic relationship if the rival is viewed as superior to an individual in domains the individual considers crucial to his or her definition of the self. DeSteno and Salovey (1996) found that individuals considered rivals a greater threat to a romantic relationship if the rivals had qualities (e.g. fame, popularity, intelligence, attractiveness, etc.) that individuals valued in themselves, especially if those qualities were also valued by their loved one. If the rival exceeded the individual in those qualities, the rival posed a particular threat.

Availability of alternative partners also can affect levels of jealousy. Rydell, McConnell, and Bringle (2004) explored how attractiveness of alternative relationship partners affects level of jealousy in relation to commitment. They found that participants in committed relationships experienced more jealousy when they were induced to consider having unattractive alternative relationship partners. However, when participants were induced to consider having attractive relationship alternatives, there was no association between commitment and level of jealousy.

Background Research on Envy

There is a somewhat substantial body of literature on envy (see, e.g. Salovey, 1991; Schoek, 1969; Smith, 2008; Smith & Kim, 2007), although there is much less theory and research specifically on romantic envy than there is on romantic jealousy. We therefore are much briefer in our review of the literature on envy.

Envy is often characterized as a negative emotion (Schoeck, 1969; Schimmel, 1997; see also Smith & Kim, 2007). However, envy can be classified into two types: benign envy and malicious envy. Current empirical findings support experiential and behavioral differences between these two qualitatively distinct types of envy (Van de Ven, Zeelenberg, & Pieters, 2009). Whereas the experience of benign envy is associated with a motivation to move up in the world and encourages an envying individual to improve his or her own position, the experience of malicious envy is associated with the motivation to pull down the envied individual in order to damage the position of the other (Van de Ven et al., 2009).

Envy is often accompanied by feelings of hostility toward the object of the envy. One hypothesis concerning such hostility was tested in a study conducted by Smith et al. (1994). These investigators predicted that the feeling of hostility experienced in envy is associated with a subjective belief of unfairness about the envy-producing differences in circumstances between the envying individual and envied person. The researchers suggested that this sense of unfairness is evoked by the envied person's advantage, which in turn is perceived by the envying individual as unjust. To test this hypothesis, subjects were asked to write autobiographical accounts of experiences in which they had felt envious and to indicate how unfair they perceived the envied individual's advantage to be. The data led

Smith et al. (1994) to conclude that hostile envy did indeed result from a sense of unfairness and/or injustice felt by the envying individual.

An evolutionary framework for understanding envy predicts sex-differentiated features in envy that are relevant to evolutionary reproductive success as well as to domains in which both men and women have faced qualitatively different adaptive problems (Hill & Buss, 2006). Hill and Buss (2006) hypothesized that feelings of envy among males and females would likely differ in the domain of sexual competition, particularly reflecting differences in qualities of mate competition. They found that women experienced more envy in situations in which the envied same-sex peers were more attractive than themselves, whereas men were more likely to experience envy when their rivals in mate competition had access to more financial resources than they did themselves (Hill & Buss, 2006).

According to Hill and Buss (2006), one functional role of envy is to alert individuals about the fitness-relevant advantages that are enjoyed by their rivals. Envy then motivates individuals to acquire the same advantages. Many individuals judge their own success in regard to resource competition based on social comparisons relative to their competitors (Hill & Buss, 2006). Thus, the envy experience is likely to occur when an individual holds an inferior position in comparison with a rival in a domain of high personal relevance (Hill & Buss, 2008; Parrott & Smith 1993; Salovey & Rodin, 1991, Smith & Kim, 2007; D'Arms & Kerr, 2008). Social competition is important for survival and reproductive success, so adaptations designed to generate distress as a response to being outperformed by competitors or rivals likely favors evolutionary selection (Buss, 1988; Hill & Buss, 2008).

Our Research

Our own focus was a bit different from that of most past studies. In particular, we were interested in developing a model of the structure of jealousy as well as of envy, and then comparing the two structures. We further were interested in how well structural variables purported to be involved in jealousy and envy would predict actual perceived levels of jealousy and envy, respectively. Our approach was to use both (a) hypothetical scenarios by which we studied participants' perceptions of third parties involved in relationships and (b) actual real-life relationship events by which we studied subjects' own past and current experiences. In the first kind of situation, participants read scenarios and rated described partners on a set of jealousy or envy-related variables, such as how much the described individual appeared to need, want, and deserve the other romantic partner (or, in the case of envy, the desired romantic partner). In the second kind of situation, subjects rated their own relationships.

Theoretical Framework

The theoretical framework for our research is an augmentation of a duplex theory of love proposed previously (see Sternberg, 1986, 1988, 1995, 1998a, 1998b, 2006). The theory contains triangular and story elements.

The Triangular Theory of Love

According to the triangular theory, love comprises three components internal to the individual – intimacy, passion, and commitment. Intimacy refers to feelings of caring, trust, equity/fairness, communication, and so on. Passion refers to needing and intense longing. Passion leads one especially to be susceptible to jealousy and envy. Commitment refers to durability – that the relationship can survive threats. All three components, we believe, are relevant to jealousy and envy. With regard to jealousy, one is more likely to feel jealous if one feels that despite one's caring, trust, and fairness, the relationship is nevertheless threatened. With regard to passion, one is more likely to feel jealous if the fulfillment of one's intense needs are threatened. And with regard to commitment, one is more likely to feel jealous if the long-term viability of a valued relationship is threatened. Similarly, one is more likely to become envious of another individual if one feels intimacy, passion, and/or commitment toward a person, but those feelings are not reciprocated and instead are directed toward another individual. However, these internal states are not adequate, in and of themselves, to account for jealousy. Hence the need for augmentation of the triangular theory to take into account an external variable, in particular, the threat posed by another to an actual or desired relationship.

The Theory of Love as a Story

Sternberg has also proposed in the duplex theory that love can be understood in terms of stories (Sternberg, 1998b, 2006). Love triangles emanate from stories. Almost all of us are exposed to large numbers of diverse stories that convey different conceptions of how love can be understood. Some of these stories may be explicitly intended as love stories; others may have love stories embedded in the context of larger stories. Either way, we are provided with varied opportunities – through experience, literature, media, and so forth – to observe multiple conceptions of what love can be. As a result of our exposure to such stories, we form over time our own stories of what love is or should be.

The interaction of our personal attributes with the environment – the latter of which we in part create – leads to the development of stories about love that we then seek to fulfill, to the extent possible, in our lives. Various potential partners fit these stories to greater or lesser degrees. We are more likely to succeed in close relationships with people whose stories more, rather than less closely match our own.

Although the number of possible stories is probably infinite, certain genres of stories seem to keep emerging again and again in pilot analyses we have done of literature, film, and people's oral descriptions of relationships. Because the stories we have analyzed were from participants in the United States, our listing is likely to show some degree of cultural bias.

The stories contain some overlap, so that people with certain stories higher in their hierarchies might be expected to have others as well higher in their hierarchies. This non-exhaustive working list of stories is based upon an analysis of love stories in literature, previous psychological research by the authors and others, and on interpretations of informally gathered case material.

Certain stories render lovers particularly susceptible to jealousy and envy. These are as follows:

1. *Addiction.* Strong anxious attachment; clinging behavior; anxiety at thought of losing partner.
2. *Art.* Love of partner for physical attractiveness; importance to person of partner's always looking good. The lover does not want to lose such a precious piece of art, or wants to attain one.
3. *Business.* Relationships as business propositions; money is power; partners in close relationships as business partners. Jealousy and envy reflect a betrayal of the business.
4. *Cookbook.* Doing things a certain way (recipe) results in the relationship being more likely to work out; departure from recipe for success leads to increased likelihood of failure. Jealousy and envy arise from actions on the part of someone else that are not part of the recipe.
6. *Fantasy.* Often expects to be saved by a knight in shining armor or to marry a princess and live happily ever after. Knights and princesses are definitely not supposed to betray each other.
7. *Game.* Love as a game or sport. Jealousy or envy may be incited as part of the game.

8. *Gardening.* Relationships need to be continually nurtured and tended to. A threat to the relationship threatens to destroy the garden that has been so carefully attended to.

9. *Government.* (a) Autocratic. One partner dominates or even controls other. (b) Democratic. Two partners equally share power. One becomes envious (of the other partner) when one's power does not match the power one wishes to have.

10. *History.* Events of relationship form an indelible record; keep a lot of records – mental or physical elements. One becomes jealous when a third person starts to change the history to become a history one no longer desires or takes pride in. The new history may be one that is taking the relationship to a future history one hopes to avoid.

11. *Horror.* Relationships become interesting when you terrorize or are terrorized by your partner. One way of terrorizing a partner is through a simultaneous passionate relationship with someone else.

12. *House and Home.* Relationships have their core in the home, through its development and maintenance. Jealousy represents a violation of home turf.

13. *Humor.* Love is strange and funny. An external relationship may not seem funny to the threatened partner.

14. *Mystery.* Love is a mystery and you should not let too much of yourself be known. Many partners may like mystery up to the point at which the mystery involves an unknown other.

15. *Police.* You've got to keep close tabs on your partner to make sure he or she toes the line, or you need to be under surveillance to make sure you behave. The police officer in the relationship is always on guard for criminal behavior by his or her partner, such as straying with another.

16. *Pornography.* Love is dirty, and to love is to degrade or be degraded. Having an adulterous relationship may help create a pornographic environment for the adherent to this story.

18. *Religion.* Either views love as a religion, or love as a set of feelings and activities dictated by religion. An outside relationship may be seen as a violation of a religious principle.

19. *Sacrifice.* To love is to give of oneself or for someone to give of himself or herself to you. Nothing betrays sacrifice quite like one's partner, for whom one has made sacrifices, then seeing someone else.

21. *Science Fiction.* Feeling that partner is like an alien –incomprehensible and very strange. But partners often do not want a weird external threat to be part of the story.

22. *Sewing.* Love is whatever you make it, unless you don't like the sewing involving a third sewer.
23. *Theater.* Love is scripted, with predictable acts, scenes, and lines. An other threatening the relationship may not be part of the script.
24. *Travel.* Love is a journey. But partners may not want to journey into adulterous territory.
25. *War.* Love is a series of battles in a devastating but continuing war. An external threat can create a very serious war drama.

So both the triangular theory (through passion) and the theory of love as a story (through the stories noted above) have elements that produce jealousy and envy. What kinds of variables produce jealousy and envy?

We expected there to be two kinds of variables that would affect levels of jealousy and envy. The first kind of variable, based on the triangular theory, would be *internal or personal* – it would involve the individuals' feelings in the relationship. The second kind of variable would be *external or situational* – things not directly under the jealous or envious individual's control, particularly, how much of a threat a third party poses to an existing or hoped-for relationship.

Empirical Studies

We conducted four studies to investigate the augmented duplex theory as a basis for understanding jealousy and envy. We sought to determine how well two kinds of variables – internal and external – would predict jealousy (Studies 1 and 2) or envy (Studies 3 and 4). We summarize those studies here. There were no significant gender effects in any study, so we do not discuss gender effects further.

Study 1: Jealousy – Ratings for Hypothetical Scenarios

In Study 1, 219 undergraduate subjects, 63 males and 156 females at Cornell University, were asked various questions regarding scenarios in which two individuals are in a romantic relationship and one of the individuals is jealous of a third party the individual perceives to be a threat to the relationship.

We compiled two jealousy surveys, Survey A and Survey B, each containing sixteen scenarios that would typically arouse some level of romantic jealousy. Surveys A and B differed only by the names used for the characters in the scenarios, which were switched in order to balance gender and thereby eliminate gender as a confounding variable in the scenarios. Each scenario involved a jealous romantic partner (JRP), the other romantic partner (ORP), and an individual who served as a third party/threat (T).

All scenarios in Study 1 involved a JRP who was in a relationship with the ORP and a T who posed a threat to the romantic relationship between the jealous romantic partner and the other romantic partner in the relationship. Each jealousy scenario was followed by twelve questions asking the participants to provide a number on a scale of one (low) to ten (high), which assessed the participant's judgment regarding the level of each independent and dependent variable in the scenario.

Two examples of jealousy scenarios, from forms A and B respectively, are provided below:

Example 1: Jealousy Form A

Victoria and Chad are high-school sweethearts who got married a year after they graduated from the same high school. They grew up in the same suburban town in Connecticut and never traveled to other places before. In high school, Victoria and Chad were known to be "the best couple," and even shared the same friend circle. They recently moved into a small apartment in downtown Chicago where Victoria is interning as a makeup artist and Chad is preparing to start a graduate program in Data Science. Victoria wants Chad to attend fashion events and parties with her but he always refuses to go because he says these events keep him from focusing on his schoolwork. They both have started making new friends in their fields and Chad is starting to feel that he no longer enjoys Victoria's company when they are spending time together. Chad finds himself bored with his marriage and would rather invest his attention on his career than on Victoria. One night after Victoria returned home from a party slightly intoxicated, she kept on talking about her friend Anthony, who escorted her to some parties after Chad refused to go. The next morning Victoria asked Chad if he would be okay with the idea of an open marriage. Chad does not know how to respond to this and is convinced that Victoria has romantic feelings for Anthony.

On a scale of one to ten:

How much does Chad want to have an intimate relationship with Victoria?
How much does Chad deserve Victoria?
How fair is Victoria's treatment of Chad?
How much does Victoria care about Chad?
How much does Chad care about Victoria?

How realistic was Chad and Victoria's relationship before Anthony entered the picture?

How much does Chad need Victoria, either practically or emotionally?

How much does Chad trust Victoria?

How big of a threat is Anthony to Chad and Victoria's relationship?

How jealous is Chad of Anthony?

How jealous would you be if you were in Chad's situation? (You might or might not react the same way Chad did.)

How likely is the relationship between Chad and Victoria to work out given all the circumstances?

Example 2: Jealousy Form B

Chad and Victoria are high-school sweethearts who got married a year after they graduated from the same high school. They grew up in the same suburban town in Connecticut and never traveled to other places before. In high school, Chad and Victoria were known to be "the best couple," and even shared the same friend circle. They recently moved into a small apartment in downtown Chicago where Chad is interning as a makeup artist and Victoria is preparing to start a graduate program in Data Science. Chad wants Victoria to attend fashion events and parties with him but she always refuses to go because she says these events keep her from focusing on her schoolwork. They both have started making new friends in their fields and Victoria is starting to feel that she no longer enjoys Chad's company when they are spending time together. Victoria finds herself bored with her marriage and would rather invest her attention on her career than on Chad. One night after Chad returned home from a party slightly intoxicated, he kept on talking about his friend Rachel, who escorted him to some parties after Victoria refused to go. The next morning Chad asked Victoria if she would be okay with the idea of an open marriage. Victoria does not know how to respond to this and is convinced that Chad has romantic feelings for Rachel.

On a scale of one to ten:

How much does Victoria want to have an intimate relationship with Chad?

How much does Victoria deserve Chad?

How fair is Chad's treatment of Victoria?

How much does Chad care about Victoria?

How much does Victoria care about Chad?

How realistic was Victoria and Chad's relationship before Rachel entered the picture?

How much does Victoria need Chad, either practically or emotionally?

How much does Victoria trust Chad?

How big of a threat is Rachel to Victoria and Chad's relationship?

How jealous is Victoria of Rachel?

> How jealous would you be if you were in Victoria's situation? (You might or might not react the same way Victoria did.)
> How likely is the relationship between Victoria and Chad to work out given all the circumstances?

All participants received all materials either through Form A or Form B. Subjects were randomly assigned to take either Form A or Form B of the questionnaire. The ten independent variables in this study were want, deserve, treatment/fairness (ORP of the JRP), care (the JRP about the ORP), care (ORP about JRP), need, threat, trust, plausibility before threat, and plausibility after threat. The two dependent variables in this study were perceived jealousy felt by the JRP in the scenario and jealousy each of the participants would experience if he or she were the JRP in the scenario. These variables are described further below.

The independent variables *want, deserve, need,* and *plausibility* were manipulated in each scenario to portray them as either high or low (e.g. high want, low need, high deserve, low plausibility), resulting in two to the fourth power, or sixteen total permutations, that is, one scenario for each permutation.

There were ten independent variables with respect to prediction of jealousy.

Want (JRP, ORP). This variable assessed the participant's judgment of how much the jealous person wanted to be in an intimate relationship with the ORP(i.e. How much does the JRP want to have an intimate relationship with the ORP?).

Deserve (JRP, ORP). This variable assessed how much the participant felt the jealous person in the scenario deserved to be with the ORP (i.e. How much does the JRP deserve the ORP?).

Treatment/fairness (ORP of JRP). This variable tested how fairly the participant thought the ORP treated the JRP in the scenario (i.e. How fair is the ORP's treatment of the JRP?).

Care (JRP about ORP). This variable tested how much the participant thought the JRP cared about the ORP (i.e. How much does the JRP care about the ORP?).

Care (ORP about JRP). This variable tested how much the participant thought the ORP cared about the JRP in the scenario (i.e. How much does the ORP care about the JRP?).

Need (JRP for ORP). This variable tested how much the participant felt the JRP practically/emotionally needed the ORP (i.e. How much does the JRP need the ORP, either practically or emotionally?).

Trust (JRP toward ORP). This variable tested how much the participant felt the JRP in the scenario trusted the ORP (i.e. How much does the JRP trust the ORP?).

Threat (T toward JRP). This variable tested how great a threat the participant felt the T posed to the romantic relationship between the JRP and the ORP in the scenario (i.e. How big of a threat is T to the JRP and the ORP's relationship?).

Plausibility of relationship (before threat). This variable tested how realistic the participant felt the relationship between the JRP and the ORP in the scenario would have been before the T entered the picture (i.e. How realistic was the JRP and the ORP's relationship before T entered the picture?).

Plausibility of relationship (after threat). This variable tested the participant's view of how likely the relationship between the jealous person and romantic partner would be to last after the T entered the picture (i.e. How likely is the relationship between the JRP and the ORP to work out given all the circumstances?).

There were two dependent variables, a main one (perceived jealousy experienced by the JRP in the scenario) and a subsidiary one (hypothetical jealousy of the participant if he or she were the JRP in the scenario).

Jealousy (scenario). This variable tested how jealous the participant felt the JRP was of the T in the scenario (e.g. How jealous is the JRP of the T?).

Jealousy (hypothetical). This variable tested how jealous the participant felt he or she would feel if in the same situation as the JRP in the scenario (i.e. How jealous would you be if you were in the JRP's situation? You might or might not react the same way JRP did.).

We were interested in the extent to which the independent variables in the model would predict levels of jealousy in the JRP. We separately modeled the secondary dependent variable – the participant's own imagined jealousy in the situation – but we do not present the results of this dependent variable because the results were very close to those of the primary dependent variable, presumably because the two dependent variables were quite highly correlated (.75).

We used stepwise multiple regression. The variables that entered into a stepwise multiple regression were, in order, (1) threat, (2) need, (3) care of the ORP toward the JRP, and (4) want. Thus, there was one external factor–threat (from the augmentation of the duplex theory) and there were three internal factors – need, care, and want – from the original triangular theory, representing passion and intimacy, respectively. The successive stepwise values of multiple R were .63, .72, .74, and .75. The respective beta weights in the final model for the four variables were .42, .24, .15, and .15, the first three of which were statistically significant at the .001 level and the last of which was statistically significant at the .026 level. We thus accounted for about 56% of the variance in the data (adjusted: 55%), with an F (4, 214) of 68.72, $p < .001$.

Study 2: Jealousy – Self-ratings

In Study 2, participants were 132 individuals, including both male ($N = 24$), female ($N = 107$) and other ($N = 1$) undergraduate students enrolled in human development and psychology classes at Cornell University in Ithaca, New York.

Two self-compiled jealousy surveys, Survey A and Survey B, were used to assess the participants feelings of jealousy. Survey A asked the participants to reflect on feelings of jealousy in a present romantic relationship and survey B asked the participants to reflect on feelings of jealousy in a past romantic relationship. Additional materials included the Sternberg Triangular Love Scale. The surveys were created by researchers using Qualtrics Survey Software and made available for online participation using the Cornell University Department of Psychology SONA System Software.

Two examples of Jealousy forms A (present) and B (past) respectively, are provided below.

Example 1: Jealousy Form A

Reflect on a time during your romantic relationship in which you experienced at least some degree of jealousy. Reflect on the situational circumstances in this relationship that led you to feel jealous. In other words, think about a time you were afraid that you might lose your romantic partner because he or she might become romantically interested in another person.

Read the following questions and rate your feelings with respect to this romantic relationship.

On a scale of one to ten:

How much do you want to have an intimate relationship with your romantic
partner?

How much do you deserve your romantic partner?

How fair is your romantic partner's treatment toward you?

How much does your romantic partner care about you?

How much do you care about your romantic partner?

How realistic was yours and your romantic partner's relationship before
another person entered the picture?

How much do you need your romantic partner, either practically or
emotionally?

How much do you trust your romantic partner?

How big of a threat is the third person to your romantic relationship?

How jealous do you feel of the third person?

How likely is the relationship between you and your romantic partner to
work out, given all the circumstances?

Example 2: Jealousy Form B

Reflect on a time during your past romantic relationship in which you
experienced at least some degree of jealousy. Reflect on the situational
circumstances in this relationship that led you to feel jealous. In other words,
think about a time you were afraid that you would lose your romantic partner
because he or she might become romantically interested in another person.

Read the following questions and rate your feelings with respect to this
romantic relationship.

On a scale of one to ten:

How much did you want to have an intimate relationship with your
romantic partner?

How much did you deserve your romantic partner?

How fair was your romantic partner's treatment toward you?

How much did your romantic partner care about you?

How much did you care about your romantic partner?

How realistic was your and your romantic partner's relationship before
another person entered the picture?

How much did you need your romantic partner, either practically or
emotionally?

How much did you trust your romantic partner?

How big of a threat was the third person to your romantic relationship?

How jealous did you feel of the third person?

How likely was the relationship between you and your romantic partner to
work out, given all the circumstances?

The subjects of the experiment were assigned to one of two surveys, creating a between-subjects design; each participant received one of two surveys that we had created, one of which studied feelings of jealousy in a past romantic relationship, and one of which studied jealousy in a present romantic relationship. Each survey asked students to reflect on a past or present romantic relationship in which they experienced at least some degree of jealousy. In other words, they were asked to think about a time they were afraid that they might lose their romantic partner because he or she might become romantically interested in another person (a third-party individual or threat). The main dependent variable was jealousy, calculated by the participants' ratings. The independent variables were the participants' levels of need, want, trust, and deservingness for the person of their romantic interest, and their romantic relationship plausibility with the person of their romantic interest. The surveys consisted of eleven questions asking the participants to provide a number on a scale of one to ten, which assessed the participant's judgment regarding the level of each independent and dependent variable in the romantic relationship they reflected on. The subjects also were asked to complete the Sternberg Triangular Love Scale (Sternberg, 1998a).

The independent variables were the same as in Study 1, except that in this case, they pertained to one's own past or present relationship rather than to a relationship in a hypothetical scenario. The dependent variable was jealousy, but in one's own relationship rather than in a hypothetical one.

The variables that entered into a stepwise multiple regression were, in order, (1) threat, (2) need, and (3) trust by the JRP of the ORP. The successive stepwise values of multiple R were .71, .72, and .74. The respective beta weights in the final model for the four variables were .66, .19, and −.18, meaning that the last variable was a suppressor variable. The first variable was statistically significant at the .001 level, the second at the .01 level, and the third at the .012 level. We thus accounted for about 55% of the variance in the data (adjusted: 54%), with an F (3, 128) of 51.27, $p < .001$. Note that after threat, an external variable, was entered into the stepwise multiple regression, the internal variables that followed – need and trust – mattered relatively little, increasing the squared multiple correlation only from .71 to .74. Why was the contribution of the internal variables so minimal?

There was one particularly fascinating, perhaps stunning result in this study compared with Study 1. In Study 1, the internal variables showed high zero-order correlations with the jealousy ratings. For example, the zero-order correlations for three internal variables – need, want, and care of the jealous person for the significant other – with the jealousy ratings were .58,

.60, and .45, respectively, all significant at the .001 level. The correlation for an external variable, threat, was .63, also high. But in Study 2, where the ratings were about oneself rather than about some hypothetical other, the comparable zero-order correlations for the internal variables, respectively, were .00, .12, and –.02. Correlations of the Sternberg Triangular Love Scale (all internal factors – intimacy, passion, commitment) with jealousy ratings were also trivial. The correlation for the external variable, threat, was .71. Thus, for others, both the internal variables (such as needing, wanting, and care) and an external variable (threat) were viewed as important, whereas for oneself, the external variable (threat) was the only one that greatly mattered. We interpreted this result in terms of the actor–observer effect (Jones & Nisbett, 1971), according to which when making evaluations about the self, external variables are particularly important whereas when making evaluations about others, internal variables become particularly important.

Study 3: Envy – Ratings for Hypothetical Scenarios

In this study, we sought to study envy in a way that closely paralleled the way we studied jealousy in Study 1. In this case, an individual in the scenario is envious of a person involved with a potential romantic partner (PRP) with whom the envious individual would like him or herself to be involved.

Participants in Study 3 were 167 undergraduate students, including both males ($N = 37$) and females ($N = 130$) enrolled in human-development and psychology classes at Cornell University. Participation was voluntary.

The survey consisted of sixteen romantic-envy scenarios. Each scenario involved an EI, a PRP, and a T. Additional materials included two self-compiled envy surveys, Survey A and Survey B, each containing sixteen scenarios that would typically arouse some level of romantic envy. Surveys A and B only differed by the names used for the characters in the scenarios, which were switched in order to balance gender and eliminate gender as a confounding variable in the scenarios. The surveys were implemented through Qualtrics Survey Software and made available for online participation.

Each envy scenario was followed by twelve questions asking the participants to provide a number on a scale of one to ten, which assessed the participant's judgment regarding the level of each independent and dependent variable in the scenario. Two examples of an envy scenario, from Forms A and B respectively, are provided below:

Example 1: Envy Form A

Victoria, Chad, and Anthony went to the same high school. During senior year, Victoria started dating Chad and they were the most popular couple among their peers. After senior year, Chad went to attend a university four hours away while Anthony and Victoria attended a college in their hometown and remained good friends. Although Victoria and Chad are still dating, they have grown apart since they don't see each other much. Recently, Victoria has been very upset because Chad has not come to visit her as often as he used to. Anthony has realized this too and knows that Chad has become very busy with classes. Anthony feels bad that Victoria does not have Chad's company, so he hangs out with her almost every day. The last few weeks Chad has been visiting more often since his semester has started to wind down. Every time Anthony asks Victoria how she is doing and if she wants to hang out, Victoria says she is too busy with schoolwork or has plans with Chad. Anthony does not hang out with Victoria as much since she leaves all her free time reserved for the days Chad comes to visit.

On a scale of one to ten:

How much does Anthony want to have an intimate relationship with Victoria?

How much does Anthony deserve Victoria?

How fair is Victoria's treatment of Anthony?

How much does Victoria care about Anthony?

How much does Anthony care about Victoria?

How realistic is a romantic relationship between Anthony and Victoria if Chad was not in the picture?

How much does Anthony need Victoria, either practically or emotionally?

How much does Anthony trust Victoria?

How big of a threat is Chad to Anthony and Victoria's potential relationship?

How envious is Anthony of Chad?

How envious would you be if you were in Anthony's situation? (You might or might not react the same way Anthony did.)

How likely is a relationship between Anthony and Victoria to work out given all the circumstances?

Example 2: Envy Form B

Chad, Victoria and Rachel went to the same high school. During senior year, Chad started dating Victoria and they were the most popular couple among their peers. After senior year, Victoria went to attend a university four hours away while Rachel and Chad attended a college in their hometown and remained good friends. Although Chad and Victoria are still dating, they have grown apart since they don't see each other much. Recently, Chad has been very upset because Victoria has not come to visit him as often as she used to. Rachel has realized this too and knows that Victoria has become very busy with classes. Rachel feels bad that Chad does not have Victoria's company, so she hangs out with him almost every day. The last few weeks Victoria has been visiting more often since her semester has started to wind down. Every time Rachel asks Chad how he is doing and if he wants to hang out, Chad says he is too busy with schoolwork or has plans with Victoria. Rachel does not hang out with Chad as much since he leaves all his free time reserved for the days Victoria comes to visit.

On a scale of one to ten:

How much does Rachel want to have an intimate relationship with Chad?
How much does Rachel deserve Chad?
How fair is Chad's treatment of Rachel?
How much does Chad care about Rachel?
How much does Rachel care about Chad?
How realistic is a romantic relationship between Rachel and Chad if Victoria was not in the picture?
How much does Rachel need Chad, either practically or emotionally?
How much does Rachel trust Chad?
How big of a threat is Victoria to Rachel and Chad's potential relationship?
How envious is Rachel of Victoria?
How envious would you be if you were in Rachel's situation? (You might or might not react the same way Rachel did.)
How likely is a relationship between Rachel and Chad to work out given all the circumstances?

All subjects received all materials either through Form A or Form B. The ten independent variables in this study were want, deserve, treatment/fairness, care (EI about PRP), care (PRP about EI), need, threat, trust, plausibility (before threat), and plausibility (after threat). The two dependent variables in this study were envy experienced by the EI in the scenario and envy the participant would feel if he or she were the EI in the scenario. All scenarios in Study 2 involved an EI who wanted to be in a relationship with a PRP and a CT who posed a threat to the potential romantic relationship between the EI and his or her PRP. The independent variables *want, deserve, need,* and *plausibility* were manipulated in each scenario to portray them as either high or low (e.g. high want, low need, high deserve, low plausibility) resulting in two to the fourth power, or sixteen total permutations, that is, one scenario for each permutation.

There were two dependent variables, a primary one (perceived envy of the EI toward the T) and a secondary one (hypothetical envy the participant would feel if in the situation of the EI).

We were interested in the extent to which the independent variables in the model would predict levels of perceived envy in the EI. We do not separately report the participant's own imagined envy in the situation because the results of the modeling were almost the same as for the primary dependent variable, presumably because the two dependent variables were quite highly correlated with each other (.77).

The variables that entered into a stepwise multiple regression were, in order, (1) want, (2) threat, (3) care (PRP for EI), (4) plausibility after the threat (T) entered the picture, and (5) fair treatment by the PRP of the EI. The successive values of multiple R were .76, .82, .83, .84, and .84. The respective beta weights in the final model for the four variables were .30, .40, .29, .12, and –.13, the first three of which were statistically significant at the .001 level, the fourth at the .01 level, and the last of which was statistically significant at the .05 level. Note that the last variable, fair treatment, functioned as a suppressor variable in the multiple regression (that is, it suppressed irrelevant variance in other independent variables in predicting the criterion). We thus accounted for about 71% of the variance in the data (adjusted: 70%), with an F (5, 161) of 77.67, $p < .001$.

Study 4: Envy – Self-ratings

In Study 4, participants were 101 individuals, including both male ($N = 23$) and female ($N = 78$) undergraduate students enrolled in human development and psychology classes at Cornell University in Ithaca, NY. Voluntary participants received extra credit in their respective classes for participating. Participants ranged in age between 18 and 23 ($M = 20.26$, $SD = 1.30$) and were 44.6% White, 31.7% Asian or Pacific Islander, 10.9% Hispanic or Latino, 7.9% Black or African American, 0% American Indian or Alaska Native, and 5.0% Other. Incomplete responses ($N = 3$) were eliminated from the study.

Two self-compiled envy surveys, Survey A and Survey B, were used to assess the participants' feelings of envy. Survey A asked the participants to reflect on feelings of envy in a present potential romantic relationship and survey B asked the participants to reflect on feelings of envy in a past potential romantic relationship. Additional materials included the Sternberg Triangular Love Scale (Sternberg, 1998a). The surveys were created by researchers using Qualtrics Survey Software and made available for online participation using the Cornell University Department of Psychology SONA System Software.

Two examples of envy forms A (present) and B (past) respectively, are provided below.

Example 1: Envy Form A

Reflect on a potential romantic relationship you want to have with a person who is romantically interested in or involved with another person. Reflect on the circumstances in this potential relationship that led you to feel envious of the other person. In other words, think about your feelings of wanting the potential romantic partner who is romantically interested in another person.

Read the following questions and rate your feelings with respect to this potential romantic relationship.
On a scale of one to ten:

How much do you want to have an intimate relationship with your potential romantic partner?

How much do you deserve your potential romantic partner?

How fair is your potential romantic partner's treatment toward you?

How much does your potential romantic partner care about you?

How much do you care about your potential romantic partner?

How realistic was yours and your potential romantic partner's possibility of a relationship before another person entered the picture?

How much do you need your potential romantic partner, either practically or emotionally?

How much do you trust your potential romantic partner?

How big of a threat is the third person to your potential romantic relationship?

How envious do you feel of the third person?

How likely is the possibility of a potential relationship between you and your potential romantic partner to work out, given all the circumstances?

Example 2: Envy Form B

Reflect on a past potential romantic relationship you wanted to have with a person who was romantically interested in or involved with another person. Reflect on the circumstances in this past potential relationship that have led you to feel envious of the other person. In other words, think about your feelings of wanting the potential romantic partner who was romantically interested in another person.

Read the following questions and rate your feelings with respect to this potential romantic relationship.

On a scale of one to ten:

How much did you want to have an intimate relationship with the potential romantic partner?

How much did you deserve the potential romantic partner?

How fair was the potential romantic partner's treatment toward you?

How much did the potential romantic partner care about you?

How much did you care about the potential romantic partner?

How realistic was yours and the potential romantic partner's possibility of a relationship before another person entered the picture?

How much did you need the potential romantic partner, either practically or emotionally?

How much did you trust the potential romantic partner?

How big of a threat was the third person to the potential romantic relationship?

How envious did you feel of the third person?

How likely was the possibility of a potential relationship between you and the potential romantic partner to work out, given all the circumstances?

The subjects of the experiment were assigned to one of two surveys, creating a between-subjects design; each participant received one of two surveys created by the researchers at Cornell University, one of which studied feelings of envy in a past potential romantic relationship, and one of which studied envy in a present potential romantic relationship. Each survey asked students to reflect on a past or present potential romantic relationship in which they experienced at least some degree of envy. In other words, think about their feelings of wanting a potential romantic partner who was romantically interested in another person (a third-party individual or threat). The main dependent variable was envy, calculated by the participants' ratings. The independent variables were the participant's levels of need, want, trust, and deservingness for the person of their romantic interest, and their potential romantic relationship plausibility with the person of their romantic interest. The surveys consisted of eleven questions asking the participants to provide a number on a scale of one to ten, which assessed the participants' judgment regarding the level of each independent and dependent variable in the potential romantic relationship they reflected on. The subjects were also asked to complete the

Sternberg (1998a) Triangular Love Scale. Provided below is an explanation of each independent and dependent variable in the study.

There was one dependent variable: *Envy.* This variable tested how envious the participant felt of the third-party individual in the potential romantic relationship (e.g. How envious do you feel of the third person?).

The variables that entered into a stepwise multiple regression were, in order: (1) threat toward the ERP by the T; (2) want of the ERP for the ORP; and (3) care of the ORP for the ERP. The successive values of multiple R were .52, .55, and .60. The respective beta weights in the final model for the four variables were .47, .29, and –.27, meaning that the last was a suppressor variable. The first was statistically significant at the .001 level, the second at the .002 level, and the third at the .004 level. We thus accounted for about 36% of the variance in the data (adjusted value: 34%), with an F (3, 97) of 18.53, $p < .001$.

The stunning difference between self and other ratings for jealousy that appeared in Study 1 versus Study 2 was replicated for envy in Study 3 versus Study 4. The zero-order correlations with envy ratings for the hypothetical other ratings in Study 3 were .54 for wanting, .58 for needing, and .48 for care of the envious person for the desired other. In Study 4, the comparable correlations were .15, .05, and .12, respectively. Correlations of the Sternberg Triangular Love Scale with envy ratings were trivial. Internal variables entered the stepwise multiple regression as part contributors only after the external variable – threat – entered. The correlation of threat with the envy rating in Study 4 was .52. Once again, as with jealousy, for others, both internal variables and an external variable were perceived as important, but for oneself, only an external variable was perceived as mattering, suggesting something akin to an actor–observer effect.

Conclusions

Return for a moment to the story of Bob, John, and Jane. According to the two-factor models of jealousy and envy we have proposed in this article, based on an augmented duplex theory of love (see Sternberg, 1986, 1988, 1998a), Bob's envy toward John, boyfriend of Jane, was very strong because he felt strongly attracted to Jane – he wanted her and cared for her deeply. Moreover, his experienced love for her was threatened by the presence of John, Jane's boyfriend. All of these factors would serve to increase his envy toward John. But there were two tempering factors in his envy – the fact that John, given his elevated status as soccer-team captain, made the relationship far less plausible for Bob and the fact that Jane did not seem to care a whit about him. Retrospectively therefore, Bob's experience fits quite well into our proposed model of envy.

We have proposed in this article that both jealousy and envy can be understood in terms of an augmented duplex theory of love. In particular, we found that for others, both internal variables from the original triangular theory (e.g. care, need) were important in predicting jealousy and envy, as was an augmented external variable, threat. But for oneself, one adjudged only an external variable, threat, to matter.

There are various accounts of what jealousy is, and many of these accounts would apply to envy as well. Some researchers have hypothesized that jealousy is composed of several different emotions (e.g. anger, fear, and sadness), whereas other researchers have suggested that jealousy is itself a specific emotion distinct from others. On the first view, it is possible that the different emotions are experienced simultaneously when an individual is experiencing jealousy or perhaps in a sequence over the course of a single jealous episode (Hupka, 1984; Sharpsteen, 1991). On the second view, jealousy is a unique, specific emotion that involves motivations to protect against a threat in a valued social relationship (Daly, Wilson, & Weghorst, 1982; Harris, 2003; Symons, 1979).

Our results also look at the question of single or multiple elements, but from a slightly different point of view. They suggest that jealousy and envy both are a blend of multiple factors that either can increase or decrease levels of experienced emotion. Stronger feelings and stronger threat can enhance jealousy; but situational factors, such as feelings of deservingness and of treatment by and care from the actual or potential romantic partner, can intensify or modify the feelings of jealousy or envy. For example, if someone has strong feelings toward a famous movie star or popular musician, that person's feelings are likely to be tempered by the fact that the relationship simply is not plausible and that the desired other almost certainly has no comparable feelings toward us. (Stalkers are perhaps among those who cannot temper their feelings of envy in such cases. Often, they are former romantic partners – Duntley & Buss, 2012.) Similarly, high-school students sometimes lose their romantic partners when the partners go off to college and meet other men or women who present attractive features that the now-former partner just cannot match. Now-former partners might do well to temper their jealousy, if they come to believe that they are not in a good position to compete. Alternatively, they might try to compete on other grounds and convince the partner they are trying to retain that they are plausible partners after all.

A surprising result of our studies was how differently people judge jealousy and envy in themselves versus in others. In others, internal and external variables are important to ratings. In oneself, only an external variable, threat, is viewed as mattering greatly. One sees jealousy in oneself as responding to external circumstances and little more. For many people, what matters for jealousy and envy, as it pertains to themselves, is how threatened they feel, not how they feel about the other. But when they judge others, they may figure that if someone does not even care that much about someone else, why should they feel jealous or envious? These findings may be related to the actor–observer effect, whereby one view internal causes as more relevant to other's behavior but external causes as more relevant to one's own behavior (Jones & Nisbett, 1971).

Our studies are initial forays into testing the augmented duplex theory and its applicability to jealousy and envy was accompanied by many of the limitations one would expect from initial forays. First, our students were all undergraduate students at Cornell University, a selective northeastern university in the United States, which was hardly a representative sample of the general population. Second, our study of the self was for the real self, whereas our study of others was entirely scenario based. Ideally, there would be a condition of real others as well, but in reality, few people are in a position to have the knowledge required to make judgments of jealousy and envy actually experienced by real others in their lives. Third, our scenarios represented a limited range of relationship variations. Future research might mitigate at least some of these limitations.

Try as one might, it is difficult to go through one's life without experiencing romantic jealousy or envy. Our four studies have suggested some of the factors that might contribute to jealousy and envy, emanating from a combination of the particular person experiencing the emotion and the situation in which that person finds himself or herself.

Acknowledgment

We are grateful to David Buss and Felix Thoemmes for comments on an earlier version of the manuscript.

References

Afifi, W. A., & Reichert, T. (1996). Understanding the role of uncertainty in jealousy experience and expression. *Communication Reports, 9*(2), 93–10.

Barelds, D. P. H., & Barelds-Dijkstra, P. (2007). Relations between different types of jealousy and self and partner perceptions of relationship quality. *Child Psychology and Psychotherapy, 14*, 176–188.

Barrett, H. C., Frederick, D. A., Haselton, M. G., & Kurzban, R. (2006). Can manipulations of cognitive load be used to test evolutionary hypotheses? *Journal of Personality and Social Psychology, 95*, 513–518.

Bauerle, S. Y., Amirkhan, J. H., & Hupka, R. B. (2002). An attribution theory analysis of romantic jealousy. *Motivation and Emotion, 26*, 297–319.

Berman, M. I., & Frazier, P. A. (2005). Relationship power and betrayal experience as predictors of reactions to infidelity. *Personality and Social Psychology Bulletin, 31*, 1617–1627.

Bringle, R. G., & Buunk, B. P. (1991). Extradyadic relationships and sexual jealousy. In K. McKinney & S. Sprecher (Eds.), *Sexuality in close relationships* (pp. 135–153). Hillsdale, NJ: Lawrence Erlbaum.

Buunk, B. (1981). Jealousy in sexually open marriages. *Journal of Family and Economic Issues, 4*, 357–372.

Buunk, B. P. (1997). Personality, birth order and attachment styles as related to various types of jealousy. *Personality and Individual Differences, 23*(6), 997–1006.

Buss, D. M. (1988). The evolution of human intrasexual competition: Tactics of mate attraction. *Journal of Personality and Social Psychology, 54*(4), 616–628.

(2011). *The dangerous passion: Why jealousy is as necessary as love and sex*. New York: Basic Books.

(2016). *The evolution of desire: Strategies of human mating* (rev. ed.). New York: Basic Books.

(2018). Sexual and emotional infidelity: Gender differences in jealousy revisited. *Perspectives on Psychological Science, 13*, 155–160.

Buss, D. M., Larsen, R. J., Westen, D., & Semmelroth, J. (1992). Sex differences in jealousy: Evolution, physiology, and psychology. *Psychological Science, 3*, 251–255.

Buss, D. M., Shackelford, T. K., Choe, J., Buunk, B. P., & Dijkstra, P. (2000). Distress about mating rivals. *Personal Relationships, 7*, 235–243.

D'Arms, J., & Kerr, A. (2008). Envy in the philosophical tradition. In R. H. Smith (Ed.), *Envy: Theory and research* (pp. 39–59). New York: Oxford University Press.

Daly, M., Wilson, M. I., & Weghorst, S. J. (1982). Male sexual jealousy. *Ethology & Sociobiology, 3*, 11–27.

DeSteno, D., Bartlett, M., Braverman, J., & Salovey, P. (2002). Sex differences in jealousy: Evolutionary mechanism or artifact of measurement? *Journal of Personality and Social Psychology, 83*, 1103–1116.

DeSteno, D. A., & Salovey, P. (1996). Jealousy and the characteristics of one's rival: A self-evaluation maintenance perspective. *Personality and Social Psychology Bulletin, 22*, 920–932.

Duntley, J. D., & Buss, D. M. (2012). The evolution of stalking. *Sex Roles, 66*(5–6), 311–327.

Edlund, J. E., & Sagarin, B. J. (2017). Sex differences in jealousy: A 25-year retrospective. In J. M. Olson & M. P. Zanna (Eds.), *Advances in experimental social psychology* (pp. 259–302). New York: Elsevier.

Guerrero, L. K., Trost, M. R., & Yoshimura, S. M. (2005). Romantic jealousy: Emotions and communicative responses. *Personal Relationships, 12*, 233–252.

Harris, C. R. (2003). A review of sex differences in sexual jealousy, including self-report data, psychophysiological responses, interpersonal violence and morbid jealousy. *Personality and Social Psychology Review, 7*, 102–128.

(2004). The evolution of jealousy did men and women, facing different selective pressures, evolve different" brands" of jealousy? Recent evidence suggests not. *American Scientist, 92*(1), 62–71.

Harris, C. R., & Darby, R. S. (2010). Jealousy in adulthood. In S. L. Hart & M. Legerstee (Eds.), *Handbook of jealousy: Theory, research, and multidisciplinary approaches* (pp. 547–571). New York: Wiley-Blackwell.

Hazan, C., & Shaver, P. (1987). Romantic love conceptualized as an attachment process. *Journal of Personality and Social Psychology, 52*(3), 511–524.

Hill, S. E., & Buss, D. M. (2006). Envy and positional bias in the evolutionary psychology of management. *Managerial and Decision Economics, 27*(2–3), 131–143.

(2008). The evolutionary psychology of envy. In R. H. Hill (Ed.), *Envy: Theory and research* (pp. 60–70). New York: Oxford University Press.

Hupka, R. B. (1984). Jealousy: Compound emotion or label for a particular situation? *Motivation and Emotion, 8*, 141–155.

Jones, E. E., & Nisbett, R. E. (1971). *The actor and the observer: Divergent perceptions of the causes of behavior*. New York: General Learning Press.

Kirkpatrick, L. A., & Hazan, C. (1994). Attachment styles and close relationships: A four year prospective study. *Personal Relationships, 1*(2), 123–142.

Knobloch, L. K., Solomon, D. H., & Cruz, M. G. (2001). The role of relationship development and attachment in the experience of romantic jealousy. *Personal Relationships, 8*, 205–224.

Mathes, E. W. (1986). Jealousy and romantic love: A longitudinal study. *Psychological Reports, 58*, 885–886.

(1991). A cognitive theory of jealousy. In P. Salovey (Ed.), *The psychology of jealousy and envy* (pp. 52–78). New York: Guilford Press.

Miller, R. S. (2014). *Intimate relationships* (7th ed.). New York: McGraw-Hill.

Parrott, W. G. (1991). The emotional experiences of jealousy and envy. In P. Salovey (Ed.), *The psychology of jealousy and envy* (pp. 3–30). New York: Guilford Press.

Parrott, W. G., & Smith, R. H. (1993).Distinguishing the experiences of jealousy and envy. *Journal of Personality and Social Psychology, 64*, 906–920.

Rydell, R. J., McConnell, A. R., & Bringle, R. G. (2004). Jealousy and commitment: Perceived threat and the effect of relationship alternatives. *Personal Relationships, 11*, 451–468.

Salovey, P. (Ed.) (1991). *The psychology of jealousy and envy*. New York: Guilford Press.

Salovey, P., & Rodin, J. (1991). Provoking jealousy and envy: Domain relevance and self-esteem threat. *Journal of Social and Clinical Psychology,10*(4), 395.

Salovey, P., & Rothman, A. (1991). Envy and jealousy: Self and society. In P. Salovey (Ed.), *The psychology of jealousy and envy* (pp. 271–286). New York: Guilford Press.

Schimmel, S. (1997). *The seven deadly sins: Jewish, Christian, and classical reflections on human psychology.* New York: Oxford University Press.

Schoeck, H. (1969). *Envy: A theory of social behavior.* New York: Harcourt, Brace & World.

Sharpsteen, D. J. (1991). The organization of jealousy knowledge: Romantic jealousy as a blended emotion. In P. Salovey (Ed.), *The psychology of jealousy and envy* (pp. 31–51). New York: Guilford Press.

Sharpsteen, D. J., & Kirkpatrick, L. A. (1997). Romantic jealousy and adult romantic attachment. *Personality Processes and Individual Differences, 72,* 627–640.

Smith, R. H. (Ed.) (2008). *Envy: Theory and research.* New York: Oxford University Press.

Smith, R. H., & Kim, S. H. (2007). Comprehending envy. *Psychological Bulletin, 133*(1), 46–64.

Smith, R. H., Parrott, W. G., Ozer, D., & Moniz, A. (1994). Subjective injustice and inferiority as predictors of hostile and depressive feelings in envy. *Personality and Social Psychology Bulletin, 20*(6), 705–711.

Sternberg , R. J. (1986). A triangular theory of love. *Psychological Review, 93,* 119–135.

(1987). Liking versus loving: A comparative evaluation of theories. *Psychological Bulletin, 102,* 331–345.

(1988). Triangulating love. In R. J. Sternberg & M. Barnes (Eds.), *The psychology of love* (pp. 119–138). New Haven, CT: Yale University Press.

(1995). Love as a story. *Journal of Social and Personal Relationships, 12*(4), 541–546.

(1998a). *Cupid's arrow: The course of love through time.* New York: Cambridge University Press.

(1998b). *Love is a story.* New York: Oxford University Press.

(2006). A duplex theory of love. In R. J. Sternberg & K. Weis (Eds.), *The new psychology of love* (pp. 184–199). New Haven, CT: Yale University Press.

Symons, D. (1979) *The evolution of human sexuality.* New York: Oxford University Press.

Van de Ven, N., Zeelenberg, M., & Pieters, R. (2009). Leveling up and down: The experiences of benign and malicious envy. *Emotion, 9*(3), 419–429.

Weiner, B. (1995). *Judgments of responsibility: A foundation for theory of social conduct.* New York: Guilford Press.

Index

action triangles, 286
actor–observer effect
   in jealousy/envy studies, 319, 325
actual triangles, 286
adaptation in evolution
   and love, 42–44, 57–58
addiction
   love as, 64, 68, 209, 291, 309
adultery, 210, *see also* Ludus love style
Agape love style, 167, 224, 230, 231
age
   and love styles, 231–232
anthropological view of love, 192, 241–243, 256
anxious attachment, 262
   and caregiving, 266
   and jealousy, 303
   and love styles, 228
   and sexual activity, 267, 268
arranged marriages, 45–46, 192
Art (love story type), 291, 309
Artificial Intelligence
   humanoid robots, 199, 200–201
attachment
   behavioral perspective, 260–262
   in Berscheid quadrumvirate model, 156
   and caregiving, 266–267, 269
   and commitment, 270
   and communal responsiveness, 100, 105–106
   cultural differences, 175
   evolutionary theories, 210, 259–262, 266–267
   and falling in love, 140–142, 143–144
   hyperactivation and deactivation, 261–262
   and intimacy, 270, 271
   and jealousy, 303–304
   and love styles, 228
   romantic attachment, 138–145, 147, 155, 270–271
   and self-expansion model, 17, 31
   and sexuality, 267, 268–269
   two-stage model, 303–304
attachment-related avoidance, 262

attraction
   evolutionary theories, 43, 46–47
   gender differences, 46–47
   of opposites, 4
   politics of attraction, 119–121
   self-expansion model, 3–4
attribution theory, 304
augmented duplex theory of love, *see also* duplex
   theory of love
   envy research studies, 319–325, 327
   jealousy research studies, 311–319, 327
   research findings, 326–327
Autocratic Government (love story type), 162, 310
automatic thoughts, 289
avoidant attachment, 266, 267, 268

behavioral approach (romantic love), 259–260
behavioral confirmation, 29–30
behavioral systems, 260
being in love, 46, 162–163, 171–172, 186, 227, 253–254
   creativity, and being in love, 186
Belief Pattern Scale for Measuring Attitudes
   Toward Romanticism, 165
Berscheid quadrumvirate model of love, 155–156
bias in research, 129–132
bisexuality, 148, *see also* same-sex attraction
body image, 127–128
brain, *see also* neurobiological perspectives
   love brain network (LBN), 67–69
   plasticity, 34–35
breakup of relationships, 14, 36–37, 53–54,
   174–175, *see also* divorce
Brief Sexual Attitudes Scale, 229
Business (love story type), 173, 291, 292, 309

caregiving
   and attachment, 266, 269
   dysfunctions, 262–263
   function and features, 262–263
   hyperactivation/deactivation of system, 264
   and romantic love, 271–272

Printed in Great Britain
by Amazon

15763368R00201